JOURNEY'S END

JOURNEY'S END

Bomber Command's Battle from Arnhem to Dresden and beyond

KEVIN WILSON

Weidenfeld & Nicolson
LONDON

First published in Great Britain in 2010
by Weidenfeld & Nicolson

10 9 8 7 6 5 4 3 2 1

A CIP catalogue record for this book
is available from the British Library.

ISBN 978 0 297 85821 8

Typeset by Input Data Services Ltd, Bridgwater, Somerset

Printed in Great Britain by CPI Mackays, Chatham ME5 8TD

The Orion Publishing Group's policy is to use papers that are
natural, renewable and recyclable products and made from wood grown in sustainable
forests. The logging and manufacturing processes are expected to conform
to the environmental regulations of the country of origin.

Weidenfeld & Nicolson

The Orion Publishing Group Ltd
Orion House
5 Upper Saint Martin's Lane
London WC2H 9EA

An Hachette UK company

www.orionbooks.co.uk

CONTENTS

20 Finale 387

LIST OF ILLUSTRATIONS

The pictures in this book come from the personal collections of the aircrew and others interviewed by the author, and are reproduced with their permission.

First picture section
Australian skipper F/O Bruce Windrim, wearing his good luck talisman of a chequered bowler hat, with his crew of Englishmen on 625 Sqn at Kelstern.
The 101 Sqn crew of F/O George Harris, pictured outside billets at Ludford Magna.
Kay Polley, newly married to navigator George Kirby. She would be a widow before she was 21.
F/Sgt Kirby with some of his 106 Sqn crew at their Metheringham dispersal site.
Sgt Peter Bone polishes his mid-upper turret at Wickenby.
F/O Reg Johnson, RAAF, on the far left, enjoying leave with the Narborough family at Carshalton under the Lady Ryder hospitality scheme for airmen far from home.
Flight engineer Sgt Edwin Watson with other crew members beside the last of the six unlucky G-Georges of 630 Sqn.
Flight engineer Sgt Frank Jones poses by the rear turret of his 76 Sqn Halifax at Holme on Spalding Moor.
Flight engineer F/Sgt Frank Etherington, of 166 Sqn.
Air gunner Harry Irons, who joined up at 16.
Sgt Henryk Drozdz, Polish flight engineer on 300 Sqn.
Sgt Ken O'Brien, pictured with mid-upper gunner Sgt Ron Poulson after O'Brien became the first air gunner to shoot down

a German jet fighter at night, winning the DFM.

The 408 RCAF Sqn crew of P/O Case line up by their aircraft at Linton on Ouse.

Wireless operator Kenneth Turnham, who was wounded by flak over Cologne, with his 115 Sqn crew at Witchford.

F/Sgt 'Scotty' Young, who baled out into Russian-held territory after the 5 March Chemnitz raid.

The 'Ya Anglichahnin' flag issued to airmen on both Chemnitz raids.

Airmen still recovering from their burns in 1946, play snooker with a staff member at Burley Hall temporary hospital, Rutland. Sgt Harry Stunell, whose bomber crashed in flames returning from Munich, is on the right. Centre is Sgt Haydn Price.

The leg burns Sgt Stunell received as he struggled free from his blazing Lancaster.

F/Lt Tony Brandreth with his Mosquito Q-Queenie.

Three English members of Australian F/O Warren Clarke's 207 Sqn crew at Spilsby.

Rear gunner F/Sgt Elias Williams, sole survivor of his crew when their aircraft was shot down on a Lutzkendorff raid.

The crew of C2 of 460 RAAF Sqn, who bombed both Dresden and Pforzheim.

Second picture section

Damage from 12,000lb Tallboy bombs on the Dortmund-Ems Canal after the raid of 23/24 September 1944.

The middle of the Hohenzollern Bridge at Cologne lies in the Rhine after it was finally wrecked by retreating German troops in March, 1945.

The blasted and burnt-out centre of Bochum after the raid on the night of 4 November.

The searing scene from an RAF film unit Lancaster as a firestorm sweeps Pforzheim, ten days after the one which destroyed Dresden.

Bomber Command maintained a constant pressure on Germany to force a surrender, despite appalling weather conditions at

RAF bases in the winter of 1944/45. Here aircrew of 630 Sqn join ground staff at East Kirkby in clearing the snow to mount another raid.

The glory of historic Dresden three years before Hitler came to power.

One of Dresden's narrow streets, looking from the Brühl Terrace towards the Frauenkirche with the Landhaus museum tower in the distance.

The same scene weeks after the firestorm.

The gaping ruins of the historic Aldstadt, heart of the firestorm.

The Ruhr Express, the first Canadian-built Lancaster, arrives in Britain for a photo call with the press.

The wreckage of the aircraft in the snow after she ran off the runway at Middleton St George and caught fire in January, 1945.

P/O Wilson managed to bring this Halifax in to land after it lost its entire nose in a collision with a Free French aircraft after a raid on Saarburcken in January.

The most-destructive bomb of the war in Europe: Barnes-Wallis's 22,000lb Grand Slam goes on display in Oxford St, London.

A fireman picks his way through the rubble of what had been a house in Nunthorpe Grove, York.

101 Sqn bombers hit a railway bridge at Bremen on 23 March.

Maps

Raids on the Dortmund-Ems Canal (Ladbergen) and Neuss, 23/24 September 1944

14/15 October 1944: the complex night operations against Duisburg (Operation Hurricane) and Brunswick

Attacks on Bochum and the Dortmund-Ems Canal, 4/5 November 1944

Dresden: night operations on 13/14 February 1945

The Dresden firestorm, 13/14 February 1945

Raids on Chemnitz and Bohlen, 5/6 March 1945

To my grandchildren Nemone, Patrick, Tilly, Freya and Dominic in gratitude for the joy of their presence and in the hope they will never know war

OVERTURE

THE crews of Bomber Command, whose Lancasters rumbled and thundered away into the lengthening shadows of mid-September as a prelude to the badly orchestrated Battle of Arnhem, were metaphorically already in the dark. They were unaware they were ending one era in the bombing war and beginning a new phase of bright destruction that would be their legacy.

As they droned ever upwards that Saturday night over the flat fields of North Lincolnshire to the faint edge of coastline they pondered on their task of hitting the fighter airfields of the Luftwaffe in Holland and northern Germany, not knowing that they were in fact the spearhead for an airborne army campaign. The failure of that battle together with the stalling of Canadian and American advances in Belgium and along Germany's West Wall, would mean the continuance of the war in Europe over the winter and into the spring. Many thousands more would now die, in khaki, in air-force blue and not least in civilian overalls and dresses. For Bomber Command would enter a third campaign to bring Germany to its knees by hammering its cities once more and the key industries and transportation links within them. It would do so with new techniques and with skills already honed in battle against a Luftwaffe now in steady decline, but by no means out of the fight.

Some of these techniques were demonstrated in this night before the Arnhem assault began. The crew of F/O Vic Farmer, a navigator coming to the end of his tour on 550 Sqn at North Killingholme, was among those detailed to attack German airfields to prevent fighters creating bloody chaos among the packed Dakotas shortly to follow. Their particular target was Steenwyck. Farmer remembers:

> We were told at briefing we were to bomb a German fighter base which, as bombed airfields could quickly be repaired, seemed to us a waste of time. We made almost a straight line for the target in darkness. The Gee packed up over the North Sea as usual and there was nothing for H2S to pick up except the Dutch coast. We crossed the coast on track and on time and as an experienced crew we were among the first to go over. Usually there would be a response as we crossed, with searchlights or flak or both, but on this occasion there was no activity at all, no flak, not even one searchlight. It was eerie just flying on into the darkness and of course it gave us no confirmation of where we were. As the estimated time of arrival approached we opened our bomb bay doors to be ready and almost at the same moment flares from PFF aircraft lit up the target straight ahead, no doubt directed by Oboe. The bomb aimer could see the airfield below and we dropped our bombs almost without any change of direction practically right on the intersection of the runways and turned for home. The following day we heard about the attack on Arnhem, so keeping German fighters on the ground even for a short time undoubtedly saved many lives.[1]

Arnhem signalled the dying of faint hope to end the war without the bloody attrition so well known to the fathers of the young men now flying in Bomber Command's Lancasters and Halifaxes. So confident was Churchill's War Cabinet that Armageddon, shortly to be unleashed from the air, would now be the fate of Germany's cities where four years before it had been Britain's, a 'dim-out' was ordered from 17 September to replace the blackout. The British bomber crews left behind a totally dark Britain for the last time as they crossed the North Sea in pre-emptive support of the paratrooper assault. Each householder and factory owner in the country from now until the war's end would only have to institute a blackout if an alert was sounded, not as a nightly routine as it had been since 1939.[2]

Bomber Command's chief, Sir Arthur Harris, would fight his

final campaign with resources undreamed of when he began his bomber offensive in 1943, or even for much of 1944. Close to 1,800 aircraft per night would now be available to the C-in-C, two-thirds of them the ruggedly reliable Lancaster with its capacious bomb bay.[3] Navigation aids were at last based in mainland Europe to guide them. The crucible of war had forged technological improvements that turned bombing from an art into a science; new, bigger and at last aerodynamic bombs would be employed from the 12,000-lb Tallboy to the gigantic 22,000-lb Grand Slam. And finally there were improvements in aircraft defence, from introduction of .50 machine guns to gun-laying by radar. The weaponry would be used against a Luftwaffe that at the point of its decline had entered the jet age.

Bomber Command would wage war by night and also by day, the latter in conjunction with the USAAF's Eighth Air Force in Britain – which had by this time outstripped the power of the RAF and Commonwealth squadrons in aircraft available – and the US Fifteenth Air Force in Italy. Day raids now became a routine for most RAF and Commonwealth aircrew and they brought fresh terrors. Airmen had been conditioned to seeing a fearsome flash in the sky signalling the end of another crew, but such victims were usually anonymous. The preponderance of daylight operations sometimes meant they were looking into the faces of pilots, engineers or gunners as they died on the edge of the stream.

It was these experiences that created other uniformed victims of the air war apart from the dead, the wounded and the captive. When aircrew returned from a particularly traumatic raid where they had perhaps seen a member of their crew die a horrible death or witnessed a fellow crew wiped out in a flash against the sky, they would usually be ordered to go again as soon as practicable so as not to lose their nerve, a test many in this age, where the necessity of counselling for post-traumatic combat stress has been recognised, might find hard to accede to. In cases where an airman had finally drained his well of courage and refused to go again he was harshly treated. By and large airmen sealed themselves in a shockproof shell in which the loss of friends was dismissed with a joke and a smile. For some it would take years to escape from the cocoon and for a few the only release was in suicide.

It was ironic that many had considered themselves a fortunate elite to be starting their tours at all at a time when there was now an abundance of aircrew as pilots, navigators and bomb aimers poured ashore from the Canadian training schools and losses declined. Airmen in this final phase were aware the skill at wreaking terrible destruction they were now poised to demonstrate had been honed by the sacrifices of their colleagues in the operational expediency of the Battle of the Ruhr in 1943 and the Battle of Berlin in the winter of 1943–4.

The new sacrifices they were now called upon to make are at the centre of this history, the surprising attrition among some squadrons at a time when the Luftwaffe was in decline, the shock of taking on German jets in combat, the remarkable escapes from what seemed the certainty of death as bombers became tunnels of fire or exploded in the blackness, the fear of being on the run from vengeful enemies. Cynically the legacy for the teenagers and other young men who made up Bomber Command would be criticism after Dresden, not alone in 1945 in experiencing the horror of the firestorm. It represented what Bomber Command could now do, apparently almost at will. Yet there were valid reasons for Churchill to order the bombing of the city and his deputy Clement Attlee to agree; the war was a long way from over when the raid was mounted; and hundreds more bombers would fall before victory was achieved. But the ingratitude of peace had yet to be spawned as the hopeful young airmen of Bomber Command prepared to use their new equipment and techniques of war to finish the job they had begun in earnest at the start of 1943.

It is now September 1944 and as the third phase of the bomber campaign begins London itself is suffering under a new onslaught, plunging from the skies without warning as the leaves of hopeful summer begin to wither and die . . .

AUTUMN

ONE

A NEW AGE OF WARFARE

THE final stage of the air war, which would see Bomber Command revive its campaign against the industrial capacity of the Reich's cities, began with a bang that was not of Britain's making, but of the Germans themselves.

The unique sound of a V-2 arriving in Staveley Road, Chiswick, on 8 September, in which the boom of its descent from the stratosphere and through the sound barrier was followed a split second later by the roar of the $3/4$-ton payload going off, heralded the rocket campaign against Britain which had been dreaded since the pre-emptive RAF strike against the German's Baltic research site at Peenemünde over a year previously.

To a War Cabinet which only the day before had heard Duncan Sandys, head of its Crossbow sub-committee dealing with the V-1 flying bomb menace, announce, 'Except for a few shots the battle for London is over,' there was a sense of shock. So much so that an immediate news blackout was ordered which lasted until 11 November. It wasn't just to deny the enemy any intelligence about where the rockets were landing; the fear was that the content of the weapon was unknown – perhaps the seeds of a new biological warfare. And it could not be determined for sure whether the new weaponry might soon be carrying atomic warheads. The Americans were after all developing the atomic bomb at this time, only because the Allies had been warned by the philosopher-scientist Albert Einstein in 1941 that the Germans were already working on one. All that was known was that the blinding bright blue flash and ear-splitting bang-bang signature of the V-2 resulted in a deep crater and lateral blast that could immediately destroy a

whole terrace in densely populated areas and spread out to demolish walls and slate roofs up to a quarter of a mile away.[1]

The first V-2 killed 3 people, injured 22 and flattened 6 houses
after landing in the roadway of the tree-lined suburban avenue.
Rosemary Clarke, aged 3, was killed in the front upstairs bedroom
of No. 1 Staveley Road when the payload ripped the house apart
just before 7 p.m. Her brother John, aged 6, was in the bathroom at
the rear and survived. 'There wasn't a mark on Rosemary,' he later
remembered. 'The blast goes up and comes down in a mushroom
or umbrella shape. In the process of that my sister's lungs collapsed.
I got a piece of bomb casing in the back of my hand which has
created a scar . . . The bathroom didn't collapse but one of the bed-
rooms next to it did, which I found very strange as a boy.'[2]

The V-2 had been launched in Holland five minutes before,
from a mobile platform because 617 Sqn of Bomber Command
had proved decisively with Tallboy bombs on the huge Wizernes
bunker in the Pas-de-Calais in July that permanent rocket sites
would be destroyed. The dawn of a new age in aerial warfare,
of country-to-country ballistic missiles, had begun. Unlike the
reaction to the doodlebugs, shot down by anti-aircraft shell and
fighter cannon, this time there was no defence.

It was hoped that one of the benefits of the Arnhem campaign,
which began nine days later, would be to seal off the rocket sites.
The failure of that campaign and the knowledge that the army
would have to wait until spring to launch a major offensive meant
that Bomber Command would now be required to contain and
demoralise the enemy. Until then it had seemed that the war might
be over by Christmas. In fact imminent German collapse had
appeared so certain to Allied staffs in August that a plan codenamed En-Dor had been set up to process released RAF and
army POWs as quickly as possible.[3] The first indications of that
expected flood had been the return of the first RAF and Commonwealth Air Force POWs from Germany, who had been deemed
by the Red Cross too sick to remain behind the wire.

Among them was pilot Nathaniel Flekser, a lieutenant in the
South African Air Force, who had assisted in digging the tunnels

for the Great Escape from Stalag Luft III in March, then had developed a duodenal ulcer, his weight falling from 205 lbs to 136. He had been handed a *Heimkehrberechtigung bejaht* (Repatriation approved) slip by the Germans, told he was among a batch of 200 prisoners being exchanged with similarly sick German POWs in Britain, and taken to a special unit near Dresden. 'Sick and wounded prisoners began to arrive from POW camps all over Germany,' he later recorded. 'Several were carried on stretchers. In all about 200 were assembled ... some suffered from burns which had melted the flesh of their hands and faces, their lidless eyes sightless.'[4] In early September the party of home-bound prisoners were taken by train to Stettin, then by ferry to neutral Sweden and finally were shipped to England in the SS *Drottingholm*, accompanied to a point mid-way across the North Sea by a German destroyer which then handed over its charges to a warship of the Royal Navy to 'raucous yelps from their horns' rather than gunfire. Back in London Flekser, who had been shot down in 1942, discovered he had £13,000 in back pay and decided to take a suite at the Savoy. It was there he learned all about the new V-weapons, from a WAAF radar operator on leave he met in the bar. He wrote:

> We ate a pleasant dinner in the elegant Savoy Grill Room. Agnes was sharing a pokey room in Soho with two girls. With as much nonchalance as I could muster, I said, 'You are welcome to share my suite.' She looked at me, green eyes probing, hesitated and said, 'Thank you, I would like that.' And so began a whirlwind romance, a time of touching, a time of joy, a time of regeneration. That night as Agnes lay in my arms I experienced, for the first time, a nightmare which was to return for many years. I dreamt I was back in Stalag Luft III, digging an escape tunnel. The acrid smell from the smoke of the lamp mingled with the must of the soil and irritated my nose. I sneezed and heard the roar as an avalanche of sand ripped down and engulfed me ... I awoke shivering.

Over the next few days as the V-weapons continued to fall, Flekser's rehabilitation continued, his WAAF girlfriend introducing him to London's monuments, museums, galleries and places steeped in history. We fed the pigeons in the shadow of Nelson's Column, strolled through Hyde Park and punted on the Thames in the late summer sunshine. The theatres were in full swing, featuring artists who I had listened to on records and read about. We saw Noël Coward in *Blythe Spirit*, Gracie Fields and Vera Lynn in variety shows ... we danced in the Savoy ballroom to the music of my favourite jazz band – Carol Gibbons and his Savoy Orchestra.'[5]

It was a long way from Stalag Luft III in Silesia, despite the sound of V-2 rockets arriving, including one on the Thames in September which blew out the windows of the Savoy Grill Room for the seventh time in the war.

F/O Douglas Jennings was another airman enjoying leave in London, who also had just returned to freedom. Jennings, a 22-year-old bomb aimer, had been liberated by the American Army near Liège after being hidden by the Resistance since he had been shot down on 21 June on his way with 57 Sqn to bomb the Wesseling oil refinery near Cologne. After a couple of days in Paris he was put aboard a Dakota carrying the King's Messenger. He remembers:

I was flown back to Hendon from Paris on 17 September 1944, the day Arnhem began and of course all the newspapers were full of it. I was taken straight off to MI9 at the Marylebone Hotel for debriefing. There was a lot of damage in London from the V-weapon offensive and while I was on survivor's leave at my mother's home in Pinner I heard a V-2 actually explode about a quarter of a mile away. There was a huge bang as it arrived without any kind of warning and it knocked down a block of flats. I think people had the attitude, 'If it's going to happen to you, it's going to happen.'[6]

Sgt Laurie Boness, an evader since being shot down in late June bombing a V-1 site at Prouville in France – his first operational trip – was in London after being flown back from Paris the same way as F/O Jennings, but two days before. He savoured each moment from stepping out of the Dakota at Hendon with other RAF aircrew now safe from the Gestapo.

> Shortly after landing we passed an American PX van where dough-nuts were being sold. They smelt so good and were particularly inviting because we had had no breakfast that morning and it was almost noon. 'Why don't you buy some?' asked the girl in the van. We quickly explained our situation – importantly, that we had no money. She disappeared for a few minutes then returned and handed each of us two doughnuts. They were delicious.[7]

That night the young flight engineer, wearing a brand-new uniform stuffed with back pay and adjusting to hearing the unex-plained boom of V-2s, was in a hostel in London specially set up by the Air Ministry for returned evaders. He remembered:

> Late in the evening a group of us went for a quick drink in a nearby London pub. In returning to the hostel we somehow missed a turning . . . suddenly one of our group panicked. 'We're lost! We're lost!' he shouted and big tears rolled down his cheeks . . . fortunately a local man, realising who we were, and having overheard the incident, walked up to the distressed fellow, put his arm on his shoulder and said, 'Don't worry, lad, I know where you are heading for,' and guided us back to the hostel.[8]

Within days Sgt Boness was back at his base at Waddington near Lincoln and reporting to 'Dixie' Dean, the engineer leader of 463 RAAF Sqn he had last seen before he took off for Prouville. 'I walked into his office, saluted, went to the operations board and picking up a piece of chalk wrote my name on it once again. Everyone laughed,' he remembered. 'Re-chalking my name up on that squadron ops board was one of the greatest moments of my life.'[9]

But others returning from life under the jackboot found their welcome could have a bitter twist. Sgt George Stewart, a 50 Sqn bomb aimer, was the sole survivor of his crew. He had clipped on his chute as flak began pinging through his Lancaster over Bochum in June 1943. Seconds later the aircraft exploded, hurling the seven

men into the night sky. Only Sgt Stewart was wearing a chute. He
says:

> I got a big wound in the front of my head which left an indentation.
> When I got back home after being repatriated I was only about ten
> minutes in front of an RAF debriefing officer and he didn't want
> to know anything. I could have been the bravest man in the crew
> and he didn't want to know what happened. He just said, 'Oh, you
> got a direct hit, right.' I was bitterly disappointed by his attitude. He
> just didn't want to know and I thought: I'm just another number.[10]

THERE was a sense of regrouping in Bomber Command as the
weeks unfolded in September, a time for reflection among senior
officers after the successes of the summer in which the bomber
boys had supported the invasion by knocking out Transportation
Plan targets to keep the German Army bottled up in Normandy,
by mounting the offensive against oil targets, by directly assisting
the armies in the field in taking out strong points, and even by
blitzing the Reich's cities at night to keep the night fighters and flak
guns in Germany. It was a period of both change and preparation
before the bomber crews were launched into the final assault of
flak, fighter and the multi-coloured fury of German targets. On
twenty-four days out of thirty there were raids by the heavies of
Bomber Command, either in daylight or at night, sometimes by
as many as nearly 900 on one target.

Tours ended and tours began with fresh blood for the new time
of testing. F/O Vic Farmer, the 550 Sqn navigator whose crew
raided a German fighter airfield before Arnhem, was one of those
now released from operations who had reasons to be grateful to a
pilot for bringing them through. He had met his new skipper at
Heavy Conversion Unit after he and the rest of the crew refused
to fly with the previous one because he had ground-looped his
aircraft on landing. F/O Farmer remembers:

> I was the first to meet him, F/O Rhys Thomas. My heart sank. He
> had a paunch, a twitch in the eye and he was over 30. My first

impressions proved unfounded. He was an ex-flying instructor, a competent pilot and in fact a superb bomber pilot. He didn't go rushing into anything and as an ex-instructor it was ingrained in him to teach people every detail had to be right before taking off. On two occasions in my opinion F/O Thomas saved us and at the end of our tour he was awarded the DFC, thoroughly deserved especially as he elected to fly operationally, a risk he could have avoided at his age by continuing as a flying instructor. The crew referred to him as Skip; in fact we never knew his first name. We went to Zoutelande on 17 September to complete our tour and the crew broke up as we went our separate ways. We never met again as a complete crew.[11]

There was little opportunity at this time on the RAF bomber bases, which stretched from Cambridgeshire to County Durham, for pilots or their crews to relax. Little chance to laze in station intelligence sections leafing through the latest reports on Luftwaffe techniques, barely time for gunners to carry out their daily inspections at dispersals surrounded by fading wild flowers, or for flight engineers to compare notes in their sections about fuel and engine management which might just save their lives.

When an opportunity arose to get off station as operations were scrubbed it was snatched. Sgt Frank Jones, a 20-year-old flight engineer who was also coming to the end of a tour, had the means of making a quick dash to the pub from his 76 Sqn base in East Yorkshire. He remembers:

We were two crews to a hut and the navigator in the crew we shared with had a Norton motorbike which we won on the toss of a coin when he was screened. We used it to ferry ourselves backwards and forwards to the pubs in Holme-on-Spalding-Moor and Howden. One night coming back with one of the gunners I think we both fell asleep on the bike because we woke up in a duck pond near where the road curved. The bike started again at first try and we got back to camp, though soaking wet.[12]

Throughout September there was the now routine tabulation of attrition at the RAF accounts centre at Uxbridge, where daily reports of missing aircrew were filed, as the pressure on Bomber Command to keep squeezing the enemy continued. And occasionally the drama of the war would be brought home to the majority of the personnel on the bases, the 1,500 ground staff at each airfield who never flew, as Lancasters or Halifaxes crashed within sight of them.

Sgt Jack Morley, a wireless operator on 101 Sqn, remembers such a day that month at Ludford Magna, when erks and WAAFs saw three Lancasters crash-land within minutes. The aircraft were returning from a raid on German strong points at Le Havre with a full bomb load because poor visibility and the possibility of hitting Allied troops had caused the master bomber to abandon the raid. Sgt Morley remembers:

We were first back in the Ludford circuit in the late evening and flying control ordered us to land on a particular runway, 02 I believe. We reported back to them that we could see the windsock and it would have meant landing downwind instead of into it. There then came a voice which we knew was the station commander's saying, 'You will land as ordered.' We knew that with 13,000 lbs of bombs on board it was going to be practically impossible to stop. The skipper told us to take up crash positions. I moved to sit on the floor in front of the main spar with my hands round my head. We were sure we weren't going to make it with the wind behind us. The pilot landed in good time on the runway but could see we weren't going to stop before we ran out of concrete with the full bomb load on, so he ordered the undercarriage up. There was a horrible noise as the belly was being ripped away. A cloud of dust came up and there were sparks everywhere. I thought we were finished. There was a dip at the end of the runway and we came over the top of it, taking all the Fido pipes with us, and crashed down the other side, coming to rest in the bottom just behind the Black Horse pub in Ludford village. By that time the floor of the aircraft had gone.

As we got out we could see another wrecked bomber* wavering on the top of the bank as if it was going to come down on us. The two gunners and me were the first out, as quickly as we could. Don Dale, the mid-upper gunner, was first to go and I followed him. Ginger Congerton, the rear gunner, had done what he was supposed to do by turning his .50 guns to the side and trying to roll out above them. But he was 6 feet 2 inches tall and his harness got caught on the guns, so while this other bomber was still wobbling above us Don and me ran up and I banged the quick release on his harness for him to drop down. The three of us then took off for flying control without waiting for anyone else. We had already had our cup of tea before the rest of the crew turned up in the crash tender. The aircraft was completely wrecked and struck off. It wasn't until the next day we realised how close we were to the Black Horse. A little plaque was put up in the pub years later saying what happened.

Another aircraft also crashed on the aerodrome at about the same time that evening. It ended up in the area of a building known as the White House at the other end of the village beyond our own pub, the White Hart. We lost three aircraft due to the station commanding officer. Shortly afterwards he was moved away.[13]

THE intense effort on a variety of targets throughout September now meant an increasing group of aircrew were experiencing war from a new viewpoint: that of the fugitive from the enemy. As was evidenced by the establishment of the sizeable London hostel for returned evaders, the chances of an airman avoiding capture had soared throughout the summer as Bomber Command was called on to raid targets in France and the Allied armies pushed forward, liberating previously occupied territories. By the early

* This was the aircraft of F/Lt Al Massheder, a Texan serving in the RCAF, who also had to retract his undercarriage to bring his aircraft to a halt. The aircraft, B-Beer, like F/O Harris's Z-Zebra, was also damaged beyond repair, and again the crew were fortunately uninjured.

autumn even airmen downed on raids in Germany itself stood a fighting chance of avoiding capture. Several did so after a raid on the Dortmund-Ems Canal on the 23rd of the month.

The canal, which carried much of the Ruhr's war material along its 165-mile length from the river port of Dortmund to the North Sea city of Emden, had vulnerable points where the water was carried over long aqueducts and so was judged a prize target by the Air Ministry. But it was always a costly one. It had been attacked four times beginning in 1940 when F/Lt 'Babe' Learoyd had won a VC for leading an assault which saw one-fifth of the bombers destroyed by flak units in the fields lining the canal. In September 1943, 617 Sqn – whose aircrew had seen nearly half of their comrades vanish in the raid on the Ruhr Dams four months before – lost another five crews of the eight that set out to try to demolish the banks of the canal at Ladbergen with a crude 12,000-lb blast bomb.

A year later the Dambusters were asked to try again in the same area north of Münster, and not far from the flat lands of Holland, where lay the aqueducts carrying the canal water in parallel branches. This time they were equipped with the 12,000-lb aerodynamic Tallboy bomb which Barnes Wallis had designed and the squadron had used to great effect bombing V-weapon targets in the summer. Their new leader, W/Cdr Willie Tait, would act as master bomber, usually known as MC, for a total force of 136 Lancasters from 5 Group. The force would include Lancasters from 9 Sqn, the only other squadron apart from 617 that had a bulged bomb bay on its aircraft allowing them to carry the Tallboy. Tait had just returned from leading an attack by 617 Sqn on the German battleship *Tirpitz* in Kaa Fjord in northern Norway, from a Russian Air Force base near Murmansk. The last of his crews were still arriving back at Woodhall Spa up to three days before the canal raid.

There was one huge problem in attacking the canal at Ladbergen. Only a few miles away lay a German night-fighter airfield at Hansdorf, near Münster. Any bombing of the canal would inevitably bring them into action, so 5 Group – whose plan it was – briefed the crews of 107 of its Lancasters to bomb the Luftwaffe airfield at the same time as the attack opened at Ladbergen to prevent the *Nachtjäger* taking off. The raid was laid on for a night when most of the other groups of Bomber Command, 549 aircraft in all, were attacking the Ruhr port of Neuss, on the opposite side of the Rhine to Düsseldorf. It was hoped this air fleet to the south would attract most of the night fighters called to orbit their beacons across Germany. To compound the confusion for the Luftwaffe controller, forty-two Mosquitos of the Light Night Striking Force would attack Bochum in the Ruhr at the same time. A spoof raid would also be carried out by a small force of Mosquitos on Rheine, a few miles to the north of Ladbergen. All the attacks were timed to open at 9.20 p.m.[14]

The operation, like most laid on by Bomber Command at this stage of the war, lacked nothing by way of bluff, counter-bluff and downright devious planning and most of the scheming worked well, the much larger raid, on Neuss, creating considerable damage in dock and factory areas for the loss of only seven aircraft because few fighters reached the inland port on time in the German controller's confusion. But as so often happened it was the most imponderable, the target-area weather, that spoiled the carefully laid plans made hours before and now cost the lives of crews on the Dortmund-Ems Canal raid.

Bomb aimers of the Dambuster squadron Lancasters who arrived over the area of Ladbergen where they expected to see the aqueducts carrying the canal, met the kind of conditions that had prevented a successful attack by their squadron in the past: thick cloud. In this case it blocked any sighting of red spot fires that had been dropped by Mosquitos. F/Sgt Peter Whittaker, a mid-upper gunner in the crew of F/Lt Geoffrey Stout, one of those who had just returned to Woodhall Spa from Russia, later reported to intelligence officers: 'Over the target there was 10/10s cloud. We were to bomb on the red marker, but after tooling around for about five minutes the MC told us to try and make individual runs over the area to try to identify the target ... we were unable to locate the target and we received orders to abandon the search and return

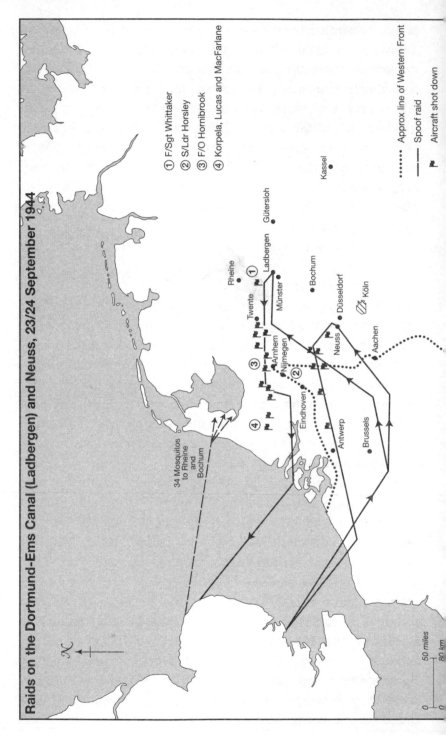

Raids on the Dortmund-Ems Canal (Ladbergen) and Neuss, 23/24 September 1944

① F/Sgt Whittaker
② S/Ldr Horsley
③ F/O Hornibrook
④ Korpela, Lucas and MacFarlane

······ Approx line of Western Front
—— Spoof raid
Aircraft shot down

Kassel

Gütersloh

Rheine
Ladbergen ①

Bochum

Twente
Münster

Düsseldorf
Köln

Arnhem
Nijmegen ②
Neuss
Aachen

③

Eindhoven

④

Antwerp

Brussels

34 Mosquitos
to Rheine
and
Bochum

0   50 miles
0   80 km

home.'[15] Fortunately others of 617 and 9 Sqns, who like Stout had descended to 7,000 feet to try to find the red flare, did spot a marker and two dropped their Tallboys accurately enough to breach each branch of the canal and others of Main Force then cratered the area, which would make repairs difficult.

But the fatal delay as most of the Lancasters milled around the area of the aqueducts searching for the TIs gave the night fighters time to arrive. The raid on the Luftwaffe airfield of Hansdorf nearby had suffered for lack of a master bomber, who failed to reach the target. There was intense highly accurate light flak hosing in flashing white streams across the airfield and only twenty-three aircraft attacked, most in fact bombing Münster itself. The diversion to keep the night fighters away from the Dortmund-Ems Canal had failed and the Luftwaffe now had its revenge. The night fighters were equipped with Schrage Musik, a development in aerial gunnery which consisted of two machine guns, or more usually cannons, installed in the roof of a twin-engined German night fighter at an angle of 70 to 80 degrees. It allowed the night fighter to creep slowly into the blind spot below the RAF machine and fire, usually with tracerless ammunition, between the glowing exhausts on either wing, thereby setting fire to a petrol tank. After a quick fatal burst the night fighter dived away from the roaring red and yellow glare of the now furiously burning bomber and looked for another victim in the blackness of the night. Schrage Musik accounted for most British bombers lost on night raids at this time and its use was never fully fathomed by the Air Ministry until the war was closing, though they realised by interrogating lucky crews who survived such attacks that aircraft were being fired on at a strange angle by unseen machines.

F/Lt Stout's aircraft became the Luftwaffe weapon's latest victim as he climbed away from the target and the later written report by F/Sgt Whittaker to intelligence officers makes it clear Schrage Musik was used although Whittaker, like the rest of Bomber Command's airmen, hadn't been told about the Luftwaffe's secret weapon. 'Shortly after leaving the target area I heard cannon shells hitting the plane, the intercom went dead and the pilot started corkscrew action,' Whittaker reported. Crucially, he continued:

> I saw no enemy aircraft about, but also saw no flak. I think we were attacked from below.
>
> I climbed down from the turret, saw flames coming from the bomb bay and with the bomb aimer [F/O W. A. Rupert] went to the scene of the fire which had burst through the bomb inspection window and flames were licking into the fuselage. There was much smoke. I ran into the navigator [F/O Clyde Graham] who seemed to be terribly wounded – he was yelling and searching for parachutes at some of which he was tugging and pulling the rip grips. He ran forward and the bomb aimer handed me a large fire extinguisher which however did not function and there was nothing we could do.
>
> We went forward after putting on our parachutes and found the navigator had collapsed on the forward hatch. We pulled him on one side, freed the hatch, and after fixing a chute to him – he was now unconscious – pulled his ripcord and pushed him out. I spoke to the pilot as I passed him. I do not know whether he had been hit, but he seemed a bit strange. He was groping around for his parachute unsuccessfully and I went back to find one for him. I heard a yell and thinking he had found his chute I returned. As I started to ask the pilot about it he pushed me away and said, 'Get out!' As I baled out I could see two chutes below me.[16]

The aircraft had passed over the border with Holland, but F/Sgt Whittaker's traumas were to continue on the ground.

S/Ldr Hugh Horsley was the skipper of a 61 Sqn Lancaster lost, K-King. He also was an unwitting victim of Schrage Musik, though in fact, unlike most others, shortly before reaching the Dortmund-Ems Canal. After evading and getting back to Britain he reported:

> We did not bomb because on our fourth leg we were hit, probably by flak (which was not seen). Both port engines were put out of commission and the aircraft could not be controlled . . . I gave the

order to put on parachutes and turned the aircraft west, heading for the English lines. I commanded the crew to jump, but at 6,000ft turned the aircraft east heading back for the German positions in case the aircraft should come down on British lines. At 4,000ft I went down to the front hatch to bale out ... I landed safely, but I am not sure where, I believe it to be due west of Duisberg, west of the River Meuse. I decided to make a North West course towards the British lines between Eindhoven and Nijmegen. After burying my parachute and harness I carried on until the next morning and finally reached British lines about 1920 hours on September 24.[17]

The keen and resourceful officer made the most of his trek through enemy territory. 'During my walk I made a recce of everything which might be of value to the army intelligence,' he reported, 'and gave details of results to various commands and intelligence officers and to Major Warren of the Inns of Court Regt, who was likely to make a recce of the area I traversed.' Horsley's 22-year-old flight engineer, P/O Charles Cawthorne, also evaded, narrowly avoiding capture by German troops. Back in Britain he reported:

After giving the skipper his parachute I baled out and above I could see another parachute coming down. I landed heavily on my left knee and my parachute caught in some barbed wire and was billowing out as a big white cloud. This evidently attracted unfriendly attention because I heard people and dogs approaching and then some shots whistled in my direction. I abandoned my parachute and ran for it.

Coming down I had more or less orientated myself by the river and gun flashes and so made off in a generally south west direction, I stopped for a breather after a couple of hours running, by which time my knee was giving me trouble. I had decided to stop in a ditch which had some straw in it and as I burrowed underneath I found another evader's parachute harness. It seemed wise to carry on a bit further. There were no woods or cover at all until finally I came to a barn at about 0400. Here I laid up. In the morning I heard voices, but shelling started in the area and drew the people away. After a time I came out of my hide and made a recce to try to fix my position. A few fields away some two truck loads of Germans were laying mines or doing some sort of wiring. I set off then down the road, but came on more Germans so returned to my barn.

P/O Cawthorne realised that German troops might soon enter the barn and even though it was now full daylight he would have to flee its beguiling security. To disguise his appearance he took off his white aircrew roll-neck sweater, soiled it with mud, and put it on again over his battledress. He found an old bucket in the barn, filled it with grass and walked out holding it, hoping he looked like a Dutch farm worker. 'I went off to the nearby village passing Germans and villagers with a "Ja",' he wrote. 'I nearly ran into a German tank.' After an hour and a half of walking, expecting to be found out at any moment, he came across a shack occupied by a young man and his mother. They hid him in a small plantation until the Germans left the area and a few hours later he was able to make contact with a British patrol.

I was given the choice of waiting for the main body to come up or to go forward with the recce unit. I chose the latter and remained with them until September 24th. While with the British troops the villagers took me to be a Hun prisoner. They cheered the army and booed me. It would have been risky to have moved out alone, although when it was known I was RAF my popularity transcended that of the army![18]

From S/Ldr Horsley's crew two were killed, two became POWs and three evaded, the third being the rear gunner Sgt R. Hoskisson. Within days Horsley and Hoskisson were back with their squadron at Skellingthorpe, on the southern edge of Lincoln and within four months one of them was dead. On 1 February Horsley was taking off from Skellingthorpe's main runway for a raid on Siegen with Hoskisson and a new crew when the port outer of his Lancaster cut. He force-landed on the airfield, but the aircraft caught fire. Before it exploded the injured Hoskisson escaped from the turret, a survivor again.[19]

For most crews whose aircraft were shot out of the sky by hunting *Nachtjäger* on the Ladbergen and Hansdorf operation on 23 September there was little chance to react before accurately aimed Schrage Musik cannon set wing tanks ablaze, rapidly ending in an explosion of orange and scarlet, killing all on board in an instant or tossing them out into the black sky without parachutes. For a few who did bale out and then evade, their attempts to get back to England would continue almost until the end of the war. One of them was F/O Oliver Korpela, a Canadian lumberjack. The 24-year-old 50 Sqn pilot had bombed the Dortmund-Ems Canal and was on his way back across Holland when his Lancaster appeared as a blip on a night-fighter radar screen. 'A cannon shell exploded in my aircraft setting it on fire,' he reported months later. 'I tried to corkscrew, but the aelirons had been shot away. I then tried to give the command to jump, but the intercom was out of action, so I signalled to the flight engineer (Sgt H. Macfarlane) to jump and then abandoned the aircraft.' In fact the bomb aimer, F/O Charles Lucas, whose position was over the forward escape hatch, had already baled out as whirling flame roared through the Lancaster and the intercom went dead. They were the only members of the crew to escape before the glowing, twisting wreckage hit the ground not far from the Zuider Zee twenty minutes before midnight. Korpela continued:

> I landed in some bushes close to Oudleusen. After burying my parachute and Mae West I started walking south, I came to a river and walked along the bank until I came to a dam which I managed to cross when the German sentry was not looking. I continued on my way until daylight when I found a hut in a field and tried to sleep. However, I was too cold so approached a farmhouse and after considerable difficulties made the farmer understand who I was. He took me in and gave me some food while his wife went and brought back five members of the Underground movement. Later a member of the Dutch police

arrived and took me to a house in a field about two kilometres away where I stayed for six days.[20]

F/O Lucas had come down at Dalfsen, east of Zwolle. After burying his parachute he also made for a farmhouse, which he watched until daylight for any sign of the enemy before making himself known and being given food. 'About mid-day a Dutchman who spoke English was brought to me and I was told I would be helped and was advised not to make for the fighting at Arnhem,' he reported in his intelligence debriefing. 'That night I was taken to the house of a policeman, where I met my flight engineer, Sgt Macfarlane, with whom I remained until liberated. We remained here in hiding for eight weeks.'[21]

F/Sgt Whittaker, the 617 Sqn gunner shot down shortly after the raid began, discovered as he hit the ground that, like the unfortunate navigator F/O Graham, he also had been wounded, in the head and the right elbow. He later wrote:

I decided to make for the south west [the Arnhem direction]. After about an hour I came to a farm at which I sought help. It was about 2300 by my watch. The door was opened by a young girl. My reception seemed a bit odd, but I was invited to come into the living room where there were some people. I was in my battledress and my air gunner insignia was clearly visible, also I said 'Englander'. While I was applying my field dressing to my elbow I noticed one of the men leave the room. It seemed to me that he might be off to fetch the Germans and I got up to leave too. The other man in the room got between me and the door and held me up with a pistol. I got him to look over his shoulder and at that moment kicked him hard in the stomach. While he was on the ground I grabbed his pistol and bolted. I ran and walked for a time, still heading south west, when a car came along heading for the farm I had left. From what I gathered later the farm in question was owned by noted NSB (Dutch Fascists) and quite possibly the car contained Germans fetched by the man who had left the house. I understand the family were 'taken care of' by the underground movement.[22]

F/Sgt Whittaker then found a farm building and fell asleep in straw, coming out the next day to the new farmhouse and 'receiving a very friendly welcome. I was given food and my wounds were dressed. A doctor was sent for. He did something to my arm. There was a crack and it was freed from the stiff, fixed position, so that the doctor could strap it up. I gather a shrapnel shard had hit the elbow, also the doctor pulled a piece of splinter from my head.' A few days later a note was smuggled to Whittaker from F/O Rupert,* the bomb aimer in his crew, asking him to join him in his hiding place, a barn in the grounds of a large farm. There Whittaker witnessed a successful arms drop to the Dutch Resistance and was joined by three Arnhem evaders, two sergeant escapers from Stalag IVB near Munich and a private from a Polish tank division. Eventually he was told he was being moved, given a bike and 'went off in a convoy of some 80 to 90 Dutchmen on the run to a marsh in the middle of which was a small island where some sort of camp had been prepared. This camp was a kind of arsenal to which supplies were brought daily.' Inevitably such a large camp was surrounded by the Germans and Whittaker was handed over to the Gestapo. His ordeals and adventures before were nothing to what would happen to him over the next months and for F/O Korpela, F/O Lucas and Sgt Macfarlane too a new, strange, terrifying war was just beginning.

IN the days following the raid on the Dortmund-Ems Canal as WAAF interpreters examined reconnaissance pictures it was obvious it had been a great success. Two Tallboys of 617 Sqn had breached each branch of the canal and caused it to drain over a 6-mile stretch. The barges that had carried a succession of coal and iron ore to and from the Ruhr were now stuck. When the Germans finally repaired the embankments Bomber Command returned in

---

* All of Whittaker's crew survived with the exception of the pilot and the wounded navigator, F/O Graham – a general's son – who was found by Dutch Resistance men dead at the base of a tree through which he had fallen and hit the ground heavily.

February to drain the canal again. As Bomber Command turned once more to attacking German industry the Reich coal heaps grew higher as a result of its inability to move the fuel the war factories craved. Between August and February as coal production in the Ruhr fell from 10,417,000 tons to 4,778,000 tons actual coal stocks in the Ruhr rose by 415,000 tons to 2,217,000, much of it piled up uselessly for lack of the means to move it to the furnaces.[23] It was a sign of the total breakdown that would eventually overtake the Reich.

But the cost of canal raiding was always high and none more so than on the raid of 23 September. The chop rate had been eleven Lancasters, nearly 10 per cent of the Ladbergen force, including one of the Dambuster squadron's aircraft. The losses were felt most keenly at Skellingthorpe, where both 50 and 61 Sqns were based. Two of 50 Sqn's dispersals were empty the next day and so were four of 61 Sqn, which also lost three Lancasters attempting to bomb the canal and one on the Hansdorf raid.* The next night 50 and 61 Sqns each lost another aircraft on a raid on Calais. The crews of both squadrons were used to spending much of their time in Lincoln, the centre of which was just a short bus ride away from the airfield's main gate and the gaps were noticeable at the bar of their favourite drinking spot, the Saracen's Head Hotel, known as the Snake Pit to Bomber Command.

Within days new fresh-faced airmen arrived at guardrooms to fill the crew rosters. There was no shortage for what lay ahead. A profusion of aircrew was now available to Harris, the anxious search for replacements finally over as average losses fell to 1 per cent because of the Luftwaffe's decline as a result of a lack of fuel and materials, denied by the attacks of Bomber Command and the USAAF. Sgt Boness, for instance, remained on 463 Sqn, but

---

* This was the aircraft of 20-year-old Australian F/O Albert Hornibrook. The crew, with the exception of the rear gunner, were lost when the aircraft crashed into the Waal. F/O Hornibrook's elder brother, Kevin, had been killed in a Berlin raid in August 1943, saving the life of his bomb aimer. See author's work, *Bomber Boys*.

never took off to engage the enemy again because so many complete crews were now arriving, his operational experience for the war remaining at half a trip. There were now so many pilots docking from the training schools of the Commonwealth Air Training Plan in Canada that there were too few crews to go around and many would-be bomber skippers found themselves remustered. Bomb aimer Sgt Frank Tolley, who was at an operational training unit in September before finally joining 625 Sqn, remembers: 'Our flight engineer, Joe Platt, was a pilot. When he finished his pilot's course there was a surplus of them and he like a number of others was sent down to St Athan to do an abridged engineer's course. He was a very good flight engineer, he could almost tell you to a pint how much petrol we had. He was a bit miffed about not having his own crew, though.'[24] The result of now having an influx of pilot-engineers also dramatically altered the futures of those flight engineers already in training. Many found their courses cut short as they were transferred to the army, to make up shortages caused by post D-Day casualties.

The wealth of aircrew was matched by an abundance of aircraft available to Harris now that the Luftwaffe was in retreat and he was no longer playing catch-up as the scythe was swung nightly among his squadrons. The commander who always believed the war could be won by bombing alone was itching to return to hitting German industry in the cities of the Reich. Since 1 April it had been the staff of Dwight D. Eisenhower, head of the invasion armies, who had called the shots at Bomber Command. As Arnhem came and went and the armies' needs for heavy tactical support lessened there were various factions putting forward different agendas for what direction the now huge RAF and Commonwealth bomber force should take.

Two days after the Dortmund-Ems Canal raid control of Bomber Command was handed back by Eisenhower to Sir Charles Portal, the Chief of the Air Staff, and thereby to Harris. Harris did what he always intended and returned to raiding the Reich's industrial base in its cities, to destroy again what the Germans had managed to repair in the interim of the bomber boys supporting the invasion armies. 'I was seriously alarmed by the prospect of what the enemy might have been able to do during this six months respite,' Harris explained in his post-war memoirs. 'It was, moreover, a period of critical importance when the enemy was getting into production a whole range of new weapons from jet-propelled aircraft to submarines which could recharge their batteries under water.'[25]

There had been many changes in Bomber Command since last he had conducted a campaign against German conurbations. Not least that techniques had improved so much single groups were now able to operate almost as independent air forces, carrying out devastating attacks on one key community at the same time as the rest of Bomber Command hit another Reich industrial city many miles away. Two aerial armies in particular, 5 Group and 3 Group, demonstrated in October how effective they now were with their own individual style of attacks. They each raided Bremen and Bonn, burning out the heart of both cities. Among the aircrew carrying out the raids there would be the usual tales of tragedy amid the awesome terrible triumph of turning the Nazi dream to ashes.

TWO

FROM ATTRITION TO PRECISION

THERE was no force dearer to Harris among his disparate troops than 5 Group, led by Sir Ralph Cochrane, a flight commander to Harris when he commanded 45 Sqn in Iraq in the 1920s.[1] Indeed so close had the men become twenty years later, as Cochrane was allowed to practise different techniques from the rest of Bomber Command, sometimes to the chagrin of other group commanders, it had led to a joke currently circulating among the bomber boys' messes. It was said that Harris had been speculating among a large group of his more junior colleagues about whom Princess Elizabeth would marry after the war. No one could give an answer, then from the back came the muffled verdict: 'I bet it will be someone from 5 Group.'

So high did the crews of the group, based south of Lincoln, now stand in the C-in-C's opinion that since April Cochrane had been operating almost his own air force with its own Pathfinder squadrons, wrested from Don Bennett, the 8 (PFF) Group commander, because Bennett did not believe it was possible to mark targets successfully at low level. The brilliantly daring W/Cdr Leonard Cheshire had triumphantly shown throughout the summer with the 5 Group 617 Sqn that it was not only possible but the path to success.[2]

Now for the return to Germany Cochrane had other techniques to display, notably a development of the group's offset-marking method, whereby a point was marked short of the actual target and crews were ordered to overshoot it, thus avoiding smoke from explosions obscuring the actual aiming point. So keen was Cochrane that his crews be individually tutored in the 5 Group methods that since February he had operated a special Lancaster Finishing School at Syerston in Nottinghamshire where airmen who had just left Heavy Conversion Units, usually the last stop before a front-line squadron, underwent a further intense course before being judged fit for battle among Cochrane's select. It could be gruelling. Sgt Harry Stunell, a 21-year-old wireless operator who shared radio lectures with George Thompson, later to win a posthumous VC, found the risks high-altitude flying could bring put him in hospital. 'I was in the sick bay in October with a suspected perforated ear drum when the rest of my crew were posted,' he remembers. 'My Australian skipper, F/Lt Jack Barlow, who we called "Pop" because he was getting on in age for aircrew and had shaggy grey hair, went with the rest of them to 106 Sqn at Metheringham.'[3]

Metheringham was not among the choicest postings in Bomber Command. It had been constructed to wartime economy standards less than a year before, its uniform black Nissen huts marching into the mist of the Lincolnshire Fens. The airfield's three concrete runways lay between the hamlets of Martin and Metheringham itself and the impact on village life of 1,500 men in air-force blue had been dramatic. Kay Kirby was one of the few civilian incomers. She had arrived in Metheringham in July as the bride of a 106 Sqn navigator, unaware that Harris strongly disapproved of wives living near their spouse's stations because of the likelihood of husbands being killed. Now Kay, barely out of her teens, had been married just over a year and the thirty-operation tour of her 22-year-old husband George was almost over. She remembers:

I met George when I was 17. I had gone with my family to a cousin's wedding at Ashford in Kent and stayed for a holiday and he was a friend of the bride's family. We went to a roller skating rink and he asked if he could write to me when I went home to London. We were engaged when he went out to South Africa to train as a navigator and we got married in September 1943 after he came back. The garden of my parents' home near Stockwell backed onto the church, but it had been bomb-damaged and we got married in the church hall. I had a full white wedding. I worked in the office of a big jeweller's and a lot of the older women I worked with gave me clothing coupons for a wedding dress. They were like mother hens. I had leave due to me so asked a manager if I could take time off unpaid to get married and he was most indignant. He never said yes and he never said no, so I took the leave and when I got back I had been given my cards. I then went to work for a silversmith's in Regent Street. They were doing a lot of contract work on clocks for aeroplanes.

We had our honeymoon in Torquay at relations of George's and I brought back a very pretty dress. When he was posted to Metheringham I went too. He asked me to meet him in the sergeants' mess and when I went in wearing the dress I brought back from honeymoon I found everyone else was in uniform of course. There was a sort of gasp of 'What's this that's come in.' My sister's husband, who was aircrew in bombers, had asked her to come up to Lincolnshire because she had been bombed out of their flat in London and she was pregnant then. I think she probably put the idea in my head that I would move to Lincolnshire to be near George. I used to go up to Lincoln from Metheringham about once a week and my sister and I would meet for lunch. I lived in the village as a lodger in the house of a large farming family, named Holvey. They had a pair of council houses that had been made into one. One of the sons was in the army, but there were another four sons, ranging from teenage to early twenties, there were two daughters, who also worked on the land, then the farmer and his wife. The two daughters were about my age.

My husband was able to visit me most days. If he didn't turn up I knew there was a briefing. When he was visiting me if anything was laid on in a hurry the others in the crew would tell him because it was only three minutes by bike from the airfield. When he was operating I could hear the aircraft revving up then the sound of them taking off. I saw them climbing above the airfield, their navigation lights showing as they set out. Then hours later as I lay in bed I heard the noise of them returning. That seemed to go on for a long time. I suppose I was a bit naïve, but I never thought he

would not come back. There was a WAAF on the camp, also a
London girl, who was the girlfriend of one of the men in George's
crew. She and I were quite friendly and she would come and tell
me they were back. Towards the end of George's tour I asked him
if he wanted me to go home to London to hear where he would be
posted. But he said 'No' because my being at Metheringham got
him away from the realities of what he was doing. He came from
a very good-living family and it was very much on his conscience
that he was killing people.[4]

The final operation of F/Sgt Kirby's tour would be to Bremen.
The inland port on the river Weser had always been a high-priority
target for Bomber Command. Bremen had been attacked in force
a total of thirty-one times, beginning with a leaflet raid on the very
first day of the war and in fact had been the final target city in
Harris's three 1,000-bomber raids of mid-1942, causing considerable damage. But as techniques improved and defences
declined, by late 1944 vastly more destruction could be inflicted
on a target involving much smaller forces of aircraft. On the night
of 18 August 274 Lancasters and Halifaxes of various groups
devastated Bremen's port area and much of the centre and north-
west of the city for the loss of only one aircraft. On 6 October 5
Group, assisted by 1 Group, was asked to return and take the
ancient Hanseatic city out of the war for good. It was a night of
a three-quarter moon, unthinkable conditions for Bomber
Command to raid in during most of the previous spring when the
Luftwaffe was at its peak of efficiency.

As F/Sgt Kirby went into briefing in the ubiquitous, semi-
circular-roofed Nissen hut in the early afternoon of that brisk
autumn day, he discovered his pilot F/Lt Douglas Stewart would
be taking an extra crew member to Bremen. Harry Stunell's
skipper F/Lt Jack Barlow, who at 35 would be the oldest man on
board, had found himself on the battle order to fly his mandatory
raid as a second-dickey pilot, gaining experience before he operated with his own crew. As the airmen lined up on the hard
benches, leaning forward attentively, they heard their squadron

commander tell them most of Bomber Command would be going to Dortmund that night, a total of 523 crews. But 106 Sqn and the other squadrons in 5 Group would be taking part in an exclusive attack to demonstrate how effective the group's new marking and bombing techniques could be.

Early illuminator aircraft from 5 Group's own Pathfinder squadrons, 97 and 83, would identify Bremen on their H2S sets, then by the light of the flares they had dropped the crews of seven Mosquitos following immediately behind would identify separate aiming points downwind of the actual targets Bomber Command wanted attacked and mark them with 1,000-lb target indicators. The master bomber would check the position of these and drop target indicators of a different colour to cancel any that might be wide of the mark. Finally the rest of Sir Ralph Cochrane's boys would approach the marking points on several different tracks and release their bombs by predetermined seconds after an aiming point appeared in their bomb sights. This was 5 Group's famous offset-marking method which prevented the actual target Bomber Command needed to hit being obscured by smoke. Having squadrons approach on different tracks allowed bombs to be distributed more evenly, fanning outwards, producing fires that quickly linked up and spread out of control. In the bomber offensive of 1943 the idea was to concentrate bombs in a circle, thus inevitably wasting a great many towards the edges of a target by crews bombing short as they were faced with walls of groping white searchlights and bursting red flak. The new 5 Group technique of area bombing would hopefully mean one single group could achieve the same destruction rate as several groups in 1943 and the early part of 1944. It had been tried on the virtually virgin target of Bremerhaven three weeks before and had struck a knock-out blow. Now it was hoped the new methods would achieve the same at nearby Bremen itself with its important three Focke Wulf aircraft factories and extensive shipbuilding yards.

At Metheringham shortly after 5 p.m. the fourteen aircraft assigned to bomb the north German city lumbered down the perimeter track, their engines snarling and barking, then one by

one lined up for the quickly flashed green signal from flying control
and thundered away down the main runway and into the rapidly
chilling autumn air. As they climbed in wide circuits over the
airfield, the sound of their Merlin engines booming and echoing
in the villages below, other luckier airmen were preparing to go to
a concert on the base. It was provided by a troupe of entertainers
from ENSA, initials that aircrew and others liked to say stood for
Every Night Something Awful, but in fact were an acronym for
Entertainments National Service Association – actors, singers and
comedians who toured air force and army camps bringing light
relief to the troops.

F/Sgt Kirby's wife Kay received an informal invitation to
attend. She remembers:

> The WAAF I was friendly with came to tell me, 'They are flying
> tonight, but I'm going to the ENSA concert on the camp and about
> the time it's over they'll be back. Would you like to come to the
> concert and we'll meet them in the sergeants' mess afterwards?'
> I had been to one or two ENSA concerts on the base or even
> concerts the RAF people had put on themselves, so I went to the
> concert with her. The crews had already taken off when we got
> there. I knew before that this was the last trip of George's tour.
> I was told it would be about midnight when George would come
> back to the mess. We had made plans for the future.[5]

The force now flying east would do so in daylight for more than
two hours; only the leg as they approached the Frisian Islands
would be in twilight though Bremen itself would be reached in
darkness as navigators followed on their H2S sets the narrowing
line from the North Sea of the river Weser. It was hoped that
diversionary raids by high-flying Mosquitos, including a small
number over Berlin, would distract the German night-fighter
controller from both the Bremen raiders and the larger Dortmund
force. That was exactly what happened, Bomber Command's
Operational Research Section later recorded with some sat-
isfaction: 'The enemy's fighters seem to have had little fore-
knowledge of the attacks.'[6]

The force tasked with putting 5 Group on the map by taking Bremen off it arrived over the city in clear skies shortly after 8 p.m. Looking down from 16,000 feet, crews could see the converging roads of the city standing out in the moonlight. Bombing began immediately and accurately. More than 1,000 tons of bombs, of which four-fifths were incendiaries, went down within twenty minutes. So close was the rain of firebombs that S/Ldr J. E. Grindon's Lancaster from 106 Sqn was badly damaged by falling incendiaries and he had to nurse his crippled plane homewards to land eventually at the emergency airfield of Woodbridge in Suffolk. An inferno soon raged throughout Bremen town centre, spreading out as planned under the 5 Group method, to engulf factories and nearly 5,000 houses. Yet only sixty-five people were killed, suggesting an efficient shelter system and wholesale evacuation of the city after the previous raid in August. 'Great fires were started and those at Bremen were commented on by Mosquito crews returning from Berlin,' the ORS boffins later reported.[7]

> The weight of the attack was shown to have fallen on the town centre, large areas of which, having escaped unscathed, were devastated. Neustadt and Alstaat were particularly badly hit, seven of the primary industries were severely damaged; [as were] the three factories of Focke Wulf Flugzeugbau, each priority; two motor transport factories; a ships pump manufacturer and two engineering works. Several unrated industries were also affected and thermal power stations and gas works, four hutted camps and the tramway depot was hit and many warehouses gutted.[8]

The economical methods of destruction by 5 Group were vindicated and Bremen was finished as an industrial and shipping centre; it would not be attacked again until the war was nearly over and it was about to be occupied by British troops. In fact so economical of Bomber Command's aircraft was the raid that only five Lancasters were lost, two to target flak, two north of the Frisians on the way out and a fifth to a fighter west of Emden. Unknown to Kay Kirby, awaiting her husband's return and a worry-free future as the ENSA programme unfolded at

Metheringham, her husband was in one of the last three.*

Kay Kirby remembers:

> That night the WAAF and I hung around a bit after the show and she went to make some enquiries. Then she told me, 'They've not returned yet.' She came with me back to the house and we stayed up half the night. The girls in the house stoked up the fire and made cups of tea. We sat there for hours then finally went to bed and the next morning she went to the camp and came to tell me they were definitely missing. My sister's husband Jimmy had finished his tour in Bomber Command and was on leave with her at my parents' house near Stockwell. In the middle of the morning I went to the post office in Metheringham and sent a telegram to them and to George's parents saying he was missing. The lady in the post office, who saw the contents, looked at me and said: 'If you want to send a telegram any time of the day or night, dear, just come down to me.' I got a wire back to say Jimmy was coming to bring me home and he did so. He went in his uniform to see someone on the camp and they told him, 'We didn't know she was here, we've got her down as being in London.' They had sent the 'Missing' telegram there. They apologised and said if they had known I was in Metheringham they would have sent someone up to me. I packed my bags and came back to my parents' house in London. My sister's baby was born in the December two months after George was lost and they named her Georgina.[9]

Mrs Kirby, not yet old enough to vote, had become one of the thousands of war widows left behind by the scythe that swept through the junior ranks of Bomber Command. Of the eight men

* Only two of the eight men aboard Lancaster PD214 have a known resting place. The second-dickey pilot F/Lt Jack Barlow, a married former bank manager, of Rockhampton, Queensland, Australia, is buried in the same grave as rear gunner Sgt Ronald Paul, a 20-year-old bachelor, of Whitehaven, Cumberland, at Becklingen War Cemetery, south of Hamburg. The others are remembered on the Commonwealth War Graves Commission's Runnymede Memorial.

aboard her husband's aircraft six were married. Sgt Stunell was released from sick bay at Syerston shortly after the Bremen raid and reported to 106 Sqn. 'I arrived at Metheringham to find my skipper had not come back,' he remembers. 'Our crew was broken up after he went missing and I joined the crew of F/O Jim Scott who had arrived at Metheringham short of three crew members.'[10] Sgt Stunell's own terrible operational ordeal with his new crew would come in January.

Just over a week after the devastating raid on Bremen 5 Group demonstrated again how effective their new bombing techniques were. Cochrane sent 233 Lancasters and 7 Mosquitos to Brunswick and once more completely destroyed the centre of an old city. Brunswick had been attacked four times before by Bomber Command in 1944, often at great cost for little gain – losing for instance 38 Lancasters out of 496 dispatched to the target on 14 January. On this occasion just one Lancaster was missing and Brunswick and its factories which fed the Luftwaffe armaments machine had been so effectively smashed that Bomber Command was able to take it off its target list. Air-raid officials in Brunswick thought as many as 1,000 bombers had been used, the damage was so extensive. Yet all this was achieved by just one group, on a night when the rest of Harris's forces were wrecking Duisburg for the second time in 24 hours.[11]

ARMAGGEDON from the air was now being visited on the Reich and in October yet another group showed how effective it could be when operating independently; 3 Group had long been the poor relation when it came to resources from Bomber Command headquarters. When the bomber offensive had begun in earnest in 1943 the group had been equipped with the Stirling, an aircraft that had its wingspan limited to 100 feet by the Air Ministry in its original design in 1936 so that it could fit in the then available RAF hangars. The aircraft's resulting 14,000-foot ceiling made it such easy meat for fighters Harris had had to withdraw his Stirling squadrons from Germany within a week of opening the Battle of Berlin in the winter of 1943–4.[12] Stirlings had then been used in mining and spoof operations and on the short-haul targets to France. In fact the last major bombing operation of the war in which they were employed had been on the marshalling yards and locomotive sheds at Laon on 22 April.[13]

But by the autumn of 1944, 3 Group was a different force indeed. Not only was it fully equipped with the Lancaster by this time, it had a new bombing aid, GH. Its squadrons would now show how successful they were at using it. GH was a combination of the navigation aid Gee – radio pulses to a positioning screen on an aircraft receiver – a system that Bomber Command had been using since March 1942, and the target-finding device Oboe. The latter had enabled high-flying Mosquitos to mark selected areas to within a 120-yard error and led to devastation of much German industry in the Battle of the Ruhr in the spring of 1943. Oboe worked by transmitting pulses from a pair of home-based ground stations to a suitably equipped aircraft and then registering, by its automatic responses, the aircraft's position over enemy territory. One station controlled the track of the aircraft over the target while the other calculated the point on the track when the target indicators should be released. However, for much of the bomber offensive only one aircraft at a time could be controlled by each pair of ground stations, so Harris encouraged scientists to find a new system. It became known as GH where, unlike Oboe, instead of the active components being on the ground they were in the aircraft, a transmitter and receiver, which enabled ranges from two ground stations to be measured. Its big advantage was that it could be used by a number of aircraft at the same time, but it required a good navigator to work out and stay on the right track.

F/Lt Philip Gray, a pilot on 186 Sqn at Stradishall, was aware the reason his crew were selected for the week-long GH course at Feltwell in Norfolk was because, as he had been told, 'That navigator of yours is dynamite.' He remembers:

> The system was accurate and relatively easy to operate. Once in the air the navigator fed the target co-ordinates into his GH radar set. With the bomb doors open for business over the target city the

navigator could then release our little bundles of deadly joy from his navigation table. He need never actually see the target. In fact Gerry [Merrick], our very capable navigator, once admitted to me that he never did see an enemy target. Lucky him![14]

However a pair of GH stations could only service up to eighty bombers at one time and in practice most 3 Group crews found themselves in the position of supporters in V-formations of three bombers, the lead one – its tail painted with distinctive yellow stripes for other aircraft to recognise and formate on –-being the only aircraft that would actually use GH. 'When he dropped his bombs in compliance with the co-ordinates supplied, the air bombers in the Lancasters on either side of the lead machine would then release their loads of destruction when they saw the second bomb leave the leader's bomb bay,' F/Lt Gray remembers. 'That was the basic plan.'[15] It hadn't always worked. In an initial trial by one Mosquito on the night of 4 October 1943 GH had proved unable to find the aiming point in Aachen. Twelve days later another GH-equipped Mosquito was sent to attack Dortmund, but its equipment failed and it had to bomb by dead reckoning. Bomber Command tried once more, in a large raid on the Mannesmann steel plant at Düsseldorf on the night of 1 November. This time about half of the sets failed, leaving only fifteen aircraft of 115 and 514 Sqns to bomb the factory on GH, but those GH-aimed bombs wreaked encouraging damage to the plant. Harris – now aware that the new equipment might overcome many of the problems of Bomber Command in finding and hitting key targets in foul weather and fearful that before its potential could be fully realised such a valuable piece of equipment might fall into the hands of the Germans, allowing them to create a countermeasure – halted its use.

He wanted all the snags ironed out before a large force of bombers was fitted with the new bombing device, then in short supply. After D-Day and the possibility of establishing GH stations in France, which would greatly increase its range, it became obvious that GH would become a valuable aid for tactical bombing of small targets, such as V-weapon sites. 'It was indeed for tactical bombing that we now intended to use GH, not primarily for precision attacks on German industrial targets, and it was for this reason that in June I made an urgent request for enough GH sets to equip one bomber group. I chose No 3 Group for this,' Harris wrote in his immediate post-war memoirs.[16] By October a third of 3 Group's Lancasters had the device, enough to allow other bombers to formate on them in daylight. 'In September, 1944, the air defence of Germany crumbled to pieces; the German army was driven out of France and the enemy's early warning system was lost,' Harris wrote.[17] At last conditions were ripe for an operational GH daylight experiment without advantage falling to the Luftwaffe.

The commander of 3 Group, Air Vice-Marshall Richard Harrison, asked to be allowed to choose a virgin target, a city entirely or relatively unbombed, to be able to show in post-raid reconnaissance that any devastation was entirely down to GH and the skill of his crews. Harris agreed. There were several towns or cities Harrison could have chosen, but in the caprice of war the dice fell on Bonn, the home of Beethoven, with its university dating from 1818 and many architecturally important buildings. Bonn had no significant war industry; its candidacy for annihilation lay in the fact that it was on the Rhine and a major railway line went through it, both making it part of Germany's north-south transportation axis. It also had hardly been touched by war so far, only being bombed once previously, by the USAAF in August 1943.

In the early hours of 18 October airmen in the string of RAF stations south of the Wash from Mildenhall to Methwold were roused from their beds with orders for a short dawn briefing. They were told they would be the only Bomber Command crews operating that day and the GH experiment was about to be launched in force. A total of 128 Lancasters drawn from nine squadrons would be hitting Bonn without benefit of pre-attack marking from the Pathfinders of 8 Group or indeed any other group. Instead the entire force would strike at Bonn just after

11 a.m. in Vics of three, the lead aircraft in each trio being the one with GH equipment. Crews were told they wouldn't necessarily be formating on aircraft from their own squadron, instead they would pick up the GH leaders, with their yellow-painted tail fins, at pre-designated rendezvous points. As in most ground-breaking forms of warfare, part of the plan went well and some of it didn't. For instance F/O J. G. Benson, an Australian pilot serving on 622 Sqn, later reported: 'The GH leader was not at the rendezvous point, but I picked him up at Bradwell Bay.'[18] From Mildenhall, 15 Sqn had dispatched fourteen Lancasters. 'The aircraft attacked the target in pairs, each pair being led by an aircraft of 218 Sqn carrying special equipment,' the squadron adjutant later recorded. 'The attack was carried out in clear conditions, but owing to the failure of some of the aircraft special equipment the attack appeared to be rather scattered.'[19]

In fact approximately half the GH-equipped aircraft in the stream of bombers, extending in a long line back along the Rhine and stacked in groups of threes between 17,000 and 18,500 feet, experienced fading of the release pulse on the run in to Bonn as they approached from the south just after 11 a.m. They decided to bomb visually, the weather being better than forecast with only three-tenths to five-tenths cloud. 'The decision was possibly premature and unfortunate as in some cases the release pulse picked up sufficiently for bombing,' 3 Group's raid analysis later found. 'Those crews who persevered were able to bomb satisfactorily.'[20] The force was carrying a total of 50 medium-capacity 4,000-lb bombs – shaped quite unaerodynamically like a huge dustbin and known to aircrew as Cookies and to the press as Blockbusters – 200 high-explosive bombs of 500 lbs each and more than 80,000 4-lb incendiary bombs. The latter were each designed to start a fire after the Cookies and other high explosive had turned buildings to combustible debris and blown the roofs off others.

As the GH leaders released their loads from gaping bomb doors the others followed, a rain of explosives and fire heading for the French rococo-style buildings of the town centre. There were no fighters, but heavy radar-predicted flak was sending up a barrage which pilots, intent on holding their aircraft steady on the long bomb run, had to ignore, minds whirling and bowels churning, as it seemed each angry black puff that exploded around their aircraft was the signal for the final fatal blast into oblivion. Seeing the growing, closing pattern of red flak flashes at night as aircraft bored on towards a target was unnerving enough, but the increasing number of daylight raids brought a new dimension of fear to aircrew. It was particularly stressful for pilots, watching death approaching across the sky on the bomb run as an anti-aircraft unit marked them and steeling themselves not to twitch on the controls. The Bonn anti-aircraft units were deemed to be efficiently fearsome – there was a flak training school there. It was easy for ground-based researchers in the comfort of a quiet office later to criticise those who had made a rapid decision to bomb visually as their GH signal faded, or others who had left the formations of GH leaders in the fierce flak to bomb alone, but the dangers of continuing or perhaps making another run in the hope the signal would pick up were not to be contemplated if one hoped to return.

Those bomb aimers who did make a visual attack now had to cope with a westerly wind stronger than forecast. It caused many aircraft loads to fall east of the Rhine, away from Bonn, which lay on the opposite bank. The outspoken Australian F/O Benson cryptically stated at debriefing back at Mildenhall, as stomachs rumbled for lunch: 'Bombed on GH leader at 1103 from 17,000ft, heading 316. On the run up one stick went down in the centre of the town. Unable to see our own bombs hit . . . The speed was too great, 50 per cent of the aircraft were in threes, the rest flying singly over the target.'[21] But F/O W. Mason, a 15 Sqn skipper, reported: 'A good concentration in the centre of the town [with] smoke to 3,000ft.' He was one of the lucky ones able to follow a GH leader with effective equipment though it didn't do him much good. 'Own bombs seen in river,' he told the intelligence officer.[22] Bomber Command's research section prepared a post-raid analysis which ran, 'The bombing hit mostly built-up areas,' then added in the light of crew debriefings, 'The result was disappointing for a GH raid.'[23]

It was true that fading of the GH signal in many of the leader aircraft had led to scattered bombing and other bomb loads had fallen uselessly in the Rhine, but the tonnage from the gaping bomb bays of the Lancaster Vic formations, where the system had worked, had wreaked enormous damage in the centre of Bonn and the fluttering thermite sticks that went down with them caused raging fires. The heart of old Bonn was destroyed, the Prussian Rhine University and many cultural and public buildings were burned out, as was a large residential area. More than 700 buildings were destroyed and 1,000 seriously damaged though the cellar-shelter system and large theatre bunker near the Rhine bridge kept casualties in the town down to just over 300.[24] RAF crews had reported at debriefing seeing four Lancasters falling to Bonn's fierce flak barrage, but it was likely that amid the red shock above the target the identical image of the same Lancaster vanishing in a puff of rolling, oily black confusion had imprinted itself on the minds of many. Only one aircraft of the 128 that had set out after dawn had been lost. F/O Kenneth Smith of 115 Sqn, a 21-year-old from New South Wales, disappeared with his entire crew.

In pure statistical terms of profit and loss the raid had been a great success for GH despite its temperamental performance. For AVM Harrison and 3 Group it meant he was now released from the general daily and nightly demands of Bomber Command headquarters at High Wycombe to pursue, like 5 Group, a virtually independent war for the C-in-C. Harrison would carry out group-strength raids with GH until the end of hostilities. They would have their own crushing effect on key German industrial targets and Reich transport links as well as splitting the enemy's defences, while 5 Group carried on its own singular campaign and the other groups of Bomber Command combined to pound the Reich's cities.

Wrecking the Reich from end to end causing collapse from within was how Harris considered the war would be won, thus removing the need for the Allied armies to storm Germany's final defences. The turning point at which Bomber Command had found itself that autumn after its support for the breakout from Normandy and the rush to the Scheldt estuary and its ports, was at first resolved with a personal decision by Harris to return to his old campaign of eroding the industrial production of Germany's cities and the spirit of the people who lived and worked in them. He recorded in 1947: 'From October 1st until the end of the war, Bomber Command dropped 153,000 tons of high explosive or incendiary bombs on the industrial cities of Germany, many of them new targets, and many other targets that had often been attacked before. In 1944 the heaviest attacks were made in October.'[25] The target cities that Harris related had 'often' been raided previously by his Command were those in Germany's industrial heartland, the well-defended conurbations all crews feared. They would face up to their terrors again in the chilling nights of autumn as Harris began a second Battle of the Ruhr.

THREE

RUINING THE RUHR AGAIN

THE towns and cities of the Ruhr that much of Bomber Command returned to in October and November were familiar territory to Harris both geographically and ideologically. The Battle of the Ruhr he had conducted in the spring and early summer of 1943 was the major opening round in his mission to prove that the war could be won by bombing alone. It had cost the Germans serious losses in coal, iron, steel and other vital war requirements as the Reich Armaments Minister Albert Speer told a conference of Gauleiters at the time. The nineteen weeks of the campaign had also debited 872 British bombers and their crews. Another 2,126 aircraft were damaged, some so seriously that they didn't fly again.[1] There were never any easy targets in the Ruhr, even though in the autumn of 1944 the Luftwaffe was now nothing like the force it had been earlier in the year and in 1943. In fact Guy Gibson, hero of the Dams Raid, had just been killed while returning from a Ruhr operation to Mönchengladbach/Rheydt where he had acted as master bomber.

It was armed with this knowledge that Harris prepared to go back to basics after being released from the control of Eisenhower's Supreme Headquarters. It was not with the blessing of his masters at the Air Ministry. There were three philosophies about which direction Bomber Command should take after the successes of the summer. The senior strategic planners of the Allied forces believed an all-out offensive should be launched against the enemy's oil installations; there was considerable evidence, after all, that such bomber attacks had had a dramatic effect in the summer on Germany's ability to wage war. The army's commanders in the field wanted Harris to employ his force on the German transportation system because the bomber boys had proved so effective in bottling up the German Army in Normandy. In fact Eisenhower's deputy, Air Chief Marshall Sir Arthur Tedder, was the chief protagonist for this policy. The third party, led by Harris himself, believed the best and quickest way to win the war was to return to raiding Germany's industrial base.

The debate ended in victory for the oil strategists, led by the Chief of the Air Staff and Harris's boss, Sir Charles Portal. Portal was not against bombing Germany's industrial cities at this time. In fact he considered that the opportunity was ripe for the British and American bomber forces to try tilting the balance with a campaign of devastating aerial attacks, as did briefly Eisenhower, though *he* basically followed the transportation target line. But Portal believed that the main aim of Bomber Command should be to deny the enemy his oil and he now proposed that a new directive be issued in which the order of priorities for the joint bombing campaign should be first the petroleum industry, second ball bearings, third tank factories and last motor transport industries. The Combined Chiefs of Staff agreed and on 14 September new orders were issued making it clear that the responsibility for controlling the Strategic Bomber Forces in Europe belonged to the Chief of the Air Staff and the Commanding General of the USAAF.[2]

Eleven days later both Harris at RAF Bomber Command and Carl Spaatz, chief of the US Eighth Air Force, received the directive 'giving clear priority to the petroleum industry, with special emphasis on petrol including storage'.[3] A further directive was sent solely to Bomber Command on 1 November telling Harris: 'In view of the great contribution which the strategic bomber forces are making by their attacks on the enemy petroleum industry and his oil supplies, it has been decided that the maximum effort is to be made to maintain and, if possible, intensify pressure on the target system.' Harris, always against what he called the 'panacea' of bombing particular collective systems, famously scribbled in the margin: 'Here we go round the mulberry bush.' He did turn to oil, but still believed the main weight of bombs should be against

Germany's industrial cities. A split now began to widen between the views of Bomber Command's C-in-C and his superior Sir Charles Portal which would have far-reaching consequences for Harris's post-war reputation.

In an autumn speech at a damp USAAF base Harris, looking like a mild-mannered civil servant in raincoat and glasses rather than a leader of mighty forces, had told the newsreel cameras:

> We propose to finally emasculate every enemy centre of war production if necessary. We are well on the way now to that end. There are possibly 40 centres which are absolutely vital to the production of war material to the Germans There are about 50 which are of considerable import to them. There are all together possibly not more than 100 and we are as I say well on the way to their destruction. Now is not the time in any way to ease up, but to put on what indeed may prove – sooner perhaps than followers think – the final threat.[4]

There was, therefore, no doubt about what he believed in and what was to follow as the days chilled in 1944.

THE new Battle of the Ruhr began on 6 October with an attack on Dortmund by 523 bombers, 293 of them alone from 6 RCAF Group, the largest number put up by the Canadians in the whole war. It took place on the same night as 5 Group was demonstrating its individual bombing technique on Bremen, which helped to divert the attention of the enemy fighter controller. He did not have an easy task in the autumn of 1944. Apart from depredations among the night-fighter arm itself, the liberation of France, Belgium and part of Holland had by now played havoc with the German warning system and consequently with the enemy's nocturnal defences. It was a clear night and there were some, unsuccessful, attacks over the target, but the German fighter force was able to claim only one victim, a Lancaster of 115 Sqn destroyed east of Cologne.

Dortmund had had a particularly effective shelter system in place for months, deep tunnels extending from the main train station to the West Park with nineteen entrances to allow up to 80,000 people inside. The walls were lined with benches, shelterers sitting opposite one another as if they were still on a train.[5] The station was the aiming point for the raid. Trains were still arriving as the Pathfinder flares cascaded over Dortmund and passengers died at the entrances to the overflowing station bunker as the tumbling bomb loads followed and exploded in lurid crimson flashes across the city centre and beyond.[6] Above, other vivid splashes of red were breaking across the sky as the flak found the bomber stream at 20,000 feet. Two Canadian Halifaxes were brought down, trailing flame over the city, G-George of 433 Sqn being hit within seconds of bombing.*

F/Lt Wilbur Pierce, another skipper on the squadron, was on the eighteenth operation of a tour that had begun at the end of July. The stresses of the raid were summed up in his log book back at Skipton-on-Swale, where he cryptically wrote: 'Heavy flak. Multi searchlights. Too much moon!'[7]

It was a night the men of 433 Sqn would indeed remember. P/0 Joseph Zareikin, an American who although he was well over 30 was so keen to do his bit in Europe's war he had gone north before Pearl Harbor and across the border to join the RCAF, was three trips away from the end of his tour in the crew of F/O W. T. G. Watson when his rear turret appeared in a night-fighter's sights over Dortmund. In its first burst it killed him with a cannon shell through the head. As Watson went into an immediate corkscrew the night fighter attempted to rake the aircraft, but Watson slipped away into the darkness and made it back to Britain.**[8]

---

* The pilot, P/O V. Valentine, survived with two others of his crew, but four died, including the wireless operator John Tazuk and rear gunner Wenford Maxwell, who unknown to them had both just been commissioned.
** Bad weather at the Yorkshire bases caused the returning aircraft of 433 Sqn to be diverted to a USAAF base in East Anglia, where the body of P/O Zareikin was removed by his fellow countrymen. Zareikin, whose brother was also lost in the air war, was interred four days later at Harrogate's Stonewall Cemetery, where many RCAF men lie.

Others from the squadron found themselves in danger from both the Luftwaffe and their own comrades. The squadron diarist, compiling 433's operational record book within hours of the raid in the breezy Canadian style so redolent of the age, reported:

> F/O T. J. Kelly, the pilot of 'X' is now a firm believer in the adage, 'It never rains but it pours' for just as he completed his bombing run his aircraft was hit by several incendiary bombs from another aircraft which broke the Perspex nose of his aircraft and injured the bomb aimer, F/Sgt N. D. Nixon. At the same time a Ju88 came in to attack, but was driven off by F/Sgt J. B. Ackerman, the mid-upper gunner. The fighter was evaded. F/Sgt Nixon's wounds were attended to by the navigator, F/O W. E. N. Burnett, who in civilian life was a pharmacist. F/O Kelly brought his aircraft back and landed at Woodbridge emergency strip.[9]

The diarist went on: 'F/O Ray Mountford also had a brush with an unidentified single-engine aircraft, but it was driven off by the mid upper gunner, W/O E. Munro, who in the heat of battle shot his own aircraft's RT aerial away.'[10] Munro would be a POW within a month.

The concentration of towns in the industrial Ruhr meant flak belts ran into one another, the reason the region was so feared by aircrew, and as the stream headed homewards from Dortmund a Lancaster of 75 Sqn was brought down near Mönchengladbach. But compared to the Battle of the Ruhr in 1943 the losses on such a well-defended area were encouragingly small, only 0.9 per cent, yet the destruction to Dortmund's infrastructure had been extensive. After reconnaissance flights the next day Bomber Command's Operational Research Section was able to report: 'Extremely severe and widespread damage was caused, industrial and transport facilities suffering especially. All the through running tracks of the main passenger station were cut and the carriage sidings were rendered 80 per cent unserviceable. The goods depot, offices and passenger station were severely hit.'[11] Dortmund's transportation links were so damaged and it was so short of housing stock after the attack that the city now closed its doors to outsiders.[12]

It had been the second major raid of the night on the Reich and there had been two more as Harris paid a due to the oil directive: more than 250 Halifaxes of 4 Group attacking the synthetic production plant at Sterkrade and 46 Lancasters and 20 Mosquitos of 8 Group hitting the plant at Scholven-Buer for the loss of a total of 9 aircraft. Another 35 Mosquitos of the Light Night Striking Force had attacked various targets, including Berlin, losing only 1 crew. A total of 1,124 bombers had struck Germany in one night at a cost of only 12 aircraft – 1.3 per cent. Yet other units of Harris's force had also been out, 19 aircraft mine-laying, 35 involved in radio countermeasures operating a radar screen, 6 dropping supplies to the Resistance and 76 Mosquito night fighters patrolling the Luftwaffe bases.

The tide had truly turned for Bomber Command. The aircraft factories were now churning out a stream of new machines which stacked up the flight line instead of merely filling the gaps caused by losses. As strength reports were sent by teleprinter to High Wycombe on 5 October they had shown 1,752 heavy bombers available to the C-in-C in sixty-seven operational squadrons and two non-operational, 1,115 of them the redoubtable Lancaster and 589 the excellent Halifax III.[13] The availability would continue to grow until the end of the war. The Reich was facing a final cataclysm only Hitler could stop yet, unsurprisingly, he was now urging the German people to increased sacrifice.

The stalling of the Canadian advance by the Scheldt estuary, the failure of Montgomery's bid to isolate the Ruhr by taking Arnhem, the bogging down of the Americans in the Siegfried Line, had given fresh heart to the Germans after a summer of doom-laden defeat. There was one other important factor that now convinced even the more rational among the civilian population that it was worth responding to Nazi calls for greater effort: the Morgenthau Plan, endorsed by both Churchill and Roosevelt at the Quebec Conference two days before Arnhem. The scheme, fathered by the American Secretary of the Treasury Henry J. Morgenthau, suggested in essence that Germany should be dismembered and converted into a country 'primarily agricultural and pastoral in character'. The Ruhr, now being subjected to Harris's new blitz, 'should not only be stripped of all presently existing industries, but so weakened and controlled that it cannot in the foreseeable future become an industrial area'. Remaining industrial plant would be removed and mines wrecked.[14]

It was an absolute gift for the Reich Propaganda Minister Josef Goebbels. In speeches and newspaper articles he was able to claim that the area bombing of Germany's cities by the RAF was the Morgenthau Plan in action. The stream of arms and munitions from the Ruhr to the front lines must be maintained in the hope that the Allies would realise they could not crush the proud German people and thereby ease their demands for unconditional surrender. He wheedled that the Allies proposed to turn the Reich into a 'potato patch'. The Nazi Party newspaper, the *Völkischer Beobachter*, was able to state, somewhat convincingly for once, that the Morgenthau Plan meant 'the destruction of German industry to such an extent that 50 per cent of the German population would be faced with starvation or would be forced to emigrate as working slaves'.[15]

Germans in every city, who could see what 'slave labour' meant by the ever present work parties of emaciated Russians and Poles and by the concentration camp victims clearing unexploded bombs, took the point.

The American Secretary of War Henry Stimson and the Secretary of State Cordell Hull had opposed the plan, Hull pointing out that 'by completely wrecking the German industry it could not but partly wreck Europe's economy'[16] and Roosevelt later declared 'the German people are not going to be enslaved', but the damage was already done. The majority of ordinary Germans now believed their only hope for the future lay in total obedience to the Nazi Party. As the rain of firebombs and Blockbusters bloomed and mushroomed the dislocation grew and German civilians became ever more dependent on the Nazis for the essentials of life. They were now stuck in a trap baited by Hitler in which the plenty and successes of 1940 and early 1941 known as 'The Happy Time' were just a memory.

IT was unfortunate, therefore, that Portal should be promoting at this very period Operation Hurricane, a two-stage plan of massive aerial assault, the first part of which would be the maximum demonstration of air power in a concentrated period against the Ruhr. In a nine-page signal to Harris in mid-October Portal's deputy, Air Marshall Sir Norman Bottomley, told him that although the overall mission of the strategic air forces and priority of targets remained as of 25 September, in other words oil, at the first available opportunity Harris and the USAAF chief, Carl Spaatz, would 'demonstrate to the enemy in Germany generally the overwhelming superiority of the Allied air forces in this theatre'. The intention was 'to bring home to the enemy a realisation of this overwhelming superiority and the futility of continued resistance'.[17]

There then followed details of how the responsibilities of Hurricane I and the later Hurricane II would be shared out. Hurricane I for the Americans would mean targets selected from the current priorities list of Ruhr synthetic oil and benzole plants. But for Harris's command the targets were to be 'areas selected from the undamaged parts of the major industrial cities of the Ruhr'. There was no equivocating now – as there had been from the Air Council in the saturation raids at the end of 1943 – and the signal went on: 'The targets for Bomber Command should be areas of one square mile in extent . . . some 2,000 bombs of high explosive should be concentrated within 1,000 yards of each aiming point. This is calculated to achieve the complete destruction (90 per cent) of the areas attacked and, as opposed to incendiary attacks, will inflict heavy casualties.' It was expected the raids, over two days, 'would have incomparably greater consequences than did, for example, the break in the morale of the population of Hamburg, which undoubtedly occurred in July, 1943. For at that time there was no conviction of impending defeat and no immediate military threat.'

It was anticipated that administrative chaos in the Ruhr would follow the attacks.

To underline the message that this was what we now call shock and awe tactics, the brief went on: 'The appearance of the concentrated bomber forces will affect the morale both of the Ruhr population and of the troops over which the aircraft pass. The unprecedented impact of this new form of attack coupled with the belief that it will be repeated may well cause a panic evacuation.'[18] It was a new philosophy that would find final fulfilment over Dresden in mid-February. Hurricane, therefore, was obviously to be a prime example of the whirlwind Harris had pledged way back in 1943 that the Germans would reap for 'sowing the wind' with their Blitz on Britain and other nations.

The directive, which arrived at Harris's headquarters at High Wycombe on 13 October, was exactly what he believed in and had been waiting for. Duisburg, which produced a third of all Germany's iron and steel, was selected for the demonstration of might. Bomber Command had not operated for 48 hours, and before dawn on the 14th the crews of 519 Lancasters, 474 Halifaxes and 20 Mosquitos had been briefed to launch themselves against the Ruhr city's considerable defences. The Halifaxes and radial-engined Lancasters of the Canadian 6 Group in North Yorkshire and Teesside had the furthest to fly so took off first. F/Lt Wilbur Pierce, of 433 Sqn, who had lost a unit comrade on the Dortmund raid he had flown eight days before, remembers:

> We were supposed to be on leave, but a maximum effort and then a standby for the second trip were on the orders. I offered to do the early trip. We went in to the bomb run at minus two minutes as 'flak bait' with the PFF markers. Previously just three or four PFF aircraft were going in which made them easier targets. A few more aircraft going in at the same time improved it for them, not so for us. We did the trip and then went on leave after the debriefing. Most went back to the same target that night.'[19]

Harris now had even more operational aircraft available than at the beginning of the month and an abundance of aircrew, but it didn't prevent squadron commanders using some crews twice against the same defences. Sgt Frank Jones, the young flight engineer on 76 Sqn at Holme-on-Spalding-Moor, who had the luxury of a motor bike to nip back and forward to pubs in the village, was one of them. He remembers:

> We did three ops in thirty-six hours. First we went to Duisburg in daylight then within a few hours we were briefed for it again as a night operation. We had only just got in from the village when we were called for the first briefing. It was obviously a very big raid, we could see so many aircraft in the sky. As it was part of the Ruhr we knew the flak would give us all a pretty good bashing. We came back, got about three or four hours' sleep, then were called again for briefing. They were only four of us senior crews on the squadron who were briefed to go back to Duisburg again within 24 hours. I don't think we found it daunting, we just thought of it as another trip. It was a different route on the night trip and took us five hours and twenty minutes there and back, half an hour longer than on the daylight, so there was deliberate re-routing to avoid some flak. It was standard Ruhr flak we met both times, in other words pretty hot. We came back, got another few hours' sleep then found we were going to Wilhelmshaven that night. They weren't very sympathetic about what sleep we got. We got used to going without sleep. We managed because we were so young.[20]

Operation Hurricane was the start of the operational tour of Sgt Peter Bone, a 22-year-old mid-upper gunner on 626 Sqn at Wickenby, and he also found his crew on the battle order for both raids. His diary, enthusiastically entered up within hours, gives an insight into the fear and fascination of young airmen experiencing combat for the first time.

> We were roused at 2.30am and had our meal at 3.45am. Briefing 4.30am – DUISBURG! Got out to C-Charlie and we took off at 6.30am. It was light as we s/c [set course] over base and soon I could see Lancs everywhere – above, below and on each side. Flew up to 17,000 [feet]. Weather fair to good. No opposition till

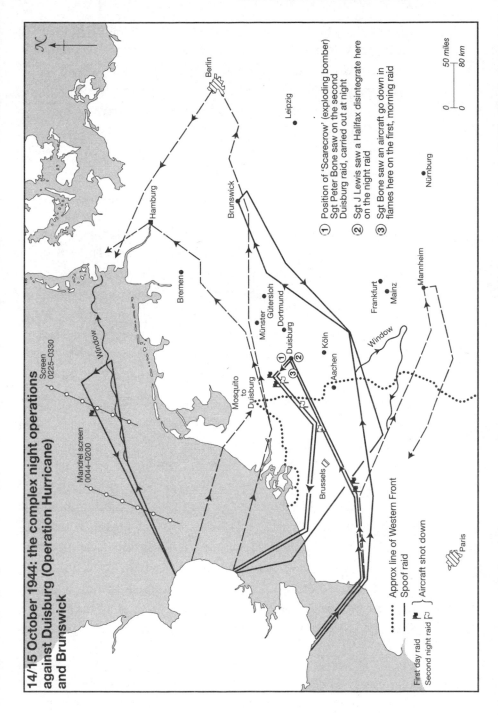

14/15 October 1944: the complex night operations against Duisburg (Operation Hurricane) and Brunswick

① Position of 'Scarecrow' (exploding bomber) Sgt Peter Bone saw on the second Duisburg raid, carried out at night

② Sgt J Lewis saw a Halifax disintegrate here on the night raid

③ Sgt Bone saw an aircraft go down in flames here on the first, morning raid

Screen 0225–0330

Mandrel screen 0044–0200

Window

Window

Mosquito to Duisburg

First day raid
Second night raid

Approx line of Western Front
Spoof raid
Aircraft shot down

Berlin
Leipzig
Hamburg
Brunswick
Bremen
Münster
Gütersloh
Dortmund
Duisburg
Köln
Aachen
Frankfurt
Mainz
Mannheim
Nürnburg
Brussels
Paris

0   50 miles
0   80 km

the target where flak was fairly heavy and they put up Scarecrows.*
Saw one kite go down in flames. Kites and shell bursts everywhere.
Felt scared. Dropped our Cookie and incendiaries freehand and
got out quick. Things quietened down on way back. Mustangs and
Spits gave cover. Passed over Walcheren Islands on way home.
Base 11.15am. BIGGEST DAY ATTACK – 1,000 Lancs. Lost
14 kites. 4,500 tons. After meal got down for some sleep. At 5.30pm
we were warned that briefing is at 7pm. DUISBURG AGAIN!
    Took off at 10.30pm.
    DUISBURG 2. Will never forget this – my first night op. Got
over target at 1.30am. First to attack at 0139. Scarecrow went up
just in front of us. Skipper was 2nd Dickey to F/Lt Hicks, a 34-
ops man. Bags of flak, and searchlights were effective but few.
Impossible to keep up search over target – whole place lit up with
flashes and flares. Down below Duisburg was an inferno. We
weaved to avoid searchlights, turned for home. Got back at 4.30am.
Interrogations, meal and bed. Very tired. First two ops done: day
and a night. Slept till 2pm. In evening wrote home.[21]

Holme-on-Spalding-Moor was a 4 Group base, south of York,
and the maximum effort ordered by High Wycombe had a total
of twenty-eight Halifaxes turning onto the main runway in the
dark for the first of the two raids and taking off at two-minute
intervals from 6.30 a.m. The few WAAFs who turned out to see
them go quickly lost them in the cloud, as the orbiting bombers
added their thunder to the rolling sound of others from bases
spread across the rich farmland of East Yorkshire. Eventually the
roaring cacophony which roused farmers and townsfolk alike from
their beds faded to a rumble as 4 Group joined the aircraft from
all other groups in Bomber Command now heading to the North
Sea. The cloud began to clear before the air armada reached the

* The myth of German Scarecrow rockets designed to simulate exploding
bombers was widely circulated by RAF station intelligence officers in 1944
to maintain morale on squadrons. But there were no Scarecrows, simply
doomed aircraft and aircrew.

enemy coast and in Duisburg that Saturday as a new shift toiled at the chemical producers, steel plants and iron works shortly before 9 a.m. the first bombs began to plummet from a seemingly endless stream of aircraft.

In less than 24 hours nearly 9,000 tons of bombs would fall on the city, which would later claim to be among the most bombed in Germany with 299 raids destroying or damaging 80 per cent of all residential buildings. Almost the whole of Duisburg would eventually have to be rebuilt. 'Over the target there was seven-tenths broken cloud, and [our] aircraft attacked at 16,000 –17 000 ft,' the 76 Sqn adjutant later recorded. 'The town was clearly seen and the markers accurately placed. The master bomber was clearly heard and his instructions were carried out. There was some light and heavy flak and several fighters were seen.'[22] The Luftwaffe did claim some victims, practically all to flak, but as Peter Bone noted only fourteen were lost, an extremely small number for a daylight attack by 1,013 aircraft, and a convincing demonstration to the Luftwaffe if one was needed that mastery of the air now lay with the Allies and was likely to remain that way.

Sgt J. Lewis, a 158 Sqn flight engineer, was looking through the astrodome of his Halifax 200 yards directly ahead of one of the flak victims, the moment it was hit in the area of the bomb bay. 'It buckled and folded amidships, right under the H2S blister, but kept coming forward on an even keel,' he later recorded. 'About 20 seconds later the two outward engines literally pulled themselves off the mainplane and fell away in a forward, gradual sinking motion.'[23] Some of the crew then began to bale out.

> Two from the upper escape hatch adjacent to the mid-upper turret, followed by two from the escape hatch in the nose. Gradually the remainder of the Halifax lost height and started to disintegrate, the outer wing sections first. The port inner engine burst into flames leaving a trail of black smoke and balls of fire. This spectacle had a peculiar macabre fascination – everything seemed to happen in slow motion. The debris surrounding the bomber looked like an

exploded diagram of the Halifax as it fell from view still holding its flight path.*[24]

Sgt Jones's aircraft attacked Duisburg from 16,500 feet at two minutes after 9 a.m., his pilot F/O Ken Carr reporting after landing back at Holme-on-Spalding-Moor mid-morning: 'Our bombs were seen to strike the west side of the aiming point. Two chimneys were hit. Large fires were seen after the aircraft left.'[25]

Meanwhile the USAAF were carrying out their own part of Operation Hurricane with a huge force of 1,251 heavy bombers escorted by 749 fighters bombing targets in the Cologne area. It too achieved great damage for little loss, only five bombers and one fighter going down. As they returned to their bases south of the Wash the RAF crews further north unlucky enough to be making a second trip to Duisburg in one day were being roused from their beds. They stumbled into their second briefing in operations blocks where the red-taped old maps now showing a new route to the Ruhr still hung and where it seemed that the rough benches had barely had time to cool. In the early evening the first of 675 bombers of this second Duisburg force rumbled out to runways once more, bound for a new onslaught on the Ruhr city beginning at 1.25 in the morning. A second wave of 330 would thunder in two hours later.

The stresses of preparing aircraft for a new attack only hours after they had returned from the first now began to show and at Lissett in East Yorkshire F/Lt D. W. McAdam discovered as he tested the engines of H-How at his dispersal point that the starboard outer was running rough. Quickly McAdam and his crew, including a young Canadian rear gunner who was beginning his tour that night, sprinted across to the dispersal of the spare aircraft all squadrons had standing by when operations were mounted. But the maximum effort order had claimed that too, so the keen McAdam and his crew dashed back to H-How and tried the

* The aircraft was that of F/Lt J. Galipeau of the Canadian 425 Sqn. Four of the crew, including Galipeau, survived to become POWs.

engines again. Finally, satisfied the trouble had been cured, McAdam lined up with the active runway and roared away down the concrete. But before the Halifax could reach flying speed the troublesome engine stopped dead. The pilot did the only thing possible. He raised the undercarriage to halt his aircraft before it ran out of runway. It then noisily careered along the tarmac shedding sparks that eventually caused a fire. The crew were not slow to evacuate the aircraft.

'I called for a check of members by trades and it was then we realised the rear gunner was missing,' the skipper recorded. 'I ran back towards the burning aircraft and found that he was trapped in the turret. Entering the wreckage of the rear fuselage I attempted to get him out from the inside, but when this failed I found an axe and a few minutes later chopped him free from the outside.'[26] The pilot and gunner joined the rest of the crew a safe distance away and eventually the bomb load went up, punching holes through hangars and maintenance buildings with pieces of Halifax. Another 158 Sqn aircraft, K-King, had earlier swung off the active runway and come to a stop with nothing worse than a broken tail wheel leg until it was showered with debris from McAdam's aircraft. It too was wrecked.[27]

It meant there were a total of 1,003 bombers airborne for Duisburg, ten fewer than in the daylight attack. This time there were also fewer incendiary bombs and more high explosive: 4,040 tons of Blockbusters and 1,000-lb and 500-lb bombs ranged alongside 500 tons of incendiaries. It was hoped the fire crews would still be struggling with fires created by the earlier raid and the new high explosive was designed to spread the blazing debris. That was exactly what happened.

'Fires were still burning from the great daylight raid,' Bomber Command's Operational Research Section later reported. 'In each instance the aiming point was accurately marked in perfect weather and the subsequent bombing was highly concentrated.'[28] Daylight reconnaissance showed the damage had indeed been enormous: 16 of Duisburg's 36 industries with a high-priority rating were damaged, together with a further 24 unrated factories.

'Five of the 14 listed public utilities were hit, notably the Thyssen gas and water works (priority 2); the two gas-driven power plants at Hamborn-Alsum (priority 2); and the Homberg gasworks,' the ORS recorded.[29] 'Widespread damage was caused to railway facilities and on the following day there were no signs of activity in any of the railways sidings or through lines. Many craters were caused in the dock area, where several barges were sunk. At least 90 hits were scored on the airfield. 1,292 acres of the town were estimated to have been devastated.'[30]

For such awesome results Bomber Command would at one time have expected to pay heavily. Yet only seven aircraft were lost over Germany and four more were lost in Britain, including the two 158 Sqn Halifaxes.* More than 3,000 Germans died in the day and double night raid on Duisburg.[31] But there had been no mass panic and resulting chaos in the Ruhr as had been the aim, the city's thirty-seven tower bunkers, two underground bunkers and fifty-three tunnels dug into slag heaps preventing the kind of death toll that Hamburg had suffered.

The devastation of Duisburg that night had not been all. Harris now had such a wealth of resources available he had been able to carry out the attacks at the same time as the 230 Lancasters and Mosquitos of 5 Group were finally wrecking the centre of Brunswick and a further 319 aircraft flew on various diversionary and support missions for the main raids. Over the 24-hour period, the RAF had flown 2,589 sorties, dropping a total of approximately 10,050 tonnes of bombs – the largest total of the war – for a loss of 24 aircraft, which was 0.9 per cent of the deployed force. 'The enemy's defence system met with unprecedented failure on this night, considering the number of bombers engaged and the depth of the Brunswick penetration,' the Operational Research Section later reported. 'Our counter-measures were elaborate and

---

* Among the forty-four bomber aircrew killed in the raid was F/Sgt Kadir Nagalingham, a wireless operator from Ceylon who was 48; and 19-year-old sergeants Gerald Neville and William Purnell-Edwards, both from neutral Ireland.

successful. Only 15 of the 1,238 returning bombers reported being attacked by fighters and flak opposition was very slight.'[32]

Operations at this stage of the war were complex indeed, but the countermeasures employed for the night Duisburg raid had been so cleverly successful they were later taught at staff colleges and found their way into the Air Ministry-sponsored RAF official history. It revealed that the deceptions had begun with the first wave flying low over France to avoid enemy radar then climbing just before crossing the enemy lines.

> At the same time a diversionary sweep of training aircraft made a feint attack against Hamburg, but turned back before reaching Heligoland. A small force of aircraft, dropping quantities of Window to simulate a large force, flew on towards the German coast and Mosquitos actually bombed Hamburg. These operations in the north were to mislead the controller into believing that Hamburg was the main target. He would, therefore, and in fact did, despatch fighters towards Hamburg and did not reinforce Central Germany from the north.[33]

The Luftwaffe had sent off eighty of its night fighters to find and attack the bombers, yet the initial plot of the first wave on Duisburg was not registered until the bombers had been over the target for two minutes. Eventually the confused night fighters pursued the first Duisburg force

> which turned left from the target and dived back towards France. While the fighters were thus engaged, the Brunswick raid, crossing the Rhine further south, slipped through. A small number of aircraft dropping Window split off from this force at the Rhine and made a feint attack on Mannheim, which was bombed by Mosquitos. Finally when the Brunswick raid was returning the second Duisburg raid came in to cover its withdrawal. The fighters were by then on the ground refuelling.[34]

The Germans lost five fighters to Mosquito intruders and claimed one bomber. At the same time 100 Group aircraft, stuffed with electronics, were picking up the Luftwaffe radio signals and frequencies for later analysis and subsequent hindrance. For their part the once victorious Luftwaffe never discovered adequate countermeasures for the now devious radio tactics of Bomber Command.

THROUGHOUT October and November the sirens wailed across the Ruhr as fleets of Bomber Command aircraft pounded its towns and cities. The list grew daily: Düsseldorf, Solingen, Hagen, Oberhausen, Neuss, Gelsenkirchen, Krefeld. But it was the home of the Krupps armaments empire, Essen, which was probably the most feared. Its rings of flak sites defending the run-in to the target had become the stuff of billet nightmares in the first Battle of the Ruhr in 1943. Crews asked to return in the autumn of 1944 found them equally daunting.

Sgt Jack Morley, the wireless operator on 101 Sqn, who had been in a crash-landing at Ludford Magna in September, found himself on the battle order for Essen on 23 October, a maximum effort involving 1,055 aircraft from all groups. More than 4,500 tons of bombs were dropped and 90 per cent were high explosive because by now much of Essen was rubble rather than combustible material. But some fires in remaining coal heaps were started and of such intensity that they were still burning two years after the war.[35]

Sgt Morley found he and the rest of the crew of S/Ldr George Harris didn't add one bomb to the infernos. He remembers:

> It was supposed to be our last trip. Everyone in the crew had done more than the thirty we were supposed to do. I had been in hospital at one time for a fortnight and the rest of the crew had done a trip without me and then trying to catch up I had done two more without them with different pilots. When we got to Essen and after we had fused the bombs the starboard outer started to overheat. There were small flames coming out of it, so we stopped the engine for a while and then restarted it, but it overheated again and we had to shut it down. Because the electrical power to release the

bombs came from that engine it meant we couldn't drop them. We flew round Essen twice trying to unload.

I could see from my wireless operator's window the flashes and smoke from bombs going off and there were flak guns all over the place. I had a little handle at the side of my wireless operator's position with which I could jettison the whole bomb bay. But it didn't work that night. We flew halfway round Essen again and then set off home with the bombs still aboard. They could have exploded at any time. We were set up to get in at the crash-landing airfield at Carnaby, which had a very long runway. It's just above sea level and we had had some practice at flying so low, so the skipper said, 'I am not going to try to land. Get the trailing aerial out, Jack, and I'm going to fly it on.' I could hear on the radio the Carnaby tower saying: 'Clear the airfield, a bomber might explode.' The altimeter didn't register below 100 feet, but the aerial extended to 50 feet and when it touched the sea it clicked over two little dials I had and I was able to shout, 'Now, George,' for the pilot to lift the nose up. Of course at that height there is no horizon over the sea and you can crash in. He flew straight onto the airfield from the sea. It was so gentle I said, 'Are we down yet, George?' and he said, 'I'm just going to turn off the runway now. Get ready to get out when it comes to rest.' He made a wonderful landing.[36]

It was not the final trip for Sgt Morley, but another, this time daylight, Essen raid two days later ended the tour of F/Lt Geoffrey Winston Woodward, a Halifax pilot on 158 Sqn with a double DFC. His squadron led the Main Force attack by more than 750 aircraft, and two 158 Sqn bombers were shot down, the price often paid by those who went in first with flak guns concentrating on them alone, before the bombs began to fall and the need for self-preservation took over on the gun sites. Woodward's wireless operator F/Lt William Clark remembers:

It was a beautiful day with a clear sky and we were the lead aircraft. Standing in the astrodome I could see massive AA fire in front. Behind was a spectacular view of RAF four-engined aircraft as far as I could see. It was very impressive. We were hit by AA fire on the port side; both engines were out of action but failed to feather. We released the bombs and were losing height. F/O Day of 158 Sqn followed us down, then broke off to the target. The aircraft was difficult to control with both props windmilling. We headed for Aachen [where the US front line lay]. AA fire followed. It was very accurate, but there was no further damage. The skipper was wonderful. We had lost height from 17,000 feet to 2,000 when he ordered us to abandon the aircraft.[37]

After the last crew member had left the bomber F/Lt Woodward baled out himself, but he was seen coming down by German troops and killed by small arms fire.*

F/O Robert Vollum, a wireless operator on the same squadron who had taken part in the 1,000-bomber raid to Essen in 1942, was on his second tour that autumn. It included five trips to the Ruhr, among them the raid that cost his comrade F/Lt Woodward his life. He remembers: 'Any of the Ruhr targets were tough because of the concentration of flak. They tried to route you away from flak, but it was such a concentrated population centre you were bound to get flak from somewhere. I had been to many of those places on my first tour and it was pretty unpleasant to go back. They threw everything at you except the kitchen sink.'[39]

Sgt Morley was at the base near Bridlington for two days as mechanics repaired the faulty engine of his aircraft after the first Essen operation. He flew back to Ludford as the second raid on the Krupps city was mounted. 'We thought we were going back to be screened. I had done thirty-two trips, but we were told we had to do another one and five days after Essen we went to Cologne,' he remembers.[40]

Cologne, the great melting pot for Ruhr raw materials of iron and steel to feed its steel fabrication plants, was the third largest city in Germany and had a population of more than three-quarters

---

* The rest of the crew landed safely to become POWs, as did the other shot-down 158 Sqn crew, that of F/Lt W. D. Harrison. But Harrison's 19-year-old rear gunner Sgt Geoffrey Johnson died in captivity in April.[38]

of a million at the start of the war. It became a regular destination for Bomber Command in late October, both as an industrial and transportation target. There were raids by 733 aircraft on the 28th, by 905 bombers two days later and by 493 the following day. So total a domination did Bomber Command now seem to have over the Luftwaffe that as the first raid was planned it was considered opposition was likely to be so slight it could be mounted in daylight. Sgt Morley remembers:

> We were told at briefing we would have a fighter escort of Spitfires part of the way along the route. We were also ordered not to damage the cathedral. To do so we had to bomb down river from it. There was the Hohenzollern bridge over the Rhine at Cologne the Germans had put out of action themselves and our objective was to hit the one bridge remaining, which was next to it. Our bomb aimer did hit the bridge. It was a wonderful feeling after we had bombed and turned away because we knew our tour was finished. When we got back to Ludford and taxied round to dispersal all the ground crew were there and the wing commander [W/Cdr M. de Everest] was waiting. He knew the sergeants in our crew were known as Harris's Rebels and he said to me, 'There's a flag here. You hold it because you are the biggest rebel of them all.' WAAF officers had cut the ties off some aircrew and sewed them onto a flag with a skull and crossbones. So a photograph was taken with me holding the flag.[41]

Sgt Frank Jones, who had begun his tour on 10 Sqn in February then after a long bout of dysentery was transferred to 76 Sqn at Holme-on-Spalding-Moor where he joined a new crew, also ended his tour with the first of the three Cologne raids. He recalls:

> The next day the skipper came to tell me the CO wanted to see me. I thought, Oh no, what's this about? But in fact he told me I was now a flight sergeant and my tour was finished. I told him I wanted to go on, because the rest of the crew had several ops to do and I wanted us to finish together, but he said, 'There's nothing I can do, this order to screen you has come from group.' So that

was it. Fortunately my crew went on to finish their tour with a replacement engineer.

We had a marvellous ground crew who couldn't do enough for us. They waved us off from dispersal on every op and were waiting for us when we returned. After I was screened I took the rest of our aircrew and the whole of the ground crew for a night out. I paid for everything and it cost me £20. The corporal in charge of the ground crew told me then I was the only flight engineer they had worked with who had finished a tour.[42]

In the three huge Cologne raids only nine bombers were lost. But although the Luftwaffe fighters were largely absent and the flak crews inaccurate, there were other dangers when a large number of aircraft were squeezed through the target area in a short time. F/O John Holmes, a bomb aimer on 102 Sqn, was on the final raid, of 31 October. He later recorded:

Over the target we made a normal run up and I released the bombs. After the distributor arm had completed its passage, I turned to the bomb panel to press the jettison bars across and from that point I can remember no more. Two hours later I opened my eyes and found that I was on the rest bed in the middle of the aircraft. The navigator was leaning over me and said that we were preparing to land at Pocklington. I learnt later that we had been hit by a load of incendiaries dropped from an aircraft flying above us. One of these incendiaries had smashed through the perspex nose of the aircraft and hit me on the head, laying me out cold.[43]

But if it seemed as though the greatest danger in this period was from so-called friendly fire, the Luftwaffe was about to prove that the RAF wouldn't always get away with it. On a raid by a mixed Halifax–Lancaster force of 749 aircraft on the Ruhr town of Bochum on 4 November, night fighters and flak brought down 32 aircraft, nearly all of them Halifaxes, 5 of them alone from one squadron.

FOUR

BLOODY BOCHUM

BOMBER Command was always a polyglot force. The overwhelming majority of its volunteers came from the United Kingdom with its many accents, but thousands had joined up overseas to fight from Britain. Canadians made up the next largest number of aircrew by far, followed by Australians, New Zealanders and finally a smaller number from the reaches of the empire such as South Africa, India, Ceylon and the West Indies. In this final phase of the offensive 46 per cent of Harris's pilots were from the Dominions. Then there were the thousands from neutral Ireland and others who had made their way from the occupied countries to strike back at their invaders, men from Norway, Holland, Poland, Czechoslovakia, Belgium and France.

It was in the bucolic, sleepy towns and villages of North Yorkshire and stretching up into Durham, that the presence of so many flyers from overseas was most obvious. The squadrons of the Canadian 6 Group were based there and bars of village pubs and shops were more likely to echo with the sharp tones of Ontario or Saskatchewan than the broad vowels of locals. The Canadians even had their own RCAF newspaper, *Wings Abroad*, printed in London, which locals could read in the pub over the shoulders of the local airmen. Slightly further south of 6 Group lay the airfields around York of 4 Group, an RAF organisation but which contained Australian squadrons. By the late autumn of 1944 the streets of Driffield, for instance, were well used to seeing the distinctive dark blue of RAAF uniforms as aircrew who had left their homes in the sun to fly Halifaxes on operations from the nearby airfield queued in the rain for the cinema, often with girls from the town.

From Canada and Australia then, the young men on the loose and far from the restraining influences of home had female hearts aflutter as they aimed for the local Yorkshire girls as their targets for tonight. But it was a group of individuals from just beyond the Channel who were among the most determined to make their mark.

Frenchmen, many of whom had been rescued from the beaches of Dunkirk in 1940, were in a small minority compared to the many flyers in Bomber Command who spoke English as a first language, but by the late spring of 1944 there were sufficient trained airmen to complete two heavy bomber squadrons, 346 and 347, at Elvington. In the Normandy campaign, where the flyers were called upon to bomb targets in their own homeland, the temptations of nearby York proved a welcome distraction and so far they had suffered moderate losses, but after a Ruhr raid on the night of 4 November many a girl was left weeping for her French lover. One-quarter of 346 Sqn's total aircrew strength vanished within a few hours.

Shop girls and barmaids who courted men from the Commonwealth also had their hearts broken. The Canadians suffered much that night, five RCAF units losing comrades, and two Halifaxes of an Australian squadron failing to return. In all twenty-eight aircraft were shot down, eighteen of them from 4 Group alone. The name of the Ruhr town was Bochum and to many of those once carefree aircrew who suffered from its defences it would become known as Bloody Bochum from that night on.

BOCHUM was at the very heart of the well-defended Ruhr, so the approach from any direction meant a battering from the flak battalions. However on this November night the planners compounded the dangers in deciding to approach the Ruhr by the once traditional route of the North Sea and Holland rather than by the dash across the Channel and over liberated stretches of Europe, where the Luftwaffe no longer had radar to warn its night fighters. Such a route hadn't been planned since August and the front line had changed drastically since then. Bomber Command headquarters placed its main hope of confusing the enemy in another raid on the Dortmund-Ems Canal at Ladbergen by 5 Group, taking place at approximately the same time as the 749 aircraft of 1, 4, 6 and 8 Groups hit Bochum. 'The enemy controllers, however, succeeded somehow in plotting the Ladbergen force off Yarmouth and plotted it for the last 60 miles over the North Sea,' the post-raid inquest of the RAF Operational Research Section recorded. 'Fighters were up over the Dutch coast and engaged the heavier [Bochum-bound] force of bombers in earnest over the Ruhr where there was little cloud cover.'[1]

The lack of cloud to dissipate provided an almost unbroken wall of searchlights as the bombers approached Bochum, which many ruefully commented on in the reflective security of their debriefings. The nocturnal air war had a terrible, exclusive beauty and the sharp, cold air that night over the Ruhr gave it a particular clarity. As the stream of bombers droned remorselessly for the white curtain of light, ahead a shower of green, glowing liquid fire dripped downwards, signalling the Pathfinders marking the aiming point. Red Verey lights bloomed to port and starboard indicating the night fighters tracking the course of the bombers. For the moment the stream was intact and as the aircraft passed through the white wall of searchlights into the arena itself bombs began to fall with great accuracy onto the town centre. Fascinated, crews looking down saw sticks of silver incendiaries twinkle then outline the streets in red and yellow as the fires took hold. It was a swift, temporary diversion from the red shock of bursting flak that spattered shrapnel across the sky and through the thin skin of airframes to find vital oil pipes and soft flesh. Captain A. Araud, one of the 346 Sqn pilots lucky enough to return from Bochum, bombed on red target indicators at 7.45 p.m. and within hours described the scene. 'Many fires were seen in the centre of the target and the streets could be seen in the glare,' he reported.[2]

W/O Harry Irons was an air gunner in a 466 (RAAF) Sqn Halifax on the raid. He was only 20, but now on his second tour because he had lied about his age, joining the RAF at 16. He remembers:

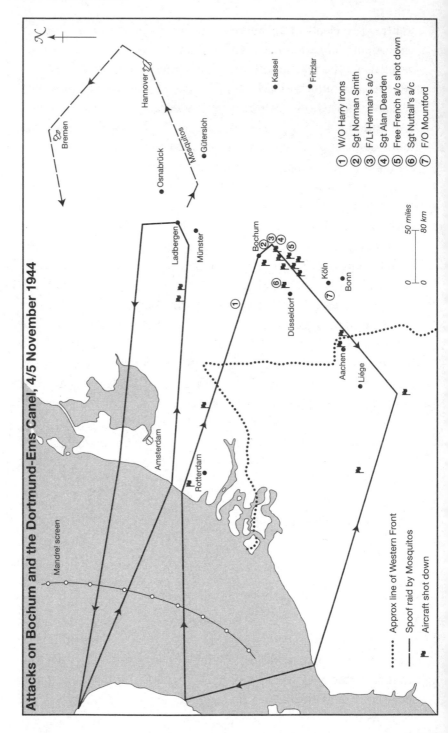

Attacks on Bochum and the Dortmund-Ems Canal, 4/5 November 1944

① W/O Harry Irons
② Sgt Norman Smith
③ F/Lt Herman's a/c
④ Sgt Alan Dearden
⑤ Free French a/c shot down
⑥ Sgt Nuttall's a/c
⑦ F/O Mountford

Kassel
Fritzlar

Bremen
Hannover
Osnabrück
Gütersloh
Münster
Ladbergen
Bochum
Köln
Bonn
Düsseldorf
Aachen
Liége
Amsterdam
Rotterdam

Mosquitos

Mandrel screen

50 miles
80 km
0

······· Approx line of Western Front
——— Spoof raid by Mosquitos
Aircraft shot down

There were plenty of fighters about. I saw quite a bit of air-to-air firing, but you never saw an aircraft actually shot down, they just exploded, especially approaching the target before they dropped their bombs. It only took a splinter of shrapnel or one bullet. The resulting explosion could be red, green, orange or blue, depending on what the bomb load was. Incendiaries went off in a whitish explosion. There would perhaps be 14,000 lbs of bombs going off at once. Some crews were lucky and managed to crash-land, but most aircraft exploded.

Even though there were aircraft being blown up on the run-in the other crews still carried on to the target, irrespective of what they had seen. It was the most amazing thing, the crews just kept going in although they could see blokes being hit. It was absolutely terrifying approaching a target. Personally I think the Pathfinders had it easier because they went in first and stirred up the nest and by the time the rest of us came in the flak gunners had got the direction and it was coming up. To look at it you thought, How on earth are we going to get through that lot? The Germans would fire a box barrage right from the start of the run-up through to the target. Sometimes you would see air-to-air firing as the German fighters went right in the midst of their own flak. You also had to look out for aircraft above dropping bombs. It was very frightening to see an aircraft above you with its bomb doors open. The pilot had to be careful if he dived to get out of the way because there were so many aircraft going in to the aiming point. There must have been a hell of a lot of collisions as a result. Then there were searchlights. If the blue master searchlight hit you about five or six others would lock on straight away. There was nothing else the pilot could do but put it into a dive and hope for the best. You just hoped the fighters wouldn't come in at that point.[3]

In fact as those bombers that had unloaded over Bochum slipped away from the glowing target and the inner ring of flak guns, the belts of searchlights were waiting on the way out to show how easily they could ensnare.

Sgt Norman Smith, a rear gunner on 166 Sqn, remembers the

moment his own Lancaster was caught near the town.

> We had just left the target when we got fastened on by a blue master searchlight and all the others joined in. The light was indescribable and painful. It just took over the whole world. It was totally overwhelming. I shut my eyes and covered them with my gloved hands, but I could still see it and all the time the pilot was corkscrewing, trying to get out of the beams and he couldn't even see his instruments. Only the navigator at his curtained-off desk had a couple of instruments to tell us where we were heading. I was afraid we were going to get hit by a night fighter and I knew there was nothing I could do because I couldn't see anything – nothing at all except this flood of white light.[4]

Eventually the corkscrewing paid off and the Lancaster slipped away into the welcome darkness.

Sgt Allan Dearden, a 21-year-old Lancashire flight engineer on 76 Sqn who had only just returned to operational flying after a crash near Norwich in January which had put him in hospital for six months, now saw the waiting night fighters pounce on the aircraft of 4 Group, of which the French 346 Sqn was part. He remembers:

> As we were coming out of the target we were slightly off-track when the mid-upper gunner, W/O Ken Hirst, reported four-engine aircraft were going down a couple of miles to starboard one after the other. He counted six aircraft going down in rapid succession, all within ten minutes or so. I'm sure they were hit by night fighters. It's quite possible some of them were from 346 Sqn as we were all in 4 Group and would have been following the same flight plan. But the wireless operator on one of the aircraft shot down on the raid, from 640 Sqn, was Freddie Nuttall who lived 250 yards away from where I now live. I knew him quite well. He was a little, red-headed chap, full of confidence. He had been an apprentice butcher. If anyone ever deserved the VC it was Freddie.[5]

Sgt Nuttall was standing alongside his pilot F/O Kees Goemans, a Dutchman, when their 640 Sqn Halifax released its load over Bochum. It was the last trip of their tour and as Nuttall searched for night fighters the aircraft turned for home. But no sooner had it settled on track than a line of flak exploded immediately ahead. Sgt Graham Korner, the crew's New Zealander rear gunner, saw the shell blasts. 'It was over on my port quarter,' he later related. 'Three bursts came towards us. Woomph! Woomph! Woomph! Then there was an explosion at the front, the whole aircraft shuddered and I heard Kees gasp.'[6] The Dutch pilot had been killed immediately as shrapnel whipped and pinged through the front of the aircraft, starting several fires. Goemans's lifeless body tumbled down the steps into the navigator's compartment, his chute spilling out and the cords becoming entangled with the navigator, P/O Ron Purcell, and his seat, which was positioned over the escape hatch. Sgt Korner clipped on his parachute, but delayed baling out because he could still hear the engines roaring. Then with no one at the controls the bomber pitched forward into a slow spiral dive which could only end one way. It was at that moment that Sgt Nuttall, who had never handled an aircraft in his life, took over, stopping the spiral before it could turn into an uncontrollable spin that would pin the crew members helplessly to the fuselage by centrifugal force. But the aircraft was still going down.

P/O Purcell called on the intercom for a fire extinguisher and the bomb aimer P/O 'Jock' Patterson came forward to make 'strenuous efforts to clear the entanglement and attempted to beat out the flames', Purcell related fifty years later. 'But because of the limited space and the difficulty of movement with the aircraft diving, we were not successful. Then, probably due to lack of oxygen, we both became unconscious. In what must have been a very short time afterwards we both sat up, almost at the same moment and we immediately made further efforts to beat out the flames, but it was absolutely futile.' As each fire was put out several more burst out elsewhere. 'When I tried to throw down the metal fire extinguisher I was using I found that it was red hot and had stuck to my hands,' P/O Purcell said. 'It had to be torn off – taking most of the flesh of my hands with it.'[7]

Sgt Korner, who had been listening to the drama on the inter-com, rotated his turret and flipped backwards into the darkness. Two other members of the crew also baled out, but on one para-chute. The flight engineer, Sgt Patrick Finnigan, who had been a replacement crew member that night, had found his parachute pack burning in its stowage and agreed to go out clinging to the back of the mid-upper gunner, Sgt Ron Heath. But as Heath pulled his ripcord Finnigan was plucked away by the jerk of the chute opening. Finnigan plummeted, arms and legs flailing, thousands of feet to his death.

P/O Patterson and P/O Purcell now realised the aircraft was doomed and stumbled, with Patterson leading, towards the para-chute stowage behind the cockpit, where Purcell, like Finnigan, also found the remaining chutes burning in their rack. 'I stamped out the flames of one and clamped it on my harness,' Purcell later related. 'I looked back to Freddie Nuttall, who was sitting at the controls to prevent the aircraft spinning. His flying suit was alight, but despite my shouting to him to come, he waved to me to go towards the rear escape hatch.'[8]

P/O Patterson baled out followed by P/O Purcell, whose trou-sers had been eaten by the flames from the thighs down. He knew he was unable to pull the parachute release with his hands because of his burns, so he pushed one arm through the D-ring and slid out of the hatch into space. 'I have no recollection of actually pulling the ripcord,' Purcell related. 'But the next moment the chute opened above me and immediately burst into flames again. The descent was an eerie experience. Although there were flak bursts above I seemed to be floating in silence and I felt no pain. This was probably due to the intense cold and the shock, but I do remember seeing our burning aircraft dive and spin downwards. This must have been when Freddie Nuttall left the pilot's seat and released the controls.'[9]

Purcell landed in the garden of a house near Düsseldorf where an old man and a boy, who had been under the impression the airman was a falling flare, picked him up and bandaged his face, hands and legs before he was taken to hospital where he underwent skin grafts.*

Purcell's survival was astounding, but there was another escape that night that ranks among the most breathtaking of Bomber Command's remarkable war. In common with most Commonwealth squadrons 466 (RAAF) Sqn at Driffield comprised only about half native-born aircrew on its aircraft, the rest made up of British or other nationalities, such as W/O Irons. But on the Bochum raid twelve Australian aircrew failed to return from two of the sixteen bombers it dispatched. One of them, F/Lt Joe Herman, was among the squadron's most experienced pilots, having braved the flak and fighters of Dortmund only two days before and now making the thirty-third trip of his tour. It was his escape without a parachute that would become the stuff of legend.

On the run-in to the target Herman's Halifax, D-Dog, was twice coned by the fearsome searchlights, but each time he managed to slide away. Then as the flak came up the former Outback gold miner warned his crew to clip on their chest chutes, though he was too occupied to do so himself. Once inside the arena Herman's bomb aimer F/O William Nicholson released the aircraft's load on the markers and the pilot then turned south-east and began the briefed letdown from 18,000 to 10,000 feet. At that moment D-Dog was bracketed by flak. One shell went through the rear spar of the fuselage just behind the mainplane then two more hit the wings, rupturing both fuel tanks. Within seconds the mainplane was burning from roots to tips. Herman gave the order he had practised many times in drills at dispersal, but hoped never to bellow in earnest: 'Bale out, bale out, bale out!' As the pilot tried to hold the aircraft steady one by one the Australian crew dropped through the escape hatches, leaving only their countryman, mid-

---

* P/O Purcell was later sent off to prison camp like his surviving comrades Patterson, Korner and Heath. The details of Sgt Nuttall's courage were revealed by the survivors when they returned from captivity, but the wireless operator, who doomed himself by keeping the aircraft from spinning while his comrades escaped, received no award.

upper gunner F/Sgt John Vivash, and the English engineer Sgt Harry Knott, who apparently was off intercom and had not heard the bale-out order as he directed a fire extinguisher at the flames licking the main spar. Herman's earphones crackled to hear Vivash reporting he had been wounded in the leg by flak. As the pilot left the now useless controls to reach for his own chute in the flight engineer's position he saw Vivash crawling towards him. At that moment Herman, out of the corner of his eye, saw the starboard wing slowly fold back in a blowtorch-like burst of blue, fuel-fed fire and the aircraft turned over on its back. As the pilot, still without his chute, braced himself against the roof the bomber exploded in a red rush of flame and he was thrown out into the night sky.

He found himself plunging through the freezing air in a shower of debris. For a moment he wondered if he could perhaps find his parachute pack among it, then realised all hope was useless. Under a three-quarter moon, effortlessly, even to his senses apparently slowly, he tumbled above the pale chill of the countryside, performing a macabre ballet between stars and landscape as hundreds of doomed bomber boys, similarly helpless, had done before him. Herman plunged and pirouetted in the night, waiting for the inevitable. He felt detached from globe and sky, a speck in oblivion. Far below the River Ruhr gleamed silver in the moonlight then disappeared as he rotated, seemingly without fear or friction, once more. Beyond him the crazed, multi-coloured epicentre of the target glowed, sparkled and pulsated in the dark and the last of the searchlights stretched down and died. A prayer turned in his mind as he whirled, expressively floating between heaven and earth. It was peaceful now, away from the scorching fire and the creaking, crashing, roaring mayhem of the bomber in its lurch of death. There was no sensation of speed, just a clean cold as the young Australian plummeted earthwards at terminal velocity of 120 miles an hour.

With a bone-jarring thump Herman made impact. In reflex action his arms shot forward to save himself and he found himself hanging, no longer twisting. There then followed one of the most bizarre conversations in the history of the air war. Herman heard

F/Sgt Vivash call out, 'Is there anybody around?' The pilot looked up, realised there was a fully open parachute above him, and replied succinctly, 'Yes, I'm down here.' Vivash then asked, 'Where, where are you?' Herman told him, 'Here, hanging on to your legs.'

Much later the two Australians worked out what had happened. As their aircraft exploded at 17,500 feet and they were tossed out into the night Vivash was knocked unconscious, unaware his pilot was free-falling less than a few feet away. He came to at less than a mile above the earth and apparently, though he did not remember doing so, pulled the ripcord. As his chute spilled out, catching the air, it swung him forward, legs horizontal with the ground. At that exact moment Herman had reached a point in his head-over-heels tumbling where he was face down and he banged into Vivash's body and automatically reached out, grabbing the extended limbs. If Vivash's parachute had been fully deployed at that point it would have already slowed the gunner down from terminal velocity to approximately 10 miles an hour and Herman, still travelling at the vastly higher speed, would have bounced off. As it was they slowed down together as the canopy opened fully and the distance to the ground was not so great that Herman could not continue to hold on. In less than five minutes Herman felt a tree brush against his face and he hit a clearing in a pine wood, immediately followed by Vivash landing on his chest and breaking two of the skipper's ribs. Herman then used the single parachute that had saved them to bind up the seven flak wounds in Vivash's legs and they began making for Holland, being caught four days later.*[10]

* The flight engineer, Sgt Harry Knott, who fortunately did have his parachute clipped on when his aircraft exploded, was captured the same day, trying to cross the River Ruhr, but the other four members of the crew, who all evacuated the aircraft safely, were buried at Neviges, near Wuppertal, on 8 November and later their remains were removed to the Reichswald Forest War Cemetery. Their mysterious deaths remain unexplained. Herman and Vivash were able to return to their homes in Australia, but Vivash was killed shortly afterwards in a motorcycle accident.

*

SEVERAL of the French 346 Sqn Halifaxes shot down that night were in fact certain to have been among the six aircraft Sgt Dearden's gunner saw falling in flames one after the other. They included that of Commander A. Beraud, who baled out but did not survive the descent and that of his comrade Lieutenant P. Raffin, killed when he landed on electricity cables. Captain Jules Roy, serving as a bomb aimer on the squadron at the time, wrote cryptically in his diary after the raid in which he had flown in F-Freddie: 'Heavy losses, 346 Sqn lost five aircraft with their 35 crewmen.'[11] In fact thirteen Frenchmen survived out of those shot down, two evading and the rest becoming prisoners of war with their former army comrades who had been behind the wire since Dunkirk.

Others in the bomber stream saw the Canadian squadrons cut down by the night fighters. F/Lt Wilbur Pierce, of 433 Sqn, remembers: 'Fighters were very active and we lost two of our aircraft. I saw F/O Mountford's aircraft on fire 100 yards away.'[12] F/O Ray Mountford was on his twentieth operation from Skipton-on-Swale with his navigator F/O Robert Madill, both from the same Ontario area. The attack by a night fighter on the Dortmund raid had been followed by a Cologne operation in which Madill had narrowly escaped serious injury when incendiaries from another aircraft plunged through their Halifax, destroying the navigation table and the Gee box by his elbow. Now as their aircraft F-Freddie approached Bonn on the way home from Bochum the pilot of an unseen night fighter equipped with Schrage Musik positioned his sight between two engines of the Halifax. F/O Madill remembers:

> He was underneath the aircraft and fired into the starboard wing, setting the aircraft on fire. I came down between Cologne and Bonn and fell into an open pit mine ... I was captured on 9 November after trying to walk through to the American lines about 60 miles away. I walked at night in the rain and hid out during the day ... very cold and miserable.[13]

F/O Mountford recalls:

> The night fighter fired upward into the starboard inner engine – an
> uncontrollable fire made us jump. I stayed at the controls and tried
> to keep the plane level while my crew baled out. When I let go,
> I was thrown out of the hatch, hit my head and was knocked out.
> I was free falling and the rush of air brought me to, just in time to
> pull my rip cord. After landing rather hard, I made a tent of my
> parachute and had a cigarette. This was now around midnight.[14]

F/O Mountford, whose flying boots and socks had been pulled
off by the jerk of his parachute opening, saw a house across the
fields from where he lay and went across to investigate.

> I walked over in bare feet, knocked on the door and when the lady
> opened it and I said, 'Englander' she took me in. There was a
> teenage daughter who could speak some English. The mother was
> very kind and bathed my feet and gave me a pair of slippers. She
> showed me a picture of her son (a flyer). He was lost over England.
> The man left the house and in a short time the Gestapo arrived
> with their guns drawn. I was a prisoner.[15]

All his crew had survived, though the bomb aimer had broken his
ankle when he came to earth.

In all, seven aircraft from Canadian squadrons were shot down.
It had been a night when the old empire had suffered much for
the mother country, the other lost Halifax from the Australian 466
Sqn claiming the lives of the entire crew except the pilot. Then
there were the casualties among Canadians, Australians and
others from the Commonwealth serving on British squadrons.
They included a 19-year-old navigator from Mauritius, Sgt Claude
Terriere, killed with the rest of his 101 Sqn crew.

The dangers were not over when the returning bombers crossed
back into friendly territory. Night raids in the autumn and winter
were always mounted in the hope, sometimes unfounded, that
reasonable weather would last until the bombers were back at
their bases. But fifty-four had been hit by flak over Bochum,
damaging fuel tanks and engines, which often had to be shut down

creating a greater strain on the ones remaining, thus reducing airspeed and causing more fuel to be used, demanding further economies. It meant several bases were now socked in with mist by the time many bombers returned. One more Canadian aircraft was wrecked when it overshot the runway on landing back in England, another Canadian Lancaster crash-landed in liberated France, a second Canadian pilot crashed in Belgium and another bomber, of 166 Sqn – which had managed to put up twenty-seven Lancasters – flew into trees in the circuit at Kirmington, injuring the Australian pilot F/O Alan Falconer and half his crew. The mid-upper gunner died the next day. Those bombers that crashed in Britain or liberated territories were not counted in the official figures released of how many bombers had been shot down in a raid and under the subterfuge of 'failed to return' the Air Ministry, already miscalculating by four, told the press twenty-four (3.2 per cent) were lost, a bad enough figure when casualties were meant to be falling.[16] But including the crashes in England thirty-two Halifaxes and Lancasters were gone from the battle order. The official telegrams went out from the Air Ministry the next morning, informing relatives across the Commonwealth from Prairies homestead to Outback sheep farm that their sons, husbands and fathers were missing. The tears the blue-edged forms invoked would perhaps have been even more bitter if relatives had known that so many of the losses were unneccessary. The decision to route the bombers over the North Sea and Holland, instead of the Channel and liberated territories, allowed the Luftwaffe plenty of warning for once that a large raid was on its way. Its controllers were not fooled by the Ladbergen-bound force and as Bomber Command's Operational Research Section recorded immediately afterwards, the Luftwaffe night fighters had trailed the Bochum force. Perhaps in some effort to protect the route planners the ORS, who also worked under the umbrella of Bomber Command headquarters, went on: 'Losses might have been severe if our aircraft had not been protected by 10/10s cloud over Belgium on the way home. As it was fighters followed the stream as far as Liege.' Severe was just how the losses were being described on

346 Sqn and its Canadian neighbours in North Yorkshire.

'Fourteen of the Bochum raiders were seen to go down in combat,' the report went on. 'Four over the target, six in the Cologne area, two over Aachen and two in isolated combats further west. Two bombers collided over the Dutch coast and went down in flames and one was coned and destroyed by Allied fire over the Charleroi-Namur area.' Damage in Bochum had been devastating. 'This raid together with that of 9/10 October destroyed 92 per cent of the built-up area.'[17]

Another Ruhr town and its industry had been wiped off the map. October and the first few days of November was the period of the heaviest attacks by Bomber Command in 1944 because in the rest of November Harris diverted his force to concentrate on the smaller targets of oil and benzol plants. He was under intense pressure from Portal to obey the priority demanded by the Allies' senior strategic planners of cutting off the enemy's fuel supplies. The reminder from the Air Staff on the 1st of the month that 'the maximum effort is to be made to maintain and, if possible, intensify pressure on the [oil] target system,' was a definite warning. Portal had been the prime mover behind Operation Hurricane, after Eisenhower had shown his interest, but it had been drawn up as a two-part plan. The second part had called for: 'The maximum demonstration of air power in time against a single target system [oil].'[18]

So far it was clear not enough British tonnage was falling on oil plants and too much on cities. Harris was forced reluctantly to switch his focus and in November 14,312 tons of bombs would plummet onto oil installations. As Bomber Command's crews had already learned, they were always well defended.

WINTER

FIVE

A TORCH TO THE OIL

CONCENTRATION by Allied air power on the targets Bomber Command now turned to in earnest would eventually bring the German war machine grinding to a halt. Starved of its fuel supplies the Luftwaffe would no longer be able to train replacement pilots and by the final weeks of the war would be forced to tow its aircraft out to their take-off points by oxen. The Wehrmacht too would be reduced to relying on boys with Panzerfausts as the Reich's much vaunted Tiger tanks eventually clanked to a standstill, empty fuel tanks echoing.

The USAAF had been bombing Germany's synthetic oil plants since May, as had RAF Bomber Command since mid-June, opening with a raid on Gelsenkirchen which had cost 6.1 per cent of the Lancaster force. Each time Harris sent out his boys to throttle oil installations in the Ruhr that summer, as he also obeyed the other demands on his bombers, it cost them dearly. The attacks had continued in August and September, gaining greater impetus when the Russians overran the Ploesti oil fields in Romania, and by the end of September German oil production had fallen to 35 per cent of the pre-attacks level with aviation fuel down to 5.4 per cent.[1] But in October there had been only three raids on oil installations by Bomber Command's 'heavies', comprising only 330 sorties in total, as the C-in-C went back to bombing industrial cities.

In November and early December Harris was forced to change direction temporarily from the way he conceived the war would be won to launch a series of heavy raids by day and by night on oil installations. He had already been asked to do so in

Hurricane II, the final part of the Operation Hurricane directive sent to High Wycombe from Portal's office on 13 October, which called for 'maximum' Allied air attacks against 'precise' targets in Germany when visually possible.[2] Bomber Command's part of the plan, which also included the USAAF Eighth and Fifteenth Air Forces, was to make 'a maximum effort against the Ruhr-Rhineland synthetic oil plants'. But there was a get-out and Harris had been using it. The directive had said Hurricane II was to begin as soon as Part One was completed 'to concentrate effort on primary oil targets and *undamaged built-up areas of the Ruhr*'.[3] It was those undamaged parts of the Ruhr's cities Harris had continued attacking.

Because winter was now here, limiting the number of days when a visual attack was possible, it was realised it would be essential to use almost the whole of the visual bombing days available to attack oil. Harris had received his reminder on 1 November. The more experienced among his crews, who had braved the flak and fighters over oil targets before, viewed with some trepidation the prospect of bombing such installations the German forces needed to preserve to survive.

On 2 November in a 1,000-bomber USAAF raid on the Merseburg/Leuna oil complex 26 were shot down in minutes by fighters and 14 destroyed by the target's formidable flak. The Americans went back to Merseburg on 20 November, on the 25th and on the 30th, combined with another raid on Zeitz. The final raid was the fifteenth in which the Eighth Air Force had hit Merseburg and this time it was even more costly, the rings of flak guns bringing down twenty-nine bombers and damaging twenty-seven more so severely they had to land at bases in France. Some 80 per cent of the US Third Air Division's Flying Fortresses were damaged by the Merseburg flak and by flak guns around other synthetic oil plants on the way in to the aiming point. It was the USAAF's last visit to Merseburg, the most dreaded of targets.[4]

The rumour mill among those who flew had been working well and it was with rapt attention therefore that Bomber Command crews called for an early briefing in the chilly dawn of 6 November now learned they would be playing their part in the new oil plan. Hundreds of eyes were riveted on the end wall of briefing huts and operations blocks up and down eastern England as the curtain on the target map was drawn back to show a route to the Ruhr and Gelsenkirchen, the very oil refinery that had cost seventeen Lancasters in the night raid of mid-June, three of them from the Polish 300 Sqn at Faldingworth. There had been operations by no more than 225 aircraft on oil plants on 1 and 2 November, but this was the big one.

The young airmen were told that in excess of 700 bombers, split fairly evenly between Lancaster and Halifax squadrons, would be attacking the Nordstern synthetic oil plant at the heart of the Ruhr with its formidable defences. More importantly it was a daylight raid, with the aircraft taking off around noon. There would be no other forces of Bomber Command hitting other German targets at that time to divert the Luftwaffe defences. Those who had been to the Nordstern oil plant before in the summer and seen their comrades suffering heavily at night couldn't help but pre-judge it as a suicide mission in daylight. Even the newer crews were aware from the gossip over a pint with old sweats in the mess that a raid to the Ruhr in daylight was not to be contemplated. After the losses two days before in the night raid on Bochum nerves were still on edge.

There were many therefore whose stomachs balked at the pre-op meal and whose fingers fumbled over zips and press-studs as they clambered into their bulky flight clothing in the crew locker room for what they considered was probably the last time.

Harry Irons, the young but experienced air gunner on 466 (RAAF) Sqn remembers the Gelsenkirchen raid well. It was his fifth Ruhr op in eight days after being posted to the Driffield-based squadron a couple of weeks before.

> They were short of gunners and just wanted a bloke on his second tour, so I became a spare gunner operating with various new crews. It was nerve-racking for me having inexperienced pilots. I do think it was luck whether you survived or not, though. If you were in the

wrong part of the sky when a shell came along it didn't matter whether you were experienced or not. I found my second tour was easier, but not over the Ruhr. There were flak guns round every town. On Düsseldorf on 2 November as we came off the target you were supposed to turn to port and I saw a Halifax apparently decide to cut across and join the aircraft coming out. Up came three shells, and hit him right in the middle and he just exploded. It was horrifying.[5]

Just four days later W/O Irons waited by his locker to go to Gelsenkirchen. He remembers:

The worst time was in the crew room when you had all your cold-weather clothing on and you were waiting for the transport to the aircraft. You looked round at everybody and wondered who wasn't going to come back. It could happen to you on your first trip or the last trip of a tour. As you were looking round at everybody in the crew room the lorry would arrive and they would call out your aircraft and out you went. It was better then because you had started.[6]

The Canadian crews of the northerly-based 6 Group had the furthest to fly and were therefore usually the first to take off, but on this occasion they followed the Halifaxes of 4 Group in East Yorkshire and Lancasters of 1 Group in North Lincolnshire. It was just after noon when the Canadian Halifaxes and Lancasters grumbled and growled down perimeter tracks at bases with quaint English names such as Middleton St George and Skipton-on-Swale, then turned onto runways and bounded away into the overcast, placing them at the rear of the stream. They met up with their RAF fighter escort well before reaching the target and to their surprise and relief the Luftwaffe failed to show up in force. There was another aid to longevity, the weather, which was hampering the flak battalions. 'Upon arrival at the target it was found that cloud of the stratus variety completely obscured the town,' 433 RCAF Sqn's diarist recorded the next day. 'Arrangements had been made to mark the target with ground marking. Since this proved impossible the master bomber gave orders for individual bombing on instruments.'[7] The Gelsenkirchen heavy flak units were proving none too accurate in the overcast. And instead of being the bloodbath crews had feared only two 6 Group Halifaxes and three Lancasters from other groups were shot down, though one of the flak victories was another 300 Sqn Polish crew which had suffered so much over Gelsenkirchen before.*

Harry Irons remembers:

> We had a huge fighter escort. It was daunting to go in in daylight to the Ruhr, especially as we had just come back from Bochum where the flak had been horrendous at night, but in daylight you could see the red flash of the shells exploding and the black puffs they left behind. As you got closer to the target the flak bursts were packed closer together. I saw the odd aircraft hit. You not only got the flak from Gelsenkirchen but the local towns as well. To get away with so few shot down we thought was pretty lucky. I think it was because we had loads of fighters with us. There was plenty of Window being thrown to put off the flak. There was a box barrage at one height. We got a few holes in the aircraft as we did on most raids.'[8]

It was an encouraging and surprising start to a new oil campaign. The small size of oil targets made them ideal for 3 Group, now that it had proved how effective it could be with the target-finding device of GH. Two days after the Gelsenkirchen raid 3 Group alone attacked the Meerbeck installation with the loss of only one aircraft, then the next day 1 and 8 Groups went to Wanne-Eickel with 256 bombers and 254 came back safely. The list of oil strikes grew on an almost daily basis: Castrop-Rauxel, the Rhenania-Ossag refinery at Harburg, the Hoesch-Benzin synthetic plant at Dortmund, another 3 Group attack on the same plant four days later, Wanne-Eickel again, Homberg twice, Castrop-Rauxel again, Sterkrade, and a 3 Group raid on Gelsenkirchen on

---

* P/O L. W. Latkiewicz and his crew all survived to become prisoners of war.

23 November. In the thirteen raids Bomber Command launched against oil installations in November a total of thirty-eight bombers were lost, an average of fewer than three per strike against such vital targets, most of them in the Ruhr with its rings of flak sites. Compared to the cost of such targets in the summer it was small indeed.

The chances of surviving a tour in Bomber Command had brightened considerably. Sgt Frank Etherington, who had now moved from 166 Sqn to a new squadron, 153, formed at Scampton, remembers:

> I wasn't ever afraid on ops, but *very* apprehensive. At that time I used to read the *Lincolnshire Echo* in the sergeants' mess and if it said 600 bombers had gone out and we lost 10 we didn't think that was so bad. We knew the odds were in our favour at that time. When we did our tour losses were relatively light; we went time after time without losing any, then there would be the odd couple of losses to make you think.[9]

Although it was no longer waging the attrition on Bomber Command it had in the past, the Luftwaffe usually showed up to defend its fuel supplies. But as stocks declined with which to train replacement pilots the poor quality of those new pilots became obvious. Sgt Allan Dearden, the 76 Sqn flight engineer, remembers being attacked by a pilot of waning enthusiasm during a raid on the refinery at Sterkrade on 21 November. 'The rear gunner, Doug Begbie, saw an Me110 coming in and called a corkscrew as he opened fire. The German tried again about three times, but he eventually got fed up and made off. The mid-upper gunner, Ken Hirst, was the kingpin of the crew, though. If it didn't have four engines he opened fire.'[10]

So confident did Harris now become that on 6 December he launched a night strike by 475 Lancasters from 1 Group and the GH-equipped 3 Group on the oil plant at Merseburg, which had proved so costly to the USAAF. It necessitated planning a devious route at extreme range to deny the Luftwaffe its numerous aircraft-locating opportunities over Germany for the fighters to gather.

The Polish 300 Sqn would be taking part and among the crews called to briefing at Faldingworth was that of F/Lt Jan Kozicki, who had only begun their tour a week before. Kozicki's flight engineer was F/Sgt Henryk Drozdz, who had been serving in the air section of the Polish Army when the Germans invaded in 1939. Like so many of his comrades he had been evacuated south through to Romania, interned and released to travel to France. He eventually arrived in Britain in January 1940, intent on avenging the rape of his homeland. He had volunteered to fly, but spent years as a ground mechanic in the Polish Air Force before being selected for a flight engineer's course. Now he was keeping an operational diary and on the afternoon of 6 December recorded the reaction in the briefing room of the Polish squadron – whose memories of the savagery of oil targets went deep – when the destination was revealed.

The long and winding course of today's flight fills us with dread. It is a little village and next to it is a large factory producing oil and motor fuels – Merseburg, a few miles to the west of Leipzig. During the briefing everyone is very quiet. Today's flight of 1,700 miles casts a gloom over the company. When I look at the faces they all look depressed, but here and there somebody tries to smile. Only to an outsider may it seem like heroism ... not here among the hundreds of people who will soon take off – for them it is not heroism, just duty ... we fly because this is an order.

It is the second time I am flying in B-Betty (the mechanic in the ground crew is Adamski, a friend from France). We take off at 5pm ... As soon as we cross the German border there is artillery to the left and to the right – it does not augur well. This flight to the target seems to last ages, but I am occupied by throwing out 'Window'. Eventually we are nearing the target. As usual battle course – full throttle and to target. Ready, steady and the bombs are gone – it is 2045 hours. The flak fire intensifies left and right, then the searchlights start – we duck to the left, then down – my stomach is in my throat. But we escape.

It was 1 a.m. before B-Betty joined the circuit at Faldingworth and made a welcome return to the runway's concrete certainty, then turned off for its dispersal pan, a long eight hours of nervous tension at an end for the crew. 'How nice it is to climb down from the plane, heave a sigh of relief and say, "One flight less to go",' F/Sgt Drozdz recorded.[11] Again Bomber Command had got away with it, only five Lancasters from all squadrons going down, but the fearsome flak damaged many more.

Among them was the Lancaster of F/Sgt James Wright, a wireless operator on 166 Sqn. He remembers:

It was only our second operation and at briefing we were told it was a very heavily defended synthetic oil plant with 400 heavy flak guns and 400 light flak guns. We lost an engine on the way to the target, but as we had already crossed the French coast we decided there was no point in turning back. It meant we arrived over Merseburg fifteen minutes late. Everything was quiet apart from the fires burning below, then all hell broke loose. It was very heavily defended and we were the sole target. We continued on our bomb run and I could see a solid wall of flak ahead. There were red bursts all over and we knew we had all those guns to ourselves. Some shrapnel from a nearby burst came through and knocked out all our radio equipment and navigation aids, starting a fire in my wireless set. I could smell the cordite from the flak burst, then saw the radio set was smoking. The fire went out, but nothing would work after that.

As soon as we had bombed the skipper put the nose of the aircraft down and we got away quick. When I looked at the radio equipment it was obvious it couldn't be repaired in the air. The navigator had to go in the astrodome and take star shots which I recorded. It was the only way we could navigate home. After a while I asked the navigator where we were and he said we were just crossing the French coast into the Channel. Unfortunately we were over the French coast at Dunkirk, which was still occupied by the Germans. We were suddenly coned and saw radar-predicted flak coming up and bursting close. It was quite frightening and again the skipper put the nose down and dived almost vertically.

The altimeter was almost off the clock. By the time we levelled out we were quite disorientated and in fact we came right up the Thames at about 4,000 feet. We were over London and all our own anti-aircraft fire started coming up. You were supposed to fire off the colours of the day, but they only gave you two Verey cartridges. I fired them off, but the guns were still active. Fortunately I had a spare box of cartridges I always carried and banged off reds one after another and the guns shut down. I think we were a bit too low to be hit and we weren't damaged, but we were up to half an hour late returning to Kirmington.[12]

Bomber Command dispatched a total of 15,008 aircraft in November and 14,312 tons of their bombs fell on oil targets, Homburg-Meerbeek receiving no less than 4,312 tons alone.[13] Way back in the summer Albert Speer had warned Hitler by letter that without greater fighter protection and increased efforts to carry out repairs an unbridgeable gap would be created 'which must lead to tragic results'.[14] In fact those 'tragic results' had now arrived. Luftwaffe day and night fighter pilots were being shot out of the sky by the US Eighth Air Force Mustangs and RAF Mosquitos, consequently creating a vicious circle of fewer Luftwaffe pilots to defend the oil targets. The bombing of oil installations would continue in January, and increase in February, though Harris had still continued bombing cities in November and begun to step up his urban raids in December on old favourites such as Essen and on new, smaller towns now on the target list as part of the new Transportation Plan against Germany's communication network.

There was one major hope for the German high command as Christmas approached and right on cue the gift arrived: the barometer fell in their favour.

SIX

A BITTER SEASON TO BE MERRY

IT was the weather that dominated Bomber Command operations as November faded into December and northern Europe headed deeper into the harshest winter within living memory. The bombed-out cities of Germany offered little protection against the freezing winds that now swept and eddied around the cellars that had become home to civilians forced to stay amid the rubble to service the declining Reich war machine And to all but the most obtuse Nazi it was obvious worse was to come, from the RAF, the USAAF Eighth Air Force in England and now the B-17s and B-24s of the US Fifteenth Air Force, growing in strength in Italy. Lt General Ira Eaker, who had begun his country's round-the-clock bomber offensive with the RAF while heading the Eighth Air Force in England, was now the commander of the Mediterranean Allied Air Forces, able to reach the southern cities of the Reich. In an interview with war correspondents on 4 December about the coming winter bombing of Germany he boasted of an 'even bigger punch' by his forces, purely because strategic targets in the Balkans and southern France had now disappeared with the Allied advance. Not even the weather would be a handicap to his bombers finding their targets, he promised, because of 'technological improvements' (in other words the secret H2X, the American name for the RAF bombers' ground-scanning radar) allowing a great number to attack in overcast.[1] Bombing through cloud that winter would result in the USAAF being no more accurate in hitting individual small targets than the RAF, which in the pragmatism of war had abandoned such a policy in 1942 for the necessity of area attacks. Ironically Bomber Command was now achieving considerable success in knocking out small plants, such as oil installations, with the growing abilities of 3 Group and its GH equipment.

The memories of Bomber Command's crews of that bleak period of mid-November through December are of the variety of targets they were employed against. They ranged from north German cities to oil installations and also to rail targets in smaller towns of the Reich as the new Transportation Plan was launched to bottle up supplies and troops headed for the Siegfried Line, where General Omar Bradley's Twelfth Army Group had by now suffered 100,000 battle and weather casualties trying to take the snow-covered Wehrmacht bunkers in the frozen forests of the West Wall.

On the night of General Eaker's prediction a total of 535 Lancasters, Halifaxes and Mosquitos from three RAF groups had hammered Karlsruhe in the Upper Rhineland and another 282 Lancasters solely from 5 Group had at the exact same time hit Heilbronn, 40 miles to the east. Both were on the Transportation List; Karlsruhe had much light industry as well and Heilbronn was not only the second most important industrial town in Würtemberg, but was also a port on the Neckar river and perhaps most temptingly had marshalling yards on a main north-south railway line. Aircrew, who even in October had battled through a blizzard on the way to Essen, particularly remember the bitter cold experienced at 20,000 feet on the Karlsruhe and Heilbronn raids.

Sgt Patrick Bell was a 20-year-old Canadian air gunner, rapidly gaining experience on 97 Pathfinder Sqn after beating off attacks by two Ju88s and then an Me109 on only his second operation, to Mönchengladbach, in September. He recalls:

Heilbronn was our thirteenth operation and we were flare force three so the target hadn't started to burn at that time. It was a very cold night and on the way back we had to climb to get over high cunim clouds. It was so cold my guns were iced up right to the breech and ice was building on the aircraft as we climbed. I was anticipating a bale-out order because the aircraft was shuddering as we tried to climb above, then as we got out of it I heard the ice flying off and hitting the aircraft.[2]

It was a night when experience paid off and Bell's pilot, F/O John Greening, was very skilful indeed. Greening remembers:

I had well over 1,000 hours of flying experience before I went on ops and this was extremely valuable to me. I was a staff pilot in Training Command for two years, stooging around training navigators when the losses were high in Bomber Command. I was stationed in the Isle of Man and Northern Ireland. A pal and I were so fed up, we really wanted to get on operations so we dive-bombed Ramsey in the Isle of Man and made a lot of noise. Of course we were on the carpet the next morning before the OC Flying and within two months we were posted to an operational training unit at Silverstone. That was how I got on ops, by making a nuisance of myself.

That night above Heilbronn was seared on his memory.

We had dropped our load and then had to climb to 23–24,000 feet to go over these huge cunim clouds which were rising to a tremendous height. I couldn't go below them because of the mountains below. It was pretty maximum height for a Lancaster, even an empty one. I vividly remember the rings of St Elmo's Fire around the airscrews. There was no question of following those famous last words: 'I'll go down and see where I am.' Once we got above the cunims it was no longer disturbed air, in fact it was very still and cold.[3]

Sgt Harry Stunell, the 106 Sqn wireless operator whose original skipper had been shot down on his first raid, as a second-dickey pilot, now had a new crew and was in the Heilbronn force. He remembers:

It was a pretty nasty night and the aircraft was being thrown around a bit. The bomb doors had been opened and we were beginning our bombing run. I was off intercom, tuned in to the radio when a Ju88 attacked and the first thing I knew of it we were in a most violent corkscrew. I switched over to the intercom, but there was no firing. The 19-year-old rear gunner, Ron Needle, had tried to open fire as the Ju88 came in behind, but his guns had jammed. He later saw it as a blessing in disguise because he was able to concentrate 100 per cent on calling for corkscrews at the exact time as we were attacked instead of trying to get a ring and bead on the fighter. There were six attacks in all and we weren't hit. There wasn't a break, we would climb up out of one corkscrew then immediately go into another. I think the fighter then went for someone else, because we were clued up. We had passed the target by this time and had to jettison our bombs 2 or 3 miles to the south.[4]

Despite the difficult conditions Heilbronn, which had been raided many times but only once before in force, was dealt a devastating blow by the efficient fire-raising techniques of 5 Group. As the master bomber criss-crossed the town he accurately controlled the fanning-out effect of bomb loads crashing simultaneously into the old town centre. The cold air outside Heilbronn created ideal conditions for a firestorm as it rushed in to fill the vacuum caused by hot air rising from the fires and such a devastating phenomenon did develop, burning out 62 per cent of the town and immolating its centre. A total of twelve Lancasters were lost in the Heilbronn raid, some by icing in the extreme meteorological conditions, but 6,000 people died in their cellars below.

A fireman in a community nearby described what he could see as he emerged from his own shelter and looked towards the old town: 'A great sea of fire. All you could hear was the roar of the mass of planes and the bang of the exploding bombs. The ground was a seething mass of fire. Everywhere explosions, which looked like little fountains of fireworks, and then larger explosions in between.' Fireman Flein made his way to Heilbronn to help, but was shocked for a different reason as he approached Beethovenstrasse. 'Two drunken soldiers came from the burning city, howling and shouting, as if they'd come straight out of the lunatic asylum. They laughed when they saw me: 'Ha! – a fireman! What good does he think he can do?' I couldn't believe it. They came from the burning city and were totally oblivious. Could it be possible that people had become so desensitised to such destruction?'[5]

A resident of Heilbronn, Hans Martin, was caught in the raid as he made for his home in Sontheim. The blast from a bomb hurled him into some ruins. He found shelter in a cellar near the central St Peter's Church, but was driven out when the iron exit door began to glow with heat from the burning building above. 'Some of the streets were blocked by burning rubble,' he later recorded. 'Electrical wires, some of them glowing, were particularly obstructive. About 60 metres in front of the Goetzentrum I fell and my leg went into a manhole. Stuck and caught up in the wires, I saw the moment coming where I would be killed by burning rubble. But someone had seen me and my cries for help were answered.' Martin stumbled on, eventually reaching the banks of the Neckar river. 'I tried to get to Sontheim along the river bank. It was burning terribly on the other side of the Neckar. In the darkness I fell into a bomb crater filled with water and had difficulty getting out. Covered in mud and freezing, I set back upon my path. As I reached the Knorr factory I saw firemen I recognised though they didn't recognise me. I was totally exhausted.' They gave him a drink of Schnapps and eventually he reached his home.[6]

A third resident described how his once beautiful town looked the next day. 'Heilbronn was wiped out, a dead city, the rubble glowing hot. We went back to the Lixstrasse to see if anything was left of our house. The cellar was full of hot ash and our cat Peter was lying dead along with the 11 dead members of the Baumann family ... We helped a neighbour to search for his family and found them sitting in the cellar – dead. They were sitting together, as if sculpted in marble.' They had died as victims in a firestorm usually did, from creeping asphyxiation by carbon monoxide as the roaring flames above greedily sucked up the oxygen to make an ascending, acres-wide cone of flame.[7] At

Karlsruhe, too, severe damage was caused, and for the loss of only one Lancaster and one Mosquito. 'Three-quarters of a mile of fire,' was how one Canadian airman described Karlsruhe to a newspaper reporter at his debriefing, but here a true firestorm had not developed and the death toll was in the low hundreds rather than thousands.[8]

Other towns were practically razed to the ground in this period, for a multitude of reasons which could include direct pleas from the Allied armies. In the previous two weeks before Heilbronn Bomber Command had been called on to help the Americans end their blood-letting in the Huertgen Forest where hundreds of machine guns in interlinked German bunkers had taken ground warfare back a quarter of a century to the scale and horror of Passchendaele. Harris was asked to bomb three German towns that were about to be attacked by the American First and Ninth Armies in the area between Aachen, the initial German city to fall to the Allies, and the Rhine. A total of 1,188 Bomber Command aircraft raided Düren, Jülich and Heinsburg to cut their communications with the rest of Germany. Düren suffered the most. After Bomber Command had left, only 13 of its 9,322 buildings remained undamaged, the town ceasing to exist within an hour.[9] The cost to the RAF of all three raids had been just four aircraft, three of them over Düren – a small price indeed, but to those who saw them destroyed traumatic enough.

The Düren raid was the first operation of Sgt Ken O'Brien, a rear gunner on 101 Sqn at Ludford Magna, and he saw one of the aircraft vanish. He recalls:

It was a daylight raid and very frightening. Over the target there was an aircraft just behind us. It was close enough for me to see the crew. They had just opened their bomb doors when they were hit by flak. The whole aircraft exploded. There was a big flash and bang because they still had their bombs on board and then just bits of aircraft falling. As our own bombs went down I could see the bombs of others exploding and lots of smoke coming up, but I was still shocked by the sight of the aircraft exploding. After debriefing at Ludford when I went to bed I couldn't sleep. I kept seeing this crew who had vanished. In fact I couldn't sleep properly for a week. But the next night we were on ops again, to Wanne Eickel. Over the target I was looking down through the open turret when a piece of flak came up and took a piece off the top of it. There was a flash as it hit and it took a while for me to get my eyes right in the dark again and then I realised the top of the turret was damaged, not too far from my head. We were diverted to Tudenham when we came back. Within a few trips I was sure I wouldn't survive my tour. I was 19.[10]

But there was one target always spoken of with dread in RAF messes, which bomber crews would fear no more at night. Essen, the home of the Krupps armaments empire, and once ringed by 400 flak guns which had downed scores of British bombers in the Battle of the Ruhr more than a year before, was hit in force on 2 December. The accuracy of the raid shocked Hitler's Armaments Minister Albert Speer. In post-war interrogations he revealed: 'The last night attack upon the Krupps works which was carried out by a large number of four-engined bombers [in fact 512] caused surprise on account of the bomb pattern.'[11] Krupps was now largely rubble and it would be nearly the end of February before production was restored to a degree that called for a return by Bomber Command, and then in daylight. Many of Essen's flak guns were being ranged against tanks on the Western Front in December and Harris's dominance over the night skies of Germany was now such that only six bombers were lost, less than 1 per cent, compared to the average of 5 per cent on Essen raids in the first Battle of the Ruhr the previous year.

However, the large numbers of flak guns remaining could still sting. Sgt Frank Etherington, the 153 Sqn flight engineer, was on the 12 December raid. He remembers:

We could see the flak coming up over the target when we felt a bump and we knew we had been hit and after the bombs went down, the nose started to climb. I had to help the pilot push down on the column. We had a second-dickey pilot with us that night, a

F/Sgt Robinson, and he was sent back to see what was happening. He reported there was a hole in the side, so I went back with my bag of tools and found a hole about a foot in diameter with a peppering of holes all the way round it. A big piece of shell had come through the port side aft of the mid-upper turret low down, shattering and twisting the tray carrying the belts of 303 ammo to the rear turret as if by a giant hand. By a miracle it had missed the push-pull rods controlling the elevators and rudders, but had severed the wires to the tailplane trimming tabs, pushing the elevators in the up position causing the aircraft to climb. I pulled on one of the trimming tab wires manually, but that made the climb worse. I'd got the wrong one, so I pulled the other one and we got back to straight and level. As we came in to land the pilot got everybody except me, who was helping him, to assume the crash position. I think he was playing safe in case the tail dropped off. We got in OK and taxied off the runway, but the whole rear section of the aircraft including the tailplane had to be replaced, we were told later.[12]

FOR those unlucky enough to be in the wrong part of the sky at the right time life could be short and the temptation for aircrew was to make it as filled with merry experience as possible before one day or night the Grim Reaper tapped on their shoulder. In the weeks of December as Christmas beckoned there were various attractions to divert the attention of young airmen, far from the restrictions and moral codes of home. Aircrew not operating could leave their stations practically at will for nights out and on a week night rest and relaxation might consist of a few beers and a trip to the pictures to take their minds off flying. Those films featuring a female star or saucy title were usually what young airmen made for, such as *She Has What It Takes*, starring Jinx Falkenburg, playing at the St George's Cinema in York in mid-December, or *Two Thousand Women*, starring Phyllis Calvert at the Ritz, Lincoln. Theatres quickly discovered they got the biggest audiences with productions such as *Design For Glamour*, advertised at the Theatre

Royal, Lincoln, as 'Showland's loveliest act'. But on Friday and Saturday nights it was the dance halls of cities such as Lincoln, York and Cambridge that brought aircrew flocking from the air bases nearby. In Lincoln, usually a sea of blue uniforms any night of the week Bomber Command wasn't operating – as its attractions served both 1 Group to the north and 5 Group to the south – a venue opposite the Theatre Royal which advertised itself as 'The Montana, where the good dancers go' was promoting several dances over the mid- to late December period and a 'Special Dance' was also being advertised at the city's Astoria Ballroom on Boxing Day, though with the strict proviso that there would be no admission after 10 p.m. – to keep out airmen who had spent too long at the pub.[13] In Cambridge the Guildhall was advertising a dance on the 20th guaranteed to 'Start Christmas with a Swing' in which Harry Parry would be turning up with his Radio Rhythm Sextet[14] and in York the Railway Institute, somewhat of a step down from the popular De Grey Rooms, was promoting dancing to Jack Carr's Melody Aces.[15]

Every six weeks Bomber Command aircrew got a week's leave, long considered necessary to ease the nervous tension of their strange life where they would experience the trauma of seeing comrades ensnared in searchlights, going down in flames or disappearing in a flash, then return to the peace of a rural billet only to be asked within days or hours to repeat the whole experience again over a new target. In their home towns they were able to impress local dance partners with their tales. But Commonwealth airmen, far from a home many would never see again, took their leaves in London. A week's accommodation in a central hotel, such as the Mascot, in Baker Street, which advertised '50 bright rooms with modern furniture, running water, telephones and gas fires' for five guineas (£5.20) a week was easily affordable on a Canadian junior flyer's pay, twice that of an RAF sergeant pilot's 13s 6d (68p) a day.[16] When not watching the nude Phyllis Dixey*

---

* The stripper meant so much to aircrew, that a Lancaster of 50 Sqn was named after her.

in her show *Peek-a-Boo* at the Whitehall Theatre or the equally sparsely attired showgirls in *Revudeville* at the Windmill Theatre, the Canadians, Australians and New Zealanders went to night-clubs such as Ciro's in Orange Street in the West End where they danced to Don Marino Barreto's Cuban Orchestra.[17] Dancing was a national pursuit in wartime. The RAF even had its own swing bands, the Squadronnaires – where the musicians had the lowest rank in the air force of aircraftsmen second class and therefore played for 3s 6d (18p) per day – and the Skyrockets and RAF Northernaires groups, which shared hangar venues at bleak Fens airfields, and were paid the same.

A dance was a guaranteed way to meet the girls who desired a winged airman on the arm as one of life's major prizes. Aircrew often had access to cars and petrol others didn't, so travelling to dances from isolated airfields wasn't a problem. P/O Jack Gagg, a Sheffield-born pilot who completed a Lancaster tour on 166 Sqn then became an instructor at 1667 HCU, in Sandtoft, North Lincolnshire, from September 1944 to early 1945, remembers his off-duty excursions well.

I had a little Morris 8 which a friend of my dad's had sold me for £15. We used to go out and milk petrol from the Lancasters. The bowser man would fill all three tanks to the brim, but the little third tank didn't feed direct to the engines, it only fed to the other two tanks so one of us would go in and switch the immersion pump on and as it was feeding into a tank already full it would come out of the overflow outlet underneath the wing where someone would be waiting with a can. As soon as I got a night off I was off to Sheffield in the Morris 8. There were police roadblocks to see what fuel you were driving on and I got stopped a couple of times, but the police were very kind as I was in uniform and they let me through.

During the war Sheffield was a marvellous place for young ladies. Most of them were working in the steel works as the young men had gone into the forces. The City Hall used to run an after-noon tea dance and that suited us very well. It wasn't sex all the time, it was just nice to have the company of a young lady. My flight commander often used to say to me, 'I haven't put you down for flying tonight, we're going to Sheffield.' If I said, 'I haven't enough petrol,' he would say, 'That's OK, we'll go out and milk one.' I was more or less engaged at the time and we used to have mess parties, very good ones as we could get grub from the farms around. We used to go in a little pub at Belton and got pally with quite a few farmers. My fiancée used to come over from Sheffield and I've even put her standing underneath the wing of a Lancaster catching the petrol.

It was a great life off operations, but it could be a bit dicey instructing at times. We lost three aircraft in one night when a thunderstorm came over as some pupil pilots were flying and they all crashed trying to get in. I used to say, 'I wish I could get back on ops,' but I didn't really mean it.[18]

Those counting down the targets in their combat tours often found the nightly chance of death acted as a subconscious aphrodisiac. F/Sgt Ron Brown, a 75 Sqn flight engineer on his second tour, remembers his pilot as 'quite a romeo'. He recalls:

There was a girlfriend at every dance. The next morning he would be wearing a different pair of knickers around his collar. He didn't care for WAAFs because their issue knickers were what were called passion-killers. When he was wounded and we went to visit him in hospital there he was sitting up in bed with a pair of knickers tucked inside his pyjama collar. The matron explained, 'He hasn't got these through amorous activities, he's borrowed them from one of the nurses'![19]

The feverish, here-today-gone-tomorrow atmosphere of wartime led some, but by no means all, to exploit a dance partner's gratitude for the sacrifices the young airman was making. A tail gunner of a Lancaster bomber explained in a post-war study:

While girls had a much stricter upbringing, they were sorely tempted when they knew there was little chance their loved one had of returning unscathed. There was no doubt that wartime did make more opportunities, and caution was often not exercised under such stress. Equally quite a lot of us chaps would play on a girl's emotions by stressing the possibility of death, even though we as aircrew never believed it would be us who got the 'chop'.[20]

There was now an epidemic in Britain of sexual diseases and ads regularly appeared in national and regional newspapers reading: 'VD. Shadow on Health' and gave indications of what to look for. Such advertising would have been unthinkable before the war. The new free and easy atmosphere even loosened the previously staid atmosphere at the BBC, Mrs Mopp, a character on the comedy show *ITMA*, which did much to maintain morale on the Home Front, revealing to fireside radios that she once went out with a reporter who promised 'to take down everything I said'. It got a big laugh from the mixed home audience.

THAT winter, from Sheffield to Lincoln to London there were few corners of the nation where an airman couldn't find a dance on somewhere. The most popular musicians in Britain were not home-produced, however, but from overseas. Glenn Miller's Army Air Force Orchestra, with its unique sound, created by replacing trumpets with clarinets and getting the clarinet players and tenor sax players to sound off an octave apart, was *the* sound of the Second World War. Since June, the air force major, who had fourteen hit numbers in five years, had been in England, his band playing at air bases and army camps throughout the UK. In December Miller decided to take his band to a new base on the Continent, starting with a Christmas concert from Paris on Allied Expeditionary Forces' radio for the front-line troops. He prepared to fly across the Channel to make the arrangements, but as December entered its second week the weather turned particularly foul. With all flights grounded Miller fretted for days before the band's representative was offered a lift with a US Army colonel in a single-engined Norseman due to leave from RAF Twinwood Farm in Bedfordshire within 24 hours. Miller jumped at it and on 14 December took off in conditions barely above freezing point.

The Norseman vanished into the mist that day and it and its famous passenger were never seen again.

Lt Howard Roth, a 20-year-old Flying Fortress pilot with the 306th Bomb Group at Thurleigh, a few miles from Bedford where Major Miller's Army Air Force Orchestra was based, met Miller the night before the bandleader disappeared.

A fellow pilot, Doug Schrack, and I had a three-day pass and went in to Bedford to stay at the American Red Cross Officers' Club. On 14 December we went to the local pubs and went back to the officers' club intending to hit the sack, but decided instead to go into the dining room and have a couple of drinks. I looked over at a table and told Doug, 'I think that's Glenn Miller.' I asked a waitress and she said, 'Yes, that's him.'

I told Doug I was going to ask Miller for his autograph. He said, 'You're stupid, you can't have a lieutenant asking a major for his autograph.' I thought about it for a while and said, 'I guess you're right.' Now I wish he'd kept his mouth shut. Holy smoke, think what that dated autograph would be worth today. When we left the dining room Miller was still there with his aide Lt Don Haynes. I believe he and Lt Haynes left in the morning at about nine. It's funny, that night I dreamed of a plane going down and right away I thought it was me. I told Doug and he said, 'Holy shit.' But it didn't foretell *my* future, it was another person's future.[21]

There have been many conjectures about what happened to Glenn Miller, including a claim by a now deceased former RAF navigator that he saw the Norseman below him as bombs were jettisoned in the Channel from returning 3 Group Lancasters. They had been recalled from a raid on railway yards at Siegen, near Bonn, because thick cloud almost to the ground made even a GH-guided raid impossible. But Ron Brown, the 75 Sqn flight engineer, who was on the raid, remembers that the bombs were dropped miles away from the Channel:

We jettisoned our bombs set to safe in the pre-designated jettison area of the North Sea, from about 3,000 feet. If the bombs had been armed, dropping them from that height you would have blown up your own aircraft. The bomb doors opened and I doubt that the bomb aimer even saw the bombs falling away, the cloud was so thick. It's a nonsensical claim for someone to make that they saw jettisoned bombs hit Glenn Miller's Norseman flying at about 1,000 feet because it wouldn't have been possible to see anyone in that weather.[22]

Sgt Kenneth Turnham, a 115 Sqn wireless operator, began his tour on the day Glenn Miller was lost and also remembers the 'atrocious' conditions. 'The Siegen operation was just like one of the old fogs in Manchester, you couldn't see a hand in front of you,' he says. 'We were recalled and given a designated area in the North Sea to jettison our bombs and that's where we did. Nobody will ever know what happened to Glenn Miller, but it's likely his aircraft iced up.'[23] An enquiry by the USAAF in fact concluded the Norseman's airframe had become encrusted with ice and it had plunged into the sea.

Glenn Miller's disappearance wasn't announced until Christmas Eve and in the aircrew pubs north of London airmen mourned his passing. Lt Roth remembers: 'The pubs we went into in Bedford were the Swan and the Silver Spoon. We used to meet RCAF and RAF aircrew in there and they were all talking about it. Fighting the war the only thing we had was the big band music and the booze.'[24]

The mysterious exit of Glenn Miller did much to enhance his band's reputation and the popularity of swing music generally. Even the Nazis, after years of condemning swing as an example of what they considered to be Negro and Jewish degeneracy, had to capitulate to its popularity after they found Luftwaffe personnel were tuning in to American broadcasts. They funded a Nazi band, Charlie and his Orchestra, which played swing tunes with Propaganda Ministry lyrics in English, for instance extolling that Churchill hated to send his bombers to see them smashed. They were recorded by British intelligence and played to Churchill, who was much amused.[25]

But there were other things on the minds of RAF aircrew apart from music and sex as December closed, not least food in cold and rationed Britain. It was perhaps uppermost in the minds of a distinctive, more staid, minority. It was the younger British and Commonwealth aircrew who often found solace in boozy nights out or chasing girls. Older airmen, sometimes married, were usually of a more reflective nature. Their chosen entertainment was more that of the pianist Dame Myra Hess, appearing with the New London Orchestra at Cambridge Guildhall in December.[26] It was the 155th of a series of wartime concerts which often had a sprinkling of RAF or USAAF flyers in the audience. In York, surrounded by RAF and Canadian airfields, there was sufficient interest for the Theatre Royal to stage a pre-Christmas performance of *Othello*, to be followed by weeks of ballet in the New Year.[27]

The content of the slightly improved rations made available for Christmas was a news item avidly looked for in the small-sized wartime papers, not least by aircrew who might be lucky enough to be spending Christmas at home. In early December, amid the usual small ads seeking 'live rabbits' for breeding as a nutrition source or the less usual prosecution of an airman and NAAFI worker for rations stealing,[28] the Ministry of Food announced that 9 ounces of sugar per person would now be available between 10 December and 6 January; that the meat ration value of each coupon was being increased from 7d (less than 3p) to 11d; and that there would be 8 ounces of chocolates or sweets available, but only to young people, who held green or blue ration books.[29] It was promised pork from South America would be available for Christmas dinner.

Aircrew on operational stations had no such problems. It was considered necessary for their morale that they were well fed. As one RAF bomb aimer explained pithily to a researcher: 'You went to war for six hours and you came back to clean sheets. When you did an operation you got ham and eggs. Nobody else did.'[30] And if aircrew had to land at one of the USAAF bomber bases so much the better. Sgt Laurie Godfrey, an English wireless operator on the Canadian 408 Sqn, remembers:

We went to Düsseldorf on Christmas Eve, 1944, and had to land at Eye, Suffolk, an American Flying Fortress base, because of the ice and snow. We were there for Christmas Day and the Americans really looked after us. We were treated very well. There was plenty of good food and I was able to go to the PX and stock up on supplies. I got lots of cigarettes, I remember, for my brother-in-law, but you could get practically whatever you wanted there. It was marvellous stuff. We were actually stuck at the American base for four days, the reason being that when we went out to the aircraft on the 26th our pilot, P/O Case, stepped out on the wing and slipped off the trailing edge, breaking his heel. It meant we had to stay there until they sent another pilot from Linton two days later to bring us back to base. We never saw P/O Case again, but on 22 January a Flt Smith, who had already done one tour, joined us to finish our tour with us.[31]

Keen to maintain morale among those who didn't fly as well as those who did, rations and their preparation were even improved in late 1944 on RAF bomber stations in 4 Group around York. A somewhat simplistic newspaper article explained that a Bomber Command catering officer, F/Lt J. McGrath, on seeing that a tired and dejected WAAF driver couldn't eat her lunch of 'greasy stew' because she had spent the entire morning cleaning out a lorry sump, the contents of which looked somewhat similar, decided variety of the kind found in pre-war urban life was the answer. 'This is the civilian outlook provided by the day's dinner menu of Sgt Ben Ball, the industrious cook,' the article went on. 'Roast mutton; stewed steak of mutton and dumplings; fried chops; roast and boiled potatoes; brussels sprouts, carrots and swedes; parsley and onion stuffing and gravy.' For dessert there was a choice of 'Baked fig rolls, steamed fig pudding, stewed prunes and custard'.[32] Even more was later promised by the RAF for Christmas Day, with 'Scotch broth, roast turkey and forcemeat stuffing; roast pork and apple sauce' plus all the trimmings, and then for afters 'Christmas pudding with custard sauce, mince pies, cheese, biscuits, celery, apples, oranges, cigarettes, beer, minerals'.[33] At the same time newspapers, with access to reports from neutral Sweden, were recording that rations for German civilians had been cut yet again.

For the thousands of bomber boys who had been shot down and taken prisoner in the savage air battles of 1943 and the early part of 1944 it would be a bleak and lonely Christmas with an uncertain future ahead, in which their lives were at the whim of the enemy. They were on the lowest rations in Germany, those of a totally non-productive adult civilian. Only the distribution of parcels from the Red Cross, which became more haphazard as the bombing offensive increased, brought hope. Fallingbostel, near Lüneburg Heath, where the RAF POWs from Stalag Luft VI at Heydekrug had arrived in the late summer after evacuation from their Lithuanian camp in front of the Russian advance, was now also the home of Stalag 357, which had been moved from Thorn in Poland for similar reasons. By mid-1944 there were some 96,000 POWs of all nationalities spread over a complex of camps at Fallingbostel and conditions were already deteriorating. They would soon become much worse as Reich territory shrank in the face of Allied advances in 1945.

Aware of what lay ahead, the RAF POWs had been saving tinned rations for months from their Red Cross parcels and prepared a Christmas Day lunch of steak and kidney pudding, shepherd's pie, meat roll, roast potatoes and peas followed by Christmas pudding and cocoa.[34] It was a similar story at other RAF POW camps, at the Great Escape camp of Stalag Luft III at Sagan, Poland, where in January the prisoners were to be forced into a march in the snow over many weeks away from the Russians, and at Stalag IVB at Mühlberg, between Leipzig and Dresden. W/O Dennis Slack had been incarcerated there since being shot down over Berlin in August 1943 and he recorded that the young prisoners, not long away from the classroom, went a stage further to celebrate Christmas. 'The paper wrappings were removed from the (Red Cross) food tins and then glued together with paste made from the klim (milk) powder. These were then formed into paper chains and we decorated the hut with them, just like we did at school.'[35]

Both among the prisoners of war in Germany and their loved ones back in Britain there were now obvious signs that the war was entering its final chapters. The Home Guard, formed in the summer of 1940 when Britain faced a real threat of invasion, was stood down at the beginning of the month and now the once stringent blackout restrictions had been further eased by allowing cars to be driven with headlights unmasked.[36]

It was all very satisfying, and there was little pity for a reeling enemy. But in the middle of the month hopes of an early end to the war, perhaps by bombing, began to look unjustified when Field Marshall von Runstedt's SS-led Tiger tanks burst through the forests of the Ardennes to try to divide the American and British and Canadian armies in a dash for Brussels and Antwerp. Von Runstedt had waited for a period of heavy overcast to thwart the bombers and made his attack in freezing mist, the same conditions that had killed Glenn Miller the day before. It came as a complete surprise to the green US 106th Infantry Division which had been in the line for only five days and 7,000 of its GIs were captured, including Kurt Vonnegut, who would experience the bombing of Dresden nine weeks later and write about it post-war in a controversial novel.

Hitler's irredeemable final thrust would keep the war going in the west, so that more German cities would die as Bomber Command reached a new terrifying level of efficiency with a still growing force of bombers. And for the moment it changed the bombing war again as transportation targets, often at the heart of cities, became the new priority to prevent supply trains reaching the front.

SEVEN

FIRE AND ICE

THE Arctic weather that had gripped northern Europe in December bit even deeper as a New Year of warfare opened, rapidly freezing hopes of seeing an early end to the bloodshed. The pressure on Harris to bomb transportation targets in the final days of December to cause a bottleneck of supplies to the Ardennes Front now revealed the weather as the true enemy, his crews flying under almost impossible conditions in which to wage aerial war. Between 16 December, when the Battle of the Bulge began, and the end of the month Harris's heavies had carried out seventeen major raids on railway installations, often bombing through thick cloud, the despair of any aerial commander. It had meant a turning away from Portal's direction to hit oil refineries and synthetic fuel plants, thus throttling the Luftwaffe and draining the potential of the Wehrmacht's tanks.

Only one raid in the oil plan had been carried out in that period, on the Scholven/Buer refineries at Gelsenkirchen in the Ruhr. Sgt Peter Bone, the young mid-upper gunner who had begun operations with the double Duisburg raids in October, was on the raid in 626 Sqn's Jig 2, the twelfth trip of his twenty-five-operation tour and it proved the most frightening. In post-war memoirs he recorded:

> We'd strayed off course due to an undetected malfunction of one
> of our electronic navigation aids and were flying over the outskirts
> of Cologne some 20 miles to the southwest and we were all alone.
> The first intimation that anything was wrong came suddenly when
> anti-aircraft shells began to burst all around us. I can still see the

port wing dissecting a hideous ball of black smoke tinged with wicked orange flame and I can still smell the cordite ... Skipper thrust the huge bomber, still heavily laden with fuel and about six tons of bombs, into a steep dive to port in an attempt to escape the lethal stream of shells coming up at us from radar-controlled anti-aircraft batteries some 20,000ft below. 'Start windowing, Fred,' he snapped [to the bomb aimer Sgt Till]. Till tore open dozens of brown paper packages stacked in the fuselage and thrust hundreds of silver strips down the flare chute. The effect was immediate. The shells ceased to be so terrifyingly close and then ceased coming altogether. Skipper was able to fly straight and level again.[1]

The crew of Jig 2 turned on to a new course to the target, which came up a few minutes later. Sgt Bone wrote:

Now we were no longer alone, but one of 324 Lancasters and 24 Mosquito night fighters. We bombed and turned thankfully for home. We were tucking into bacon and eggs in the mess by 10 that night. Half an hour later I was sitting on my bed in the Nissen hut I shared with 13 other young men and writing in my diary, 'I didn't like that trip.' Next day we found that a large sliver of flak had entered the starboard side of Jig 2, crossed the passageway between Bert [Sgt Bray] our wireless operator and the navigator [Sgt Duncan McLean], cut through the leads of the H2S and exited through the port side to embed itself in the port engine, fortunately without putting it out of action. It was by sheer chance that we had got away with only minimal damage and no injury to any crew member. But if there hadn't been solid cloud beneath us, we would have been immediately coned by numerous searchlights from which there was almost never any escape.[2]

The severe cold that ushered in the New Year not only brought problems of icing in the air and often turbulent cloud, but also increased the chances of aerodrome accidents as aircraft skidded on icy runways or suffered engine failure on take-off because of ice cutting off the fuel supply. F/O Douglas Jennings, the bomb aimer who had evaded the enemy after being shot down in June and arrived back in London in time for the German V-2 offensive, was posted to 9 Sqn at Bardney in Lincolnshire on New Year's Day and found immediate evidence of the weather raising the operational stakes. He had had great difficulty persuading the air force to break the golden rule of not allowing fliers who had been helped by the Resistance to go back on operations for fear they might fall into the hands of inquisitive Germans. He remembers:

I was keen to get back. I had done the training and yet I had been sent to an OTU to start training again. I thought it was a complete waste. I decided to do something about it and in the mess I accosted an air vice-marshal who had stripes up his sleeve from wrist to shoulder and poured my heart out and luckily for me he took pity on me and sorted it out and I was posted to 9 Sqn. I must have been barmy, but at the time it seemed the right thing to do.

I had got myself a little car and arrived at Bardney in style. As I drove in I could see there were bits of aircraft spread about the aerodrome . . . I thought, Welcome back, Doug. I suppose it was a bit daunting, but often before I was shot down in 1944 when there were mass take-offs at night the planes would be droning over the airfield and there would suddenly be a crack and a bang and two of them would fall out of the sky. That happened quite a lot. There always seemed to be something going on.

It was a very severe winter and there had been severe icing conditions the night before I arrived at Bardney and two crashed on take-off, I believe. One never actually got off.* I think it must have skidded, and it ended up in a ditch. Most winters seemed to be bad. We were housed in Nissen huts at Bardney with a stove in the middle that used to get red-hot, but three or four yards away from it the air was stone cold. We got used to the cold temperature

* This was the aircraft of F/O J. W. Buckley, RAAF, which crashed at 0750 just off the Bardney main runway in severe icing conditions. Only the flight engineer was injured, but three minutes earlier the Lancaster of F/O C. S. Newton, RCAF, had dived into the ground within sight of the airfield after losing power to both port engines shortly after becoming airborne and all the crew were killed with the exception of the bomb aimer.

in billets. I felt sorry for the ground crews stuck out in the middle of the aerodrome trying to change engines, load bombs and fuel aircraft with icy fingers. Those poor devils really suffered.[3]

Apart from the two aircraft lost on take-off two other 9 Sqn aircraft would fail to return from the raid the day F/O Jennings arrived, which had been on the Dortmund-Ems Canal and its munitions-supply barges. He remembers: 'In the mess that day I can't say people were gloomy because of the losses. They were conditioned to that kind of thing. I suppose they were shocked in their own minds, but aircrew in those days got so used to losing friends that they never really expressed it. If you ever asked, 'Whatever happened to Charlie?' for instance, they would just answer, "Oh, he's gone for the chop. Roll on." '[4]

However what had happened in one of those missing Lancasters became the talk of the mess in weeks to come. It had resulted in a posthumous VC, the second in Bomber Command's trans-portation campaign in nine days.* The Bardney VC winner, F/Sgt George Thompson, a former grocer's boy and the son of a Perth-shire ploughman, had been a wireless operator on 9 Sqn since the autumn, in the crew of New Zealander F/O Harry Denton. Denton, like the rest of 9 Sqn, was briefed to attack the Dortmund-Ems Canal between 10,500 feet and 12,000 feet for maximum accuracy and effect by the aerodynamic Tallboy bomb they were carrying, which it was hoped would breach the Ladbergen viaduct, last attacked in September and now repaired. But attacking from such a low bombing height inevitably meant a greater threat from both heavy and light flak. Denton's bomb had just been released in the clear, freezing-cold air when a heavy shell went through the aircraft in front of the mid-upper turret. Fire broke out and dense

---

* S/Ldr Robert Palmer, the 24-year-old master bomber for a raid on the Cologne marshalling yards on 23 December, won a posthumous VC for continuing with his bomb run to mark the target accurately even though his flak-hit 582 Sqn Lancaster was ablaze. The aircraft hit the ground after bombing, only the rear gunner surviving.

smoke filled the fuselage. The nose of the aircraft was then struck and the slipstream rushing in cleared the smoke, revealing a scene of devastation. Most of the Perspex nose had been shot away, gaping holes had been torn in the canopy above the pilot's head, the intercom had been cut and there was a large hole in the floor of the aircraft. Bedding and other equipment was alight and one engine was on fire.

The announcement of Thompson's VC in late February caught the public imagination, vividly assisted by Britain's national newspapers, and this report from the *Daily Herald* captures the spirit of enthusiastic wartime reporting. 'The gunner (Sgt Haydn Price) was unconscious in his blazing mid-upper turret. Thompson went down the fuselage into the hell of the flame and explosions and pulled the gunner from his turret and edging round the hole in the floor carried him from the flames.'[5]

The newspaper continued that Thompson then went to rescue the rear gunner, Sgt Ernest Potts, trapped in his burning turret.

Despite severe injuries he moved to the rear of the fuselage, extricated the helpless gunner with great difficulty and carried him clear. Still he thought his duty was not done. Exhausted he clambered back perilously through the burning fuselage to warn the captain of the condition of the crew. The flow of air through the hole in the floor caused him intense pain and frostbite developed, but he made it. So pitiful was his condition that his captain did not recognise him, but through burnt, cracked lips he croaked out his report.[6]

Denton made for the Allied lines, where he was again hit by ground fire, and crash-landed in a field not far from Eindhoven, where six of the crew were hospitalised. The rear gunner, flames from whose clothing Thompson had beaten out with hands he had already injured putting out the fire in Price's clothing, died of his injuries the next day and Thompson succumbed three weeks later.

The mid-upper gunner, Sgt Price, whose life Thompson had saved, would be undergoing treatment until long after the war.

Sgt Harry Stunell, the wireless operator who had lately survived an attack by a Ju88 on the Heilbronn raid and had trained with George Thompson, would share a burns hospital with Price over several weeks. Stunell's own severe injuries had been contracted in a horrifying crash following a raid on Munich, seven days after Thompson's heroic action.

WHILE Harris demonstrably complied with the urgent demands to wreck the enemy's supply network and cut off his fuel supplies he quietly held on to his core belief that the war could still be ended by massive blows to the enemy's heavily populated major centres of industry which would tip the balance into final collapse from within by a demoralised people. He had been allowed, by the Air Ministry directive of 25 September, to carry out such large city raids 'when weather and tactical conditions are unsuitable for operations against specific primary objectives'. Surely there could be no clearer picture of such conditions than the ice, snow and plummeting temperatures of early January and Harris seized his chance. On the 2nd he sent 514 Lancasters against the old enemy of Nuremberg, the target that had set the scene the previous March for Bomber Command's bitterest battle of the war in which ninety-five bombers and one Mosquito intruder were shot down, killing more airmen in one night than in the whole of the Battle of Britain.

F/Sgt Henryk Drozdz, the 25-year-old Pole who had escaped from his devastated country to fly as a flight engineer with his fellow refugees from Nazi tyranny on the all-Polish 300 Sqn, took part in the raid and recorded the minute-by-minute events in his diary.

Always ahead of time we race to the briefing room to satisfy our curiosity – where to today? The answer is short and simple – Nuremberg. The briefing becomes noisy and I do not like either the turmoil or the target. It is the home town of Alfred Rosenberg, the author of racial ideology of Nazism, and besides the prognosis is not good for tonight – 96 planes did not come back from the last sortie to that city. According to the briefing the flight should be easy – they always see everything as easy (from the ground).[7]

His skipper, F/Lt Jan Kozicki, turned his Lancaster onto Faldingworth's duty runway just after 3 p.m. and thundered into the gathering gloom, the heavily laden bomber lifting slowly into the overcast, engines straining at 3,000 revolutions per minute, then turning crosswind to orbit base for the navigator to call out the compass course for the first leg of the night. The force would not be taking the route through the Cologne gap that had proved so fatal in March, but making use of liberated territory as far as Strasbourg to avoid German reporting points for night fighters. The journey down to the south-east of England and across the Channel into France was uneventful. F/Sgt Drozdz wrote:

> The constant hum of the engines make you sleepy and you could fall asleep if you did not have to watch the clocks and other instruments. We are flying at 6,000ft, but the clouds are very low – less than a hundred metres above the ground. This shroud envelops the earth and keeps us apart. We are flying above the clouds and suddenly we see a tower. It must be the tower of Reims Cathedral. It is a wonderful sight – all you can see is this slender spire like God's finger pointing the way.[8]

The drone of 2,000 engines beating in unison rolled wave-like across the rural patchwork below and on to Strasbourg then over the German front line, once more inducing fear in the ranks of field grey beneath its path as former victorious soldiers now speculated in troubled agitation if it would be their city Bomber Command would strike that night, their home that would be turned to ashes, their family reduced to living in cellars like so many before and as the people of Warsaw were now doing, the city centre bombed heavily in 1939 now totally destroyed after the recent Resistance uprising. 'The earth is sleeping. Underneath we can see white patches of snow. It is winter below us – brrr! Here in the plane at 19,000ft it is warm and cosy,' F/Sgt Drozdz wrote. But he admitted there was already nervous tension when I think of the target – Nuremberg. How long do we have to wait before we see the long-awaited markers, the red and green lights on parachutes . . . We are in the second wave, there are others in front of us, maybe they will start some fires so that it will be light. My legs are shaking, there are searchlights in front. A beautiful silver-white cone of 10 searchlights is lying in wait for the audacious. It does not last long though and I don't know why this sinister cone of light goes out. Thank God for that. But that was just the beginning, the prelude, now the main performance. Flak blasts away, but gradually grows weaker. Now one after another come the Lancasters. It is light as daytime, not a single cloud in the sky. Underneath us the city appears. This is something I will never forget – the whole city of Nuremberg lies under our feet with its thousands of streets and alleyways. We can see everything – every street and block of houses. We cross the river – left turn – 'Keep it steady' shouts the bomb aimer. Centre of the city and the bombs are gone. I try to see the results of the bombing, but a huge pall of smoke and fire begins to envelop the whole. Quickly we leave the target. It is a splendid view – I have never seen the like of it before – it is magnificent. Oh, something is not right. Behind us something is on fire and goes down – probably one of the planes, now another one already past the target. I can see it clearly breaking up into four pieces . . . This is not good, shivers go down my spine and automatically I check my engines . . . We are going full speed, the further the safer. Below us to the right something else is burning, but we are going ahead. Flying at the speed of 200 while slightly descending is good tactics as far as the fuel goes. I am still elated by the sight of the target which is still aflame and of the ground itself which is clearly visible with its mountains, snow, houses and other buildings. I am sure every Kraut's skin creeps at the sound of the formidable armada.[9]

Under a rising moon the Pathfinders had carefully marked the centre of the city. The Lancasters that followed them destroyed the eastern half of the centre and flattened much of the industrial area in the south. It was a textbook area attack and old Nuremberg died with much of its industry. This time there had been no ascendent Luftwaffe to wage attrition among the bombers and the price in terms of bombers lost over the city had not even reached double figures.

But there had been the usual crop of collisions and near misses in the crowded sky over Lincolnshire as the Lancasters returned. The circuit at Faldingworth almost overlapped that of Wickenby, both of them satellite airfields to No. 14 Base headquarters at nearby Ludford Magna where 101 Sqn operated its special radio-jamming Lancasters in proximity to RAF Kelstern. Just to the west of Faldingworth lay another Bomber Command airfield, Hemswell and a few miles to the south was Scampton. F/Sgt Drozdz now saw how dangerous so many heavy bombers flying orbits in close proximity could be.

> We are over the base. Having reported our arrival we fly in a circle and at this moment it seems that over Wickenby something in the air caught fire. It is a huge fire which breaks up and falls down in big trails. Could it be that some planes collided? I become more watchful to what goes on around me. One more circle and 'Prepare to land'. The longed-for 'Power-off' moment of waiting and then we feel Mother Earth beneath our feet. We land and disperse. We learn that in fact two planes collided over Wickenby.* In the interrogation room we learn that one plane has not yet returned and is 'Missing'. This is T for Talimena. I feel sad when I see Halinka crying in the interrogation room. It was her sister's fiancé, Captain Janas,** who flew in that plane. Their wedding was due to take place in two weeks' time. He probably did not come back.[10]

---

* M-Mother of the Hemswell-based 150 Sqn collided at low level with N-Nan of 153 Sqn, from Scampton. Both aircraft came down at Sudbrooke 3 miles north-east of Lincoln, not far from Wickenby. None of the fourteen crew aboard was able to bale out in time.
** The Lancaster of S/Ldr B. Janas exploded near Luxembourg, killing him and his crew.

The toll for the night on such a long-distance and normally well-defended target had been just seven Lancasters. If Harris had been interested in retribution rather than waging what he saw as efficient war he might have considered his crews had been avenged for the massacre in the moonlight of the previous March. But Nuremberg's night-fighter defenders were not finished with Bomber Command, as they would demonstrate in two months' time.

In fact the statistics would not comfort crews for long as they contemplated their tours in January. Three nights after Nuremberg Harris dispatched a mixed force of 650 Lancasters and Halifaxes to Hanover, the first occasion since October 1943 that a large raid had been mounted on the city. This time the *Nachtjäger* found the stream and twenty-three bombers were lost, 4.7 per cent, the kind of figure that had been routine in 1943 and early 1944 and drained Bomber Command to the point of despair. The damage was not commensurate with such loss, bombs falling all over the city in the poor weather conditions.

F/Sgt Eddie Hilton, a wireless operator on 51 Sqn at Snaith, had completed seven operations in the crew of P/O Alan Leach by the beginning of January, but was grounded when the Hanover operation was planned because he had a severe head cold. Instead F/O Lionel Wilson, an Australian who had completed his tour, took his place. Wilson was older than most aircrew at 32. He was also married, as was the Yorkshire mid-upper gunner, F/Sgt Walter Burton. The flight did not begin well. Sgt Don Thomsett, Leach's rear gunner, recalled later that there had been a magneto drop on the Halifax and as the time came and went for F-Freddie to move from dispersal and join the growling queue along the perimeter track the ground crew were still working on it. It was fixed just in time for P/O Leach to join the tail end of the squadron and he took off at 4.47 p.m., ten minutes after the last aircraft navigation lights had faded from the circuit. 'We flew to the south coast to join the bomber stream and quickly reached 16,000ft, which previously had been a drag, but on this day she made the climb easily,' Sgt Thomsett remembered. 'The stream appeared very tight, there was a Lancaster sitting right on our tail at our height and another close to the port side.'[11]

Less than three hours later they were over the target where yellow and blue tracer was criss-crossing above the arena of crimson bomb bursts lighting up the cloud below. The quick red glare of heavy flak was interspersed with the telltale downward trails of yellow and orange flame which marked the final journey of aircraft and their crews. Three already had fallen to Hauptmann Georg Greiner, the ace commander of 1V/NJG1 with forty-five victories now, when his radar operator gave him another contact and he approached to tuck his Schrage Musik-equipped Me110 beneath the port wing of P/O Leach's Halifax. Sgt Thomsett recorded:

> Suddenly our mid-upper gunner was on the intercom saying, 'Fighter to port.' He could not engage as his tail fin inhibitors had put his guns to 'Non Fire'. I saw the Me110 so close that I could see the dark outline of the pilot. My sight with the Me110 illuminated in it also gave me a Lancaster at 100 yards. I gave the order to 'Corkscrew to port' to give me a better firing angle and our plane dropped out of the sky violently.[12]

But by now Hptmn Greiner was tucked beneath the Halifax's wing with the angled sight to his cannon between the two port engines and followed P/O Leach downward. 'I can remember being very surprised that a heavy bomber like a Halifax was capable of such daring and dangerous evasion manoeuvres,' he later recorded. 'Only because of my oblique-directed weaponry was I in the position to keep my relatively close distance as with this armament – visor vertical above me – I could not lose the opponent.'[13] Sgt Thomsett later wrote:

> There was a terrific explosion. I thought we had hit another plane in the stream. The skipper gave the jump call. I tried to line up my turret with the fuselage, but the power had gone. I had to mechanically turn the turret. Opening the door I saw fire rushing through the fuselage. On finding my parachute I banged it on and

tipped myself backwards out of the turret. One thing I forgot to do was to unplug my intercom; the wire could have broken my neck. Fortunately I was upside down and my helmet was pulled straight off.

As his chute snapped open Sgt Thomsett looked down straight into the target.

There were planes above, bombs coming down and flak going up. The smell of cordite was overpowering. I could hear the silk of the parachute making a crackling noise and I spent most of my time on the journey down trying to lay back to see if the chute was on fire. I saw I was close to houses and fires, then the roofs came up so quickly that my boots caught the apex of a house. The chute slackened and I fell, landing in front of an apartment block in Hanover-Herreshausen.[14]

Sgt Thomsett was taken to the local police station and eventually, after being beaten up by some civilians, sent to the Luftwaffe interrogation centre at Dulag Luft and on to Stalag IIIA at Luckenwalde. The rest of his crew, including the unlucky F/O Wilson, had not survived. Two other 51 Sqn crews were also lost over the target. F/Sgt Hilton discovered the next day that his crew was missing. He had to operate as what was known as a 'spare bod' among airmen, filling in for missing members of different crews, his last operation taking place in the middle of March.

Hanover was the last operation of F/Lt Arnold Derrington, an English navigator on 466 RAAF Sqn, whose tour had begun in the warm days of August. He remembers how cold it was that night in January. He says:

We knew before we took off it would be the last operation of our tour. We were pretty experienced by that time of course and this was the second trip we had made as PFF support. I had already been invited to do a second tour, but my father had died the previous October and as the eldest son of four children I didn't feel like doing that. This last trip was among the most memorable because of its problems. The heating packed up in the aircraft and the temperature was registered as minus 44° Fahrenheit. It was absolutely freezing. I was well dressed up in several layers of clothing, but I could feel the cold striking through. I could only wear thin gloves as I needed to use a pencil and my hands were nearly numb with the cold. We weren't getting a regular supply of oxygen, possibly through ice building up in oxygen tubes. Over the target there was moderate flak, but Hanover was covered by 10/10s cloud. The bomb aimer had to blind-bomb, from the picture on the H2S screen. We were relieved they were gone and we were on our way home and we were very glad when we got back to Driffield. Within a week we were sent on leave and within a month I learned I had been awarded the DFC.[15]

The Hanover raid cut a swathe through the Canadian squadrons, eleven of the Halifax and Lancaster crews of 6 Group going down. The aircraft of F/O Wally Weitendof, a skipper on the Canadian Pathfinder squadron, 405, attached to 8 Group, nearly became the twelfth. F/O Weitendof had lined himself up on the bomb run when he was hit by an incendiary bomb from another aircraft. 'There was a huge flash and loud explosion immediately in front of me and about a foot ahead of the windshield. I distinctly recall saying to myself, "This is it, you're dead." I must have let go of the controls and found our aircraft was going down fast when the rear gunner called me to say our starboard inner engine was on fire and the flames were about even with his turret.'[16] Flame retardant was rapidly pumped into the starboard inner with the Graviner button, the propeller feathered to prevent drag, and the aircraft brought onto an even keel. The bombs were dropped and the skipper, freezing in the draught from the shattered windscreen, turned for home. As the defunct starboard inner controlled hydraulic pumps and a key generator, he now had no wireless, no flaps or brakes.

RAF Woodbridge in Suffolk had been established for just such emergencies, with a runway a third longer than the average 2,000 yards and a width of 250 yards compared to the routine 80, and the navigator worked out the correct heading. Weitendof remembers:

> The crew covered me as much as possible with blankets so I could do my job. We made visual contact with our Aldis lamp and got immediate response in green. Our landing lights were working, but I had to bring her in at about 140 knots because we had no flaps. Soon after touchdown our landing lights picked up a Mosquito bomber and two men waving their arms like mad. I had no choice but to swing the Lancaster to miss them and we did by a few feet.[17]

The next day, when the airframe fitters had examined his aircraft, the young skipper discovered just how lucky he had been to survive. 'An RAF flight sergeant told me, "If you had not gone into that steep dive the incendiary bomb could have caused an explosion as a 640-gallon tank of 100 octane is close by. The wind over that hole was so strong it caused a low-pressure area, enough to suck the burning incendiary out".'[18]

Among the crop of wrecks at Woodbridge that morning was another bomber downed by its own air force. The Halifax was one of four lost on the Hanover raid from 158 Sqn. Three of the Lissett squadron's aircraft were shot down by night fighters, but T-Tommy was struck from underneath by a Lancaster 20 miles from the aiming point. T-Tommy's bomb aimer, P/O P. A. J. Carroll, saw the impact.

> I was about to commence the run-in to the target, but before I could select 'bomb-doors open', I saw one of our aircraft being chased by a German night fighter. In taking evasive action it came up beneath our aircraft and smashed into the under surfaces. I was thrown hard against the Perspex nose and was pinned down. The whole of our aircraft was vibrating terribly, while through the Perspex I could see the fires raging below. I thought, 'This is it'.[19]

A gale swept into the aircraft through a hole in the airframe, as big as a table, caused by the collision and the temperature on the navigator's gauge in the nose of the Halifax immediately dropped to minus 30°F. The navigator, F/Sgt G. Huband, who had clipped on his chest chute as the aircraft pitched forward, later recalled: 'The terrible vibration stopped and as we came out of the dive we saw a starboard engine fall from its mountings leaving wires hanging and sparks flying.'[20] The intercom plug of the bomb aimer had come out in the impact and without communication, freezing cold, and pinned to the Perspex nose by centrifugal force in the plunge, Carroll was convinced the front of the aircraft had been blown away with him in it until the pilot, F/O W. McLennan, managed to pull the aircraft out of its dive. F/Sgt Huband remembered: 'As our best course of action seemed to lie with remaining with the mainstream we held our course and dropped our bombs on the outskirts of Hanover.'

McLennan then had to try to bring home an aircraft with few instruments and a nose twisted so far out of line the Halifax was attempting to fly in circles. The radio was also out of action, so the wireless operator F/Sgt M. Spivey took off his protective gloves and tried to repair the wiring, but his fingers developed frostbite in the piercing cold. The navigator was able to take star shots with a bubble sextant and eventually, after switching on the IFF transmitter which indicated the aircraft as Allied, the pilot spotted searchlights pointing to the Suffolk emergency airfield. But as the aircraft now had no hydraulic power the wheels could not be lowered. 'To our alarm we could see a 4000lb bomb still resting in the bomb bay,' F/Sgt Huband remembered. 'In desperation I pulled at an electrical junction box and the bomb went, taking with it the bomb bay doors.'[21] A few minutes later, nearly three hours after his ordeal began as he approached Hanover, McLennan hit the runway at Woodbridge. As he careered along to the screeching of tearing metal another engine broke away and the aircraft slid off the concrete to come to rest in a snow bank near the airfield boundary. McLennan was awarded an immediate DFC and the wireless operator, who had to have the worst affected of his frostbitten fingers amputated, a DFM. The bomb aimer and navigator were decorated later.

*

FORTY-EIGHT hours after the Hanover raid Harris sent a similar-sized, all-Lancaster force to Munich, which brought more tangible results, further damaging the already battered centre and some industrial areas to such a degree that Bomber Command would never feel the need to return, with a total of 70,000 in the city now bombed out. A letter eight days later from an aristocratic resident to her daughter, Fey von Hassell, a prisoner in Buchenwald concentration camp as a result of the July bomb plot against Hitler read: 'I am afraid that the last letter I wrote will never arrive, because I sent it just before a horrifying air attack on Munich . . . Of the Munich we used to know, there is practically nothing left.'[22] The raid had been mounted in two waves, almost two hours apart and in ten-tenths freezing cloud all the way across France almost to the target. It was a night for collisions again, claiming many of the fifteen aircraft lost. A 460 Sqn bomber was hit by another east of Paris, barely making it to the south coast emergency airfield of Manston; Lancasters from 405 (RCAF) and 635 Sqn collided near Nuremberg killing all fourteen crew; two 626 Sqn airmen were killed in a collision with a 150 Sqn Lancaster which managed to fly away south of Laon; and another bomber hit a 106 Sqn Lancaster over the target itself. On board was wireless operator Harry Stunell and his tour was about to end in a horrifying manner.
Stunell remembers:

We were told at briefing that Munich was Hitler's favourite city and that the Nazi movement had been founded there. It was certainly very heavily defended, fringed by a number of night-fighter airfields. Once we got to the target I could see a huge amount of fire below; it was like a contorted Turner landscape. It didn't pay you to look at it too long, gunners particularly were told not to be held by the awesome stuff that was going on below. I had been looking through the astrodome and the bomber stream seemed a bit raggle-taggle. They weren't well ordered and aircraft were moving dangerously near as if they were going to go across the stream. We had released our bombs and just completed the thirty-second wait for the photograph when someone spotted a Lancaster coming towards us. I was off intercom at the time and the first I knew was we were upside down and going down almost vertically. I was dragged out of my radio compartment and was pinned to the floor – which had now become the roof – by the centrifugal force. I had no idea what had happened, but I thought, This is it, I'm going to die, and I just accepted I couldn't do anything about it.

The pilot and the flight engineer eventually managed to pull it out of the dive and I got back to my seat. Apparently the other Lancaster had just flicked our wing. The pilot, Jim Scott, had called out, 'Prepare to abandon aircraft,' in the dive and the front escape hatch had been jettisoned. Once I'd gathered myself I looked for my parachute pack to clip on but it had disappeared. It was a shambles in the aircraft. It was a freezing night and there was a gale whipping through the fuselage from the front. You could hear the roar of it. The maps were flying around and my spare trailing aerial had flown out of its housing and was unravelling. I went forward and saw the navigator, Ken Darke, sitting on the step by the open hole. I lifted up the flap of his flying helmet and shouted, 'Ken, I've lost my parachute, I'll have to go out on your back, hanging on to the straps.' I could see he was terrified by the prospect, so I went back and as I was doing so actually tripped over my chute.

I heard the flight engineer say that the rivets of some of the upper wing panels might have popped in the dive because I think he noticed some vibration on the upper mainplane surfaces. The decision was made to head for Juvincourt in France. There was no other discussion on the intercom about what had happened, perhaps because of the trauma. We seemed to be gradually losing height in a blizzard and the mid-upper gunner told the skipper, 'I can see some trees just beneath us.' I thought, We're going to pile up. I immediately put my feet up to the edge of my wireless operator's table, grabbed hold of the tubular support between the floor and the roof and shoved myself into the back rest of my seat as hard as I could.

As soon as we struck the tops of the trees we were on fire with a whoosh! I was in the middle of the flames. I couldn't see anything apart from fire and if I'd put my hand in front of me I wouldn't have seen it. I felt blobs from the melting Perspex astrodome above me falling on me and I thought, This is the way out. There was a bar across it for the navigator to rest his sextant when taking star shots. It caught the clips of my parachute harness, impeding me. I knew my clothing was on fire from the waist down and I had great difficulty struggling through. I thought I would jump down onto the port wing, but it was gone and I fell quite a long way to the ground. On the ground I couldn't make out anything either because the fire was so tremendous. Even the forest had started to burn in the howling wind that night. There was a great roar of flames and of course the trees must have been soaked in petrol. I rolled in the snow to put out the flames from my burning clothing. Then I was on my hands and knees and could feel brambles under the snow. I crawled about 50 yards away and lay on the ground looking at this Lancaster burning from end to end. It looked as if the front two-thirds were being consumed absolutely by fire.

I stumbled through the snow with third-degree burns to my legs, hands and buttocks. After about three hours I saw a winking light. I made for it and eventually came across a barn with a door slap-slapping in the wind and a lantern inside. The barn was full of sheep and I thought I could keep warm among them, but they skedaddled straight away. I lay down in their straw. It was very painful because my legs were like raw meat and the sharp ends of the straws were sticking into me.

I think I slept because I was so exhausted, then I heard period-ically the sound of a bell. I went outside and could work out the direction. I was on a high hillside which was part of a bowl surrounding a village. I knew I would have to find help or die. I staggered and crawled along and saw a farmer in the village street driving some cows. People were then coming from all directions. They thought I was a German. I had left my dog tags above my shelf at Metheringham which was a chargeable offence, but I got some English coins out and they realised I was RAF. The bell I had heard was the angelus bell being rung in the village church. The farmer who had been driving his cows, Lucien Giroux, took me to his house and his wife cared for me. I was in the village of Méligny-le-Grand, near Commercy.

Unknown to me Ron Needle, the rear gunner, had also survived. He had managed to exit from his turret after the crash before the fire reached it, then we had got out of the forest in different directions, each believing we were the sole survivor. He was found after me, suffering from frostbite, and later had a leg amputated. After a few days two American trucks came and took me and Ron to Commercy, where there was a 14–18 War French hospital being used by the Americans for Battle of the Bulge wounded. It was very crude, all trestles and planks and while I was being treated I looked sideways and saw these American surgeons taking a bloke's leg off. I was put on the critically ill list and kept everybody awake for about three nights shouting out in my dreams. I was there a couple of weeks and was put in a plaster cast from my waist down.

I was eventually put in an ambulance train at Commercy. It had a central passageway with angle brackets to take three rows of stretchers on each side. It travelled through the night to Bar-le-Duc and we kept being shunted into sidings. It was an endurance in itself. We finally got to Cherbourg and the wounded were put aboard a hospital ship and reached Southampton then put in an American Nissen hut hospital at Cirencester. I should really have been taken to the plastic surgeon Archibald McIndoe's hospital at East Grinstead, but they had to get me in somewhere quick and when the RAF arrived the American surgeon said, 'I've started skin grafts and you can't have him.'[23]

THE battle in which the weather was as great an enemy as the Luftwaffe fighter and flak units continued against city targets in January, Magdeburg, Duisburg and Stuttgart being hit by large forces. Occasionally the *Nachtjäger* would muster sufficient numbers in the right area to inflict grievous loss, 17 Halifaxes in a stream of 320 being lost on Magdeburg – 5.3 per cent, another statistic Bomber Command had considered confined to the previous year. At the same time smaller forces would hit oil targets, though 573 Lancasters virtually destroyed the oil plant at Leuna on the night of 14 January. And in the dreadful winter conditions collision proved an ever present danger. On the night before the Leuna raid F/O A. L. Wilson, skipper of the Halifax Y-Yorker on 51 Sqn, was hit by a Free French Halifax of 347 Sqn at a turning point over France while coming back from Saarbrücken. The operational diary of 51 Sqn, written up by the adjutant's staff at freezing Snaith a few days later recorded simply: 'The captain, after looking down at the DR compass at Position H looked up to see a Halifax aircraft coming from starboard. The tail fin of this aircraft cut the nose of the aircraft straight off and the navigator and bomb aimer,* who had no chutes, fell out of the aircraft.'[24] In the clinical accounting of war there was no further mention of the two airmen who plunged – like so many before them unable to clip on their chest chutes in time – helplessly and agonisingly to their deaths.

But later analysis revealed what torments lay ahead for F/O Wilson immediately after the collision and in the hours to come. Y-Yorker plunged 1,500 feet before the pilot could bring the aircraft, now missing 9 feet of its nose, under control. He got the aircraft up to 11,000 feet, but there it stalled and now back down to 7,000 feet Wilson struggled to bring it home as a freezing gale swept through the fuselage from the gaping hole in front. The Leicester-born skipper had only been on 51 Sqn since the start of the year, seeing his Australian namesake on the squadron go missing only three days after he arrived, but fortunately he was an experienced pilot with several raids on 578 Sqn in his log book. As the icy blast contracted his muscles Wilson had to try to hold the aircraft steady despite dents to the propellers causing constant vibration through the airframe. Few of his instruments were working and the radio had to be turned off five minutes after the collision because sparks shooting from it threatened to start a fire.

---

* The navigator, P/O Thomas Whitehouse, 21, who was married, is buried in Berthenonville Churchyard and the air bomber, P/O David Hauber, 22, in Rouen.

But the wireless operator had already managed to send off a distress signal and as the stricken bomber crossed the sea searchlights on the south coast pointed to the airfield at Ford, in West Sussex, which had facilities for crippled aircraft and wounded crews. Wilson brought in Y-Yorker two hours and ten minutes after leaving the target and the next day his visibly shortened aircraft on the flight line provided a remarkable testimony to his escape. The Free French aircraft that collided with him wasn't so lucky. It crashed north-west of Paris and the pilot and two other crew members were killed.*

WHEN they weren't flying in those first grim weeks of 1945 aircrew were dragooned into clearing snow from key points on their spartan, hastily built stations. Bill Porter, a 21-year-old NCO navigator on 625 Sqn in North Lincolnshire, remembers:

> Kelstern was a pretty bleak place to be. It is one of the highest places if not the highest on the Lincolnshire Wold. There wasn't a pub in the village, I remember, but there was a good bus service to Grimsby and occasionally we went there. We arrived at Kelstern in January and between then and leaving in April we saw nothing but cold weather. At one stage we were snowed in and we sergeants and flight sergeants aircrew had to dig our way through the snow from the airfield to the main road to Ludford Magna so that we could get some supplies in. It was a case of 'You are not flying, chaps, so you can dig out the snow.' It was a pretty grim situation. We were in Nissen huts at Kelstern, with half a hut to a seven-man crew, and you had to go wandering out to find showers.[25]

On the Continent too soldiers and civilians alike shivered as they waited for a thaw in the piercing weather. None suffered more than evaders, trying to make their way home through enemy lines. Many of those shot down on the costly Dortmund-Ems Canal raid of 23 September, such as F/O Lucas, F/O Korpela,

* The pilot, Adj. E. Jouzier, the navigator, Cne R. Brachet, and the rear gunner, Sgt E. Malterre, are all buried in their native France.

Sgt Macfarlane and F/Sgt Whittaker, were still trapped in enemy territory.

Bomb aimer F/O Lucas and his engineer crewmate Sgt Macfarlane had spent weeks being hidden on a barge by the Dutch after coming down near Zwolle, then in January returned to the Resistance in the area where they had been shot down and met a downed RAF Typhoon pilot, a USAAF B-17 flyer and finally their Canadian pilot, F/O Korpela. They decided to try to make it back to the British lines, despite the freezing weather, and Lucas's stoical, factual report back in Britain later gives little indication of the hardship they suffered that bitter winter.

> We hid in a hole in the ground made by the Underground and food was brought to us by a farmer. Whilst there we met a Dutchman who was working as an agent for the British and used this hole for wireless transmitting. He took us to a friend of his who took us to the front line. We walked south for three days and then stopped at a house at Zelheim. We then split up and lived in nearby farms ... From March 27th I and the American were hidden upstairs in a house at Zelheim with Germans billeted down below. On April 1st we were liberated by the British 21st Army Group.[26]

But the greatest ordeal was probably that of F/Sgt Whittaker, the 617 Sqn air gunner, who had been captured by the Gestapo when the Dutch Resistance camp he and two RAF escapers from Stalag IVB were sheltering in was surrounded in October. The RAF men were then kept in prison in Doetinghem for seven weeks, 'slowly starving', he reported to IS9, the evaders' debriefing unit of MI9 based in the Great Central Hotel opposite Marylebone station.

> Early in the eighth week of our stay at Doetinghem we were taken by some *arbeitscommandodients* to the station for entrainment to Hamburg. We found that our cattle truck had a ventilator about three feet by ten inches and after the train had started we prised this open, and one by one, clambered through it, dropping off the truck when the train was going about 25mph. I decided that from

now on I would travel alone . . . I made across country by the aid of the stars in a generally north west direction. I wanted to get away from the railway and thought that the Arnhem direction would bring me towards our troops.

The starving Whittaker sheltered in woods overnight then sought help from a farm where he was given food and taken to another farm in the Varesveld area to await eventual liberation. He was extremely weak from his ordeal in Gestapo hands, but after being nursed on the local produce gradually regained his strength.

I spent about seven weeks being fed like a fighting cock on milk, butter and eggs. On March 31st I heard the sound of an approaching battle and in the evening went off to meet the troops. It was a bit rough as I was under two fires, however I was able to give the British troops of 43 Division the location of a German 88mm which was giving them trouble. From the forward troops I was passed down to IS9.[27]

F/Sgt Whittaker eventually returned to 617 Sqn, but by that time operations were practically over. For Harry Stunell, the 106 Sqn wireless operator who had been so terribly burned when his aircraft crashed returning from Munich, the pain continued as he slowly recovered.

I was transferred to a huge mansion house hospital at South Cerney where a very old lady who was a physiotherapist used to come with a large container of wax which was then melted. I had to put my hands in to make a fist and finally she taught me how to walk again. I went on to Weeton near Blackpool then Rauceby, near Sleaford and eventually to a huge mansion hospital at Burley-on-the-Hill, near Oakham, Rutland.

It was there I met Haydn Price, the mid-upper gunner in the crew of George Thompson, the wireless operator who got the VC. George had saved his life, pulling him out of his burning turret. All his helmet had burned away in the fire and his head was all red and raw when I met him. His burn-disfigured ears required re-fashioning from flesh taken from other parts of his body. I did my training with George Thompson and Haydn Price told me George's pilot asked George if he'd like to go for a commission. He was interviewed and this board asked him what his father's profession was. George answered, 'Farm labourer'. They asked him where he lived and he said 'A cottage.' They asked him if his father had any financial means and they grilled him so much, George got up and told them he was proud of his father and walked out of the interview. Four weeks later he was good enough to be up for the VC.[28]

Most of the evaders brought down on the Dortmund-Ems Canal raid in September, such as F/Sgt Whittaker, had been the victims of Schrage Musik, though it was unknown to them. By January, the time when Sgt Stunell's aircraft was lost, it was all too evident that the German night fighters had some secret device that allowed them to shoot down British bombers without being seen and at last air gunners were being given some clue as to what to guard against. But the lie of 'Scarecrow' shells was maintained and gunners in targeted aircraft were being officially blamed for not being alert enough rather than excused because of the Luftwaffe's upward-firing cannon. Air gunnery in Bomber Command had changed much since the attrition of 1943 and early 1944 and now there was a new edge to combat. The jet age had arrived.

EIGHT

TRACKING THE FUTURE

THE shock of seeing a weird, red-tailed, enemy-pursuit plane curving death across a black sky at three times the speed of a laden Lancaster or Halifax raised fear to a new level for the teenage gunners of Bomber Command. The strange, propeller-less aircraft of the Luftwaffe's latest advances in the air war had been reported by a photographic reconnaissance Mosquito as far back as 25 July when F/Lt A. E. Wall of 544 Sqn had been attacked by an Me262 at 29,000 feet near Munich.[1] Three days later Mustangs of the US Eighth Air Force spotted an experimental flight of rocket-engined Me163s near the oil target of Merseburg.[2] But it was not until October that the public, or in fact the rank and file of the RAF, heard about the German threat to tilt the balance in the air war. Newspapers in Britain broke the story on 2 October, *The Times* revealing: 'The newest German aircraft, the jet-propelled Messerschmitt 262, known as The Swallow, is being encountered with ever-greater frequency over Holland and North-West Germany ... At the moment the twin-engined machine could hardly be described as a menace, for it has yet to shoot down a British or American fighter.'

The story, a mere single column to curb any incipient alarm, went on: 'When more experience has been gained it may prove a more formidable opponent and those who did not already know of its existence must have been relieved at the recent official announcement that the RAF also possessed a jet-propelled fighter, for experts are almost unanimous that within a measurable distance of time jet propulsion will play a big part in both war and commercial aviation.'[3] Air warfare had indeed changed for ever with the arrival of the jet age. It was not until November, however, shortly after the operational debut of the first official combat Me262 unit, Kommando Nowotny, was established at Achmer near Osnabrück* that jets began to feature consistently in combat reports of either the USAAF or RAF Bomber Command. The Me163 rocket-powered fighter only carried enough fuel for five minutes' combat and proved perhaps more of a menace to the Luftwaffe than the Allied bomber fleets due to its predilection to blow up on take-off. But the twin-engined Me262, the most promising in a series of twelve jet or rocket-powered aircraft that underwent development for the Luftwaffe, proved more formidable. Its success was only limited by the poor skills of novice Luftwaffe pilots, their training cut short by USAAF and RAF throttling of their fuel supplies in the continuing oil campaign. By the middle of March it would be seen as *the* plane that could save the Reich. 'According to a Führer decision production is to be concentrated on the Me262,' the German Propaganda Minister Josef Goebbels recorded in his diary on 16 March. 'This can stay in the air for 70 minutes and uses a sort of diesel oil of which 44,000 tons are available ... A Mosquito will be simply torn apart by a hit from an Me262. Four hits finish off a bomber.'[4]

However, the Me262's advent in night skies was at first treated with some scepticism by intelligence officers debriefing dismayed gunners at RAF and Commonwealth bomber stations. For instance reports of sightings on the Düsseldorf operation of 2 November in which gunners claimed to have shot down eight jet-propelled fighters under a full moon were given little credence by boffins who prepared the subsequent night raid analysis for Bomber Command headquarters. 'The alleged jet-propelled [aircraft] may have been self-destructive projectiles,' they reported.[5] Days later, after the horrifying Bochum operation of 4–5 November they were beginning to be slightly less sceptical, but remained

---

* The unit was headed by Major Walter Nowotny, an ace who claimed 258 victories, all but the final three on the Eastern Front. He was shot down and killed by a P51 in November.

unconvinced, summing up: 'Peculiar projectiles were encountered over the target and on the long leg out, looking and behaving like aircraft, but only 34 were reported to have launched any attack and 21 were alleged to have been destroyed. Probably the fire of our crews merely helped in the destruction of these phenomena.'[6] In fact it was not until mid-January that an RAF gunner was officially credited with and rewarded for shooting down a Luftwaffe jet at night. F/Sgt Ken O'Brien, the 101 Sqn teenager who was certain he would not survive his tour after seeing a crew vanish in exploding flak in November, received an immediate DFM for the action, which took place during a raid on a synthetic oil plant at Zeitz, near Leipzig. As with all oil targets it was hotly defended and 10 of the 328 Lancasters that set out failed to return. Not surprisingly the Luftwaffe had put up its latest aircraft to guard it.

Ken O'Brien remembers:

The mid-upper gunner Ron Poulson called up to say, 'I'm sure I've just seen a plane go by.' He had seen two red trails coming out of it and couldn't think what it was, but he said, 'It's gone now.' It had passed down our starboard side in the opposite direction. I suppose it took it a long time to turn to come after us, then after about ten minutes it was back. I saw it approaching at a hell of a lick and I called out, 'Corkscrew starboard,' and I didn't even get the 'Go' out before the pilot had whipped the Lancaster over. I was already firing at the fighter and as we went into the corkscrew I gave him another blast and there was a flash in the sky and bits of burning aircraft falling down as he exploded. We used to calculate the distance on the ring sight using known wingspans, but because the Me262 had such short wings it was a lot nearer than I thought. Two minutes after I shot it down the special operator, who had been busy jamming, called up to say, 'Keep a good lookout because there are fighters about.' He had heard the radio traffic on his set. We had corkscrewed and in the middle of the plane he hadn't noticed. We had a real laugh about it.

When we got back and went into debriefing, I told them, 'By

the way I've fired my guns,' because I had never done it before.
For instance on our squadron we never tested our guns on the way
out over the sea. I was asked, 'What for?' and I told them about
the fighter and that it was one of those jets we had been warned
about. They said, 'Oh it was you was it, we've already had confirmation. We've been getting reports right, left and centre.' Apparently I was the first in Bomber Command to shoot down a jet at
night and I learned not long after that I had been awarded the
DFM.[7]

The raid had been a considerable achievement in terms of
damage, destroying the northern half of the benzine-producing
plant. A report within days in the station newspaper of North
Killingholme, from where 550 Sqn had dispatched twenty-eight
Lancasters to Zeist, revealed that crews had arrived over the
remote, snow-covered plant to hear

> a Master Bomber having his finger out and issuing precise and
> clear instructions, in a strong Canadian accent, to bomb the multi-
> coloured markers that were seen to be going down plumb on
> the centre of the target. A glorious glow developed, nine major
> explosions and a super major one at 2218 belching forth flame and
> black, oily smoke. As one gunner said enthusiastically, 'It's worth
> it when you get a prang like that at the end of it [8]

The Polish airman F/Sgt Henryk Drozdz saw that explosion.
Zeitz was the thirteenth raid of his tour with 300 Sqn and it had
begun uncertainly. Crews had been kept waiting in their aircraft
for two hours as Bomber Command headquarters assessed the
latest meteorological reports. Drozdz, who had seen two aircraft
collide just two weeks before, was apprehensive as his Lancaster
eventually took off into thick overcast. He wrote in his operational
diary:

> We are surrounded by milky clouds which is quite unnerving, green
> lights are flickering at the ends of the wings – the navigation lights.
> It goes on for quite a while, it is so unpleasant in the clouds,
> especially as 350 planes took off at the same time. We really need

some good luck. Feeling of relief as it gets lighter. It is fantastic – we are skimming over the top of the clouds – then again we plunge into them, but only for a moment and then we see beautiful blue sky at sunset. It is difficult to believe that 10,000ft below us there is fog and clouds and generally bad weather and here it is so glorious. In a short while we are leaving these cloud 'mountains' and changing course towards Leipzig which is heavily defended, the same as Merseburg. In spite of the fact that our target is almost the same as Merseburg the nature of our sortie is quite different – total surprise.

We have reached our target. There are flares and hell breaks loose again. It is the same as last time, even worse, as hundreds of searchlights light up the sky. I think we will have fun and I am getting my parachute ready just in case. This time we seem to be flying faster to our target. I strain my eyes, but it does not help, my knees are shaking slightly. There seem to be thousands of fireworks, sparklers and lights going off – it seems like daylight – the damned searchlights make a ring round the target. Please God save us from this hell, it is terrifying. We are getting closer and closer. Thousands, millions of flashes and lights – to the left and to the right – the searchlights are everywhere. The whole aircraft is lit up, we choose a path. 'Bomb doors open' sounds in the earphones. Another moment and then the dry crack of jettisoning bombs: one, two, three and so on – total weight 9,700 pounds. When they are all down not only our plane is lighter, but our spirits too. It is still light as in daytime, the artillery fire is still going on but we are leaving the target area. For the 13th time I am marvelling at the view. This is perhaps the one and only, similar to Nuremberg, sight. You can see everything, fires everywhere as if after 100 lightning strikes. Oh! Now there is a huge blast, a mere two minutes after our bombs fell (it is now 2218 hours).[9]

Conditions over Zeitz had also been ideal for the night fighters – both conventional and jet – the fires and searchlights below turning a thin layer of cloud into a glowing screen which made the bombers easily visible from above. Canadian rear gunner Sgt Al Hymers was on the tenth trip of his tour with a mainly RCAF crew from 12 Sqn at Wickenby. All of them had had a premonition they would not be returning that night and over the target Hymers had 'a nasty feeling' his aircraft was being stalked. He recalled many years later:

> I swung my turret around and looked down and there was the hunter, a Messerschmitt 410. He was tilted up about 25 yards away. I directed my guns down immediately and opened fire. At the same time I yelled for the skipper (F/O William Kerluk) to corkscrew. This all happened within a heartbeat. The fighter opened fire. I saw his four cannons blink once. One cannon shell took the two guns out of my turret on the left side. One hit under my feet and blew out the hydraulic lines and the intercom. One hit the tail and one I'm sure went up the fuselage and killed the navigator. All this happened just like that. I opened fire. I yelled for the skipper to corkscrew star-board. All he heard was, 'Corkscrew' before the cannon shell cut off the intercom. He's yelling, 'Which way? Which way?' I could hear him but he couldn't hear me. It was all over in seconds.[10]

Shortly afterwards the intercom came back on.

> I told the skipper the enemy fighter was directly below us and we had about ten seconds to live. I told him to corkscrew or dive to the clouds or something. The last words he said were, 'I'm afraid to move it. The controls are shot up.' I said, 'Here he comes,' and the Me410 tilted up and opened fire. He hit us in the gas tanks and we started to burn. The flame was coming down the fuselage and out through my turret.

Fortunately Sgt Hymers was wearing a new seat-type parachute pack which was now being issued to rear gunners because it was realised many had been unable to bale out in time by having to rotate their turrets and reach their chest-type chutes stowed in the fuselage. As Sgt Hymers struggled to unplug his oxygen and intercom leads the flames were hitting him in the face. 'I tried to get my face out of the flames, so that I could unplug. I leaned out of the doors,' he recorded. 'The wind caught my parachute harness and I couldn't get back in to unplug anything. So I let go and everything pulled loose . . . I could see the Lancaster going away. I could see the Messerschmitt 410 coming back . . . After a long pause the parachute opened.'[11] Sgt Hymers landed in countryside in deep snow and came across his badly burned Welsh wireless operator, F/Sgt Gilbert Harris, to whom he tried to give a dose of morphine. Instead the 19-year-old Harris, in terrible pain, went to get help and shortly afterwards Hymers heard shots.* Hymers himself was eventually captured after evading for several days.

F/Sgt Drozdz made it safely back to Faldingworth. To fool the Luftwaffe, the risk had been taken of not plotting the usual return route above liberated France, but across Germany, into the Ruhr and Holland. Drozdz recorded in his diary:

It seems to me that the whole flight leads over dangerous territory. Slowly losing height we are approaching a 'gate' between two heavily defended objects: Osnabrück and Münster. Again this time our Wladzio [P/O W. Kossowski] is infallible – it is his good navigation that allows us to squeeze silently between these two spots bristling with gun barrels. Now only shore defences remain in the 'bag of fear'. Silently, silently we are edging forward. Moment of relief when under our feet the blue-black mass of the North Sea smiles ominously. This is not as threatening as the thousands of bullets lying in wait for our lives. Still a few hundred miles over the depths of the sea bristling with menacing waves and in the distance lights of our safe haven – England. This flight is quite different – this is not the usual monotonous return. It is quite wonderful. After safe landing I can look back on it as a beautiful and exhilarating flight with thousands of dangers, but now behind us. But? . . . not everyone was so lucky – Ensign Bakinowski** does

* German authorities reported that the bodies of all but Hymers had been found in the aircraft, including that of F/Sgt Harris. It appears he was among the countless aircrew shot by the enemy in this final phase of the bombing war.
** In fact W/O R. Bakinowski became a POW as did three of his crew including Sgt M. Sasin when their Lancaster was shot down.

not come back. His fate is shared by Sasin, friend of Bolek. For Bakinowski it was his 26th sortie . . . Can you believe that you will never see them again? They were not my close friends, but it is still strange, especially as it seems they had a premonition about this flight – Bolek's friend said goodbye to him. He never did this before other flights. God, how dismal it seems! He flew 26 sorties and always returned and today it was different. That's flying – you return 100 times and on the 101st you land in Abraham's bosom.[12]

IT had been a costly night generally for Bomber Command. A larger, mostly Halifax, force of more than 370 aircraft had been bombing Magdeburg while the Zeitz force was approaching its target and flak and fighters had accounted for 17 of them. But the Luftwaffe fighter controller had concentrated on the Zeitz force and 15 *Nachtjäger Gruppen* of approximately 300 aircraft were airborne. The dangers were not over when the Zeitz bombers had cleared Germany and two crashed in France. The crew of one, a 576 Sqn Halifax, eventually baled out following damage caused by two Me262s. The other aircraft, a Pathfinder from 582 Sqn, was abandoned near Clichy after severe damage from a night fighter over the target. The rear gunner, 21-year-old Sgt Nicholas McNamara, who had left neutral Ireland to fight fascism, had been wounded in the attack and the crew got him out of the rear door with a makeshift static line attached to his ripcord. The rest baled out safely but McNamara did not survive and his body was found on a freezing hillside. Four of the crew were decorated for their efforts in trying to bring the bomber home.

Zeist particularly, therefore, had provided a successful opportunity for the Luftwaffe and the version of its new jets now operating as *Nachtjäger*. The Me262 was primarily a single-seat aircraft for day use, but as the New Year dawned two-seat trainer versions had been turned over to the Wilde Sau ace Oberleutnant Kurt Welter* to set up his Kommando Welter as an answer to the

---

* By war's end Oblt Welter had claimed in his jet 25 Mosquitos and 2 four-engined bombers shot down by night and 2 further Mosquitos by day.

night-bomber fleets with which Harris was currently ruining the Reich at will. Specialist radar operators, who now joined the pilot in the Me262, had a new FuG 216 user-friendly interception radar in which only one indicator tube had to be monitored. Then there was *Naxos*, a homing device that recognised bombers' H2S transmissions.

Ironically F/Sgt O'Brien's aircraft, like the rest of the Lancasters in the specialist 101 Sqn, had an extra liability that made it easier to find them: the very transmissions from the three radio sets each aircraft carried for jamming the Luftwaffe ground controller's instructions to his *Nachtjäger*. Once the pilot of an Me262 was in visual contact, destruction of the bomber was usually certain. The jet had four 30-mm cannons in the nose, giving it an enormous punch, and also a stand-off firing range advantage against the bombers' defensive weapons of machine guns.

It was because 101 Sqn's aircraft were more likely to be shot down that the squadron had been chosen in April 1944 to introduce the new Rose turret in Bomber Command, which allowed a more even contest between attacked and attacker. The cursed short-range, four Browning .303-inch (7.7 mm) machine guns were at last replaced by the new twin .50-inch (12.7 mm) machine guns, which provided a longer striking distance and more formidable destructive power. It was a move that had been instigated by the 1 Group commander AVM Sir Edward Rice and Harris himself, who finally tired of Whitehall intransigence – the same tardiness that had given the Germans the lead in jets even though the RAF officer Frank Whittle had first developed jet propulsion. Harris allowed Rice to go directly to the Gainsborough firm of Rose Brothers to develop a defensive turret for the RAF with the same power as the USAAF enjoyed. 'We should never have got it if we had not ordered it on our own and in an entirely irregular way,' Harris later recorded.[13]

The turret was introduced after consultation with air gunners from 1 Group, who suggested greater visibility by having virtually the whole of the face of the turret open to the night sky. They also pointed out that the larger turret with virtually no impediment to the front would mean gunners could now bale out over their armament, rather than having to rotate the turret to exit through the rear doors, a factor that would save many lives in the nightly combat conditions in which split seconds decided between life or death.

The .50 guns and the greater vision provided by the Rose turret proved so successful the turret was gradually fed through many squadrons in 1 Group, approximately 180 of the group's Lancasters being adapted before the end of the war, though other groups had to continue contesting Luftwaffe cannon with the .303-calibre bullet that was standard in the infantry rifle. Apart from the increase in hitting power, the .50 machine gun exponentially increased the maximum range of an air gunner, from 3,000 yards by the .303 to in excess of 7,200 from the larger weapon. Effective range by the .303 was considered by many Bomber Command experts, however, to be as low as 300 feet. Night fighter pilots knew they could if necessary open an attack out of harm's way from whatever most RAF air gunners were equipped with. Oberleutnant Heinz-Wolfgang Schnaufer, who ended the war as the Luftwaffe's highest scoring living night-fighter ace with 121 victories, told RAF interrogators that he initiated combat at very long range on light nights and he was very worried when he heard that some RAF bombers were being equipped with the .50 gun.[14]

Attacks from below, usually from the deadly Schrage Musik, were opened at a distance and in 1944 the .50 machine gun had been introduced in a refinement known as the Preston Green Ventral to guard against the as yet unexplained strikes from underneath. W/O Harry Irons, the young air gunner who took part in the daylight Gelsenkirchen raid in early November, had initially found himself posted to 77 Sqn at Full Sutton in October to operate the Preston Green .50 and soon discovered its snags. He remembers:

The squadron had this mid-under gun on some Halifaxes which didn't have the H2S fitting. It wasn't a success because it was bitterly, bitterly cold. There was no heating and the gun just froze up. I remember I was told, 'Wait until a fighter attacks you and see what happens.' It was just a fixed gun really, you could move it slightly from side to side and forward and back, but not much. The range of fire was very limited; it was only ideal if a Jerry came underneath. I only did a couple of trips with it and was posted to 466 Sqn.[15]

The .50 was far more effective in the rear gunner's Rose turret, and if a night fighter was taken on at a short distance – such as a fast-closing Me262 – the hitting power was considerable. Ken O'Brien, who shot down his from close range, says: 'Apparently I only used fifty-nine rounds.' His success was marked by an invitation to his crew from the Rose Brothers factory to see the turret's manufacture. He remembers:

The Rose turret was made on the basis of about one a month because they were producing a lot more war material as well. We had a few drinks with the owner in his bar, which was in a cricket pavilion in the middle of a field, and we toured the works. A few of the lads were making dates with the girls in the factory and we phoned up the base at Ludford Magna to see if we could stay the night, but we were told we had to return, even though we weren't flying.[16]

A gunnery review by 1 Group as the war closed gave fulsome testimony to the effectiveness of the Rose turret – and today poses the question about how many bombers might have been saved from mid-1944 if all groups had been equipped with it.

It is a fact that since the turret went into operation, on April 20/21st 1944, the number of times that Hun night fighters have achieved surprise against aircraft fitted with the turret have been negligible, so few in fact that the surprise attacks delivered against the Rose Brothers turret can be counted on the fingers of one hand.

Regarding the efficiency of control and the hitting power of the guns several Hun pilots, could they but talk, would give fitting and no doubt remarkable testimonials. As for the third aim in the design of the Rose Brothers turret there are living gunners today, sole survivors of their crews, who can testify to the success of the emergency exit through the large cut-away clear vision panel.

Shortly after the advent of the Rose Brothers turret a squadron of this Group was selected to be equipped with another revolutionary project, namely AGLT.[17]

The unit was 460 RAAF Sqn, who at 181 was in the major league for aircraft losses in the Second World War, as was 101 Sqn, who lost 171.*

The Air Gun Laying Turret resulted from an appeal by the Air Ministry as far back as Spring 1943 for a system to allow a target to be tracked and fired on in total darkness, the enemy's range being accurately computed. It was considered this advantage might well reduce the alarming – and apparently growing – ability of the Luftwaffe to create flaming destruction among the bomber squadrons. It wasn't until the autumn of 1944, however, that such a system went into production, six months after attrition by the Luftwaffe had reached its peak. The problem had been handed over to the Telecommunications Research Unit at RAF Defford who came up with an installation in the navigator's compartment of a Lancaster consisting of a transmitter/receiver operating through a scanner attached to the standard bomber Fraser-Nash 150 rear turret. Pulses from the radar scanner to the navigator's unit were relayed to a cathode ray tube next to the gun sight. Later the process became automatic, the range information being fed electronically directly into the gun sight, with the navigator's 'running commentary' only being retained for the benefit of the rest of the crew. The gunner simply manoeuvred his weapons to place the 'blip' in the centre of the gunsight's reticule, and opened fire when the range was appropriate. Windage, bullet drop and other factors were already calculated by the sight. The boffins codenamed the system Village Inn,

* The highest number of total losses was suffered by a squadron from one of the smaller nations by population in the Commonwealth: 75 RNZAF Sqn had a total of 193 of its bombers shot down.

the title above the bar in 460 Sqn's officers' mess anteroom.

Crews of 460 Sqn whose Lancasters were equipped with Village Inn were quickly impressed, particularly those selected for small-force operations dropping sea mines, where once the aircraft reached release height they were easily picked up by ground-based enemy radar systems. F/O David Francis, a 460 Sqn navigator who did thirty-three ops between November 1944 and April 1945, remembers:

A Bomber Command crew would normally only do two or three mine-laying trips in a tour. We did seven. We had an exceptionally good H2S set in our aircraft which was essential for accurate dropping of the mines and I think we were a good crew and that was why we got called on for these precision mining operations. There would be six, seven or eight aircraft meeting over Flamborough Head then you would go down and continue across the North Sea at wave-top height so the German radar couldn't spot you and you would lose sight of each other as you went to different areas for mining and would be completely on your own. You then climbed to lay the mines which is when they knew you were there. You would home onto a bearing and distance, then at a set point at a certain height, course and speed you would drop your mines. The Luftwaffe could send as many as six aircraft after you because you were on your own.

On 19 January 1945 we had laid our mines in the Kattegat and about an hour afterwards the wireless operator saw on his Fishpond* set six single-engined aircraft coming up to attack. We knew FW190s were operating out of Denmark and Norway, so the rear gunner was able to set his automatic gun-laying turret sight to 34 feet, covering the wingspan of the 190. One came in on the tail and the rear gunner opened up and he sheered away. He didn't hit us, then two more seemed to indicate they were coming in to

* Fishpond was an extension to the H2S radar system. It allowed the wireless operator, who had the cathode-ray set on his desk, to see blips of fighters approaching from below up to 30 miles away.

attack, but didn't come close enough. It was obvious we were pretty alert and we went into cloud.[18]

Once more, on 3 March, the crew were attacked while mine-laying in the Kattegat. 'The wireless operator saw on Fishpond six fighters coming up. Some fired at us without hitting us and we corkscrewed into cloud and escaped. We relied on the wireless operator to look out for fighters,' F/O Francis remembers. It was while the crew were mine-laying in the Kattegat a third time, on 4 April, that the new gun-laying equipment truly proved its worth, however.

Again the fighters came up after us and the rear gunner laid his sights on AGLT to 34 feet and when the radar blip in the centre of his sight reached the circle of diamonds on the outside of the sight he fired. He saw an explosion and burning stuff flying off right, left and centre, so claimed it as one destroyed. The Luftwaffe was still a great threat to us. In mine-laying they knew we were a small force so could afford to send up more fighters after us. We were sitting ducks really.[19]

In fact on this occasion 1 Group were the sole force providing mine-laying aircraft. They dispatched thirty Lancasters. Three were shot down, a 10 per cent loss rate.

THERE could be no weak links in a bomber crew. Each man, whether pilot, navigator, bomb aimer, flight engineer, wireless operator or gunner, depended upon the other equally, without regard to rank, to do his job efficiently if the crew were to have a chance of surviving. It was the reason why relatively few operational airmen 'went LMF' and quit, the need not to let the others down being a stronger call than the desire to live. But when fighters found the bomber stream it was the keen eyesight and reaction of gunners that made them paramount among a crew. Some were outstanding.

The top-scoring gunner in Bomber Command was F/Lt Wallace McIntosh, a Scot who joined the RAF to escape the poverty of an itinerant farm labourer. By the end of the war he had shot down five enemy aircraft individually and three in combination with another gunner in the crew, a total that would have handsomely qualified him as a fighter ace. But it was the Canadians who provided many of the top-scoring gunners in Harris's forces. P/O Peter Engbrecht, who had served officers himself as an RCAF batman before remustering as an air gunner, sailed home bound for Manitoba in early 1945 with a Conspicuous Gallantry Medal for his skill at shooting down Luftwaffe fighters during his tour with 424 Sqn. The RCAF newspaper *Wings Abroad*, which parochially always gave the home town of its subjects for provincial consumption, interviewed him at the Torquay Repatriation Depot, running a story headed 'Sharp Shooter Leaves' in which it detailed:

> Four and a half enemy nightfighters went down before the guns of P/O Peter Engbrecht, CGM, Whitewater, Man., mid-upper gunner with a Halifax squadron of Canadian bomber group during his first tour. On his very first operation his aircraft was attacked 14 times over enemy territory. The kite got safely back to base after beating off all the attacks. Two of the attackers fell to Engbrecht's four blazing guns. He reported that in over 40 fighter attacks during the tour his aircraft was never touched. 'We always saw them before they opened fire and usually we got in the first bursts,' he said.[20]

In fact Engbrecht and the rear gunner in his crew, F/Sgt Gordon Gillanders, together were credited with nine confirmed and two probable kills of enemy aircraft during their tour, which began with the costly Mailly-le-Camp operation of mid-1944, and were undoubtedly the most successful gunnery team in the Commonwealth during the war. But Sgt Laurie Godfrey, the wireless operator on the Canadian Halifax squadron, 408, at Linton-on-Ouse, who had spent Christmas on an American base, served with two other Canadian gunners who were also among the top scorers in Bomber Command He knows his gunners saved his life on the

tralian skipper F/O Bruce Windrim, wearing his good luck talisman of a chequered
ler hat, with his crew of Englishmen on 625 Sqn at Kelstern. Left to right, wireless
rator Sgt Ted Steen, navigator F/O Bill Porter, mid-upper gunner Sgt 'Lucky' Simmonds,
ineeer F/Sgt Joe Platt, bomb aimer F/Sgt Frank Tolley and rear gunner Sgt Jim Slater.
er and Simmonds were just 18.

101 Sqn crew of F/O George Harris, pictured outside billets at Ludford Magna. Left to
t, flight engineer John Wood, gunner Don Dale, wireless operator Jack Morley, navigator
Arthur, Harris, bomb aimer Dai Jones, gunner Vic Congerton and ABC operator
.York

Kay Polley, newly married to navigator George Kirby. She would be a widow before she was 21.

F/Sgt Kirby (bottom left) with some of his 106 Sqn crew at their Metheringham dispersal site. Only Sgt Ronald Paul (third from left, next to skipper F/Lt Douglas Stewart) and an Australian second-dickey pilot they were taking for experience on the fatal final trip of the tour have known graves.

ve left Sgt Peter Bone polishes his mid-upper turret at Wickenby.
ve right F/O Reg Johnson, RAAF, on the far left, enjoying leave with the Narborough
ily at Carshalton under the Lady Ryder hospitality scheme for airmen far from home. The
se and garden were later destroyed by a V-weapon.

ht engineer Sgt Edwin Watson (far right) with other crew members beside the last of
six unlucky G-Georges of 630 Sqn. This one crashed at East Kirkby with double engine
ıre. The skipper lost an arm.

Above left Flight engineer Sgt Frank Jones poses by the rear turret of his 76 Sqn Halifax at Holme on Spalding Moor. He did three operations in 36 hours in the intense period of mid-October, including bombing Duisburg in daylight then at night.
Above right Flight engineer F/Sgt Frank Etherington, of 166 Sqn. The whole tail section of aircraft had to be replaced after flak damage over Essen.

Left Air gunner Harry Irons, who joined up at 16. By the time he was 21 he had survived two tours and was a warrant officer with the DFC.
Right Sgt Henryk Drozdz. The Polish flight engineer on 300 Sqn saw two Lancasters collided near his base as he returned from bombing Nuremberg.

Sgt Ken O'Brien, left, pictured with mid-upper gunner Sgt Ron Poulson after O'Brien became the first air gunner to shoot down a German jet fighter at night, winning the DFM. The twin .50 machine guns of 101 Sqn's new Rose turrets gave them a hitting power Bomber Command had long needed.

408 RCAF Sqn crew of P/O Case (centre) line up by their aircraft at Linton on Ouse. less operator Sgt Laurie Godfrey is in the top row on the far right. F/Sgt Dan Shutka, and F/Sgt Tom Romanchuck, bottom right, won immediate DFMs for the firmed shooting down of two night fighters over Oberhausen with two more 'probables'.

Wireless operator Kenneth Turnham (second left), who was wounded by flak over Cologne with his 115 Sqn crew at Witchford.

Я англичанин

" Ya Anglicháhnin " (Pronounced as spelt)

Пожалуйста сообщите
сведения обо мне в
Британскую Военную
Миссию в Москве

Please
communicate
my particulars
to British
Military
Mission
Moscow

Left F/Sgt 'Scotty' Young, who baled out into Russian-held territory after the March 5th Chemnitz raid. He was accused by the Red Army of being a spy and thrown into prison returning to Britain until eight weeks after the war had ended.
Right The 'Ya Anglichahnin' flag issued to airmen on both Chemnitz raids.

ve Airmen still recovering from their burns in 1946, play snooker with a staff member at *l*ey Hall temporary hospital, Rutland. Sgt Harry Stunell, whose bomber crashed in flames *r*ning from Munich, is on the right. Centre is Sgt Haydn Price, who was pulled from *b*lazing turret in a raid on the Dortmund–Ems Canal by F/Sgt George Thompson, the *l*ughboy VC' who died from his own burns three weeks later.

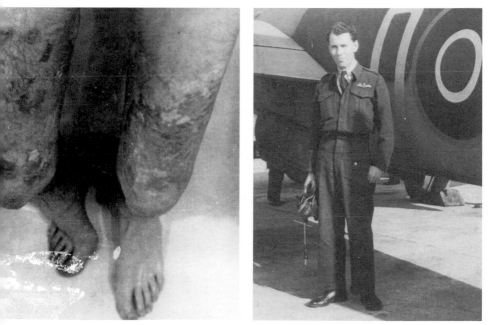

The leg burns Sgt Stunell received as he struggled free from his blazing Lancaster. *F/Lt* Tony Brandreth with his Mosquito Q-Queenie. It was written off in a crash *l*ng *after* being badly shot up by flak.

Above left Three English members of Australian F/O Warren Clarke's 207 Sqn crew at Spilsby. From the left, mid-upper gunner Sgt Ken Freeman, flight engineer Sgt Frank Bricknell and wireless operator Sgt Jim Kenny.
Above right Rear gunner F/Sgt Elias Williams, sole survivor of his crew when their aircraft was shot down on a Lutzkendorff raid.

The crew of C2 of 460 RAAF Sqn, who bombed both Dresden and Pforzheim. From the top and left to right wireless operator Neil Hawkins, pilot Gus Rowe, navigator Dave Fran mid-upper gunner Phil Lovett, flight engineer Ron Purchase, rear gunner Ossie Hanna, bo aimer Keith Lamberton and unknown mechanic.

crew's fourth operation, to Oberhausen, on 1 November 1944. Godfrey remembers:

> We underwent four attacks by fighters. Our two gunners shot down two of them and two others were claimed as probable. The rear gunner, Dan Shutka, sighted an Me410 attacking a Lancaster and the Lancaster was corkscrewing, which left the enemy aircraft open to our gunners, Shutka and F/Sgt Tom Romanchuk. It must have been pretty close to us because the .303 machine guns we had only gave you a range of about 400 yards. Apparently the Me410 was seen to go down in flames. Then we were attacked again, this time by an Me110. It broke away as Shutka opened fire.[21]

Four minutes later F/Sgt Romanchuk saw an Me410 aircraft positioning itself on the port beam. Both gunners opened fire and the enemy aircraft went down in flames as hits were registered. Two minutes later they were attacked once more, this time by a twin-engined fighter which broke away when Shutka fired.

> They were two very good gunners who kept their eye on the job. I was in the nose of the aircraft in the wireless operator's position below the pilot and my first indication we were under attack was the shout, 'Corkscrew, port go!' on the intercom. As we went down and to the left I was lifted up in the aircraft and then found myself being pressed down as we came back up. I couldn't hear any gunfire because it was all behind me, all I knew was that we were corkscrewing. Then it happened again and again. I suppose by opening fire the first time we had given our position away. After three or four times of going into a corkscrew I just hoped for the best. It was a very bad night for us, but as it turned out a lucky one. There just didn't seem to be time to think about things, it was a matter of hoping. I couldn't see anything, after all. It was perhaps worse for me and the navigator next to me because we couldn't do anything. After that it seemed to quieten down, but you couldn't relax, because night fighters could sometimes follow you all the way back. You couldn't take it easy until you were actually on

the ground. When we went into interrogation back at Linton the navigator was able to give the intelligence officer the times of the attacks and I found out then it was four attacks in six minutes. The gunners both got immediate DFMs.[22]

Three nights later, on the Bochum operation that cost Bomber Command dearly, the alert F/Sgt Shutka saved his crew again. Godfrey remembers:

It was a very clear night and the fighters were up with the search-lights because there wasn't so much gunfire coming up. Just after we bombed a Ju88 came in and the rear gunner called a corkscrew. It was low down because I believe it had the upward-firing guns. As it got a bit closer the rear gunner, F/Sgt Shutka, recognised him and opened up from about 70 yards away. He must have been a bloody good shot because he saw him going down.[23]

At the end of November during an attack on Duisburg Shutka saved his crew once more. 'We were attacked by a Ju88, but it was driven off,' Sgt Godfrey recalls. 'All I heard, of course, was "Corkscrew, corkscrew, starboard or whatever" but our rear gunner opening up shifted him away. I think generally when German night fighters approached they didn't pursue it if the gunners were alert; they were looking for someone half asleep.'[24]

With the advent of German jets, the odds against a gunner being able to react in time were vastly increased, whether by night or by day. Once an Me262 pilot had a bomber in his sights the rapid closing speed usually made the result a foregone conclusion. On the last day of March 1945, Me262s of III/JG7 were vectored from their airfield 75 miles away at Parchim in Mecklenburg as a heavy daylight raid approached the Blohm and Voss U-boat construction yards in Hamburg. More than 100 bombers of the 490-strong force were from the Canadian 6 Group, and the Luft-waffe Gruppe, largely composed of *Experten* who had survived many battles, swept in as the bombs rained earthwards through ten-tenths cloud. They downed eight Lancasters and three Hali-faxes within minutes, all but three from the Canadian squadrons.

A few of those attacked returned to tell the tale. F/Sgt Bert Vardy, a 24-year-old mid-upper gunner in the all-RCAF 428 Sqn crew of F/O D. M. Payne, claimed one jet destroyed, and later told *Wings Abroad*: 'It happened just after we dropped our bombs. The 262 ripped in from one side.' The newspaper reported: 'Vardy and the rear gunner, F/Sgt Earl Casey, both opened fire with long bursts. The fighter never had a chance to fire its guns. It dived away smoking and disappeared in cloud. Other bomber crews saw it partly in flames.'[25] The crew would suffer an even more nerve-racking and lasting ordeal in the last weeks of the war.

From 408 Sqn at Linton-on-Ouse, F/O Ken Blyth was on the nineteenth operation of a tour that had begun only eight weeks before. Blyth was 21 and the flight engineer 26, but most of his crew were little over 18 and all looked so young they were dubbed the 'Cradle Crew' on the squadron, a story that appeared in the RCAF newspaper. Eventually F/O Blyth had the name painted on the nose of his Halifax. But what they lacked in years the crew made up for in experience and after each operation, before they exited their aircraft, Blyth had them practise bale-out procedure, so that they could do it at speed in a situation where seconds separated life from death.

The Hamburg operation had not started well for the Cradle Crew. They had had to take off late with a spare aircraft which used so much fuel trying to catch the rest of the bomber stream that F/O Blyth knew they would probably have to land on return at a forward airfield. They arrived over the target six minutes late and bombed alone shortly after 9 a.m. Blyth recalls:

> We had barely closed the bomb doors when we were attacked. The tail gunner later reported he had seen a spot on the turret Perspex and the next thing an Me262 came out of the sun and we had been hit. Its 30-mm cannon shell blew off two of the guns on the tail turret and bent another. The cone of fire centred on the port wing and port outer engine. We were on fire and totally out of control. I saw two of the jets go under the wing; apparently only one had done the damage.[26]

The young skipper ordered 'Put on Parachutes' and the crew went into their oft-practised drill, the pilot finally finding himself over the forward escape hatch. F/O Blyth remembers thinking:

> Damn it! Can I get through that small hole with this seat chute on? Here goes. Soon I was falling. The ripcord pulled away and there was a crackling sound. I was afraid to look up, fearing my chute was on fire. On our previous trip I had seen such an event happen to a member of a nearby aircraft. I felt so helpless. Finally I realized I was OK. I looked up at that mess of beautiful silk parachute and said a silent prayer ... My first thought was of the Cradle Crew, which I could see in the distance, strung out like a Monday morning wash. I started counting 1, 2, 3, 4, 5, 6, plus myself 7; everyone accounted for, thank God.[27]

The training had paid off. The crew were quickly captured by German military personnel, though one of them had to be rescued, badly cut and bruised, from civilians who were intent on beating him to death.

Jets had triumphed once more against the techniques and equipment of the Bomber Command Tail-end Charlies. Gunners, whose short training could propel them into combat within three months of joining the air force, were the equivalent in Bomber Command of the Poor Bloody Infantry of the First World War. They continued to bear the blame for aircraft losses at night, even though the *Nachtjäger's* equipping with Schrage Musik – from which there was little defence – was only just being appreciated by senior officers. The official 1 Group headquarters' monthly summary of air combats in November urged: 'An all-round search is even more necessary since the Huns are now using Me110s, Ju88s, and He219s carrying upward-firing cannon. Since those do not use trace, unless the fighters are seen, probably the first indication of trouble will be strikes.'[28] February's report criticised gunners for not being alert, now that the menace of Schrage Musik was established.

> There were nine occasions on which fire from an unseen fighter was the first indication of an attack being made. Each and every

month gunners are warned to guard against surprise attacks, are briefed before each operation to co-operate, mid-upper with rear gunner in each crew, and to get their search plan on the top line, not to relax their vigilance and to maintain their search until dispersal point is reached on return. Yet in spite of these constant warnings, pleadings and advice we still get as high as 21 per cent of these attacks made by the Hun pilots being surprise attacks.[29]

But there was also blame for gunners for being *too* quick on the trigger. Rear gunners, particularly, had the loneliest and possibly the most stressful job in a bomber, their faces and upper bodies often open to the night sky, expecting any second to see the flash in which a night fighter would snuff out their lives. The temptation to fire first was extreme and sometimes they got it wrong. For instance following an operation to Hanau on 6 January 1945 F/O J. I. Bell of 427 RCAF Sqn submitted a combat report after his bomb aimer had his nose blown off by fire from another Halifax 300 yards away which had been taking evasive action. Bell's mid-upper gunner had turned his turret to the forward position and 'as he did so this aircraft opened fire as it crossed from port to starboard,' Bell reported. 'The mid-upper feels sure that this aircraft was a Halifax, so therefore ceased to fire. Bullets recovered from the wings of [our] Halifax proved to be 303. The bomb aimer was struck in the face as he moved forward to the nose position to take over the VGO [Vickers gas operated machine gun].'[30]

There was already a testy signal lying on the desk of a gunnery officer at 1 Group headquarters following a similar incident during the Nuremberg operation four nights before. The message came from PFF headquarters and pointed out that Lancaster O-Orange of 582 Sqn had been fired on by the rear gunner of another bomber while outbound, seriously injuring O-Orange's air bomber. The time and place tallied with a report by a 166 Sqn gunner. The signal concluded somewhat sarcastically: 'Could you investigate and if necessary take steps to prevent gunners of 166 Sqn trying to shoot down our aircraft?'[31] In fact three of the seven Lancasters lost that night were from 166 Sqn; little wonder that gunners tended to be nervous as they saw aircraft nearby blasted from the sky by night fighters. A week later 1 Group's investigators were able to report to the Pathfinder HQ:

> Whilst the aircraft recognition of the gunner concerned is to be deplored and his state of 'nerves' considered to have been such that his judgement was distorted, there is one small factor to justify the gunner's action. Immediately prior to Lancaster O crossing our bomber from starboard to port, up, an enemy fighter had been reported by the rear gunner flying on a reciprocal course on the port beam level. It is understood that the rear gunner of our Lancaster was under the illusion that Lancaster O was the night fighter attacking our aircraft.[32]

It was not an unusual incident as more bombers were squeezed into smaller parts of the sky to overwhelm target defences, and the advent of jets, where reaction time was a split second, increased the fear factor. There was also the possibility that the bomber riding alongside you might be a captured RAF machine and in fact the Luftwaffe's KG200 was set up in 1944 to fly such aircraft. W/O Alan Adams, a mid-upper gunner from 102 Sqn, languishing in Stalag IVB at Mühlberg in the winter of 1945, was shot down by a bomber in RAF markings while on a Frankfurt raid. He and the rear gunner were the sole survivors. He remembers:

> There was the usual banter on the intercom as we were nearing Frankfurt am Main, then I noticed a four-engined bomber coming a little too close to us for comfort. As the mid-upper gunner I had the clearest vision of the crew. I called up the skipper, Bob Fiddes. He took some evasive action, but the aircraft, which I could see had British markings, refused to leave us. Our instructions were not to fire at four-engined aircraft as no other types of planes were on this operation. Bob reminded us of this just as the rear gunner, Sandy Currie, also now commented on the closeness of the bomber as we levelled out from the evasive action. Suddenly the aircraft opened fire on us, blasting us with cannons, not the usual Browning machine guns which our bombers carried. Fire started at the front

and also below me, just behind my turret. The plane continued in level flight for a few seconds, then went into a steep dive. 'Bale out,' shouted the skipper. I immediately got out of my turret, clipped on my chute, which was in its proper place by my side, and started to crawl to the main exit at the rear. I felt the cold rush of air as I opened it and looking up I saw Sandy just rotating his turret to leave. He must have seen me too as he gave the thumbs-up signal. My parachute opened just before I hit the ground. I am not sure how long I lay there, but I came to, staggering around in the darkness in what seemed to be a field. I had already lost my chute when I was approached by two German soldiers, pointing rifles at me. They took me to a farmhouse, and then I was taken to a small army barracks and on to Dulag Luft. I have often wondered if other crews described the type of action in which we were shot down. Was the plane that fired at us made up of reclaimed parts of aircraft and put together to infiltrate the stream of bombers?[33]

Whether to fire first and identify later remained a problem until VE-Day, and there was no lessening of criticism for Tail-end Charlies by senior officers. The average air gunner, often the youngest member of a crew, must have felt he was getting it from all directions in the closing months of the war, but the greater blame for losses had always lain in Whitehall. In the winter of 1943–4 firm action and provision of resources by the Air Ministry could have saved thousands of young lives among the fresh-faced ranks of Bomber Command by earlier introduction of AGLT combined with the .50 Rose turret.

However, the improvements would have made little difference against a Luftwaffe predominantly equipped with jet fighters. Bomber Command had cause to be thankful in this last phase of the aerial offensive that Hitler and his hierarchy had squandered diminishing resources on the V-weapons with their inadequate payload – though possibly the aim was for them eventually to carry biological or atomic warheads – instead of investing in jet combat aircraft. The Me262 would continue to be a threat until the last days of the war, but in the freezing winter of 1945 all that lay ahead. Another event was about to take place in February that would prove to be the albatross the bomber boys would be forced to carry as their bitter legacy. The name of the target was Dresden.

NINE

THE MAKING OF ASH WEDNESDAY

THE RAF Pathfinder bomber crews who arrived over Dresden shortly after 10 p.m. on 13 February 1945 found a city apparently asleep. Not a searchlight flickered, not a flak gun fired. By dawn its old centre had ceased to exist. The firestorm that Bomber Command created and fed in the course of two heavy raids on the same night burned the heart out of the historic Saxon capital and certainly killed in excess of 20,000 people. It was largely the reason the Command's brave young airmen were not awarded a separate campaign medal at the end of the war and why their leader Sir Arthur Harris was ignored in Churchill's victory speech to the nation.

Yet it was Churchill himself who wanted Dresden bombed as part of Operation Thunderclap, a series of heavy raids planned on four German cities which it was hoped would help to push the Reich into a final state of collapse. The Thunderclap concept had first been put forward in a memorandum to other Allied Chiefs of Staff by the Chief of the Air Staff, Sir Charles Portal, in the late summer of 1944. He suggested that a massive raid should be launched against Berlin, where it was expected to cause '220,000 casualties, 50 per cent of these (or 110,000) may expect to be killed. It is suggested that such an attack, resulting in so many deaths, the great majority of which will be key personnel, cannot help but have a shattering effect on political and civilian morale all over Germany.'[1]

Tellingly he then added, 'Immense devastation could be produced if the entire attack was concentrated on a single big town other than Berlin and the effect would be especially great if the town was one hitherto undamaged.'[2] As the days shortened the Thunderclap idea was temporarily shelved, though Portal remained committed to the idea, his office promoting the similarly engendered Ruhr-targeted Operation Hurricane to Harris in October. Hurricane had been designed to achieve 90 per cent destruction of the city areas attacked and to inflict heavy casualties that would break civilian morale. Eventually Thunderclap came up again as the Russians launched their new offensive in the east, which would eventually end in the battle for Berlin. The Joint Intelligence Committee submitted a report to the War Cabinet on 21 January warning that the Russian offensive might well stall if the Germans, now marshalling their reserves – expected to amount to forty-two divisions within weeks – were able to position them on the Eastern Front swiftly, the critical time being mid-February.[3]

Churchill then minuted the Air Minister Sir Archibald Sinclair asking 'whether Berlin, and no doubt other large cities in East Germany should not now be considered especially attractive targets'. Sinclair consulted with Portal who said attacks in support of the Russian advance should in certain circumstances have priority. In fact towards the end of January Portal had written to the Deputy Chief of the Air Staff Norman Bottomley urging that after other obligations had been fulfilled, 'We should use available effort in one big attack on Berlin and attacks on Dresden, Leipzig, Chemnitz, or any other cities where a severe blitz will not only cause confusion in the evacuation from the East, but will also hamper the movement of troops from the West.'[4] Bottomley, told of Churchill's minute, then wrote to Harris on 27 January spelling out that Portal considered it would not be right to mount a series of knock-out 'Thunderclap' blows solely to Berlin in the near future. But that subject to 'the overriding claims of oil and other approved target systems within the current directive' there should be a 'big attack on Berlin and related attacks on Dresden, Leipzig, Chemnitz'.[5]

Sir Archibald Sinclair replied to Churchill's minute the same day saying the Air Staff had now arranged to direct available effort against Berlin, Dresden, Chemnitz and Leipzig.[6] Churchill, the prime mover for such attacks, then flew away to Malta on his way to the Yalta Conference where he would be able to tell the Russians what was being done by their British ally to aid their offensive. Portal would also – fortunately, like Churchill, for his post-war reputation – be out of the country when the Dresden firestorm was created, leaving the Vice-Chief of the Air Staff, Sir Douglas Evill, in charge. However, because of a Russian request at Yalta on 4 February for Allied air attacks against communications, Portal signalled Bottomley the next day asking for objectives east of the western bombline to prevent accidental overshoot onto Allied positions.[7] Bottomley replied within hours giving 'Berlin. Dresden' as suitable transportation and industrial areas. On 6 February Portal replied that the Vice-Chiefs of Staff had approved the new bombing priorities.[8]

The die had now been cast for Dresden, not by Harris who would take the blame, but by the deputies of the Allied Chiefs of Staff. Clement Attlee – who as leader of the first post-war government would decline a request by Churchill in 1946 that Harris be recognised with a peerage – chaired the committee of the War Cabinet that approved the raid while Churchill was on his way to Yalta. As part of Thunderclap Berlin was attacked by the US Eighth Air Force on 3 February, the heaviest raid the city suffered in the whole war, causing 5,000 civilian casualties as almost 1,000 Flying Fortresses tried to hit railway links it was thought were transporting the 6th Panzer Army to the Russian Front. The Eighth would now join RAF Bomber Command in attacking Dresden.

IT WAS with a wealth of resources that Harris turned to the task he had been given. The strength of his flight line was reaching its optimum and a total of 1,406 Bomber Command aircraft would be over the Continent and Germany itself on the night chosen to create chaos in the old Saxon capital known as the Florence of the Elbe. So impressive were the C-in-C's means that he was able to mount two mighty raids on Dresden in one night and assign just one group to the first. The force chosen was Harris's favoured

5 Group, now operating virtually as an independent air force with its own Pathfinder squadrons.

Dresden fitted neatly Portal's written desire to the Allied Chiefs of Staff at the end of the previous summer to find a big town 'hitherto undamaged' for a massive demonstration of Allied air power. Like Chemnitz, also in the Thunderclap list, it was known to be packed with German refugees and troops being moved up to the Eastern Front, vastly swelling its pre-war population of 650,000. The potential for cataclysmic, street-blocking, defence-overwhelming mayhem, always Bomber Command's intention, was at a peak. Dresden had been attacked only twice before, in minor raids by the USAAF, and never by Harris. What was not known by the Allies was that the city authorities had woefully neglected the building of air-raid shelters except for themselves. Even the local SS commander, Martin Mutschmann, whose men had been used to construct a secure bunker in the garden of Dresden's Gauleiter, had been angry enough to fire off a protest to Himmler in late 1943 reading: 'I do not think it right that such a bunker be installed in the Gauleiter's garden of all places, because the greater part of the population still has no access even to a properly constructed air raid shelter.'[9]

There was a false sense of security among the populace that the city would not be attacked because of its history and splendid architecture. They were surrounded by much that could lend validity to that view. The eighteenth-century Zwinger Palace, used by the kings of Saxony, the dominating Frauenkirche Cathedral where Bach played, the Brühl Terrace where Europe's café society had strolled between the wars. But much of it was literally built on sand – the local sandstone that would melt in the intense heat of the firestorm. It was because of Dresden's past and eighteenth-century links with porcelain china, now moved up the Elbe to Meissen, that the Nazis were able to portray it so successfully as a city of peace. However, by 1945 there were 127 factories in Dresden, making radar components, fuses for anti-aircraft shells, engines for Junkers aircraft and cockpit parts for Messerschmitt fighters. The Zeiss-Ikon optical factory and the Siemens glass works were within the confines of the city. The Dresden factories were considered so important for their precision work they had been allocated their own manufacturing code. The 1942 *Dresden Yearbook* described it as 'one of the foremost industrial locations of the Reich'.[10] A 1953 US report concluded that there had been 110 factories in the city in which 50,000 workers toiled for the Nazi war effort. Whether 127 or 110, those factories alone would have made it a suitable target for Bomber Command, but the current compelling attraction was the fact that the Saxon administrative centre was only 90 miles from the Eastern Front and that the city was a key junction through which ran both the north–south and east–west axes of the German railway system. By late 1944 twenty-eight military trains a day had been passing through just one of its four railway stations and four freight marshalling yards.

IT had been intended that the USAAF would hit Dresden first with a big daytime raid on 13 February, Shrove Tuesday, the traditional day for carnivals in peacetime Europe before the beginning of Lent. But bad weather postponed their attack until the next day, so it was Bomber Command that in fact led the way. Much had been learned at High Wycombe by this stage of the war and the operational planning for the night of 13–14 February was a masterpiece, timed and co-ordinated to the minute. Two attacks, not one, would be mounted on Dresden three hours apart. The first, by 5 Group which had demonstrated over Bremen and Brunswick five months before its new marking technique resulting in awesome results with little wastage of effort, was scheduled to begin at 10.15 p.m., to start fires that it was hoped would have turned into a conflagration by the time the second raid arrived to spread the burning debris. Early illuminator aircraft from 5 Group's own Pathfinder squadrons, 97 and 83, would identify Dresden on their H2S sets, then, by the light of the green marker flares and hundreds of white magnesium candles of flame they had dropped, the crews of eight 627 Sqn Mosquitos would mark the Ostragehege soccer stadium near the city's main railway bridge, the Marienbrücke, with red spot fires. The master bomber, W/Cdr Maurice Smith, would check the position of these and if satisfied would call in the Main Force of 5 Group. As usual the group's bomb-laden aircraft would approach the marking points on several different tracks and release their bombs by pre-determined seconds after the aiming point appeared in their bomb sights, allowing bombs to be distributed evenly, fanning outwards, producing fires that it was hoped would quickly link up and spread out of control. It was known as sector bombing.

Harris not only had huge resources at this stage of the war for bombing the enemy but also to confuse him: 100 Group would provide a long Mandrel screen from north to south behind the Western battle front to blind enemy radar; a spoof force of Window-dispensing aircraft would provide a feint in the Mainz-Mannheim area; groups of high-flying Mosquitos would bomb Magdeburg, Bonn, Nuremberg and Dortmund; and virtually all the Halifaxes of 4 and 6 Groups, more than 350 aircraft, would be hitting the synthetic oil plant at Böhlen – 70 miles to the north-west of Dresden – fifteen minutes before the attack on the Saxon capital opened. There was no doubt among those tasked with the attack on the fuel facility, in the heavily defended Leipzig area, why they had been chosen. Harry Irons, the second-tour air gunner who had been asked to try out the Preston Green Ventral gun at Driffield, was now on 158 Sqn at Lissett and remembers:

> We knew we were going as a diversion for the night fighters while the other bombers were attacking Dresden. We were told at briefing we would be there to catch it from the night fighters. The skipper I was with had only done one trip, as a second dickey. They stuck me in there because I had some experience. But everybody had the same chance over a target whether you were experienced or not. It was just luck.[11]

The first of 5 Group's Pathfinders arriving over Dresden might

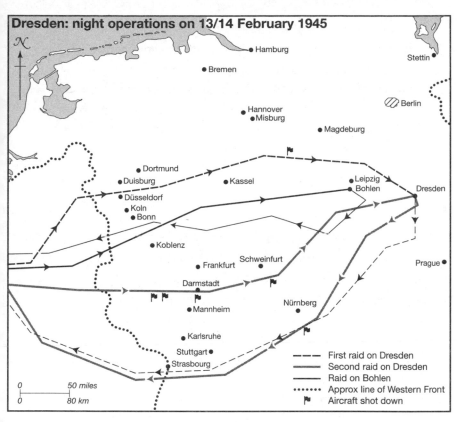

Dresden: night operations on 13/14 February 1945

- ---- First raid on Dresden
- —— Second raid on Dresden
- —— Raid on Bohlen
- ······ Approx line of Western Front
- ⚑ Aircraft shot down

0 — 50 miles
0 — 80 km

Hamburg · Stettin · Bremen · Berlin · Hannover · Misburg · Magdeburg · Dortmund · Duisburg · Düsseldorf · Koln · Bonn · Kassel · Leipzig · Bohlen · Dresden · Koblenz · Frankfurt · Schweinfurt · Prague · Darmstadt · Mannheim · Nürnberg · Karlsruhe · Stuttgart · Strasbourg

well have considered they had reached the wrong target had it not
been for the evidence on their H2S sets. They had flown for four
hours above ten-tenths cloud without moonlight and Dresden,
eerily silent, was still covered by a thin layer of stratus. F/O
John Greening, who had battled through dangerous atmospheric
conditions on the Heilbronn raid in December, was by now an
experienced Pathfinder. He remembers:

> I was primary blind marker. There wasn't a gun fired when we
> went in. It was amazing, whether the Germans there thought
> Dresden wasn't the target and they didn't want to disclose their
> presence I don't know. There was no flak at the start whatever.
> The bomb aimer on Pathfinders was really a radar operator. He
> wasn't down in the nose, he made a blind drop from his position

165

in the cabin as a radar operator, there was no bomb aiming involved. I can't recall anyone in the crew reporting fires starting as we left because it was so early on in the raid. We were one of the first over the target and there would have been nothing to show except a few target indicators burning. We just hoped we had dropped our TIs where we should have done and I think evidence shows we probably did.[12]

Sgt Patrick Bell, his Canadian mid-upper gunner, also remembers: 'It was pretty quiet over Dresden at that stage. We actually dropped our markers 400 feet off from the aiming point and I don't remember seeing anything happening as we left.'[13] In fact F/O Greening's debriefing back at Coningsby reads: 'Nine-tenths strat.cu. [stratocumulus cloud]. Target located on H2S. Dropped our green TI and bombs as briefed, but distributor arm did not move when bomb teat was pressed until tapped, causing five second delay in actual release.'[14]

The exact moment of the first green target indicator being dropped through the cloud over Dresden was witnessed by a teenager at the bakery south of the Grosser Garten where she lived and worked. Eva Beyer got out of bed just after 10 p.m. to see a strange green light shining through her window, which faced north-west towards the bend in the Elbe. The puzzled 17-year-old, who like most of Dresden's citizens had never experienced a night raid, went outside and then saw other green and white flares of 97 Sqn's primary blind markers. 'The Christmas Trees were in the sky and I knew then what it was,' she later recorded. 'I ran through the house waking everyone. Another five families lived in this building and together we totalled 11 women, six children and one man.' They stumbled down to the cellar.[15]

As the flares lit up the thin cloud the eight Mosquitoes piloted by the low-level markers of 627 Sqn roared in exactly on time. They had taken off from their base at Woodhall Spa an hour and a half after the Main Force Lancasters, but arrived a few minutes ahead of them, as planned, because of the wooden aircraft's much greater airspeed. W/Cdr Smith in his own Mosquito now called up the marker leader for the operation, F/Lt William Topper, who was sporting the ribbon of a DFC awarded just ten days before. Unusually a wire recorder had been fitted in three 'Link' Lancasters of the Pathfinders and there is, therefore, an exact record of what was said as silent Dresden, frozen in time, waited to die.[16] Topper pushed the control column of his aircraft forward, the nose of the black aircraft pitched down through the cloud towards a green target indicator and the altimeter rapidly began to unwind towards 3,000 feet. 'Do you see the green yet?' Smith asked him. 'Okay, I can see it,' the diving Topper replied. Then at 800 feet his navigator released a 1,000-lb TI. The bomb hit the ground just 100 yards to the east of the Dresden Sports Club stadium on the Ostragehege fields. As he climbed away from the city, his twin Merlin engines reverberating in roaring echo over the rooftops, another Mosquito Pathfinder shouted, 'Tally ho,' to warn off other aircraft and swooped down to drop its own red marker. Within three minutes the football stadium was ringed by blooming, pulsating splashes of crimson. As the last marker splattered across the AP the thin film of cloud across Dresden began to roll away just as the forecasters had predicted it would. The 250 Lancasters of Main Force were at that moment less than 15 miles from the city, roaring in right on cue at 3 miles a minute. The pilot of a Pathfinder Lancaster of 97 Sqn slightly ahead of them and at 18,000 feet, codenamed Check 3, was now asked by the master bomber: 'Can you see the glow?' The reply came swiftly: 'Check 3 to Controller. I can see three TIs through cloud.' 'Controller to Check 3. Good work, can you see the Reds yet? Over.' 'Check 3 to Controller, I can just see Reds.'

W/Cdr Smith called up the droning Lancasters of 5 Group, codenamed Plate Rack, and issued to each pilot fifteen words that tripped through the earphones of their leather flying helmets to blot out old Dresden and begin a furore that has lasted to this day. 'Controller to Plate Rack Force. Come in and bomb glow of Red TI as planned.' In fact as the leading Main Force Lancasters were now almost on the city the red TIs passed out of sight of the pilots high up above the protruding nose of their Lancasters. Their bomb aimers, who had also heard the master bomber's instructions in their earphones, took over as the pulsating target indicators crept down the sights in the clear Plexiglass forward bubbles of the bombers, which themselves seemed to be floating at that moment in the darkness. There was still no flak as the first bombs went down at ten minutes past ten and within minutes fires had begun to take hold. S/Ldr D. B. Wright of 49 Sqn, who bombed only six minutes into the attack from his briefed height of 13,300 feet, recorded back at Fiskerton: 'There was a considerable glow below cloud.'[17]

Gunner Robert Lee was among the 26,000 Allied POWs held near Dresden who were dispatched on daily working parties into the city. He was held captive in the Schillerschule at Freital to the south-west. The sector-bombing technique honed by 5 Group, in which bombers approached the red markers on different headings to create a wedge of destruction, alerted him by their roar as several passed close by. 'Those first waves of Lancasters were flying low,' he later related. 'We'd not had anything remotely like that before. The noise just went on and on ... a slow crescendo and then dying away, then another crescendo with the next wave coming in. I saw no anti-aircraft fire at all ... The bombers had a clear run in.'[18]

Victor Klemperer, one of Dresden's few remaining Jews who had long before been dismissed from his university post because of his religion, had just sat down to drink a cup of coffee with his 'Aryan' wife at their quarters assigned for Jews at 1 Zeughaus-strasse on the eastern side of the Aldstadt, the old town, south of the Elbe, when they heard the humming of 5 Group approaching. They had had much to think about. A friend had warned them only hours ago of a final round-up of Jews that would certainly take Klemperer to Auschwitz. They hurried to take shelter in the cellar and he wrote in his diary for that night about those first bombs on Dresden:

The light went out, and explosion nearby ... Pause in which we caught our breath, we knelt down between the chairs, in some groups there was whimpering and weeping – approaching aircraft once again, deadly danger once again, explosion once again. I do not know how often it was repeated. Suddenly the cellar window on the back wall opposite the entrance bursts open, and outside it was as bright as day. Someone shouted: 'Incendiary bomb, we have to put it out!' Two people even hauled over the stirrup pump and audibly operated it. There were further explosions ... And then it grew quieter, and then came the all-clear. I had lost all sense of time. Outside it was as bright as day. Fires were blazing at Pirnaischer Platz, on Marschallstrasse, and somewhere on over the Elbe. The ground was covered with broken glass. A terribly strong wind was blowing ... [19]

Within fifteen minutes 880 tons of bombs had fallen on central Dresden, 57 per cent high explosive to blow walls and roofs apart, the remaining 43 per cent incendiaries to torch what lay inside. As the last of 5 Group's Lancasters banked away from the target those fires were now glowing inside wrecked four-storey buildings. Eventually they would burst through shattered roofs and link up from west to east in the Aldstadt, fed by the westerly wind. Fatally, most of the residents were still sheltering in their cellars below, where many would die from carbon monoxide poisoning as the firestorm began and sucked out the oxygen it needed. The bombing had been so concentrated in time and space it had claimed a Lancaster of 463 Sqn, flying in a lower wave.*

A fireman, Alfred Birke, who had driven north-west from the parkland known as the Grosser Garten, arrived on the eastern edge of the Aldstadt close to Victor Klemperer's home shortly after 11 p.m. and recorded the scene. 'Flames shoot from the facades of buildings ... At the Pirnaischer Platz I encounter three naked bodies, a woman and two children. I take care not to drive over them.' He noted that puzzlingly he hadn't 'met a living

---

* F/O Norman Fernley-Stott, a 20-year-old Australian, was killed with all but the rear gunner when his aircraft crashed to the north of the city. They were the only air force casualties in the first attack.

soul'.[20] But as midnight approached the eyewitness Otto Griebel, a Communist painter, had emerged from his cellar shelter in the Neue Gasse in the same area and tried with a friend to make for his home a few streets away: 'Everywhere we turned the streets were on fire. The spark-filled air was suffocating, and stung our unprotected eyes ... Entire chunks of red-hot matter were flying at us. The more we moved into the network of streets, the stronger the storm became, hurling burning scraps and objects through the air.'[21]

Gunner Lee watching with his comrades in Freital remembers: 'Before long there was a massive glow over Dresden ... It was quite clear to us from where we were standing that after that first raid the whole of the old town at the bend of the river was on fire.'[22]

Those now out on the streets fought to escape the roaring, hot wind sweeping all the way from the Zwinger Palace to the Rathaus. The attack by 5 Group had achieved all that had been demanded of it, creating a vast target indicator out of Dresden for the Lancasters of the second wave. Those 529 aircraft, from 1, 3, 6 and 8 Groups, became airborne shortly before 5 Group's aircraft had reached the city. Among the first to take off was a Lancaster of the all-Polish 300 Sqn. As it climbed out of the Faldingworth circuit just before 10 p.m. it collided with a 550 Sqn Lancaster from North Killingholme over Wragby, Lincolnshire. The shocking red glare in the cloud as both bomb loads exploded lit up the outlines of other bombers across miles of sky. Their crews recognised the phenomenon for what it was, fourteen lives literally snuffed out in a flash. Another four Lancasters would be lost on the raid, but several would make forced landings in France as they ran out of fuel on the way back from this maximum-range target.

AS the first Dresden force winged its way west and homewards rear gunners would report to their skippers from up to 100 miles away that they could still see the target burning. Harry Irons, the rear gunner on the Böhlen oil plant raid, which had been scheduled to open at 10 p.m., fifteen minutes before 5 Group's squadrons unloaded on the Elbe city, also saw the glow of Dresden to the south-east. The raid on Böhlen, a huge undertaking in itself, had not gone well. The fears of crews that they were bait for the Luftwaffe had not been realised, only one aircraft being lost, but unlike the improving conditions at Dresden there was particularly cold weather in the Leipzig area and heavy cumulus cloud with accompanying turbulence. As a result the bombing had been scattered. W/O Irons remembers:

> The weather was very bad, icing was a problem. I saw a red glow in the sky behind me just after 10 p.m. and it was Dresden. Dresden was a huge fire and that was just the beginning of it. It was bitterly cold in that rear turret. The Perspex panel had been taken out so that you could see better. There was always a problem with the oxygen mask, with saliva dripping down into the tube and freezing. It would cut off your oxygen supply without you knowing it and you would just go out, so you had to keep trying to break the ice. We had heated suits and I had an Irvin jacket and leather gauntlets as well as everything else. We didn't get attacked, but we had a hang-up with a 500-lb bomb that night and had to land at Manston in Kent. We were short of fuel.[23]

The Lancaster of the deputy master bomber, F/Lt Phillips, from 7 Sqn, was the first to mark the target after it was lit up by the Pathfinder blind illuminators. The bomb aimer, F/Lt Andrew Maitland, had spotted a good gap in the cloud cover through which he could see some ground detail from 17,000 feet. He called for bomb doors open as he picked up the aiming point and gave his 'Left, left, steady, right, steady' instructions to bring the target down the bomb-sight reflector plate towards release point, then hit the button in his hand. 'I was still looking for our target indicators cascading over the aiming point when all hell seemed to be let loose,' he later recorded. 'There was a very large flash and a God Almighty crash and bang as the shrapnel from anti-aircraft shells tore into our aircraft. I knew we had been hit and hit badly and as the aircraft shuddered and started losing height, my heart seemed to stand still.'[24] Maitland grabbed his parachute and fumbled it onto his chest harness, expecting the 'Bale out' order at any second. The flak burst had peppered the fuselage in a hundred places behind the pilot and wounded the H2S set operator in the leg, from which he was losing a lot of blood. As F/Lt Phillips fought to regain control of the aircraft, the engineer leaped forward to push the Graviner button and put out the engine fire with the automatic extinguisher. The Lancaster was down to 7,000 feet before F/Lt Phillips was able to haul it back onto an even keel.

The battered bomber turned away westward for home and the set operator, F/Sgt T. Kelly, now bandaged up from the aircraft's first-aid kit, insisted on going back to his table to assist with the navigation. Once the aircraft was safely over the North Sea Maitland went to see him and to suggest he take a rest from his H2S set. 'This brave, young man, although looking quite pale and ill, looked up at me and said: 'I feel not too bad now, so I will just continue as we haven't far to go,' Maitland recorded.[25]

'Oh what a wonderful feeling as our aircraft struggled across the English coast and we headed towards Oakington with everybody keeping their fingers crossed that our wheels would come down.' Fire engines and ambulances were alerted at the Rutland base as the Lancaster slid down the approach path on three engines, the runway coming into view and rapidly widening. 'We screeched on the tarmac surface and the undercarriage held,' Maitland recalled. 'I felt like kissing the ground as we got to the bottom of the steps.'*[26]

IN Dresden the firestorm had now reached its fearsome apex after being fed by the second, larger force of bombers which had reached the city at 1.21. They had had no trouble finding it; the beckoning fires were visible from scores of miles away as a red glow in the cloud. They also discovered that not all Dresden's flak guns had

---

* F/Sgt Kelly was whisked away to Ely RAF hospital and within weeks learned that he had been awarded the Conspicuous Gallantry Medal for sticking to his post.

been moved to face the Russians on the Eastern Front, though Bomber Command's Operational Research Section later described the defences as 'negligible'.[27] The Pathfinders had been ordered to bomb the Altmarkt, but this was already well ablaze. The master bomber, S/Ldr Peter de Wesselow, and his marker leader, W/Cdr Le Good, decided as they criss-crossed the target to have markers released on so far undamaged parts of the city, to the west and south-west, on Friedrichstadt and on Löbtau, near where the Hauptbahnhof lay, in whose vaults many hundreds were sheltering. As the bombing spread with inevitable overshoot, high explosive and incendiaries rained on the parkland of the Grosser Garten to the south-east, to where many had fled from the earlier bombing.

The 460 Sqn Lancaster of F/O David Francis was among the first in Main Force to reach the city. The navigator remembers:

We took off from Binbrook at 9.30 p.m., so it was well after midnight when we got there. It had been cloud all the way to Dresden, but as we came to it the cloud opened up and the whole of Dresden was spread out below us in the bend of the Elbe. We were at the front of that attack and there were no target indicators going down from the Pathfinders. The target was not burning heavily to any extent at that time. Our bomb aimer was going to bomb visually on the aiming point of the marshalling yards and as we ran up to it and bombed the TIs went down. There was very little anti-aircraft fire coming up at that point and there were no fighters. The fires really took hold after we left. At about 100 to 150 miles away on the way back we could still see the glow behind us. Nobody commented on it. The only way you could do your job was to think of it as just a target. The firestorm was certainly unexpected. When we got back it was realised it had been a very successful raid in Bomber Command terms.[28]

F/Sgt James Wright, the 166 Sqn wireless operator whose skipper had taken on the defences of an oil target by himself in December, was halfway through his tour in 1 Group when he was briefed for Dresden. 'We were in the second phase and we could see the fires from a long way away as we approached, but at that time they weren't the most intense fires I had ever seen,' he remembers. 'Most of the major targets were fires and to me it was just another raid.'[29]

But by the time the final Lancasters of 3 Group arrived over Dresden its firemen were battling uselessly against the roaring flames, the narrow, cobbled streets of the Aldstadt an inferno with few gaps as the individual furnace of each four-storey building in the close-packed streets swept yellow flame and burning red debris skyward to link with that of its neighbour. The firestorm was now almost a living entity, growling and grumbling as it invaded every court and alley of the old centre with searing, shooting tongues to seek and devour combustibles it needed to survive. Furniture, photographs, family records, families themselves, disappeared as the fiendish whirligig danced on, spinning scraps of torched paper like halted conversations high into the burning sky. The more it flourished the more oxygen it needed and rapidly the air was drawn out of the cellars beneath Dresden to where its citizens had descended for lack of proper air-raid shelters. As the temperature grew, they suffocated.

The Lancasters of 3 Group were among the last to unload, the final bombs going down at 1.55 a.m. Wireless operator Sgt Kenneth Turnham in a Lancaster of the group's 115 Sqn, remembers:

> We were quite a long way back in the second wave. The crew remarked they had never seen such an intensive fire before; usually you just saw the explosions of bombs ahead. By the time we were over the target it was a mass of fire. It was just like a bush fire spreading and was the most impressive target I saw. As a target it was so clear. The glare was so bright it was like daylight. We were at 20,000 feet and at that height there was no buffeting from the heat. We dropped our bombs in the middle of the fire and put the nose down to get away. Our skipper, Richard Briggs, was known as 'First Back Briggs' on the squadron because instead of making a slow descent with the stream to the coastline he used to dive to

about 3,000 feet, giving us airspeed, then fly all the way back at that height. The night fighters wouldn't come that low and the ack-ack radar would have a hell of a job picking us up. He was a clever skipper. When we got back it was obvious it had been a very successful raid. It wasn't a doddle, no target was a doddle, but when you get a target lit up like that as you approach there's no way you are going to miss it.[30]

Sgt Derek Jackson was a 19-year-old air gunner in the same group, on 149 Sqn: 'The Dresden operation was my most memorable operation for obvious reasons,' he says. 'We were in the second wave of course and the city was well alight – no flak, few searchlights and the master bomber flying around directing the bombing after target marking by the Pathfinders. On the way home the glow in the sky could be seen 100 miles away. It was also my longest trip, nine hours.[31]

Lothar Metzger, a child in Dresden during the war, wrote about his experiences more than 50 years later. After the first raid he had come up from his cellar shelter, which had been damaged by a bomb, with his mother, sister and twin babies to find their fourth-floor apartment didn't exist any more.

> We fled into another cellar overcrowded with injured and distraught men, women and children shouting, crying and praying. No light except some electric torches. And then suddenly the second raid began. This shelter was hit too, and so we fled through cellar after cellar. Many, so many, desperate people came in from the streets ... Explosion after explosion. It was beyond belief, worse than the blackest nightmare. So many people were horribly burnt and injured. It became more and more difficult to breathe. It was dark and all of us tried to leave the cellar with unbelievable panic. Dead and dying people were trampled upon ... The basket with our twins covered with wet cloths was snatched up out of my mother's hands and we were pushed upstairs by the people behind us. We saw the burning street, the falling ruins and the terrible firestorm. My mother covered us with wet blankets and coats she found in a water tub.[32]

Victor Klemperer, situated on the eastern edge of the Aldstadt, had become separated from his wife in the second raid. He had scrambled out of his cellar because it had become dangerous and sheltered in a passageway as further waves of bombers passed over. 'Bangs, as light as day, explosions,' he cryptically recorded in his diary later. 'I had no thoughts, I was not even afraid. I was simply tremendously exhausted. I think I was expecting the end.' He rested in a crater, then in a telephone kiosk. 'I saw only flames everywhere, heard the noise of the fire and the storm, felt terribly exhausted inside.'[33]

Otto Griebel, who lived in the same area as Klemperer and saw the firestorm beginning an hour after the first raid, had managed to battle his way north through the flames to the Brühl Terrace alongside the Elbe. He looked back south towards the Aldstadt and saw the familiar buildings starting to disappear in smoke and flame. To the north, across the river, much of the Neustadt was burning, though this had not been part of the sector bombing plan.[34]

A companion of Klemperer's that night also realised that safety lay only by the river, where the raging fires could not draw out all the oxygen, and shouting, 'We must get through to the Elbe, we'll get through,' set off with a child on his shoulders. Klemperer recorded:

> A group of people were clambering up through the public gardens to the Brühl Terrace, the route went close to the fires, but it had to be cooler at the top and easier to breathe. Then I was standing at the top in the storm wind and the showers of sparks. To the right and left, buildings were ablaze, the Belvedere and – probably – the Art Academy ... Within a wide radius nothing but fires. Standing out like a tooth on this side of the Elbe, the tall building of the Pirnaischer Platz [not far from his home], glowing white. The storm again and again tore at my blanket, hurt my head.[35]

The 248 Lancasters of 1 Group bombed between 0123 and 0152, their attack ending just three minutes before the final bombs of 3 Group. Sgt Joe Williams, a 22-year-old rear gunner in

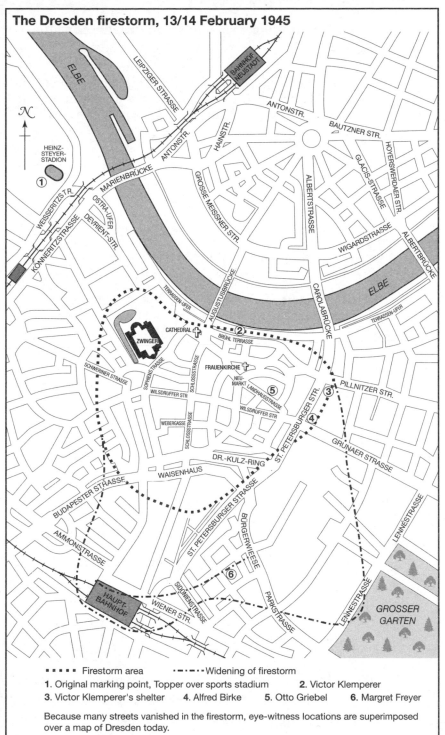

The Dresden firestorm, 13/14 February 1945

•••••• Firestorm area   ·—·—·Widening of firestorm
1. Original marking point, Topper over sports stadium   **2.** Victor Klemperer
3. Victor Klemperer's shelter   **4.** Alfred Birke   **5.** Otto Griebel   **6.** Margret Freyer

Because many streets vanished in the firestorm, eye-witness locations are superimposed over a map of Dresden today.

1 Group's 625 Sqn, remembers his aircraft released its load at 0135. He says:

> As we approached our bombing run we could see the target was a mass of fires. When I looked down the streets were dark lines criss-crossing in a sea of flame. I hadn't seen anything like that before. It was obviously a very severe raid. There was no flak. It seemed to me that there was only one flak gun, a 105 mm or 128 mm, firing. The bursts were a different, deeper yellow/red than other flak. As we cleared the target the bomb aimer shone his Aldis lamp into the bomb bay to make sure all the bombs had gone and he said, 'The Cookie's hung up.' The pilot said, 'We'll drop it on the way out.' From my position in the rear turret I said, 'Let's go round again, there's no flak.' 'No,' said Jim, the pilot, 'we'll drop it.' I said again, 'Look, there's no flak, we've brought it all this way, let's go round again.' For the first and only time my captain said, 'Shut up, Joe.' We ditched it, probably 10 miles out from the target. The wireless operator lifted a little lever under his seat which dropped the whole bomb rack. I saw the flash as it exploded and then a massive fire started. I've no idea what the Cookie hit. At approximately 180 miles from the target I asked the navigator how far we were away and he told me. We could still see the glow of Dresden and beside it to the right with a distinct gap was our miniature glow.[36]

In the final months of the war scientists who made up Bomber Command's Operational Research Section were given much evidence after a raid to show how it had gone and what could be learned to make the Command even more efficient. The night Dresden died yielded not only the wire recording of the initial target marking, but also a film shot by two cameramen in a 463 Sqn Lancaster, from the 1 Group base Binbrook. The Lancaster, Y-Yorker, skippered by F/Lt G. C. Skelton, had circled the city from just before 1.30 at 14,500 feet as the cameramen, W/O Buckland and Sgt Pease, recorded the scene, then added its own bombs to those below. '5 Group blazed a trail in magnificent manner,' Skelton reported back at Waddington. 'The whole of

Dresden appeared to be on fire. We orbited the target for eight and a half minutes to allow the film unit to do a good job.'[37] The images, Bomber Command Operational Film No. 257, show the fire increasing in that time, the seemingly innocent twinkling of incendiaries contrasting with the angry flash of exploding Cookies, and one long street particularly – probably the north–south route towards the Pragerstrasse and Hauptbahnhof – clearly outlined as a solid stream of flame. Within days the film had been released to be shown to the British public as well, on newsreels at their local cinemas.

A bomb aimer in 625 Sqn, F/Sgt Frank Tolley, says:

> Their aircraft must have been very close to our own because their film was the scene I saw. As we came up to the target I could see the huge fires. I thought, Why are we here, there is nothing we can do, just release our bombs and go; there was no target marker as such. After we turned away for home the rear gunner could still see the fires for a long way.
>
> About a week later I was on leave and went with my now wife to the cinema and the film of the Dresden raid was on the newsreel. It was just as I remembered it and I thought, This could even have been taken from our aircraft.*[38]

But not all airmen in the bombers over Dresden looked out on the inferno. F/Sgt Bill Porter, the navigator who had had to clear snow at Kelstern and was in the same crew as F/Sgt Tolley, says:

> As we approached I didn't hear anything about the fires. I was enclosed in my little curtained-off navigator's compartment with a 24-volt lamp. I didn't go out to look at the target, but I did with the next one, Chemnitz. I could hear the commentary and it was suggested I might want to see what was happening. I did so. I could see the searchlights, the flak coming up and the mess below and

---

* The operational record book for 625 Sqn shows F/Sgt Tolley bombed in the exact time frame and similar height band as F/Lt Skelton's film, at 0135 from 16,000 feet.

I thought it was pretty scary. I was frightened and I didn't go to look again. I had false security enclosed in my little navigator's position behind my blackout curtain. That was my war.[39]

In the streets below there was now not just the raging red inferno of the Aldstadt, but also several independent large fires including a lake of flame in the area of the Friedrichstadt marshalling yards, west of the Dresden Sports Club stadium at Ostragehege, initial marking point of the first raid. The areas of Johannstadt and Striesen in the east between the Elbe and the Grosser Garten were ablaze and even the suburbs of Räcknitz and Plauen to the south had taken bomb loads. A total of 962 tons of high explosive and 791 tons of incendiaries had gone down in this second attack and the Lancasters that carried them had arrived without warning, the first raid before midnight having knocked out the air-raid alert system.

Sgt Ken O'Brien, the 101 Sqn rear gunner, who had just been awarded the DFM for shooting down a jet night fighter, was also in the second raid and remembers:

It was a firestorm before we arrived. There were special bombs being used which exploded below rooftop height and before hitting the ground.* Coming back I could see the fire that was Dresden for a couple of hours. It never seemed to disappear. While still over Europe heading back we saw the USAAF on the way to Dresden and I thought, They've had two raids and now they are about to get another before they have had time to move.[40]

F/Sgt Frank Bramley, a Toronto-born gunner on 431 Sqn, saw gunfire along both the Eastern and Western Fronts after his Canadian-built Lancaster turned for home at 20,000 feet, leaving

---

* This was a development of the small bomb container used to house bundles of 4-lb incendiaries, which had opened immediately in the bomb bay on the bomb aimer's electrical signal, scattering the incendiaries earthwards. In late 1944 a new container was designed that was more aimable, itself falling then bursting apart shortly before impact.

what his skipper described at debriefing as 'a whole city ablaze with fires'.[41] Bramley added to the evidence of approaching German defeat now being presented to the British public by making a CBC broadcast three days after the raid from his base at Croft, near Darlington.

> Smoke billowed over the target in vast waves. The flak emplacements were almost useless by the time we were over the city and our Pathfinders put down very brilliant and accurate ground markers. From what I could see everyone grouped their bombs close around these target indicators. The result was that when we left the fires were more intense than ever. I doubted if any of the Nazis below would need any anti-war education after this was over. But when our Iroquois Squadron aircraft wheeled around for the homeward flight my principal feeling was one of amazement that there was an even greater line of fire on the eastern horizon. The skipper, F/Lt George McNeil, of Regina, said over the intercom that this must be the Russian Front ... By swivelling my mid upper turret I found I could see large lights reflected in the sky over the Western horizon. They were the flashes of our much nearer guns. It was a wonderful thing to see proof that Nazi territory was becoming so narrow.[42]

The roaring, crackling, searing multi-coloured flame of the firestorm spread from the Aldstadt to the south, towards the Hauptbahnhof and ending inside the northern perimeter of the Grosser Garten as the last of the bombs rained down. The sole routes of refuge from the burning central area were north or south. The woefully neglected shelter provision of Dresden meant that the only escape in a big raid was by holes previously made in cellar walls for inhabitants to flee from basement to basement until they could exit near the Elbe or the Grosser Garten. But there were no direction signs underground and most of the few still conscious as the fires above greedily gobbled up the oxygen were unable to find a way out. Both the guilty and the innocent died, as the civilians of London had died in the 1940–41 Blitz and were even now dying from the V-2 onslaught, by drowning from burst water mains and from injuries as collapsing masonry buried them alive.

One of the most harrowing accounts by a survivor of the firestorm is that of 24-year-old Margret Freyer, who had recently suffered a full day's interrogation by the Gestapo for being overheard criticising Hitler. She had escaped a cellar at Struvestrasse on the edge of the firestorm area after it spread south towards the Hauptbahnhof and the Grosser Garten. The station and its deep vaults were only three streets away to the south and the open areas of the Bürgerwiese parkland which led onto the larger Grosser Garten were just two streets away to the north-east, yet she narrowly reached safety in the confusion of roaring flame, intense heat, whirling sparks and fierce winds that swept the unwary off their feet. Shortly after making a dash from the cellar, where those who remained were afterwards found as corpses, she fell into a bomb crater, then clambering out, stumbled on blindly.

> The firestorm is incredible, there are calls for help and screams from somewhere, but all around is one single inferno . . . I stumbled on to where it was dark. Suddenly I saw people again, right in front of me. They scream and gesticulate with their hands and then – to my utter horror and amazement – I see how one after the other they simply seem to let themselves drop to the ground . . . Today I know that these unfortunate people were the victims of shortage of oxygen.

She herself fell for lack of life-giving air, but crawled on. 'There's a breeze! I take another breath, inhale deeply, and my senses clear. In front of me is a broken tree. As I rush towards it I know that I have been saved, but am unaware that the park is the Bürgerwiese.'[43]

The contemporary account of Margret Freyer, who blamed Hitler for what happened to Dresden and not the RAF, is from the southern edge of the later firestorm area before the fire spread further south and burned itself out. It has proved much harder for historians to find accounts from those caught in the middle. Some had tried to take refuge in emergency water tanks in the Aldstadt where their drowned bodies were later found. Many hundreds of others, further south, had fled to the subterranean passageways of the Hauptbahnhof, built on several levels, and this is where they died as the firestorm overtook the station and casually drew away the air as it flicked on, smothering them. A woman refugee from Silesia who was helped through the station complex hours later described the scene. 'We passed through the basement. There must have been several thousand people there. All lying very still.'[44]

At his school prison camp at Freital to the south-west of Dresden, Gunner Lee had watched the second attack on Dresden, standing alongside one of his German guards, as column after column of explosions rose from the pulsating red glow. 'I remember the guard saying to me, "Dresden was so very beautiful," and I said to him, "London was also beautiful," he later recorded. 'I was thinking of the heap of rubble that had been Chelsea Old Church.'[45] It was now Ash Wednesday, the official start of Lent, and ashes and sparks of what had once been Dresden were still falling on the wretched shelterers by the Brühl Terrace along the Elbe as dawn came. The intense heat of the firestorm had also condensed into cloud as it met the cold air above the city and rain began adding to the survivors' misery, turning the ground on which they stood to mud. Among them was Victor Klemperer who had been reunited with his wife and in the late morning they trudged back towards the glowing heart of Dresden, almost blind from the ash-laden air, to look for their home in the Zeughausstrasse on the eastern side of the Aldstadt. First he removed the yellow star from his clothes, which had marked him out as a Jew. "We walked slowly along the river bank,' he recorded. 'Above us building after building was a burnt-out ruin ... masses of the empty, rectangular cases of the stick incendiary bombs stuck out of the churned up earth ... At times the dead were scattered across our path.'[46]

They slowly and with difficulty made their way to the Jewish quarter where they found their home was now a heap of rubble. An ambulance drew up nearby and an attendant gave Klemperer eye drops with the kind words, 'Now Dad I'm not going to hurt you.' As Klemperer walked away

> after a few steps I heard the ugly hum of an aircraft above me coming rapidly closer and diving. I ran towards the wall [around the Jewish quarter], threw myself to the ground, my head against the wall, my arm over my face. There was already an explosion and little bits of rubble trickled down on me. I lay there for a little while longer. I thought, 'Just don't get killed now!' There were a few more distant explosions then there was silence.[47]

The USAAF had begun its contribution to Operation Thunderclap on Dresden.

The Flying Fortresses had arrived over the still burning city shortly after noon, but in the smoke and cloud covering Dresden only one group, the 379th, was able to find its target. It was the Friedrichstadt marshalling yards to the west of the city and near where Kurt Vonnegut had sheltered with his fellow US POWs, in a deep abattoir numbered Slaughterhouse 5, during the two raids of the previous night. Other groups in the 316-bomber force found that their view was obscured by clouds so they bombed Dresden on radar, and incendiaries and high explosive were widely dispersed over the city. Weather conditions were now such that more than sixty aircraft became separated and bombed Prague 60 miles away in error while others bombed Brux and Pilsen. The next day the Americans returned, the 1st Bombardment Division being diverted from its primary target of the Böhlen synthetic oil plant because it was obscured by cloud and bombing Dresden instead. They failed to hit the Friedrichstadt marshalling yards and, as on the previous raid, bombs were scattered over a wide area. But one stray bomb destroyed the guillotine in the courtyard of the prison in the Südvorstadt suburb in the south of the city where it is believed more than 1,000 people were executed in the course of the war for a range of offences from resisting the Nazis to defeatist talk. Another bomb destroyed the prison's north wall, killing several prisoners but allowing others to escape.

After the American raids the lines of bombed-out refugees

leaving the city grew. The bombing of Dresden had saved Victor Klemperer and other Jews because the Gestapo headquarters in the Hotel Continental, just to the south of the Hauptbahnhof, had been destroyed in the RAF raids, together with all its records on those the Nazis considered unworthy of life. Free from the telltale yellow star Klemperer joined the lines of refugees with his wife and became just another bombed-out citizen of the Reich seeking temporary papers.

The beginning of that sorry trail of the homeless out of the city was seen by Gunner Lee in Freital. He and his fellow prisoners were routinely roused at 6.30 a.m. and marched into the city to sort out materials for the Borners company, which dealt in scrap. 'We used to see Russian prisoners drop dead in the street,' he recorded. But 14 February, the day after what would have been in more peaceful times a carnival, was etched with a different horror.

> There we were marching up the Dresdner-Strasse, on our way to Borners. They're coming the other way. They're already pouring out of Dresden. Fleeing – and it's scarcely dawn. An endless column, right the way through Freital, down towards Dippoldiswalde. A carnival scene. People dress up, don't they? Specially children. Clothing ragged, burnt. Hair singed. Black with soot and dirt from the smoke and the fire and the dust. Eye sockets red. Faces streaked white, where tears are washing away the soot. And these are the lucky ones. They are the ones that have managed to get out.[48]

Those who hadn't got out were found in their cellar tombs over the next few days and either burned on pyres in the Altmarkt, where SS men from the concentration camp at Treblinka supplied expert help, or buried in the Heidefriedhof cemetery. According to the official German report, *Tagesbefehl* (Order of the Day) No. 47 issued on 22 March, the number of dead recovered by that date from all four raids, RAF and USAAF, was 20,204, including 6,865 who were cremated on the Altmarkt, and the total number of deaths was expected to be about 25,000.[49] It would be far fewer than the 40,000 who had died in the firestorm in Hamburg in the summer of 1943, which Armament Minister Albert Speer thought if repeated might end the war.

But his fellow minister Josef Goebbels, who would soon be smarting at the destruction of his own headquarters in Berlin by an RAF Mosquito raid on the night of 12 March, now saw a great opportunity. As the cities of the Reich had turned to ashes in this final phase of the air war and it was obvious that the Luftwaffe was unable to keep its oft-repeated early promise that the homeland would not be bombed in the way they were bombing other nations, the Propaganda Minister had found himself in a dilemma. He could hardly cavil at the serious harm being done to Germany while still maintaining that it would be the final victor. However now – in an attempt to force the Allies to call off the bomber offensive – he had his agents simply multiply by ten the Dresden casualty figures and protest that a jewel of world architecture whose 'few' factories 'mainly manufactured toothpaste and baby powder', had been lost. As early as 25 February a Reich Propaganda Ministry leaflet with photographs of two burned children was released under the title *Dresden – Massacre of Refugees*, stating that 200,000 had died. By the end of March the Propaganda Ministry had made it precisely 202,040, which simply added a nought to the known *Tagesbefehl* figure.

Goebbels's hypocritical outcry was taken up by the media in Switzerland and in Sweden by the *Svenska Morgonbladet* and splashed in United States newspapers. It was helped by a blunder of the Allies themselves. In a briefing at SHAEF headquarters in Paris on 16 February Air Commodore Colin Grierson of the RAF press office had told journalists: 'First of all they [Dresden and other towns] are the centres to which evacuees are being moved. They are centres of communications through which traffic is moving across to the Russian Front, and from the Western Front to the East, and they are sufficiently close to the Russian Front for the Russians to continue the successful prosecution of their battle. I think these three reasons probably cover the bombing.'

One of the reporters asked whether the principal aim of bombing Dresden had been to cause confusion among the refugees or to blast communications carrying military supplies. Grierson answered that the primary aim was to cut communications to prevent the Germans transporting military supplies, and to stop movement in all directions if possible. He then added, apparently casually, that the raid also helped in destroying 'what is left of German morale'. Associated Press correspondent Howard Cowan subsequently filed a story saying that the Allies had resorted to terror bombing.[50] 'Terror' bombing was not the phrase that Grierson had used and Cowan's take on it was denied in a report by SHAEF on 17 February, but nevertheless the growing disquiet in neutral countries and now in the US itself led its citizens to protest that the American policy of 'precision' attacks – rather than the area bombing of the RAF – had changed. General Carl Spaatz, head of the US Strategic and Tactical Air Forces, which included the Eighth Air Force, was asked to reiterate that the US only bombed military targets.[51] He did so and the blame for Dresden and the killing of civilians was firmly laid at the RAF's door. Yet the USAAF conducted much of its bombing campaign in north-west Europe through cloud, often hitting residential areas, and the bombing of Prague in mistake for Dresden was hardly an example of precision.

On 6 March the Dresden storm was further agitated when the MP for Ipswich, Richard Stokes, like the Bishop of Chichester a long-time opponent of RAF 'carpet bombing' – an opposition shared by very few – asked a key question in the House of Commons, the first time bombing strategy had been raised since the bishop's protest a year before.* He asked if 'terror' bombing was now the open policy of the government and read out the Associated Press dispatch, so that it would become a matter of public record in Hansard. The Joint Under-Secretary for Air, Commander Brabner, replied: 'We are not wasting bombers or time on purely terror tactics.'[52]

Now the AP report was completely out of the bag in Britain a steady stream of newspaper articles from neutral countries was reproduced in the British press, keeping the debate alive. On

* See author's previous work, *Men of Air*, p. 102.

28 March Churchill, mindful of future relationships with America and countries such as Switzerland and Sweden, put aside his war leader hat and took up that of the politician. It was time for a scapegoat for the furore – which let us not forget was begun by Goebbels – and that scapegoat would be Harris.

Churchill penned a minute to his Chiefs of Staff reading: 'It seems to me that the moment has come when the question of bombing of German cities simply for the sake of increasing the terror, though under other pretexts, should be reviewed.' Ignoring that it was he not others who wanted Dresden bombed he went on: 'The destruction of Dresden remains a serious query against the conduct of Allied bombing. I am of the opinion that military objectives must henceforth be more strictly studied in our own interests rather than that of the enemy.'

Giving a solid clue to the fact that he was under pressure from the Americans and (Goebbels-promoted) views in the neutral press, he concluded: 'The Foreign Secretary has spoken to me on this subject, and I feel the need for more precise concentration upon military objectives, such as oil and communications behind the immediate battle zone, rather than mere acts of terror and wanton destruction, however impressive.'[53]

It was a breathtaking about-turn by the man to whom Britain and the free world owed so much. Churchill had been an instigator of the bomber offensive, then enthusiastic supporter for years, telling Parliament in 1942 shortly after Harris took over at High Wycombe that aerial attack on Germany was 'going to get continually stronger until, in my view, it will play a great and perfectly definite part in abridging the course of this war, in taking the strain off our Russian Allies'. He continued that rather than sympathy for the Germans of the kind shown for Britons in the Blitz neutral nations would say of the RAF bomber offensive on Germany: "serve them right". That is the view of the civilised world.'[54]

To his credit, Portal, who also had urged a 'severe blitz' on Dresden and as Chief of the Air Staff gave Harris his orders, refused to accept the minute and requested it be withdrawn. First he had his deputy Norman Bottomley show the minute to Harris.

Harris was justifiably incensed, replying to Bottomley on 29 March that 'To suggest we have bombed German cities "simply for the sake of increasing the terror though under other pretexts" . . . is an insult both to the bombing policy of the Air Ministry and to the manner in which that has been executed by Bomber Command.' The reply went on for several pages and towards the end Harris makes the telling point: 'Attacks on cities like any other act of war are intolerable unless they are strategically justified. But they are strategically justified in so far as they tend to shorten the war and so preserve the lives of Allied soldiers. To my mind we have absolutely no right to give them up unless it is certain that they will not have this effect.' The next sentence, in which Harris echoes the words of the nineteenth-century German Chancellor Bismarck over the price of Pomeranian soldiers' lives for the Balkans, has so often been taken out of context and used to condemn the air strategist as an unfeeling brute. Yet he was making the point – certainly undiplomatically in a manner now unthinkable in this age of spin – that bombing was always intended to save Allied soldiers. It read: 'I do not personally regard the whole of the remaining cities of Germany as worth the bones of one British grenadier.'[55]

Churchill, who could be irrational at times, was convinced by Portal's representations, backed by Harris's letter, that he had made a great error and on 1 April substituted the minute with one that took out the tendentious phrase 'terror bombing'. The new memorandum read:

> It seems to me that the moment has come when the question of so-called area bombing of German cities should be reviewed from the point of view of our own interests. If we come into control of an entirely ruined land there will be a great shortage of accommodation for ourselves and our allies . . . We must see to it that our attacks do not do more harm to ourselves in the long run than they do to the enemy's immediate war effort. Pray let me have your views.[56]

However, the rot had begun. Within months Dresden would be part of the Communist bloc and the Russians – who also had wanted the ancient city destroyed – would later employ their own propaganda against the USAAF/RAF bomber offensive as a symbol of capitalist barbarity. It was the final nail in any hope of a separate campaign medal for Bomber Command.

The myths of Dresden would flourish over the years. That it was an act of vengeance for the bombing of London, that up to half a million people had died. Wars are not successfully prosecuted by vengeance and the number of casualties has recently been reviewed by a German government commission, finally to end speculation used by the extreme right. The commission was made up of thirteen prominent German historians, headed by Rolf-Dieter Muller. In October 2008, ahead of the report's publication, Muller said: 'In the course of its research the commission has so far identified around 18,000 victims of the air raids in Dresden ... The commission estimates that a maximum of 25,000 people lost their lives in the February attacks.'[57]

The plethora of falsehoods about the attack have been a permanent burden to the brave veterans of Bomber Command, who have had little thanks for laying their lives on the line every time they took off into the unknown to save Britain by hitting the enemy where they were told it would count. Because they lived through this period and remember public attitudes then their views about Dresden are important in weighing the evidence today. 'I've never regretted being on it,' says James Wright. 'It was just something we had to do at the time. In a war you have no control over these things. It was a long time ago and unless you were there at the time you cannot appreciate what life was like and what we were up against. There was light and heavy flak flying about as we went in to the target. We didn't consider it a particularly easy target.'[58] Bomb aimer Frank Tolley says: 'Today I don't think we should apologise for the Dresden raid, but I regret it had to be done. I feel very sad about it, but it would be hypocritical to apologise. Circumstances were such that it had to be.'[59]

His fellow crew member, Bill Porter, says:

Dresden lay on a main railway line linking Berlin with Berchtesgaden, was a great junction on the east–west axis and so was an important target to take out. The fact that there were 130 small precision engineering works in Dresden as was revealed much later would have made it a target for that reason alone, but we didn't know that then. What happened because we set the city on fire was that those works were lost to the Germans.

I don't have regrets for bombing Dresden. It was my third operation and we were told at briefing that it was a transport centre. I think it was pretty bad that in February Churchill was asking Harris why he hadn't bombed Dresden and in March he was asking why we had. I stayed in the air force after the war and on a course in 1952 it was demonstrated to me what incendiary bombs did by candles being placed in a biscuit tin about an inch apart. They started lighting them from the centre outwards and they didn't have to light many before the whole thing was aflame. That's what incendiary bombing does.[60]

Ken O'Brien remembers:

Many years later I met a British prisoner of war whose camp was close to Dresden. He said they were cheering because the RAF were hitting the city. It was another step towards the end of the war. Afterwards on the station we were told there had been a concentration of German troops at Dresden.

Today I think about it that we were told to go, so we went. This was true of all our targets and of course the Germans attacked Coventry, York, Hull and places like that and look what London got. I think that the name Dresden has people thinking of Dresden china and so on.[61]

Derek Jackson visited Dresden by invitation in recent years and was thanked by a German Jew who considered he would not have survived had it not been for the attacks on the city.

During the time I was in Dresden I was asked many times if we should apologise for the bombing and each time I said, 'No way.' Dresden was just another target to us and at the time we were only trying to finish the war as soon as possible. What has to be remembered was at that time the Germans were murdering 10,000 Jews a week in God knows how many extermination camps – end of story.[62]

Even the eminent German writer W. G. Sebald, who criticised the decades of silence from Germany about Allied bombing, urged:

As we think of the nights when the fires raged in Cologne and Hamburg and Dresden, we ought to remember that as early as August 1942, when the vanguard of the Sixth Army had reached the Volga and not a few were dreaming of settling down after the war on an estate in the cherry orchards beside the quiet Don, the city of Stalingrad, then swollen (like Dresden later) by an influx of refugees, was under assault from hundreds of bombers, and that during this raid alone, which caused elation among the German troops stationed on the opposite bank, 40,000 people lost their lives.[63]

The attack on Dresden achieved its aim of dislocating the city as a rail transport and communications centre for the Eastern Front, the ensuing chaos then spreading to cause bottlenecks throughout Germany as all transportation-targeted raids did. A single railway track was reconnected in the city within days by a Herculean effort of General Erich Hampe, who headed a special section for repairing air-raid damage to the Reich's railways, using much POW labour, but for weeks there was no railway telephone system for instance. A total of 23 per cent of Dresden's industrial buildings were destroyed or severely damaged, along with more than 50 per cent of its houses. In total, 80 per cent of the buildings in Dresden suffered some form of damage and many workers were busy carrying out repairs to their homes, rather than attending to their lathes. There is the example that half the 14,000 employees of Dresden's biggest employers, Zeiss-Ikon, were absent in the rest of February.[64] In the clinical accounting of conflict, colossal damage had been achieved in Dresden by a total of 7,100 tons of bombs of all types dropped on the city during the war, compared to the cost in Allied effort and lives of 67,000 tons of bombs that fell on Berlin or the 44,000 tons on Cologne.

MANY who castigate Bomber Command and its leader for the bombing of Dresden use as the basis for their argument that the war was nearly over. The war was far from over – or indeed decided with absolute certainty – when the raids took place in mid-February. Montgomery's and Patton's armies would not be across the Rhine for another five weeks and the Russians were only just across the Oder. There were fears right to the end that the Nazis, who had given the Allies a severe bloody nose with the Battle of the Bulge beginning only two months before – causing 81,000 American casualties and 1,400 British   might produce some new terrible weapon far worse than the V-2 rockets then falling on London.

The only reason President Roosevelt had sanctioned the Manhattan Project, incidentally the day *before* Pearl Harbor, was because he had been told Germany – the birthplace of modern physics – was developing an atomic bomb. It was a reasonable conjecture that the German scientist Werner Heisenberg would succeed. After all, nuclear fission had been discovered in Germany, the Nazis had had sole access for years to the only uranium mines in Europe, and since 1940 the world's only heavy-water plant, in Norway, had been a German possession. The possibility of a Nazi atomic warhead being unleashed remained till the final surrender. In a post-war book Portal acknowledged this as he touched on Dresden, writing: 'There was the threat of other new weapons, there was even the risk of nuclear attack.'[65] The need to finish the war quickly was paramount in February 1945. As far back as the previous February the Reich Propaganda Minister Goebbels had told a confidential meeting of all Gauleiters: 'Retribution is at hand. It will take a form hitherto unknown in warfare, a form the enemy, we hope, will find impossible to bear.'[66] On 25 September, in a speech reported in the Reich Propaganda Ministry circular *Tatigkeitsbericht*, Hitler had told some of his troops: 'God forgive me if I have to turn to that terrible weapon to end the conflict.'[67] He could not have been referring to the V-1 or V-2, since they had already been launched against Britain. He may have been referring to a bomb that would release nerve gas, but it is likely he was referring to a nuclear weapon and Germany may have been further along the path to achieving this than has so far been released. Certainly the U-234 was on its way to Japan with highly radioactive material when it was captured by the US Navy in May. The contents of huge, gold-lined, sealed containers on the deck have never been revealed.[68] If the war in Europe had continued through the summer it is possible not only the Western Allies would have been in the nuclear club.

In fact, by the time Churchill penned his unappreciative memo to his Chiefs of Staff at the end of March the war on land was looking a lot more predictable than it had been in the middle of February. But falling in action was far from over in Bomber Command. Harris's young crews had been suffering much attrition since the beginning of the year. Between 1 January and 8 May 1,080 RAF and Commonwealth Air Force bombers were lost in Europe. A total of 664 of those went down after Dresden.[69] New crews were still arriving at the bomber stations, some just in time to die.

TEN

RECORD AND REVENGE

THE improvement in weather conditions in February meant the Bomber Command war machine stepped up a gear as Harris tried to make good the shortfall in High Wycombe's target list caused by the ice and snow that had gripped his bases the previous month. There were only five days or nights in February when the squadrons were not out in force, often as many as 1,000 aircraft being split between various targets at once. But the glacial conditions of January had severely restricted the training programme and there was a shock for crews who had begun their tours in the autumn and were beginning to view with hope the prospect of finishing intact. Early in February notices went up at the bomber boys' bases throughout eastern England that the length of a first tour was now thirty-six sorties, not the thirty it had officially been for the previous three years. 'This is, of course, to offset the shortage of crews coming through,' the statement at 467 RAAF Sqn's flight offices at Waddington read. 'With the very bad weather in January the training programme was held up for long periods.'[1] The collective groan could be heard almost to Berlin.

The severe weather had indeed disrupted the training programme and had added to the dangers on the few occasions when Bomber Command had been able to operate, as the Munich raid had proved. Crews considered that not only had they two enemies at this time, the Germans and bitter winter itself, but their individual trips were taking longer now that the battle front was moving further east. On the long-distance Dresden operation in which crews had had to battle against a 70 mph headwind on the return flight, several bombers had run short of petrol and had to put down in France – one being wrecked, and another two had been destroyed trying to land in Britain.[2] It took all the skill of a flight engineer to eke out the fuel on a long-distance trip, where bombs on target, not fuel, was the priority. Some engineers were outstanding. Sgt Ron Wood, who completed a tour on 626 Sqn at this time, found himself rapidly promoted in the week after the Dresden operation as attempts were made to reduce forced landings. He remembers:

> The Lancaster on average would do .9 or .95 miles to the gallon. I was getting 1.1, sometimes a bit more. One day I was told to report in best blue to the CO's office at Wickenby and was driven with him to Bomber Command headquarters. I was taken before Butch Harris. He had my log books in front of him and quizzed me for what seemed like two hours about how I could get 1.1. He then told me that for my efforts I was given seven days' leave and while I was at home I got a telegram appointing me to commissioned rank with another seven days' leave and clothing coupons to follow. Within two weeks of going back to my squadron I was engineer leader of 1 Group as a whole.[3]

Each aircrew trade had its own section office on a Bomber Command airfield and in the engineers' hut tips on how to get more miles per gallon from a Lancaster were eagerly discussed in February 1945, as long-distance targets in icy conditions became a regular feature. Sgt Edwin Watson, a flight engineer on 630 Sqn at East Kirkby, remembers:

> We used to go to our own small section room after morning inspection. We had talks there about the different matters affecting us engineers and I remember they used to pass round a huge container of cod liver oil capsules. We had to take about four of these damn capsules every day, apparently to keep the cold away when we were flying. I remember squatting in there one day near the stove when it jumped off the floor and the top flew off, filling the room full of fumes. One of the pilots had hooked a Verey

cartridge onto a long piece of wood and dropped it down the chimney.[4]

Any practical joke or humorous story was welcome to raise the spirits and an oft-repeated air force tale had particular relevance as forced landings became more likely from fuel shortage. It told of a crew whose compasses and wireless were shot away during a night raid on Germany and who found themselves lost in thick cloud above the occupied area of the Netherlands. In the first light of dawn they discovered they were flying above level pasture and made a perfect wheels-down landing. A peasant walked by and by gestures a crew member asked where they were. 'Olland,' the local replied. The crew then set fire to their bomber and were inspecting their escape maps when a man in familiar dark blue uniform cycled up and in perfect English asked if they needed an ambulance. They then discovered they were in the area near Boston known as Parts of Holland. The salutary story, apparently based on a true case, made many changes as it went the rounds and even turned up in *Tee Emm* magazine attributed to a Spitfire pilot.[5]

For those who had been approaching tour-end and now found themselves facing an extension to peril the story had a hollow ring. Edwin Watson had been within one trip of being officially tour-expired, on paper at least, when the new edict came in, but was finally screened in March after doing eight more ops. He says:

Once you saw your name on the battle order you had a queasy stomach. No aircrew could sleep before they took off to my knowledge. You knew it could happen that you got the chop. I did thirty-eight trips as a first tour because I did three trips as a spare engineer with other crews, then it was rumoured they wanted to put it up to keep the experienced crews on the squadron. They weren't losing as many in that last winter. Our last operation was on an oil refinery at Böhlen. We had been told before we went it would be our last.[6]

The youngsters who had just arrived on squadrons took the raised trip requirement with more equanimity. They were keen to get started and, unlike their more experienced colleagues, did not think it unfair that the air force could with one hand exact such harsh punishment on those who refused to complete a tour then with the other raise the number of trips required for that tour apparently at a whim. Scottish farmer's son Sgt John Simpson was among the new breed who had spent years trying to get on operations only to be shot down on his first trip.

He says:

I wanted to have a go at the Germans after seeing what they had done in the Fall of France and bombing London and Glasgow and other places and thought the RAF was the most effective way. So I volunteered in December '41 and, after medicals and interviews, in April 1942 I was classified as fit for training as a pilot or observer and was placed on 'deferred service' which was estimated to be about three or four months. But it was November 1942 before I was actually called up for aircrew. I was five months in London waiting for a ship for Africa for training then eventually started a pilot's course in Rhodesia. I was halfway through it when I was dropped off it and offered training as a navigator or bomb aimer. I thought if I could be a flight engineer it would be the nearest to flying the kite, so I asked for that and was sent home to start the course at St Athan.[7]

In February 1945 Sgt Simpson was posted to 218 Sqn at Chedburgh, Suffolk, and within a week was briefed for a 3 Group daylight raid by eighty-five aircraft on an oil plant at Gelsenkirchen, in the Ruhr, to be filmed from a 463 Sqn Lancaster. It was the day after Sgt Simpson's twenty-second birthday. He remembers:

I felt quite contented about going, I figured you never get shot down on your first op, but before I took off a pilot who had done several ops, but wasn't doing this one, asked where the target was and when I said Gelsenkirchen he replied, 'Oh, I didn't think they would give you such a hard one for your first operation.' As we went into the target I could see black puffs of flak bursting all around us. I was busy pushing out Window, and the bomb aimer was calling out to the pilot, 'Left a bit, right a bit,' and so on and eventually, 'Bombs gone.' We were hit by a flak burst at virtually the same time in the front of the bomb bay. The wireless operator, Sgt Doug White, called out, 'We're on fire, we're on fire,' and I grabbed an extinguisher and went back. To this day I've never seen anything like it. The fuselage was a mass of flames and I think the control wires were melting because the pilot had trouble handling the plane. In not more than a minute or so the pilot called out, 'Emergency. Jump, jump. Emergency. Jump, jump. Good luck, chaps.'

The pilot, F/O Johnny Muschamp, had done two trips as a second dickey. His father was a group captain and had come through the First World War and survived the Second and his son was killed on his first operation as a skipper. We were in a steep dive by this stage and the bomb aimer, Jim Halsall, who was the first to go, couldn't get out because the anti-G force was pushing us up towards the roof, but I gave him a push and then I went out after him. The navigator, Bill Porter, came behind me. The wireless operator was coming forward with the mid-upper, Sgt George Hogg, following. The wireless operator later said there was an explosion and he came to swinging on his parachute. When I went out I was tumbling over and over and when I pulled the D-ring it unexpectedly came away in my hand. I thought, 'Oh, God, the chute will not open now and at home they'll never know what happened. I thought that was it, then there was a tug and the parachute was open above me. I was so glad I could have climbed up and kissed it.

I made a pretty heavy landing in a field almost on top of the flak site that shot us down. I had cracked ribs, a cracked ankle, some cuts and burns on the face and a few bruises. A soldier from the flak site came across with a rifle. We had been told at base that Hitler had ordered all Allied airmen who came down to be shot, so I was looking round unsuccessfully for a brick or stone to defend myself. The soldier shouted, 'Americano,' and I said, 'No,' so he said 'Englander,' and being a good Scotsman I said, 'No.' He tried

'Canadian' then decided to give up. I was taken to the orderly room of the flak site. They were cock-a-hoop, fortunately, about shooting us down. In fact there were some girls there in civvies and they helped with my wounds. An hour or so later I was handed over to the Gestapo and then transferred to a nearby police station.

The navigator was brought in shortly afterwards. His face had been badly cut by the pack whipping up when the chute opened. He was followed by the wireless operator and finally the bomb aimer arrived. As the first out he had landed in the middle of Gelsenkirchen and been set on and beaten up by civilians, so he was a bit of a mess. In fact he died only five years after the war and his mother always said it was as a result of his injuries.

En route to the police station a Gestapo officer asked me: 'Why do you bomb women and children?' I told him: 'You started it,' and I got a good thumping from him. I knew if I had tried to defend myself or retaliate I would have been shot, being ringed by ten armed soldiers. We were in the police station three or four days. While I was there a Luftwaffe officer came to see me and told me my pilot and the two gunners* had been killed. He seemed sympathetic and I thought that was quite decent of him.[8]

John Simpson's troubles were far from over. In March and April he would be on the receiving end in RAF bombing raids and would twice be strafed by USAAF fighters before he reached a prison camp.

THE film of the Gelsenkirchen operation, in which the unlucky Sgt Simpson's aircraft was the only one to be shot down, yielded little intelligence as the bombing took place through thick cloud guided by GH. But there was a wealth of other filmed material for Bomber Command's senior officers to see at this time. The RAF Film Production Unit, formed in September 1941 to provide

* F/O Muschamp and Sgts George Hogg and Thomas Darragh are buried in the Reichswald Forest War Cemetery. Only Muschamp had reached the age of 21.

a historical record of the air war, was an extensive organisation by 1945. It spotlighted RAF activities at home and overseas, covering at various times the Middle East, North Africa, Canada, the USA, South-East Asia and Gibraltar and Malta as well as operations over Western Europe. Its cameramen usually had civilian experience and were given an air gunner's course before being posted to film operations. The headquarters were at Pinewood Studios, but the film unit attached to Bomber Command was based at Waddington near Lincoln with the Australian 463 Sqn. Aircraft carrying cameramen in this final stage of the air war also took a full bomb load.

The remarkable films they took became part of bi-monthly RAF newsreels known as the Gen, shown at camp cinemas throughout the world. Each ten- or fifteen-minute newsreel promised something stimulating as the title rolled over a whirling propeller and a clarion call from a bugle made the audience sit up. The clipped, upper-class tones of the commentator then bellowed out, sometimes in RAF slang, a diverse range of activities on and off the ground that month. In January 1945, for instance, there was film of the first WAAFs arriving in India and dogfights over Belgium as the Luftwaffe shot up Allied airfields on New Year's Day to great effect. In March Bomber Command was in the spotlight, shown dropping the 12,000-lb Tallboy bomb on the *Tirpitz*.

It was at home that the activities of Bomber Command were best appreciated. Most bomber airfields down England's eastern counties were lonely places with only the village pubs for solace if the truck into town had already filled up with the guardroom queue and left. So the camp cinema, which could range from a purpose-built concrete building, such as the one at Kirmington, to a temporary adaptation, like the hastily extended part of the airmen's mess at East Kirkby, was popular with both men and women. Hollywood films were shown free, with the Gen as a supporting programme. As the cigarette smoke from rows of blue serge uniforms curled lazily to the corrugated-iron ceiling, airman eyed WAAF and WAAF eyed airman. The Gen provided both of them with visible proof that their everyday lives were a link in

201

a chain of air force effort in which all pulled together that ended with bombs on target, bringing the war's end ever closer. A WAAF who had cheerily driven crews out to their Lancasters a week or so before or an erk whose fingers had turned blue as he changed engine magnetos in the cold could now see those same aircraft unloading over Germany. Watching the on-screen testimony to their usefulness made a change from the alternative of stuffing felt toys for local children or sitting in a ring round the gramophone at music appreciation classes, typical activities both on offer at snowed-in RAF Kelstern that winter.[9]

The film taken by the air gunner-cameramen of Bomber Command revealed a true picture of how hard the Reich was now being hit. Sometimes it was taken at great cost, thirteen members of the RAF Film Unit being killed in the course of the war. To obtain clear pictures the film unit Lancasters of 463 Sqn usually had to bomb from as much as 10,000 feet below the other aircraft in the stream and stay in the target area far longer, at constant risk of being hit by falling bombs. One of the young cameramen, James Hill, remembers: 'We arrived by Lancaster over a Bomber Command target with the Pathfinders then stayed for about twenty minutes as Main Force bombed. I'm surprised the casualty rate wasn't 100 per cent.'[10]

Just over a week after the Dresden operation a film unit-equipped Lancaster of 463 Sqn took a film of a night attack on Pforzheim. It is the iconic image of a frighteningly efficient RAF night raid in the latter stage of the bomber offensive, a bomb-aimer's view mesmerising in its intensity. Lakes of fire are joined by glittering ribbons of what were once streets of factories, shops and homes as Cookies flash, lighting up rolling clouds of smoke. Three hours later those fires would reach their zenith, linked in an all-consuming inferno. The raid killed a greater ratio of the population than the RAF's double blow on Dresden, yet comparatively little has been written about it, largely because of the Dresden backlash, initially inspired by Goebbels, obscuring objective analysis of the bombing war over the decades.

*

A YEAR or even months before, Pforzheim would not have been chosen for attack as it was, but the air war had now reached a stage where the smaller towns of the Fatherland would be pulverised for whatever industry or transport links they contained until the Reich had finally ceased to resist. In late June 1944, as the search continued for what would be worth attacking in future and what not, an RAF intelligence analysis had concluded that medieval Pforzheim on the northern edge of the Black Forest was 'one of the centres of the German jewellery and watch making trade and is therefore likely to have become of considerable importance in the production of precision instruments'. A German industrial guide published in August reported that 'almost every house in this town centre is a small workshop'. Certainly the time when workers in a Reich town would be allowed to continue with such peaceful activities as making jewellery was long gone and intelligence analysis before the raid suggested the craftsmen of Pforzheim, a third of whose citizens were members of the Nazi Party, were making fuses for V-2 rockets. All this apart, a north-south railway linking Pforzheim with Karlsruhe and Ludwig-shafen went through the town, it was the hub of a road system and it lay at the confluence of the Enz and the Nagold rivers. Destruction of the centre would therefore be likely to cause another bottleneck in the Reich network of transporting troops and armaments. That centre would be ripe for creating a firestorm because of its closely packed buildings in narrow, winding alleyways.

A firestorm was exactly what happened. The 1939 German census of people available for war work had shown Pforzheim had a total population of 79,000. On the night of 23 February 20,277 died, one in four of the population, compared with total deaths of approximately one in twenty collectively in the double-strike Dresden raid.[11] The efficient airmen of 5 Group, whose sector-bombing technique had lit the torch for Dresden, did not operate that night. The ability to create a firestorm was left to 1 and 6 Groups led by the Pathfinders of 8 Group, and a South African was appointed to be master bomber, Major Edwin Swales, of 582 Sqn, at Little Staughton, Huntingdonshire. Swales, whose close friend at the base, S/Ldr Robert Palmer, had been killed eight weeks before, winning a VC on a Cologne raid, had just had his portrait painted by the RAF war artist Sir William Rothenstein as a typical Bomber Command airman. But Swales was far from typical; he was already judged extraordinary, having being recommended for a DFC for his coolness on the very same Palmer VC-winning Cologne raid when his own aircraft was attacked five times by Luftwaffe fighters. As Swales went over the final details of the Pforzheim raid the *London Gazette* was carrying confirmation of his DFC that day. Swales, who had fought in the Western Desert in 1942 before re-mustering to aircrew, was within two trips of finishing his forty-five-operation Pathfinder tour when he took off for Pforzheim.

He was joined by 350 Lancasters of Main Force. They climbed out of their airfield circuits in poor conditions as the sun was setting and flew below cloud right across France, ascending as they entered south-western Germany to bomb. It was hoped the low approach would delay Luftwaffe reaction, but night fighters of II/NJG1 got into the stream as it arrived over the town from 7.50 p.m. The master bomber's aircraft was twice attacked as he orbited the target, his gunners unable to warn him because he was issuing instructions on VHF to the bombers. His aircraft was badly damaged, but Major Swales continued to control the bombing accurately, following the last of Main Force homeward. There was no flak to spoil bombing runs, because of the continuing need for all the 88-mm guns that could be mustered to face front-line tanks, and within twenty-two minutes 1,575 tons had fallen on the town centre. The hail of bombs caused the loss of two Lancasters, hit from above as they crossed the target in the converging stream. Canadian F/O R. D. Harris of 550 Sqn managed to bring his badly damaged aircraft back to the emergency airfield of Manston in Kent, but it crashed on landing, the crew escaping without injury. F/O D. R. Paige of 625 Sqn didn't make it home. He got back over the front line and France before he and his crew had to abandon their Lancaster.[12]

F/O David Francis, the 460 Sqn navigator, who had been in

the second wave of the Dresden attack, also took part in the Pforzheim operation. He says:

> It was only ten days later and I remember huge fires. Within three or four minutes of turning away from the target, as we were silhouetted against the fires, I imagine, we were attacked by an Me410. The rear gunner called starboard corkscrew and we could feel the vibration of the shells hitting. The starboard outer was hit and caught fire. We went into cloud and feathered it, but each time we came out of cloud we were attacked again, but not hit. This went on all the way to the French coast before the attacks ended, for about three-quarters of an hour to an hour. I think we all thought, Any time now he is going to be lucky. It was very tense. At the coast we got into cloud and I think we were at the end of the fighters' range because we didn't get any more attacks and got back to Binbrook.[13]

In planning the attack Bomber Command headquarters had assumed that because the Nazis had forgone defence of its citizens in Dresden in favour of employing the flak guns on the Russian Front the same would apply in Pforzheim and therefore a low-level attack could be mounted for greater accuracy. As a result, most crews were briefed to bomb at 8,000 feet. F/Sgt Jack Dunlop, a New Zealand navigator on 166 Sqn, remembers: 'We literally bounced across the target area because of air disturbance caused by bombing.'[14]

As in Dresden, although the initial fires were impressive, the incendiary bombs took time to fully establish uncontrollable fires ascending through each floor of wrecked buildings and it was not until 11 p.m. that the firestorm was at its height, raging in red and yellow growling fury through the narrow, cobbled streets of the town centre, then rising to make a funeral pyre of Pforzheim. It was fed by ice-cold air rushing in from the surrounding area to fill the vacuum created by the scorching, rapidly ascending air inside. A soldier in Pforzheim, Wilhelm Riecker, described what it was like as shelterers came out from underground to escape the heat.

They dunked blankets and towels in [a] bucket, wrapped them around themselves, and ran through the flames to the Enz River, where they doused themselves again with water, since the heat and flying sparks were incredible. Sedan Square converged the flames from all the streets leading into it and then let the scorching force escape towards the bridge. The flames shot over it into the city centre and there the mushroom rose steeply, drawing all the fire into its shaft. During this hour the radiant heat was so intense that people were jumping into the wintry cold river.[15]

By the time the firestorm took hold Edwin Swales was dead. He had got as far as Valenciennes, 250 miles from Pforzheim and well beyond the front line, then ordered his crew to bale out, but before he himself could jump the aircraft plunged into power lines. For his bravery that night he was awarded the Victoria Cross, the war's last Bomber Command VC of twenty-three awarded to bomber boys since 1940. The citation in the *London Gazette*, which had not caught up with his acting rank of major, read:

Soon after he reached the target area he was engaged by an enemy fighter and one of his engines was put out of action. His rear guns failed. His crippled aircraft was an easy prey to further attacks. Unperturbed, he carried on with his allotted task; clearly and precisely he issued aiming instructions to the main force. Meanwhile the enemy fighter closed the range and fired again. A second engine of Captain Swales aircraft was put out of action. Almost defenceless, he stayed over the target area issuing his aiming instructions until he was satisfied that the attack had achieved its purpose. It is now known that the attack was one of the most concentrated and successful of the war.

Captain Swales did not, however, regard his mission as completed. His aircraft was damaged. Its speed had been so much reduced that it could only with difficulty be kept in the air. The blind-flying instruments were no longer working. Determined at all costs to prevent his aircraft and crew from falling into enemy hands, he set course for home. After an hour he flew into thin-layered cloud. He kept his course by skilful flying between the layers, but later heavy cloud and turbulent air conditions were met. The aircraft, by now over friendly territory, became more and more difficult to control; it was losing height steadily. Realising that the situation was desperate Captain Swales ordered his crew to bale out. Time was very short and it required all his exertions to keep the aircraft steady while each of his crew moved in turn to the escape hatch and parachuted to safety. Hardly had the last crew-member jumped when the aircraft plunged to earth. Captain Swales was found dead at the controls. Intrepid in the attack, courageous in the face of danger, he did his duty to the last, giving his life that his comrades might live.[16]

Major Swales's aircraft was one of twelve lost in the raid, mostly brought down by night fighters, who had followed the stream out of the target. From 431 RCAF Sqn F/Lt B. M. Kaplansky, who had seen the centre of Pforzheim as 'a mass of flames' when he bombed halfway through the raid, was attacked no fewer than eight times by an apparently novice *Nachtjäger* pilot who must have thought the Lancaster was easy meat because only one of its rear-facing guns was serviceable, yet he was unable to draw a bead on the corkscrewing aircraft. Kaplansky told intelligence officers back at Croft:

Homeward a Ju88 was first sighted in the glow of fires, starboard quarter down at 600 yards. We corkscrewed to port. The rear turret and one gun in the mid-upper turret was u/s. The enemy aircraft came in three more times. The mid-upper gunner fired a long burst as we were corkscrewing and tracer was seen by the rear gunner to enter the enemy aircraft. He broke away to the starboard quarter down and came in on his fifth attack at 150 yards. The mid-upper gunner again opened fire and strikes were seen on his rear fuselage. He broke away to port down and came in 200 yards below and broke away to starboard. He came in again from starboard below and broke away to port, followed by another attack from port 250 yards away and he broke away to port and disappeared. During these attacks the enemy aircraft did not open fire.

Kaplansky won an immediate DFC for what was considered 'excellent airmanship'.[17]

The RCAF newspaper *Wings Abroad* also had other gunners to compliment for their skill and daring as it encouraged all those who flew with 6 Group:

> Two Canadian gunners in an RAF Lancaster proved themselves during Bomber Command's recent attack on Pforzheim. They are Sgt E.W. Farris, 19, of Fredericton, New Brunswick, and Sgt G.J. Cleary, 20, of Montreal. They were completing their twelfth op when a Jul88 turned to attack them after shooting down one of their bombers. They met the fighter's attack with a concentration of fire and sent the enemy down in flames. Before they had time to watch results a twin-engined fighter intercepted them. They poured fire at the second machine, which broke off its attack.[18]

The next morning as the burned body of Major Swales was found still gripping his aircraft controls, they were also counting the dead in Pforzheim. Friedrich Adolf Katz, who would eventually be mayor of the city rising from the ashes, gives a glimpse of the horrors in a contemporary report. 'Herr Oswald is dead, whose Jewish wife was taken away just a few days ago. The director of the Reichsbank, Blume, is dead. There is a huge bomb crater where the Reichsbank once stood. The whole family of Richard Kraft is dead, with whom I often discussed the hopelessness of the situation, and Herr Luplow, who felt so safe under concrete nine metres under the ground, is also dead.'

He was surprised, however, at how quickly people could recover.

> As long as the attack lasted people sat with their heads bowed. However, as soon as it was over, people breathed out, freed of an enormous pressure and full of energy and vigour. Of course I met many completely broken people, who were utterly distraught by the loss of their friends and family and their entire possessions and who could only cry and complain, but I spoke to just as many who were making determined plans for rebuilding everything and for

getting back on their feet. This will slowly dwindle as the grey everydayness returns. But what is distinctive is this powerful flame of life. I have never before seen how life and death belong together, how life grows out of death.[19]

The post-war British Bombing Survey Unit estimated that 83 per cent of the town's built-up area was destroyed, probably the greatest proportion of destruction in one raid during the war.[20] Pforzheim, which had been known in the Reich as Goldstadt (town of gold), had been reduced to such complete rubble it was days before the air-raid shelters could be opened to reveal the corpses of the bankers, lawyers, jewellers and watchmakers who carned the place its title. The Enz river through the town was full of the bodies of those who had drowned in its icy waters trying to escape the inferno. As the rubble was cleared to the outskirts it gradually grew into a hill, known as the Wallberg, which now overlooks Pforzheim.* A former resident, Gotthilf Beck Ehninger, returned from captivity in a British POW camp after the war to find his town ruined. His reaction was: 'I said to myself: "You did this, you're responsible," because of the way the younger German generation had allowed Hitler to take power.'[21]

But immediately after the raid there was no such impassivity. Goebbels's exhortations in print and broadcasts for the previous eight months that 'fighter and bomber pilots who are shot down are not to be protected against the fury of the people' had found ready acceptance among his fellow Nazis and among the recently bombed a moral excuse for venting their torment.[22] Those who had suffered loss in the firestorm, and the Nazis who fed on their anguish, were to wreak a terrible revenge within weeks.

*

* A new plaque placed on top of the Wallberg in 2002 referring to the raid as a horror of the Second World War, a war fomented by Nazi Germany, is a sign of the raw feelings still present in Pforzheim. Unlike the one it replaced there is no reference to the production of military equipment that went on in the town.

THE devastating success of raids such as those on Dresden and Pforzheim was due in considerable measure to the radio counter-measures war by which the RAF confused the Luftwaffe as to its intentions. Harris had set up 100 Group at the end of 1943, tasked with blinding enemy radar on the ground and in the air and diverting the attention of what was left. The group now consisted of thirteen squadrons equipped with Halifax, Stirling, Wellington, Mosquito, Beaufighter, Lightning, Liberator and Fortress aircraft. They were employed in creating Mandrel radar screens to hide an approaching force of bombers, dropping Window to make an airborne element seem more mighty than it was, gathering infor-mation on night-fighter wavelengths and jamming those fre-quencies. In the case of 100 Group's fighter elements aggressive Ranger patrols were mounted over *Nachtjäger* airfields to shoot down Luftwaffe aircraft at their most vulnerable time of take-off and landing, and intruder missions were launched whereby the Serrate homing device locked onto *Nachtjäger* radar transmissions, turning the hunters into the hunted. The high-flying Liberators and Flying Fortresses of the group had a particular role. They were packed with Jostle equipment, powerful transmitters for continuous wave-jamming of German R/T traffic.

The crew of such a Flying Fortress were returning from a Jostle patrol in support of an attack on the Lutzkendorf synthetic oil refinery on the night of 14 March when events unfolded in which they would be asked to pay the price for Pforzheim. Light flak coming up from near the shattered city set an engine of the B-17 on fire and the skipper, F/Lt John Wynne, ordered his nine crew members to bale out. He went to follow them but became so tangled up in his oxygen tubing that by the time he had extricated himself the fire was out. He arrived back alone at 214 Sqn's base at Bassingbourn as the rest of his crew were being captured. The navigator and bomb aimer were safely sent to a POW camp, but the other seven were kept in Buhl prison before being transferred to Pforzheim, a few miles to the north-east. On 17 March they were locked overnight in the boiler room of the Neuen Schule in the village of Huchenfeld on their way to captivity by the

Luftwaffe. Earlier that afternoon, aware that the airmen were on their way to Huchenfeld, the Kreisleiter of Pforzheim, Hans Christian Knab, told his Hitler Youth commander Max Kochlin to get hold of his boys for 'a demonstration' that night. Knab also told the commander of the SA at Dillweissenstein that his men would be taking part. A Luftwaffe guard had been in place outside the boiler room for only half an hour when a crowd of up to fifty civilians arrived and demanded access to the airmen, saying, 'We want to avenge our women and children.' The guard was powerless to stop the mob from bursting in and dragging the flyers outside on to Forstrasse.

One of the prisoners was F/Sgt Norman Bradley. He later reported:

As soon as we got outside the building I realised in all probability we were going to be hung or shot, so I decided to hang back with a view to escaping. I heard a scuffle in front of me as though another member of the crew was trying to escape. It might have been more than one. I tried to hang back and so did F/O Vinall with the two men who were holding him. There was another scuffle in front and it looked as if one of the members of the crew got away. The Germans who were holding us ran forward to give assistance and Vinall and I took the opportunity of hiding between a wall and a car. I heard two screams of pain. Vinall moved forward in the shadow and I followed him. The last thing I heard of him was his shouting to me to follow him. I shouted back that he was going the wrong way as he was going in the direction of the shooting, and I heard nothing more. I ran across some fences and wire netting and escaped across a field and into the woods. There were about six shots fired when Vinall shouted to me the last time. Later, while I was crossing the wire fence I heard further shots from automatic weapons, several bursts. I was later captured about 22 miles the other side of Pforzheim. The day after I was captured two of my guards told me that two members of my crew had been shot.[23]

The other crewman who had escaped was F/O Tom Tate. He remembers:

They wanted to kill us in the school, but the mayor of the village refused, saying that blood would be on the heads of the children for all time. So we were dragged outside and down the hill. When I realised we were about to be killed, a sudden burst of energy overcame me and I ran for it. I was barefoot and exhausted, but somehow I got away. The next day I was recaptured by the German Army and taken to a POW camp by two Luftwaffe escorts. I was treated according to the Geneva Convention and assured that my comrades were safe. One of my escorts even handed me a pair of boots. He explained that a woman in Huchenfeld, hearing of my plight, had sent them to me.[24]

The gunfire Bradley and Tate heard was the final sound in the lives of four of their crew – air gunners F/O Gordon Hall, F/Lt Sidney Matthews, F/Sgt Edward Percival and F/O Harold Frost – who had last been seen being forced towards the Huchenfeld cemetery. The flight engineer F/O James Vinall was recaptured the next day, and locked up in the police station at Dillstein, only a few yards from the Hitler Youth barracks. Kreisstabführer Niklas, a major in the Volkssturm, ordered Vinall to be released into his custody. Vinall was taken outside, where he was beaten about the head with a stick until he fell, then a Hitler Youth shot him in the back of the head.* After the war an Allied court sentenced the ringleaders of the POW massacre to hang and fifteen others were jailed for up to fifteen years.[25]

THE improved weather conditions in February brought other devastating RAF raids to German towns. Thirty-nine per cent of the built-up area of Worms was destroyed on 21 February. Kleve

---

* In 1989 a former German officer and retired pastor had a memorial plaque erected to the five murdered airmen. Six years later Tom Tate returned to the village by invitation as a gesture of reconciliation and met the woman who sent him the boots.[26]

was battered out of existence the night before an attack by the Fifteenth Scottish Division. Wesel, also on the Rhine battlefront, was so devastated in four raids on four successive nights from 16 February to prepare for an eventual crossing of the Rhine that only sixty buildings in the port were undamaged by the time the crossing took place. The old industrial town of Mainz lost more than 5,500 of its buildings, including most of the historic Aldstadt, in a raid by 458 aircraft on 27 February. The target list in February also added to the mounting casualty figures of Bomber Command, for instance fourteen Lancasters going down in an attack on Dortmund on 20 February. One of them was from the Polish 300 Sqn at Faldingworth where the flight engineer F/Sgt Henryk Drozdz, whose first operation had been to Dortmund at the end of November, recorded what he had seen on this second trip. He wrote:

We take off late but the visibility is good so the flight is not tiring. Somehow the flight is different than the first one – then it was daytime, today we are surrounded by night. It is a beautiful moonlit night. Wrr-wrr ... monotonous and menacing sound in my ears. Four Merlins like four night birds of prey rumble this wonderful tune of confidence and power. There are thousands, millions of stars and hundreds of these rapacious birds of prey are flying to Dortmund for a feast. 'Bombs gone.' We spend only a short time over the target. It looks the same as before: light as day, below us red explosions of 4,000lb bombs and we are above that. The night 'birds of prey' are returning, but not all of them. Below us and to the rear I see a Lancaster on fire. It is eerie – it's breaking up and falling, it could not hold on, maybe it is one of ours? We are returning by moonlight, here and there above us we see white streaks – it's the night fighter planes. You have to be vigilant. The three hours of return flight pass quickly. Let us land safely without further thrills.

Mother England greets us with thousands of lights. Here and there friendly beacons blink. We descend to 4,000ft. The ground can be clearly seen. We pass several airfields till at last the familiar letter 'FH' – Faldingworth. We land, but not everyone is so fortunate. Lieutenant Konarzewski with Lt Janczar's crew did not come back. One crew less. I feel sad for them – they shared my billet. I am especially sorry for 'Grandad' Jakimowicz.* He could easily have been my father, such a fine chap. May they rest in peace! It is all for 'Your freedom and ours'.[27]

The next night 18 aircraft were missing, 7 being lost over Duisburg and 11 out of 349 being destroyed in the Worms attack. The character of one man in the Duisburg attack would return to haunt F/Sgt Peter Bone, the mid-upper gunner on 626 Sqn who had begun his aircrew training as a putative navigator. In a private recording made two years after the war he said:

It was impossible to get to know more than a fraction of our fellow aircrew because of the sheer numbers. I think there was another reason: it was easier to handle losses if one didn't know too many bods, as we called each other. So most remained just names on the Battle Order and faces that never became more than just familiar. Most soon vanished from memory. One name and face however I'll never forget. It was that of Roderick Donner. He had been on my navigation course in Winnipeg a year earlier. He was probably ten years older than most of us and I think I regarded him as a kind of older brother. There was always a friendly grin behind that moustache and he smoked a pipe, which seemed to me to indicate stability.

Although I didn't know it Donner was home on compassionate leave for the birth of his first child. He just had time to bring his wife and baby boy home from hospital before catching a train back to Wickenby. There he found his crew were on the Battle Order that night ... T2 never came back.

In fact I wrote in my diary that night: 'Good bods, Pyatt, Donner etc. Cleaned bike, wrote home, had crumpets and cocoa for supper in the billet.' And that was all. At the time I gave no thought to

* F/Lt J. Konarzewski was killed but five of his crew, including F/Sgt W. Jakimowicz, baled out to become POWs after their Lancaster was hit by flak over Bergish-Gladbach, eventually exploding in the air.

Donner's personal life and probably gave no thought to whether he was married or not. He was just a 'bod' whom I liked from a distance, but who was suddenly gone like so many others.*[28]

W/O Harry Irons, the young 158 Sqn air gunner, was on the Worms attack the same night as the Duisburg operation. He remembers:

The pilot was a German Jew serving in the RCAF. He had left Germany before the war, but he didn't have an accent, he spoke perfect Canadian English. None of us knew he came from Germany but on the bombing run that night he called up to say, 'Chaps, I am just going to bomb my own town. This is where I was born.' It was a very clear night and you could see a lot, the fighters coming in amid the flak and everything The most amazing thing was that the blokes just carried on going straight in to the target even though they could see planes being shot down. The flak was very thick. I couldn't believe you could fly through it and come out the other side practically unscathed. I saw a huge explosion on our port side which I believe was an aircraft. I was the mid-upper gunner and I could see a lot of fire down below. You got the best view of all from the mid-upper turret.[29]

W/O Irons, who had joined the air force at 16, was now coming to the end of his second tour, one of the lucky few to survive so many operations, and six days after the attack on Worms he was called to briefing for the final time:

The gunnery officer on the squadron told me before I went that it was going to be my last trip. I did ask to go back for a third tour immediately afterwards, but they wouldn't have it, they said, 'You've done enough,' and I think they were right, my nerves were shattered by then. They sent me up to Kinloss to 19 OTU to be an

---

* F/O Roderick Donner, husband of Joyce Donner, of Bognor Regis, Sussex, is buried in Reichswald Forest War Cemetery with the rest of his crew apart from the 20-year-old Canadian rear gunner; W/O Bob Pyatt lies at Nederweert.

instructor. You always had a chit when you went to see the CO and when I reported to him on my posting I was gradually tearing this chit into teeny pieces and dropping them on the floor. When the CO saw that he said, 'I don't think you are suitable for here', and they posted me to Blackpool. They said, 'You were a tailor so you can go on a sewing machine.'[30]

In the subjective world of the combat airman in the wrong part of the sky the attrition in Bomber Command could seem no less in the closing months of the war than it had been in 1943 or 1944. Sometimes squadrons were severely punished with little to show for it. On the night of 2 February 5 Group sent 250 Lancasters and 11 Mosquitos to Karlsruhe, another gateway to the Black Forest near Pforzheim, but difficult marking conditions in cloud meant only a few bombs hit the town. There were no German casualties, yet fourteen bombers were lost.

Sgt Patrick Bell, the 20-year-old Canadian air gunner on 97 Sqn, was on the raid. 'It was our twenty-first trip and was a very hot target with lots of flak. All the way into the target I could see the red bursts of the flak exploding. I can't believe now I had the courage then to fly through stuff like that. It was just terrible with searchlights waving across and everything firing. I consider we were very lucky.'[31]

Among the fourteen bombers missing, no fewer than four were from 189 Sqn, which had only been in existence since October in the final expansion of Bomber Command. Of the four only the rear gunners in each survived, saved by the new seat pack now being issued. One of them was Canadian F/Sgt Donald Clement. His RCAF skipper, 22-year-old F/Lt Norman Blain, had arrived over the target area to find like most that night that there were no Pathfinder target indicators. As F/Lt Blain debated the next move with his bomb aimer he flew past Karlsruhe with his full bomb load still on board. F/Sgt Clement remembers:

About three minutes after leaving the target area we were hit from below. Nothing was seen and the only indication was four or five quick thuds; then a big explosion and fire which only lasted a few seconds. I had my hands covering my eyes and face then everything was quiet.

I looked around and discovered that I was freefalling from three miles up in the rear turret and I knew it would be about ninety seconds before I hit the ground. I reached behind to open the sliding doors and discovered that all the framework, doors and the Plexiglass had been blown away in the initial blast. All that remained was what I was sitting on and the gun mechanism. I tried to push and kick the turret away, so I could pull the ripcord. My feet were stuck and all the kicking and pushing would not free them. My time was running out. What I did next was not what I wanted to do, but I had no choice. I bent forward as much as possible to help free my seat-type parachute, then pulled the D-ring with both hands ... As the chute opened the remains of the turret disappeared and my legs were not injured when it pulled free. As I drifted down my thoughts were on the rest of the crew. I figured no one could survive an experience like that.*[32]

Falling gently through the cold night air towards an uncertain future the 21-year-old air gunner discovered he had been hit in the fleshy part of the shoulder by the night fighter whose Schrage Musik had exploded the aircraft's bomb load. As the ground came into view he inflated his Mae West. He remembers:

The chute caught the edge of a tree and my feet were on the ground. The chute was quickly pulled down and taken to the nearest bushes and trees. There I stayed for about two hours, resting and planning the next move. It was about 11.45 when I came down and I had to figure out where I was. In the distance I could see a slight glow in the sky which was the target area of Karlsruhe and I estimated it to be about 12 miles away. Using the escape map and compass it was evident I was north-east of the target area. The Rhine would be about 20 miles to the west. I didn't think there would be a chance

* F/Sgt Clement was correct. The remains of his comrades, with whom he had completed twenty-three operations, are buried in Durnbach War Cemetery after being found individually near Heidelsheim.

of crossing a bridge without getting caught; my best bet was due
south to Switzerland.

F/Sgt Clement cut up part of the parachute to make bandages
for his shoulder wound and took off his flying suit and uniform
insignia, hiding them as best as he could.

The large, grey woollen scarf I had was perfect for a hat and neck
wrap. It was now about 1 a.m. and I was feeling more confident
that no one saw me coming down. I heard one German plane circle
round, but could not see it . . . Next I heard a rumbling noise getting
closer and then a locomotive went by about 100 feet away . . .
I walked through the woods till daylight, found a dry spot and
stripped to the waist. I was in good shape from the waist down,
but the rest of me was not a pretty sight. I picked out bits of clothing
from the open wound in my shoulder and wrapped it up with chute
material as best I could. After getting my clothes back on I checked
my escape kit thoroughly and went over my map. There was a
river running east and west and then the city of Pforzheim in the
general direction I was going to take. On the way I filled my water
container and put a purifying pill in.

Eventually F/Sgt Clement reached the river and after checking
that no one was around came out from cover to see there was a
bridge ahead with a city or large town on the other side. He
decided to go back under cover until night came.

There was a walking trail parallel to the river that I thought would
give a better view and a spot to rest till after dark. I had just gone
a short distance down the trail when around a bend I came face to
face with a German soldier. We made eye contact and I lowered
my head and almost touched shoulders as we passed. I expected
him to say something, but not a word was said. He was the first
person I had seen. I left the trail and went down a hill and rested
till after dark.

F/Sgt Clement crossed the bridge in the night and saw a sign
reading Pforzheim, then Stuttgart 30 kilometres, which gave him

an exact pinpoint. Over the next night and a day he kept travelling south at night, resting up during daylight. His only food was parsnips he found in a field and on 5 February a civilian turned him in to the authorities. He was taken to the POW hospital at Rottenmunster and finished the war in Stalag VIIA at Moosburg, where he joined other Canadians, Australians, New Zealanders and Britons from Bomber Command's 'heavies' being shot down in the final, crushing phase of the bombing war.

But apart from those in four-engined Lancasters and Halifaxes there were crews of other aircraft from the Bomber Command flight line which were now adding considerably to the rubble mountains of the Reich's towns. And, unlike their comrades in the squadrons of the four-engined, they were suffering proportionately little for it. The Mosquito pilots and navigators in the Light Night Striking Force would have been happy to know their nocturnal jabs irritated Goebbels most of all.

ELEVEN

STING OF THE MOSQUITO

REALITY was an infrequent visitor in the last chapter of the National Socialist Party that Josef Goebbels would finally visualise as the Twilight of the Gods. The Armageddon now taking over the Reich, which in a more rational regime might have produced a suspicion of justice for the misery the Nazis had inflicted on other nations, in fact drove the Propaganda Minister to new extremes of vengeance. In February he wanted all British and American pilots in POW camps shot and Germany to renounce its signature of the Geneva Convention. This he believed would have the dual effect of stopping Allied bombing and of deterring German soldiers from surrendering in the West for fear they would be executed in turn by the Allies.[1] Goebbels did not have a problem with defection on the Eastern Front. Russian troops were now exacting such a revenge for the country's 26 million war dead that few prisoners were being taken.

There was no doubt that bombing, which for two years had prevented German industry expanding sufficiently, was at last bringing that same industry puffing and clanking to a halt. It had forced war plants into smaller, camouflaged premises, into forests and even below ground. Factories were not now started up because of nearby resources or technical capacity but merely because of geographical position. When the time came for the finished part of an aircraft or tank to be shipped to another plant to marry with other components it was likely to be held up in a siding because of RAF bombing of transportation targets elsewhere. Eventually it too would be smashed to smithereens in its box car. By the autumn of 1944 the war industries were living off accumulated stocks of materials and it was clear to all but men such as Goebbels that eventually stocks would run out. In early March Speer told Hitler the German economy was doomed. He was ordered to operate a scorched earth policy as the Russians had in the successful German drive towards Moscow in 1941, destroying every factory or food source in the Allies' path, thus condemning the threatened German population to starvation. Speer, who had privately decided to disobey, went to see Goebbels, who recorded on 14 March: 'Speer's view is that economically the war is more or less lost. At the present rate the German economy can hold out for another four weeks and then it will gradually disintegrate ... He is very much opposed to the scorched earth idea. He says that if the life-lines of our food supply and our economy are to be snapped, it is not for us but for our enemies to do it.'[2]

In the dogma-dominated world of Josef Goebbels, defeat was unthinkable. He considered Speer had been too influenced by what he had seen on the Western Front 'and cannot look at these matters from the necessary distance'. Goebbels's verdict was: 'At times like this it is essential to take an adequately long-distance view of things. Looked at close to the impression they give is naturally terrible sometimes.'[3] In fact what was now happening to Germany as a result of the Nazis' policies could not be more terrible. The question must therefore be asked: did Goebbels know of some new frightful German weapon – as yet unrevealed as wartime secret papers are released – that would definitely turn the tide? Certainly he urged Hitler now to use Tabun nerve gas in the field.[4]

Whatever weapons were possibly becoming available, given enough time, their use on the Allies was not likely to cause Goebbels sleepless nights, but the bombing war did. The mounting chaos being caused to Reich industry, fuel supplies and transportation by Bomber Command in 1945 impressed and depressed him. In the final, surviving volume of Goebbels's diaries which run from 27 February to 9 April there are fifty-one references to RAF and American bombing operations. On 28 February he wrote: 'Once more a series of very heavy air raids thundered down on the western areas of the Reich,' and admitted: 'We are completely defenceless against this raging enemy air war.'[5] The next day after recording further heavy air attacks he wrote in desperation: 'The less said on the question of the air war the better.'[6] And on 22 March: 'It is hardly worth recording the daily series of air raids which thunders down on the Reich hour by hour. There is hardly any defence to be seen. One can imagine what the effect is on public opinion.'[7] The following day he admitted: 'In the West the air war is the alpha and the omega,' and continued, 'among most sections of the German people faith in victory has totally vanished. People wonder whether a counter-offensive in the East is possible at all. They give nothing whatsoever for the prospects of our air defence.' He commented that refugees from the East put 'a better face on things than those from the West. Those from the West are too worn out by air raids for their morale still to be totally intact.'[8] It was this collapse that Harris had been aiming to achieve for more than two years.

Ranged against Reich industry, its transportation network and its oil supplies in the winter of 1945 were the ninety-six heavy and light squadrons of RAF Bomber Command; their brothers in arms based in England, the USAAF Eighth Air Force, now mounting raids by more than 1,000 bombers at a time with almost as many accompanying fighters; the USAAF Fifteenth Air Force from Italy which could hit targets in southern Germany and Austria with 500-bomber raids; and even the Red Air Force. In 1945 the Soviet war machine produced 20,900 aircraft of all types; 7,500 alone were set aside for the final battle to take Berlin. But it was the threat from the Anglo-American air forces in Britain that was most obvious to the average German. The British wartime investment in creating seven hundred of what we would think of in size as municipal airports today had brought a new tag for England by the Americans stationed here of 'the biggest aircraft carrier in the world'. The USAAF and RAF bomber squadrons sometimes competed for the sky over eastern counties and as 1945 progressed the increased air traffic could produce unforeseen problems.

F/Lt Peter Johnson, a tour-expired Lancaster pilot, was

instructing in 1945 at 1167 HCU at Sandtoft, North Lincolnshire, when the USAAF dropped in. He remembers:

> On 16 January a force of USAAF Flying Fortresses had to abort their mission because of bad weather and were ordered to land at RAF fields in Yorkshire and Lincolnshire. Thirty-six of them were supposed to divide themselves between Sandtoft, Lindholme and Finningley, but they all followed one another into Sandtoft. They were spread all over the grass, parked simply everywhere. Fortunately the airfield was built on sand so there was no danger of them getting bogged in. Suddenly Sandtoft had 360 extra airmen to feed and nothing to give them. The Americans got onto their bases and within an hour or two a convoy of US lorries came up, loaded with supplies. That night, as they were still socked in, they wanted to be let loose on Doncaster, but only had their flying clothing, so we fixed them up with whatever we could find in the way of old tunics and trousers. They went out wearing bits of RAF blue with American khaki and looked quite a sight. Before they flew off the next day they stuffed our pockets with US cigarettes and candy and, of course, left a load of American tinned food behind. There were cans of peaches and pineapples we hadn't seen in a long time. We lived like kings for weeks.[9]

But perhaps the most economical air force ranged against the Reich was the Mosquito Light Night Striking Force of Air Vice-Marshall Don Bennett's 8 (PFF) Group. Harris disliked Bennett's title for his twin-engined bomber squadrons. It was the 'Light' that irritated Harris, a heavy bomber man and a keen advocate of the Lancaster, and he suggested 'Fast' instead of 'Light' might be more appropriate, but 'Light' stuck. In fact there was nothing light about what the Mosquito could deliver. The Mk B XVI version could carry a 4,000-lb Cookie to Berlin, two-thirds of the bomb load a Flying Fortress usually transported to the same target and with only one-fifth of the crew. The twin-engined aircraft would also suffer far fewer losses, staying away from trouble because of its high cruising airspeed of 405 miles per hour and the height bands at which it could operate. The Wooden Wonder, developed by de Havilland in 1941, had been a winner for Bomber Command since early 1943, when it had proved invaluable as a carrier of the Oboe signal to mark targets in Germany for Main Force. In January 1943 Mosquitos had bombed Berlin in daylight, interrupting a radio broadcast by Goebbels, and when the heavies of Bomber Command had been forced to withdraw from attacking the Reich capital in March 1944, because of heavy losses, Mosquitos had continuing carrying the bombing war to Berlin as part of the LNSF. By 1945 the LNSF had become an air force in itself. The Mk B XVI, which had a swollen bomb bay to accommodate the oil drum-shaped Cookie, ensured raids in strength to Berlin that could carry out substantial nocturnal damage became a routine in the closing months of the war.

News of the united force of light bombers was revealed to the air-minded public in *Flight* magazine as 1944 closed. 'LNSF is run by the Pathfinder Force and all crews are required to go through the specialised Pathfinder training course. This special training is the root of the wonderful accuracy obtained by LNSF crews in their bombing attacks on the enemy,' the magazine related excitedly, explaining that the raids involved flying for protracted periods at great height.

> To help in this matter a pressurised cabin version of the Mosquito was evolved especially for the LNSF and was designated the Mk VI [it was actually the Mk B XVI in bomber versions]. It was realised that puncturing of the pressure cabin by flak or bullets would cause grave physical damage to the crew if the normal inside pressure was much above the atmospheric pressure obtaining and thus it was decided to pressurise the cabin only to 2lb/sq.in over the external atmospheric pressure. In effect this gives interior cabin pressure equivalent to that of a height about 5,000ft below that at which the aircraft is flying. At extreme altitudes this is a very valuable asset in combating fatigue and discomfort, and maintaining a reasonable reaction period. The Mosquito VI is fitted with Merlin 70 series engines. Ceiling is over 36,000ft and it has a maximum speed of over 400mph, whilst range is over 1,500 miles

for the bomber version and over 2,000 miles for the PR type. Bomb load is one 4,000 pounder or six 500 pounders – one under each wing and four in the bomb bay.[10]

Not surprisingly, among pilots and navigators keen to carry out a second tour competition was intense for that tour to be on Mosquitos. There was also a much higher chance of survival than on the heavy bombers of Main Force, so the RAF made the requirement for completing a Mosquito tour fifty operations. It was more than a fair bargain in the survival stakes where a Mosquito could outpace any conventional night fighter and usually soar way above the flak. Six of Bennett's squadrons were eventually equipped with the Mk B XVI.

The LNSF was indeed a unit of glamour in the eyes of the press and public and its crews were aware of it. Among those who had managed to wangle a posting to the new unit was 22-year-old F/Lt Percy Brunt who had spent a long time as a staff pilot at the training unit RAF Ashbourne in Derbyshire. He became engaged as he began his tour on 692 Sqn in this final period of the bombing war and his letters to his Wren girlfriend Rosalind Newman-Newgas, who was stationed in central London, evoke a time of longing and anguish now forgotten. 'Since my last letter we have become a squadron of film stars!' he wrote in late October. 'The newsreel bods are making a film of the Light Night Striking Force – that's us in case you don't happen to know. Take off, landing, formation, beat up and also briefing were filmed and we have all decided against Hollywood as the directors are a binding lot of BFs – they haven't the slightest glimmer of a clue.'[11]

On 3 November after taking part in a raid on Osnabrück he wrote: 'Had a hell of a binding morning, had to go to the dentist through losing a stopping last night while stooging over the Third Reich. But they lost a lot more though by all appearances.' Four days later he was describing the previous night's 'hell of a party for which everybody has been preparing for weeks. It went with a big swing. The idea was of the aircrew entertaining the ground staff as we all had to contribute one day's pay and give them all a really good time.' A really good time had included all ranks standing round the officers' mess piano and singing the squadron song. It went:

> *We fly alone when all the heavies are din-ing*
> *692 will be climbing*
> *We still press on*

and ended:

> *It's always the Reich, no matter how far*
> *One bomb is slung beneath*
> *The crew they are a twitching*
> *It's not fear of ditching*
> *It's 12 degrees east*
> *One engine at least!*

In December Rosalind was due a few days' leave and the young pilot wrote: 'I made enquiries about a room in Hunts if you would like to come up during your long weekend.' On Thursday 14 December, when fog had socked in the Bedfordshire air bases including Twinwoods Farm where Glenn Miller was about to take off for Paris on his final flight, F/Lt Brunt wrote: 'By this time tomorrow I shall be feeling a little more human because you will be just about being F.O.S. preparing to come up here. As far as I can arrange everything at this end is in order, the only thing is that I am not yet certain when I shall get off on Friday evening.' Rosalind did apparently make it, but their reunion was brief. In the afternoon of Sunday F/Lt Brunt took off with 43 other Mosquito crews for a spoof raid on Hanau while 850 heavies were between them bombing Duisburg and Ulm. On return to Graveley his aircraft overshot the runway and crashed among trees. The wreckage of the wooden aircraft caught fire and both Percy Brunt and his married Canadian navigator, F/Sgt Roger Sutherland, were killed His fiancée's subsequent diary entry for 19 January 1945, the first she was able to make after the crash, reads: 'I miss my darling so much. Why does one have to go on.'[12]

F/Lt Brunt's loss was particularly cruel in an area of Bomber Command operations where survival was more likely than in most. Of the 27,000 sorties flown by the Light Night Striking Force only 108 ended in the loss of the aircraft. In the final months of the campaign losses were down to 1 per 2,000 sorties. The group's Mosquitos attacked Berlin on 170 nights, sometimes with as few as six aircraft. From 1 January until 20 April, when Russian artillery began bombarding the capital in the final assault, 3,900 Mosquito bomber sorties were dispatched to the Big City, dropping more than 4,400 bombs, including 1,479 Cookies. The apex was the night of 21 March 1945 when there were 139 Mosquito sorties against Berlin, 42 of the crews bombing the city, returning to base then handing over their aircraft to armourers and petrol bowser attendants for other crews to take the same aircraft back to the Big City that night. The nuisance raiders, which for two-thirds of the time operated when the rest of Bomber Command was grounded, didn't just go to Berlin. Mosquitos also made 'Siren Tours' over Germany, each aircraft bombing targets in four different towns in one sortie.[13]

They could strike with apparent immunity, but they didn't always get away with it. The 105-mm anti-aircraft gun had been introduced by the Luftwaffe in the middle of 1943 and in 1945 declining numbers tended to be sited around Berlin, to catch the high-flying Mosquito. The 105-mm Flak 38 weapon could hurl a 33-lb charge up to 37,400 feet, exploding with a lethal radius of 50 feet.[14] Even the 88 mm was a threat to Mosquito crews when they were called on to operate at lower heights or they dived on the bomb run, as was usually the case.

W/Cdr Robert Bray, who had completed two tours in Bomber Command by the middle of 1944, volunteered for a third tour beginning in March 1945 as the CO of 571 Sqn, part of the LNSF. He flew eight missions, ending on 26 April, bringing his total number of operations to ninety-four, and even at that stage of the war found that enemy flak could still be deadly. He remembers:

All but two of the eight were to Berlin. The LNSF were putting a considerable force of nuisance raiders over Berlin at that time to maintain the pressure and keep the population awake. We dropped a 4,000-lb bomb on each occasion. On my ninetieth operation on 21 March I took part in the biggest LNSF operation to Berlin to date, bombing at 27,000 feet as part of a force of 100 Mosquitos, and there was no flak seen at all. But even at that period of the war the defences could still be considerable and on my next operation, on 4 April, an aileron cable was cut through by flak over Berlin at 23,500 feet and on the operation after that, flying at 22,500 feet on 10 April, I was hit by flak once more over Berlin, in the port wing.[15]

However, damage to and losses of the Mosquito were still slight and such apparent inability to down the small but deadly nightly raiders on Berlin and other German cities in 1945 irritated Goebbels mightily. As his diary opens on 27 February he writes: 'During the night the cursed Englishmen return to Berlin with their Mosquitos and deprive one of the few hours' sleep which one needs more than ever these days.'[16] It was a theme that would continue without a break, often by eighty or ninety aircraft, until Berlin came within Russian artillery range. But it was the night of 13 March when the air war suddenly became personal for Goebbels. After recording that 'These Mosquito raids are becoming heavier and more distressing day by day, above all they are doing great damage to the Berlin transport system,' the Propaganda Minister wrote painfully:

This evening's Mosquito raid was particularly disastrous for me because our Ministry was hit.

'The whole lovely building on the Wilhelmstrasse was totally destroyed by a bomb. The throne-room, the Blue Gallery and my newly rebuilt theatre hall are nothing but a heap of ruins. I drove straight to the Ministry to see the devastation for myself. One's heart aches to see so unique a product of the architect's art, such as this building was, totally flattened in a second. What trouble we have taken to reconstruct the theatre hall, the throne room and the Blue Gallery in the old style! With what care have we chosen every fresco on the walls and every piece of furniture! And now it has all been given over to destruction. In addition fire has now broken out in the ruins, bringing with it an even greater risk since 50 bazooka missiles are stored underneath the burning wreckage. ... I am overcome with sadness. It is 12 years to the day since I entered this Ministry as Minister. It is the worst conceivable omen for the next 12 years.[17]

It was indeed, delivered with efficiency by the economic Wooden Wonder of the LNSF.

NO aircraft in the Second World War was more adaptable than the Mosquito. Geoffrey de Havilland's design dates from 1938 and was not initially well received by the Air Ministry, but the speed of 392 mph the prototype demonstrated in its first official test flight in February 1941 quickly led to orders, particularly when it was realised it would use labour not then directly employed in the war effort, Britain's furniture makers. In fact flaps, flap shrouds, fins, leading edge assemblies and bomb doors were produced a short distance from Harris's headquarters in High Wycombe, Buckinghamshire, a town that had a well-established pre-war furniture-manufacturing industry. Among the firms making fuselage shells was the Parker Knoll company famous for its armchairs, supplied before the war to the more earth-bound warriors in the RAF.

The Mosquito had first proved its worth with Bomber Command as Harris's offensive got under way in early 1943. Its then 30,000-foot ceiling made it the ideal Pathfinder aircraft to carry the Oboe signal – restricted by the curvature of the earth – to the Ruhr's cities, thus enabling the devastation of the heavy industry within them. Among the many subsequent uses for the Mosquito, sometimes known as the Timber Terror because of the load it could deliver, was as a photo-reconnaissance aircraft, low-level Pathfinder, fighter/bomber, mine-layer, anti-shipping strike aircraft, clandestine courier to and from neutral Sweden and night-fighter intruder. It was in this role that it had turned the tide of attrition against Bomber Command by switching the hunting Luftwaffe *Nachtjäger* into the hunted. A total of 7,781 of all types were built during the war, being used by Coastal, Fighter and Bomber Command, but it was night intruder operations, whether with Fighter or Bomber Command, that could be among the most dramatic.

F/Lt Tony Brandreth was a Mosquito intruder pilot with 613 Sqn, based near Cambrai, northern France, from November 1944. Most operations were planned to find enemy traffic of any kind as part of the Allied Transportation Plan. He remembers.

Trains were the prize target. We were deliberately seeking out railway lines and it was surprising how much you could see at night. Generally in a patrol area we would be on the prowl at about 2,000 feet – you could spot trains by their smoke. Some were well guarded by flak wagons at the rear, sometimes at the centre or front. Because of train noise the gunners wouldn't hear you coming on the initial attack. I had great respect for those fellows; whereas we could stalk a train in the darkness for subsequent attacks they were sitting ducks, but they stuck to their guns to make things difficult.[18]

On the night of 29 January the pilot was patrolling Coesfeld, west of Münster while other Mosquito crews were bombing Berlin. He recalls:

There was a high moon shining through a veil of high cirrus and I observed the glint on a spread of railway tracks forming a railway junction in this small town – an unmissable target. I positioned appropriately and attacked with our four .303 Brownings and four 20-mm Hispano cannon and two of our four 500-lb bombs. Unseen flak came up as we were climbing away – no tracers – and five irregular thumps indicated flak hits. Three took bites out of the sides of the rear fuselage and two others punched a hole about 16 inches in diameter through each of the wings – near the trailing edges and almost symmetrically – with resulting damage to aelirons and flaps. The aeliron control on the control column went all floppy and the aircraft was gradually turning over to starboard. I shouted to my navigator, Les Day, to bale out. At the same time I was trying to do something about our predicament. With aeliron control hard to port, maximum port rudder and extra revs from the starboard engine, corrective action seemed to be lifting the starboard wing, so within seconds I cancelled the bale-out order just as Les was reaching to jettison the exit door.

Our attitude was crabwise but at least level, with engines de-synchronised. I could only turn with difficulty to port – daren't risk a turn to starboard because the aircraft could flick over out of control. It was all a bit dodgy; however the flak hits had miraculously missed the engines, fuel tanks and Les and me. To get onto a heading for base we made a painfully wide 300 degrees turn to port – further into enemy territory in the process. Background rustle to and fro in the R/T headphones indicated that enemy radar might be picking us up, which prompted a climb to 6,000 feet, to hide in a layer of cloud. I didn't want to be jumped in our delicate condition.

In due course we reported our damaged state to base and requested plenty of room on the circuit. By this time I had almost got used to our bizarre style of flying and checked that the under-carriage was OK. I daren't try the flaps. They were certainly messed up and I was apprehensive about final approach at a higher speed than usual in no-flap mode. Nevertheless it would be lower speed than cruising, meaning less airflow over already critically messed-up control surfaces. All was OK until the last 300 feet when sure enough the starboard wing started to drop gradually beyond my control. I couldn't allow the wing tip to hit the ground first – would be messy – so I shoved the nose down sharply to get the starboard wheel on the runway as soon as possible. There was a huge thump and the starboard undercarriage folded as did the other one. In prang circumstances the prop blades would normally be curled back, but not this time. I have a clear recollection of the props ripping off and spiralling ahead into the darkness. There was much grinding and crunching. Les hit the engine foam tits and it all went quiet. The aircraft had slewed off the runway and described a full circle on the grass to end up pointing in the direction in which we landed. The aircraft was written off. Nothing like laminated monocoque plywood for getting you home! But I was vexed beyond words not to have spared Q-Queenie, in the last few seconds, the indignity of being written off.[19]

Two weeks later F/Lt Brandreth found himself in trouble again over Germany.

On the night of 14 February we were on low-level night patrol flying a course we had selected that crossed a succession of six railway lines to the west of Mönchengladbach and Krefeld. I spotted smoke from a train too late to get down to it and immediately did a tight turn onto a reciprocal course, hoping to find it again. In the process I flew even lower, only to be caught in a single searchlight beam from starboard at a very shallow angle. It was instantly accurate and must have been radar-controlled. I flew even lower and low-angle flak tracer was streaming over the top of us. It was a hairy few seconds before we got away as I sensed that, on this dark night and with the distraction of the beam, we were too damned close to the ground for comfort. We didn't find the train again.[20]

F/Lt Frederick Crawley was a navigator who had completed a tour on Halifaxes in 1943, winning the DFC, and in September 1944, as he began a second tour that took him to the end of the war, considered himself lucky enough to be fulfilling that requirement on Mosquitos. He was based at Upwood, Hunts, on 139 Sqn. The squadron was part of 8 Group's Light Night Striking Force, but often provided Pathfinders for Main Force. He says:

In operations I found the difference between the Halifax and the Mosquito startling. The performance of the aircraft was very comforting. No longer the long slog back against the prevailing wind, a much shorter time in the target area and not too much interference from night fighters and flak. Speed was of the essence ... If they were going to find you there was not very much time and normally there would only be one chance ... Of course we had losses. I can remember one Mosquito being caught by an Me262 in the Berlin area for example, but it is my opinion more aircraft were lost from malfunction and bad weather, particularly at base upon return, than enemy defences. Mosquito operations were frequently flown in atrocious weather. One such I remember vividly: taking off and almost immediately in cloud with thunder and lightning, using radar to circumnavigate cunim clouds, finally to emerge in clear skies at around 25,000 feet with wonderful white tops of rolling clouds and being suspended in space with no sensation of movement.[21]

Alf Rogers was a Mosquito intruder navigator with 515 Sqn at Little Snoring, Norfolk, part of 100 Group. His eleven-month operational tour, which took him right to the squadron's disbandment at the end of the war, consisted of hampering the Luftwaffe night-fighter effort by patrolling a pre-selected *Nachtjäger* airfield as the Bomber Command stream passed overhead. 'Invariably when a Mosquito arrived the aerodrome switched off all lights and closed down,' he remembers. 'As a result the number of enemy aircraft destroyed was very low. The value of intruding was not so much that enemy night fighters were destroyed, but rather that they were persuaded to stay on the ground.'[22]

Navigation in a Mosquito was a world away from course-plotting in a heavy bomber, where the navigator had his own curtained-off area, a selection of instruments and a table to work on. His opposite number in the light aircraft had only his lap on which to balance a map and little more than a pencil, a ruler and a rudimentary Dalton wind and course calculator strapped to his knee. The fact that operations were always at low level, thus reducing the field of vision, didn't help at all. W/O Rogers remembers:

A typical night intruder op began by crossing the North Sea at less than 500 feet. In this way we were too low to be detected by German radar. The Dutch coast was crossed at a point 5 miles north of Egmond. From there on navigation was by map reading which could be difficult on a dark night. Water features showed up quite well, so these were used as pinpoints. After crossing the coast the next turning point was the distinctive mouth of the Ijsell river on the eastern side of the Zuider Zee. Then on to the Dortmund-Ems Canal. Next Dummer Lake. Then Steinhuder Lake. Depending on which aerodrome was being visited the intruder would turn off at one of these points and head for the target. If the target was in southern Germany the route would be via Belgium. That involved another problem as the Allied armies moved in. They created several Artillery Zones where the gunners were free to fire on any aircraft flying lower than 10,000 feet. Intruders never flew higher than 2,000 feet, so they had to avoid these zones to avoid being shot down down.

Even without facing artillery fire, enemy or Allied, flying at low level was a dangerous enterprise at night, particularly across the North Sea on the return journey. The navigator recalls:

On one such occasion flying monotonously on we were feeling a bit tired and drowsy. After a while I glanced across at the instrument panel – not something I was in the habit of doing . . . I saw that we were in a shallow dive and the altimeter was reading Zero. I called out to the pilot, 'Watch your height,' and he pulled the nose up sharply. I have often wondered what made me look at the pilot's instruments at that precise moment. And how many crews did we lose as a result of a momentary lack of concentration due to fatigue?

Although we had no illusions that we were involved in the serious business of war it was nevertheless in many ways a happy time. We were privileged to be flying in the finest aircraft of that era – the incomparable Mossie – and for that reason we were envied by many other aircrew. There was a lively sense of humour among the crews which helped to make squadron life enjoyable and there was a great spirit of comradeship which was in itself a source of fun. Of course life was not all fun. It was not fun to wake up in a morning to see a friend's bed empty and then watch in silence as the adjutant came into the hut to pack up your friend's kit and to know you would never see him again. Then there were times when we returned from an operational flight at perhaps three or four o'clock in the morning to hear that one of our aircraft was missing. A little later, having a meal in the mess, a few of us would sit around the table talking about the crew and hoping. Eventually as the daily life of the aerodrome began we would face up to the fact that there was no use in waiting and hoping any longer and make our weary way to bed. That wasn't fun either.[23]

Occasionally intruders carried bombs, either high-explosive or incendiary, to drop on Luftwaffe night-fighter bases as a further incentive to the control tower to keep the lights turned off and prevent take-off by the *Nachtjäger* as the bomber stream flew towards the night's targets or returned. If the intruder crew had failed to find the Luftwaffe base then the load was dropped on any other legitimate target that presented itself, never being brought home. Goebbels's depression about the enormous effect bombing was now having on the Reich's ability to wage war was well-founded when even Mosquito intruders dropped explosives. The growing might of RAF Bomber Command as the weather improved in February, and as even a relatively small bombing force such as the LNSF made its demands on the ordnance factories in fact led to a bomb shortage. A law of diminishing returns was now evident in bombing industrial cities. Dortmund and Essen were still being attacked by the RAF in February – as was the Dortmund-Ems Canal, which carried coal to the steel-works – but as Harris pointed out in his immediate post-war memoirs he was 'compelled to use a huge bomb-load to destroy what remained' as there was but rubble left and therefore little to burn. He stressed that he had warned

that the time might come when we should need an enormously large supply of heavy-case high explosive bombs than before, when our main weapons had been the 4lb incendiary and the 4,000lb blast bomb – this latter was of course essentially a weapon to use against intact buildings and was no great use against already ruined cities in which life was mostly going on in cellars and only the essential factory buildings had been partially restored ... I found my warning had been disregarded. For the last six months of the war we were therefore faced with a desperate shortage of high explosive bombs and had to live all the time from hand to mouth, doing our best with our own supply and with what the Americans could let us have in spite of their own shortage.[24]

Harris had not only long pressed for more 500-lb and 1,000-lb HE bombs, he was also keen to try new weaponry from Barnes Wallis, who could do little wrong for the C-in-C since the employment of his remarkable bouncing bomb on the Ruhr Dams in May 1943. Production had been authorised for two types of aerodynamic Tallboy bomb immediately after the Dams Raid, but manufacture of the larger prototype had been stopped and not restarted until July 1944. Now it was at last available in small numbers and was provided for 617 Sqn, known to the press as the Dambusters because of their success with Wallis's bouncing device. The huge bomb, weighing 22,000 lbs, became particularly useful in destroying communication targets as Harris's crews continued the Transportation Plan to bottle up the German armies and cut off their supplies. In the pre-nuclear age it was the most destructive missile in the history of warfare.

TWELVE

BREAKING THE CHAIN

THE Reich's communications network, which Bomber Command dramatically bled dry, turned to scrap and simply halted from the beginning of 1945 to the spring, had key points that merited key weapons. High on the Transportation Plan target list in the closing months of the war was the Dortmund-Ems Canal, which was carrying coal-laden barges for the war plants of the Ruhr and towards the end even sections of the new long-distance, Schnorkel-equipped U-boats, manufactured in different Reich areas under Speer's industrial dispersal plan. The German economy ran on coal and without it ceased to function. Barnes-Wallis's smaller Tallboy bomb, the 12,000-lb capacity, had proved successful in September, draining more than a 6-mile stretch, but both Bomber Command and the Germans knew they would be returning every time the canal was repaired, which meant operations at great risk. The canal had been raided in force three times since September, each operation unplugging the repaired waterway.

On the night of 7 Februay as barge traffic began flowing once more, the whole of 5 Group was tasked with breaching the canal at Ladbergen yet again, this time with delayed-action bombs, which it was hoped would hold up repair work. It was a debacle. Bomb aimers were unable to see where previous bombs were dropping for lack of explosions and in fact not one bomb landed on or near the canal banks, all falling in nearby fields. The efforts of 177 Lancasters and 11 Mosquitos was all for naught. It was fortunate that losses were small, only five Lancasters going down. But in one of them was a remarkable airman, the youngest-ever

CO to be appointed to lead a heavy bomber squadron. Promotion in Bomber Command was usually swift, particularly for skippers, as attrition worked its way through the ranks of the young and keen. However, W/Cdr Keith Douglas had had a particularly rapid climb. He was appointed to command the Australian 467 Sqn at 22, a full two years younger than the also outstanding and boyish W/Cdr Guy Gibson when he led the Dambusting 617 Sqn. Douglas was among the most experienced skippers in Bomber Command on the night he was killed, his 124th trip. There were eight men on board, including a second navigator, when the aircraft was shot down. Five baled out, four to become POWs, but the wireless operator was able to evade. P/O James Strickland, who had joined the RAAF straight from school, told his story to intelligence officers after being brought back into British lines by advancing troops on 30 March.

> Fifteen minutes after we had bombed the target I felt the aircraft give a terrific lurch and then the pilot gave the order 'Bale out, Bale out'. I baled out from about 10,000ft and eventually landed in a ploughed field which I believe to be some 30 kms south of Münster. I hastily got rid of my parachute, harness and Mae West, which I hid in a ditch. By the aid of a compass I immediately made off in a westerly direction. It was a pitch black night and travelling was difficult. I walked for a short while before filling up my water bottle and kept walking mostly through fields until 0500 hours when I decided to lay up in a ditch until evening came. Cold and cramp decided me to move on during the day. Although we had been told at lectures this was a risky procedure, I felt that lying up for so many hours would result in cold and stiffness. I moved for the next few days in daylight as well as at night. Although I passed a number of civilians and soldiers on my way no one appeared to take the slightest notice of me. I had taken off the tops of my flying boots and put my heavy blue sweater over my battle dress. During the day I walked along the roads and through the small villages I came to. At night I made my way across country. On one occasion I was discovered by a farmer asleep in his barn. He was an elderly man

who walked with a limp. He appeared to be very cross and told me to come along with him. My feet had become very sore from walking and I was feeling cold and semi-numbed. I got up and walked along at his side while he pushed his bike. Having travelled some little way along the road I found he was taking me off to a nearby village. By this time my circulation was beginning to function more normally and I decided to leave him and make my way across the fields. He shouted to me at the top of his voice. I moved off as quickly as possible and hid myself in some straw. I stayed here until I got warm enough to move on again.[1]

By the afternoon of 12 February the exhausted and starving Strickland had reached the Dutch community of Winterswijk. 'On walking through the village I met a number of German soldiers,' he reported. 'As I passed them I looked straight at them with a view to allaying suspicion. It worked. I noticed a grocer's shop with advertisements for Lux and Persil in the window and entered.'[2] After much persuasion the Dutchman behind the counter allowed the evading airman into the rear of his premises. 'A girl in the room gave me soap and hot water,' he said. 'I shaved and cleaned myself up. Before I left I was given some sandwiches and told to make for Varsseveld via Aalten where I should meet some people who would help me on my way.' As night came Strickland knocked nervously at a house outside Varsseveld. 'A woman came to the door. I said "Englander". She appeared reluctant to let me in, but one of the people in the room who spoke a little English heard me and called for me to come in. From this house I found shelter and was eventually brought back to our lines by an advance British "recce" which had entered the district.'[3]

Strickland had actually seen the mid-upper gunner, F/Sgt B. Bean, jump from the stricken aircraft and believed the rest of the crew had got out too. But the bodies of Douglas, the bomb aimer P/O John Nanscawen and the navigator P/O Monty Stuart were later found and are buried in the Reichswald Forest War Cemetery. They joined the 4,050 of their comrades killed while serving in Britain with the squadrons of Bomber Command, often as skippers, where their tenacity was legendary.

Harry Stack, an Australian bomb aimer who completed a tour with 550 Sqn at North Killingholme, had become close friends with P/O Stuart, a 33-year-old Tasmanian, and at one time they had hoped to team up in the same crew. He remembers:

> I did an observer's course in Australia before going to the UK. I volunteered there as a bomb aimer after tossing a coin with my best mate Monty Stuart to see who would be navigator or bomb aimer so that we could fly together. I lost the toss. Monty was in hospital in Stranraer, where we were doing an advanced flying course after our initial warm-up commando course in Northumberland, when the postings came out for operational training unit, so I had to leave without him. Monty went to 463/467 Sqns, more or less all Aussies, and we used to see each other in Grimsby now and again. Monty was killed on his twenty-ninth op. I was told after the war that the bomb aimer had been badly injured in the head and Mont was trying to put a parachute on him and toss him out. Of course the skipper was doing his best to hold the kite stable while this was going on, but apparently they just ran out of height.[4]

Australian airmen were usually met with kindness and gratitude by Britons, in the knowledge the young men had volunteered to come from the other side of the world to fight Europe's war and many would not be returning. Civilians were often prepared to share rations with them and offer accommodation in their leaves, keenly aware that the young men barely out of school would undoubtedly be missing home, despite the fashionable bravado. Organisations such as Lady Frances Ryder's Colonial Hospitality Movement provided English homes for Australian and other Commonwealth aircrew to spend their leaves in. F/O Reg Johnson, an Australian pilot who came to Britain in October 1943, began his operational tour in February 1945 on 218 Sqn at Chedburgh, Suffolk. Soon after arriving from Australia he met hospitality from an English family. He remembers:

The first major civilian social contacts for me, and probably for many others of us, was through the Lady Ryder Scheme where we were invited in pairs to spend a week in an English home. I had Christmas in a house in Carshalton, outer London. Cocktail parties, walks on Epsom Downs, honorary membership of the squash club, contacts with young ladies known to our host, and sumptuous meals. Those were the highlights. We were welcomed back on later leaves. This house was later destroyed by a V-1. No casualties, but I lost touch with a gracious family.

Another time we went to a stately home near Oxford, where we two Aussies were a little too unpolished to mix with the upper crust. Consequently we enjoyed a wonderful leave with the game-keeper, the kitchen staff and two young refugee boys. My other contacts with local people came by taking a leave pass rail ticket to, for example, Exeter, from where I walked or hitch-hiked to wherever lorry drivers were willing to take me. This led to several informative travels such as detours to see interesting churches, sharing a Cornish pasty lunch or simply finding a place to stay for the night.[5]

Arrival on a squadron meant his contacts were more local. 'I really felt a part of England and not a stranger,' he says. 'I visited and stayed at the homes of my crew except that of the Scottish mid-upper gunner. This was good for the parents and for us their visitors to be seen as a happy team. The downside was often when we were about to leave the mother would say to me, 'Look after my boy, won't you.'[6]

All were aware it was usually simply luck that divided those who would live from those who would die. The aircrew of 467 RAAF Sqn must have thought they were jinxed indeed the next time they were briefed for a raid on the Dortmund-Ems Canal, on 3 March. 'Disaster,' the normally restrained squadron operational record book reads. 'This target has cost us another CO and this time also two other crews. Australian W/Cdr Eric Langlois had the new gunnery leader with him, Australian F/O R.E. Taylor who had just arrived. The CO was on the eighteenth trip of his second tour and it certainly was a shock to find him missing.'[7] Yet again the whole of 5 Group had been employed to breach the canal and a total of seven Lancasters were shot down as the night fighters gathered, white, yellow and blue tracer flashing across the sky as red target indicators glowed through the cloud. One crew even claimed to have shot down a V-1, probably on its way to Antwerp. It was some recompense that this time the canal was breached in two places and remained out of action for the rest of the war.

No sign was found of Langlois and all but two of his crew and they are remembered on the Runnymede Memorial. Like so many aircrew shot down in the final weeks of the war they seem to have been murdered by the Nazis. The new squadron Gunnery Leader F/O Taylor, who had replaced a tour-expired gunner to fly with Langlois for the first and last time, was captured at dawn by two Volkssturm soldiers and put in the cells of a local airfield then eventually taken to Stalag VIIA where he was liberated by the Americans two months later. Back in Britain he told RAF investigators that after Langlois's Lancaster was set on fire in the bomb bay:

> The captain orders bale out and all acknowledge. No one seemed injured and the aircraft was in perfect control. Fighters set us on fire. Destroyed the enemy aircraft Me110. Saw it burning on the ground when we landed. Crashed about two minutes from the target on the German side of the canal. The bomb aimer [F/O J. H. Willmott] and I know that one other member of the crew, believed to be the engineer [F/Sgt John Scott], landed between the bomb aimer and I, as I saw him walking away from his chute, but I have not heard of him since. The fate is unknown of the rest of the crew. They should all have got out as they had plenty of time to do so. I baled out from the rear turret and there was only the captain left when I went out. I was told by a French worker that four Australians and one Englishman were shot by German SS near Dortmund.

F/Sgt Scott, the only RAF man among the five missing from the Langlois crew, was the youngest on board at 19 and the former milkman was on his ninth operation in a crew well into their second tour when he disappeared. After the war the RAF Missing Research and Enquiry Unit began an investigation into what had happened to the five missing men, but abandoned their investigations for lack of evidence a year later.

It seemed that luck indeed, both on and off the ground, could be the sole arbiter of who survived. Aircrew on the Australian squadron and others maintained faith in their talismans and rituals to prevent fate singling them out. Most Bomber Command flyers were superstitious, though many would deny it if pressed. Simple actions such as a particular farewell riposte to the WAAF crew bus driver or the positioning of a civilian scarf had to be exactly repeated on every trip once one operation had been successfully completed and so many others stretched ahead.

F/Sgt Frank Tolley, the 625 Sqn bomb aimer whose aircraft had flown so near the official film Lancaster on the Dresden raid, remembers his own Australian skipper's particular ritual. 'Bruce Windrim had a bowler hat which someone had given him in a pub. He had it painted in the airfield obstruction colours of black and yellow squares and he wore it on every raid on top of his flying helmet. It was a talisman for him.'[8] In late February it became obvious to all bomb aimers on the squadron how fickle fate could be, F/O David Cooper, air bomber in F/O Jamieson's crew, being killed by a flak sliver shortly after dropping a Cookie on Dortmund. F/Sgt Tolley says:

> I remember him being killed and the crew coming back with his body in the aircraft. On another raid, a daylight, one of our bomb aimers had a particularly lucky escape. We had been debriefed and as we were leaving to go to the mess this other crew came in and the bomb aimer, F/O Taylor, was carrying his chute and it was torn to ribbons. He used to put on his chest pack approaching the target to rest on over the bomb sight and on this raid a piece of flak 2 inches wide had gone right through it. The strange thing was he wasn't injured, the chute absorbed the shock. He was going on leave the next day though and that's when the rot would set in. A

lot of bomb aimers decided to wear their chutes over the target after that, including me.[9]

To maintain morale superstition could even become part of station policy. Sgt Edwin Watson, the 630 Sqn flight engineer whose operations ended in March, remembers that early in his tour at East Kirkby his crew returned from leave to be told that the squadron's G-George had just been lost and a new aircraft, PD317, had been delivered which was also now coded G, despite the fact that the squadron had lost five Georges already. 'Because of the short life span of her predecessors crews weren't keen to claim her,' he recalls. 'At this stage we had completed eight ops as a crew flying five different aircraft. A decision was made that we should go for PD317.'[10] The aircraft demonstrated it was cursed on its first operational flight. 'Once airborne we found that both Gee and H2S navigation aids weren't working, also the radio receiver ... The wireless operator was successful in rectifying the receiver – in doing so he found a goodwill message inside from a lady factory worker, not unusual,' Sgt Watson recalls.[11] The crew had to abort the operation, but flew other successful operations in it. Another crew was then given G-George for the Munich raid of 7 January. The aircraft lost an engine on take-off and after jettisoning the bomb load the skipper tried to land, but the aircraft cartwheeled along the runway as another engine cut. The pilot was found strapped in his seat yards away from the wreck, minus an arm. The squadron refused to code an aircraft G-George for the rest of the war.

Sometimes, for no apparent reason, a crew member would know with hollow certainty as he prepared for an operation that he would not be returning. An Australian pilot on 49 Sqn, F/O Tom Hawkins, remembers such a day in February 1945.

Our normal practice after breakfast was to go to the Flights and find out what the flying programme was. The big question each time: 'Is there a war on tonight?' closely followed by: 'Are we on?' and the answer to this determined what our activities would be for the remainder of the day. As it happened, there was an operation planned for that night, and our names were down for it. So we slipped into our usual ops routine. However, for the first time something was niggling at me and I did not feel at ease. This feeling stayed with me during the day and by briefing time I was quite unsettled. Briefing over we collected our gear and waited for the crew bus to take us out to the aircraft. By this time I was feeling most despondent, but had not mentioned anything to my crew and do not know even now if they were aware of it or not.[12]

In his seat in the aircraft F/O Hawkins then went through the start-up routine, beginning as always with the starboard inner engine. The prop turned a few times on the electrical power from the plugged-in trolley accumulator, but refused to fire. After waiting a few moments F/O Hawkins tried again with the same result. Both the inboard engines drove hydraulic pumps and generators so the pilot then tried the port inner, but again it wouldn't catch. Finally he tried the starboard outer, again without success. 'Ken [the flight engineer] and I looked at each other with disbelief,' F/O Hawkins recorded. The squadron commander's car arrived and the crew were asked to leave the Lancaster so that the ground crew could try to start it. Again each engine failed to fire up. The rest of the squadron was by now well on its way, there was no spare aircraft that night, so F/O Hawkins's sortie was scrubbed. 'I felt an enormous load had been lifted from somewhere deep within me and it was with a considerable feeling of relief that I went to bed that night,' F/O Hawkins wrote. 'We flew on ops the next night and apart from the usual nervous anticipation that everyone has, there was no sense of despair as on the previous night and it never happened again.'[13]

THE attacks on the Dortmund-Ems Canal were only part of the effort to dislocate, starve and bottle up the German war effort. There were others on the eastward-stretching Mittelland Canal, on railway centres and on other key points as the German armies, desperate for supplies denied by Bomber Command, retreated. It wasn't hard for the enemy to guess where the Command was headed. A raid by 165 Lancasters and Mosquitos on the Mittelland Canal on 20 February had to be abandoned by the master bomber as the bombers orbited the waterway's junction with the Dortmund-Ems Canal at Gravenhorst because the area was covered in cloud. The next night the force returned and the canal was rendered totally unserviceable, but the Luftwaffe were waiting and thirteen Lancasters crashed, 7.9 per cent of those dispatched. One of them was skippered by the station commander at Coningsby, G/Cptn Anthony Evans-Evans, who at 43 was well beyond the normal age for combat flying. The senior officer, whose flight lieutenant brother had been killed in October, was caught by a night fighter over Holland. Only one gunner survived.

Albert Speer was much impressed by Bomber Command's campaign against waterways and railways, as was the US Strategic Bombing Survey whose report was published after the war. It concluded:

> The attack on transportation was the decisive blow that completely disorganized the German economy. It reduced war production in all categories and made it difficult to move what was produced to the front. The attack also limited the tactical mobility of the German army ... The railway system was supplemented by a strong inland waterways system connecting the important rivers of northern Germany, crisscrossing the Ruhr and connecting it with Berlin. The waterways carried from 21 to 26 per cent of the total freight movement. Commercial highway transport of freight was insignificant; it accounted for less than three per cent of the total ... The attack on the waterways paralleled that on the railways; the investigation shows that it was even more successful.[14]

The very much smaller British investigation into the results of the bombing war was somewhat more critical of the costly campaign against canals. It decided that Ladbergen and Gravenhorst had not been the best targets for destroying Germany's water network and it would have been better to wreck the Münster Locks on the Dortmund-Ems Canal, the Datteln Locks on the Wesel-

Datteln Canal and the Rothensee ship lift and any bridge over the Rhine.[15]

The successes of the Transportation Plan throughout February and March were built on earlier sacrifices made in the dreadful weather conditions of late December and January. F/O Robert Vollum, the wireless operator on his second tour with 158 Sqn, made his last operational trip of all to a transportation target on 29 December. Two separate forces bombed railway yards in Koblenz, one of the main centres serving the Ardennes battle front, following up a USAAF attack the previous day. A total of 85 Lancasters of 3 Group attacked the Lutzel yards north of the city and 162 Halifaxes of 4 Group, including F/O Vollum's aircraft, attacked the Mosel yards near the city centre. The signaller remembers:

It was a horror. Near the target area we heard over our earphones a navigator or bomb aimer in another aircraft giving his pilot in plain language their height, course, speed and the target ETA. Shortly afterwards we saw an aircraft in front of us hit by flak and start to go down. The pilot I was with, S/Ldr Salter, was flabbergasted at what he heard because of the danger of predicted flak. On our return we found that several of the squadron's planes had been hit by flak, but fortunately had returned safely.[16]

Civilian casualties were slight and a report from Germany later revealed: 'The whole railway system was blocked ... The Koblenz–Lutzel railway bridge was out of action for the rest of the war and the cranes of the Mosel harbour were put out of action.'[17]

It was seldom that the spirit of 'press on regardless', often used in jest by members of Bomber Command, was not paramount. It was never more obvious than in a crew commanded by S/Ldr Wilbur Pierce, of 433 (RCAF) Sqn, taking part in a transport target operation in the dreadful weather conditions of mid-January. The diary of the Canadian crew's English flight engineer, W/O Fred Haynes, was written within hours of them participating in the attack by 150 aircraft of the Canadian 6 Group on the railway yards at Grevenbroich while the rest of Bomber Command was operating against oil targets. The flight was beset by what airmen termed gremlins, from take-off.

> This was our old hunting ground again, only a new target, also our best effort yet. We took off at 15.45. As we climbed up to height over base we noticed oil pouring from the port inner engine. As we were losing approximately one gallon of oil every two minutes we feathered the engine. We decided to carry on as oil had stopped coming out and then unfeather it for the climb as we were only at 5,000ft.

The bomber flew on down England's eastern edge losing a little height for speed and cutting a corner so as not to lose the stream, then at the pre-determined climbing point for the operation the propeller blades were unfeathered and the control column pulled back for a rapid ascent. 'After 20 minutes the oil pressure started to fluctuate so we feathered immediately,' W/O Haynes wrote. The artificial horizon was also out of action.

It took much courage to continue to fly all the way to a target on three engines, particularly when that target was in the flak belts of the Ruhr, but that is what S/Ldr Pierce did. 'By the time we reached the target we were at 14,000ft instead of 18,000ft,' the diary goes on. 'There was yet again a most brilliant display of TIs. We bombed one and half minutes early on the skipper's advice to get away from the bombs falling from above. As we bombed photo flashes were bursting all around us, also light and heavy flak. I could see the bombers in the stream well above us.' S/Ldr Pierce put the nose down to clear the target and build up flying speed. He had to fly around Brussels, still under siege from V-weapons, because the aircraft, Y-Yokum, was now down to 10,000 feet. 'We didn't want to take the chance of being fired on by our own troops in mistake for a flying bomb,' Haynes wrote. 'Eventually we arrived over base, a little late but we had made it.'[18] Both the pilot and his navigator were awarded immediate DFCs.

*

IN the last week of February the USAAF and the RAF's Second Tactical Air Force continued the onslaught on transportation while Bomber Command turned to oil targets. Operation Clarion was launched on 22 February, a concentrated effort to wipe out in 24 hours all the means of transport the Germans still possessed. Nearly 9,000 aircraft – fighters, bombers of all weights, and fighter/bombers – took off from bases in England, France, Holland, Belgium and Italy to deliver a blow over a quarter of a million square miles of Germany. Railway targets, from marshalling yards to signal boxes and level crossings, were attacked as well as canal locks, bridges and vehicles of every kind on the road or in depots.

But key targets still needed to be destroyed and only the bombs available to RAF Bomber Command could do it. The most effective way to close a railway line was similar to breaching canals: destroy a viaduct that carried it. The movement of trains to and from the Ruhr depended on eighteen bridges and viaducts. Three of these were particularly critical: the Bielefeld viaduct, carrying the line from the biggest rail yard in Germany at Hamm to Hanover; the Altenbeken viaduct near Paderborn, carrying the line from Soest to Hildesheim; and the Arnsberg railway viaduct over the river Ruhr, not far from the Mohne Lake which 617 Sqn had breached in 1943.

As the Allied armies swept towards the Rhine, destruction of the three viaducts became vital to trap troops in the Ruhr pocket. Bomber Command had been trying since mid-February. Both 9 and 617 Sqns were equipped with Lancasters with bulged bomb bays able to take Barnes Wallis's aerodynamic Tallboy bomb. Thirty-six of them had been dispatched on 14 February to hit both the Bielefeld and Altenbeken viaducts, but the raid had had to be abandoned because of cloud, one 9 Sqn aircraft being shot down. There had been another attempt on the Bielefeld viaduct alone on 9 March, but again the operation had to be abandoned because the target was obscured. Five days later 9 and 617 Sqns set off again to destroy the Bielefeld and Arnsberg viaducts. This time an aircraft of the Dambusters squadron was carrying the larger of

Wallis's Tallboys, the 22,000-lb version which would become known as the Grand Slam. It was designed to penetrate the ground at almost sonic speed, create a camouflet or cavern with its earthquake-like explosion and shake what was above apart and into the hole. A near miss would be sufficient.

At exactly one and a half minutes before four in the afternoon F/Lt C. B. Craper, the bomb aimer in S-Sugar of 617 Sqn, dropped the first Grand Slam released in action from precisely 11,965 feet over the Bielefeld viaduct. Other aircraft released the smaller Tallboy. 'Our bomb was a 30 yard undershoot,' Craper reported back at base. 'We saw one direct hit and one 50 yard undershoot.'[19] The Grand Slam, together with the Tallboys, had worked: more than 100 yards of the viaduct collapsed, closing the line from Hamm to Hanover for the rest of the war. The technology of bombing had leaped forward once more.

A Canadian flight engineer on the raid, F/O H.R. Short, was interviewed by his country's press corps in Britain to tell his countrymen what an explosion by the new wonder weapon in this pre-nuclear age looked like. 'Three bombs fell almost simultaneously,' he said. 'There was a terrific flash from the centre one. A gigantic pall of black smoke and a fountain of debris rose hundreds of feet into the air. The centre one was one of the new 22,000 pounders. The blast from it made that from the 12,000 lb bombs which fell next to it seem small.' A fellow Canadian on 617 Sqn, air gunner F/O F. L. Inglis, said: 'If it didn't blow up the objective nothing will.'[20]

The 22,000-lb bomb had been a great success, but 9 Sqn crews had had to abandon their attack on the Arnsberg viaduct. F/Lt Douglas Jennings, the bomb aimer who had arrived for a second tour at frozen Bardney on 1 January to find two crashed aircraft, was on the raid. He remembers:

> The target was cloud-covered and we couldn't bomb, so we had to turn for home with our Tallboy still on board. As we did so one engine developed a fault, so we trailed the rest of the squadron. We couldn't get in at Bardney because of fog, so we were diverted

to Waddington. But we couldn't get in there either. We were milling about in the fog trying to land and I remember on approach we took a very close look at a very large hangar that came looming out of the murk.

We had to take avoiding action and were sent on to the emergency airfield at Carnaby. There was lots of runway for an aircraft with a heavy load and a faulty engine. We stayed there overnight and they told us they had sorted the engine out, so we took off, but almost immediately after we got airborne the engine failed. There we were trying to climb with three engines and a very heavy bomb load. Once we got flying speed it was OK, but the initial take-off was a bit of a problem. It was an anxious moment for the pilot; the rest of us just hung on, grinned and hoped for the best. It was all right after we got a bit of height and we got back to Bardney.[21]

A total of 41 Grand Slams and 854 of the smaller Tallboys were used before the end of the war. Two Grand Slams were dropped on the Arnsberg connection on 15 March, though not close enough to destroy it. The Dambusters went back four days later, this time with three times the number of such bombs, and blew a 40-foot gap in the viaduct. The bomb was then used successfully on submarine pens which had proved impenetrable so far. But not all operations with the large and smaller Tallboys went well and the opposition was usually fierce.

Douglas Jennings took part in a daylight attack on 23 March by eleven Tallboy-carrying Lancasters on the Bad Oeynhausen railway bridge, halfway between Osnabrück and Hanover, when the Luftwaffe showed up with jets. He remembers:

We had an escort of forty-five fighters. We happened to be lead aircraft that day, so we could hear the commentary from the fighter controller, but none of the other people in our flight behind us had that. We heard the intercom come into action as an attack by an Me262 started. There was all kinds of shouting, such as 'Let's get him', but in a moment he had gone. What he had done was get way above the fighter escort, then come down in a dive at a colossal speed and taken a pot at the last aircraft in our column as we went into the attack on the bridge. It all happened in a blink. He came down out of the blue. The crew of the last aircraft saw him coming at the last minute, started to take evasive action, but the Me262 managed to damage the tail plane and disappeared on his dive. The pilot had to jettison the Tallboy.

All these bridges were well defended because they were vital to the German Army at that time and they wanted to keep their lines of communication open for ammunition going up and themselves getting out. We had just dropped our own Tallboy on the bridge when we were hit by flak. It must have exploded just outside the aircraft and peppered us, because a piece went through my blister in front, then went somewhere between the pilot and the engineer and through the top canopy. Pieces also peppered the petrol tanks and we started streaming petrol from the wings. Another piece went through the body of the aircraft and cut the hydraulics. People in the flight told us they could see petrol vapour as it leaked out from the wing tanks. Because of the damage to the hydraulics our skipper put the wheels down to make sure they worked, but then he couldn't get both up again. In fact we came back with one down and one up. Eventually we used the emergency air bottle to get the other down and we got the magic green lights on the panel. As we touched down at Bardney we were a bit worried that the undercarriage might not hold up, but it did. When we taxied round to dispersal we saw the petrol was just pouring out onto the tarmac. It was then I saw the flak hole in my blister. It had come in on the other side to where I was crouched over the bomb sight. That was a bit of luck.[22]

The same time that 9 Sqn was attacking the Bad Oeynhausen bridge, more than 100 Lancasters were attacking a railway bridge at Bremen, led by the Dambusters squadron. F/Sgt Frank Tolley, the 625 Sqn bomb aimer, recalls:

We were in support of 617 Sqn aircraft carrying the 10-ton bomb, with a bridge as the aiming point. I was peering through the bomb sight ready to release on the bridge when this aircraft slid underneath us from port to starboard with part of his port wing on fire.

He seemed to be no more than 30 feet away. I was a bit shaken by seeing him and I had to wait for him to slip away before I released the bombs. I knew we would miss the bridge and in fact they fell towards streets of buildings. If I had hit the bridge the skipper would have probably got an immediate DFC instead of the one he got at the end of the war.[23]

Sgt Ken O'Brien, the 101 Sqn rear gunner, was in the same stream.

As 617 Sqn were carrying Tallboy bombs they were asked if they could keep up to our speed with such a big bomb, but the nearer we got to the target the further back they were. The 101 Sqn aircraft were flying in a Vic formation and all the tailplanes had been painted white. We were in the port Vic. The 101 Sqn aircraft to starboard of us in our Vic was shot down straight away. It was hit by flak and went straight down. On the squadron afterwards the talk was that the crew had baled out and were pitch-forked to death.* Baling out over a target in daylight they wouldn't make it.

We were hit by flak too. In the tail you can feel the aircraft jump and I heard on the intercom we had been hit. We lost the starboard outer engine, and the other outer engine was damaged and our flight engineer, Geoff Wheeler, was wounded in the groin. The crew wanted to get him to the rest bed, but he wouldn't go. He said, 'My job is to keep the engines going and get us back.' He was very groggy and was offered morphine, but he wouldn't take it, he wanted to stay at his post. We took a straight course home on the three engines. The idea was to get across the Channel and put down at the first airfield we could, but we managed to get all the way home and the whole trip there and back took five hours and

---

* This was the aircraft of F/O Ralph Little, an American serving in the RCAF. He and all his crew were killed, their aircraft coming down at Stottenhausen, just south of the target. The only other aircraft lost on the raid was also from 101 Sqn, that of F/Lt R. P. Paterson RCAF. He survived with two others of his crew when his aircraft exploded after being hit by flak near Delmenhorst, in the Bremen suburbs.

forty minutes. When we landed at the airfield an ambulance came out to meet us and took Geoff off to hospital. His flying boots had been taken off and I carried them into debriefing. The WAAF intelligence officer looked around and asked us, 'Where's the engineer?' I lifted his boots up and said, 'He's here.' I had to explain he had been wounded. Geoff was in hospital quite a while and we had a replacement engineer for our last two trips. Geoff was awarded an immediate CGM for looking after the engines and getting us back.[24]

The bridge was put out of action, the Tallboys of 617 Sqn falling cleanly towards the railway line, as the rear gunners of other Lancasters watched them go. F/Lt Jennings remembers:

When the Tallboy bomb went we used to go up like a lift. You definitely knew you no longer had it and because we were operating in daylight I could see clearly where it went to. You could see it falling, right the way down to the target. You could say with some justification at debriefing that it hit the target, or near it or missed it completely, whereas when I was bombing at night earlier there was a bang and a flash and you didn't know where the bombs were.[25]

It was the second time within 24 hours Bomber Command had been called to attack communications in the Bremen area as Montgomery waited to launch the final phase of the land war with the crossing of the Rhine from a 25-mile front in the Wesel sector on 24 March. It was as vital for the Allies to break the chain of communication as it was for the Wehrmacht to keep it open and bridges were always well defended by Luftwaffe flak, if not always fighters.

F/O J. W. Conaghty of 467 RAAF Sqn discovered just how accurate that flak could be in an attack on a railway bridge and marshalling yards at Bremen in the afternoon of 22 March. On the bomb run at 18,000 feet a heavy flak shell burst right in front of the pilot, blowing in the windscreen, wounding Conaghty in the chest, damaging the nose and also injuring the engineer,

Sgt J. Duffill. After a freezing journey home, Conaghty told intelligence officers:

> After being hit I felt myself losing consciousness and I told the crew to bale out, but I recovered complete consciousness very quickly and cancelled the order in time to stop them. I lost 2,000ft before recovering. I told the air bomber to let the bombs go and we stayed in the gaggle. The engineer had been hit just before me. He tried to carry on, but couldn't stand up and he collapsed. He was given first aid by the navigator, who put a tourniquet on his arm and gave him morphia. He never complained and asked about his instruments all the way home and checked that his engine drills were being carried out.[26]

Conaghty was back on the battle order within a few days and Sgt Duffill also recovered to fly on an operation to Pilsen in mid-April.

The Allied campaign against German transport in the final months of the war was crucial in bringing about final collapse in Germany, not least because it prevented coal shipments, the lifeblood of German industry. The post-war report of the US Strategic Bombing Survey was glowing in its tributes to what had been achieved, essentially by RAF Bomber Command. It revealed:

> Beginning in December there was a sharp fall in production in nearly all industries; week by week the decline continued until the end of the war. Although coal traffic (about 40 per cent of all the traffic carried by the German railways) held up better than miscellaneous commercial traffic, the decline was both more easily traceable and more dramatic. By January, coal-car placements in the Ruhr were down to 9,000 cars a day and in February virtually complete interdiction of the Ruhr District was achieved. Such coal as was loaded was subject to confiscation by the railroads to fuel their locomotives; even with this supply, coal stocks of the Reichsbahn itself were reduced from 18 days' supply in October 1944 to $4\frac{1}{2}$ days' supply in February 1945. By March some divisions in southern Germany had less than a day's supply on hand, and

locomotives were idle because of lack of coal. The German economy was powered by coal; except in limited areas, the coal supply had been eliminated.[27]

The bottling up of the German Army in the Ruhr, in which Bomber Command played its part by bombing railway viaducts, would in April result in the surrender of 325,000 members of Field Marshall Walther Model's Army Group B. It was a capitulation greater than Stalingrad.

The Luftwaffe too were now heading for final defeat. But as the attack on the Bad Oeynhausen railway bridge had shown, they were by no means finished in March, despite Goebbels's constant complaints in his diary about Goering's inefficiency. The force that had decimated Bomber Command in the Battle of Berlin in the winter of 1943–4 could still occasionally wreak savage destruction on the heavy bombers with the new jets as they did in daylight over Hamburg at the end of the month. Units equipped with the older Ju88 night fighters were so starved of fuel and experienced pilots they were now less often seen. But in early March Goering approved an operation with those very aircraft which took the war back to Britain. It caught RAF and Commonwealth bomber crews at their most vulnerable time.

THIRTEEN

NIGHT OF THE INTRUDER

IT was no accident that the 2,000th night of the war was chosen by the Luftwaffe night-fighter arm for a symbolic gesture of attrition to show that it was not finished yet. Bomber Command could now be guaranteed to be aloft every night as the weather conditions improved and a plan was devised to follow the tired bomber boys home and catch them as they looked forward to landing, breakfast and bed at their bases.

It was a lesson taken up from the Mosquito intruders that had been harassing with growing menace those same *Nachtjäger* over their airfields in Occupied Europe and Germany since December 1943. The Luftwaffe had also had previous experience of how effective their own night fighters over England could be. Morale in Bomber Command had taken a dip in the autumn of 1943 because of a two-month campaign by the *Nachtjäger* of mounting patrols over the command's airfield in Lincolnshire as the bombers returned from Germany and shooting down tired crews almost within sight of their welcoming billet. At the height of its success the campaign had been called off on the personal orders of Hitler because he wanted the Luftwaffe to concentrate on bombing, one of his more absurd directions among many.

On the night of 3 March 1945 more than 200 night fighters were on standby with full tanks at airfields close to the Western Front, ready to follow any bombers returning from raids on Germany. That night 200-plus Halifaxes of 4 Group had bombed an oil refinery near Kamen with great accuracy and no loss, and 212 Lancasters of 5 Group had been bombing the Dortmund-Ems Canal for the price of seven Lancasters. As was usual crews under training had been employed on a diversionary sweep across the North Sea towards Holland, dropping Window at regular intervals to confuse the Luftwaffe controller into thinking they were the actual bombing force. Some novice crews would now die before they had a chance to start an operational tour.

An early intimation that something unusual was about to happen was seen by a skipper heading west over Holland after the 5 Group attack. F/Lt Leslie Hay, who was on the penultimate operation in his tour with 49 Sqn, recalls seeing, 'beacons on the Dutch coast, the type which the night fighters orbit before being vectored onto the stream. The beacons were usually single, but this was a double one and to me meant only one thing – the fighters were waiting to move in.' F/Lt Hay went into a dive and wave-hopped all the way home.[1] The Luftwaffe's *Unternehmen Gisella* was about to begin.

F/Sgt Frank Horsley was a wireless operator in a crew completing their conversion onto four-engined bombers. They had set out from 1658 HCU at Riccall near York with four other Halifax crews under training when they ran into one of the early hunters from *Gisella*. He remembers:

> We had been dropping Window for quite a while on what was a very cold night when the two gunners saw a Ju88 and immediate evasive action took place. During the dive coring – that was oil freezing – occurred in three engines and at about 1,000 feet I began sending out SOS messages. The navigator announced that we were about 40 miles from the Dutch coast and George Robson, our very experienced pilot, asked us if we should carry on towards the Netherlands or try to restart the engines to return. We all agreed with his decision to try to get home and at the lower altitude the engines started and we returned safely to Riccal.[2]

Behind them, in the stream of bombers coming back from Germany, were the Ju88 night fighters, their navigators shadowing the Lancasters and Halifaxes on their radar sets. As the fleet reached the English coastline and gradually dispersed into gaggles heading for different bases from North Yorkshire down through

Lincolnshire, the night fighters picked up the blips of individual aircraft and followed as they switched on their navigation lights, until airfield blue perimeter illumination glowed ahead. Then they took up orbits waiting for a victim on final approach who would not have the height to corkscrew out of danger. From just after midnight the bombers began to fall, marking a trail of blazing destruction. The first to go down was a 12 Sqn aircraft on a training flight out of Wickenby, caught to the east near Alford. It plunged with such force the engines shot out of their mountings and buried themselves 10 feet into the earth. F/O Nicholas Ansdell and his crew had no time to bale out. Within forty minutes another 12 Sqn crew still under training was shot down a few miles to the north of Wickenby near Blyton. Again there were no survivors.

Not only were the intruders blasting aircraft from the sky, but in the textbook fashion of Mosquito crews, raking airfields with cannon and machine-gun fire to make Flying Control turn off runway lights and cause greater confusion. At Waddington, south of Lincoln, 467 RAAF Sqn, which had lost its CO and two other crews in the raid on the Dortmund-Ems Canal that night, had just landed the last of its returning bombers when the Luftwaffe arrived. The squadron adjutant recorded the next day:

> The enemy fighter came in very low, machine-gunning the station and with extraordinary luck hit our incendiary dump. A July 4th exhibition followed, explosions lighting up the station and sky. The firefighters had to be recalled from the scene when it was thought the Cookies might be set off. All personnel were cleared to the shelters. It was eventually found there was only one casualty, a fire hose knocked out the front tooth of an airman.

The operational record book continued laconically: 'Interrogation of crews by torch light.'[3] Intelligence officers had an unexpected crew on their hands, kinsmen from 466 RAAF Sqn who baled out over Waddington when the night fighter shot up their Halifax.

At Fulbeck only 10 miles to the south Australian F/O Les Hammond of 49 Sqn was on final approach in a damaged Lancaster without radio or brakes. He fired a red Verey light to signal he was landing, but there was no reply. The skipper used the entire runway to bring his aircraft to a halt and turned off into the grass overshoot area. 'Engine noises then sounded overhead and the next thing we saw was a Ju88 on a steep turn right at us,' F/O Hammond remembers. 'My first thought was the illuminated target we had given him ... his aircraft was outlined by a string of horizontal muzzle flashes and we will never know where his bullets landed ... there wasn't a single hole in the old kite.'[4]

A Lancaster of 189 Sqn, which shared the Fulbeck base with 49 Sqn, had already been shot down, the aircraft diving into East Rudham railway station near Fakenham, Norfolk, before F/O Sidney Reid or any of his crew could get out. It did not do anything for morale on 189 Sqn – which lost fifteen Lancasters between January and May – that Reid died on the last leg of a trip when he had so successfully beaten the Luftwaffe over Germany. The RCAF newspaper *Wings Abroad* had already interviewed him, later reporting:

> Five enemy nightfighter attacks in less than 15 trips were fought off by the RAF Lancaster piloted by F/O Sidney Reid, Orono, Ont. and navigated by F/O Thomas Nelson, Hamilton, Ont. On an attack on the synthetic oil plant at Politz, Reid's crew exchanged fire with an enemy fighter, but the Canadian pilot threw the aircraft into a corkscrew and the Nazi missed. F/O Reid took part in all the operations against the great oil plants at Merseburg, Politz and Brux.[5]

The beacons of destruction continued to flare along eastern England. A Lancaster of 460 Sqn at Binbrook, north of Lincoln, crash-landed in farmland at Langworth not far from the city after being surprised by a Ju88 while on a training flight. The mid-upper gunner was trapped in the crash and as the rest of the crew struggled to free him the night fighter came back and strafed them in the light of the burning bomber. The flight engineer, Sgt Alan Streatfield, was killed as was the Australian wireless operator, F/Sgt Robert Davey. The Ju88 then shot up the car of Observer Jack Kelway of the Royal Observer Corps on the Welton to

Spridlington road, but moments after Kelway died the Ju88 crew were killed too, hitting telegraph wires and crashing as they attempted to climb away.

Three of the ninety-five-strong Windowing force of crews under training were attacked as they returned. Just before 1 a.m. a Lancaster of 1654 Heavy Conversion Unit at Wigsley, Nottinghamshire, crashed near Mansfield; another of the same unit was attacked over its home airfield, the rear gunner baling out, but the pilot managed to land away; and another training aircraft, of 1662 HCU at Blyton, was attacked near Doncaster, the skipper landing safely. It was the squadrons based at airfields of 4 Group around York who perhaps had most to remember about that night, however, particularly the two Free French units at Elvington. A Halifax of 347 Sqn was caught inbound to Elvington at 1.05 a.m. and crashed near Cranwell and ten minutes later another of the squadron's aircraft was lost 7 miles south of York: Then an aircraft of the sister 346 Sqn, which had been diverted to Croft because of the intruders, was shot up at 2,500 feet and crash-landed near Darlington.

Sgt Leonce Vaysse, who had escaped from Tunisia to join 347 Sqn as a flight engineer, was in his billet on the base when the Luftwaffe roared overhead. The base loudspeaker system had already announced raiders were likely, ordering all lights out. 'Warm and cosy in my bed I didn't take the alert seriously until I heard the rattle of cartridges on the tin roof of our hut,' he remembers. 'I hurried into my clothes to go out and spent the rest of the alert in a trench. The German plane, which had gone very low so as to machine-gun the Halifaxes that were landing, hit a tree.'[6] The Ju88, flown by Oberfeldwebel Hugo Boker, of XIII/NJG3, clipped the tree at 1.51 a.m. when turning back in towards the airfield for another strafe then struck Dunington Lodge on the B1288 road, killing two women in the house. The remains of the blazing Junkers and its crew of four came to rest in an adjoining field. Oberfeldwebel Boker, Feldwebel Martin Bechter, Hauptmann Johann Dreher and Feldwebel Gustav Schmitz were the last Luftwaffe airmen to die in Britain in the

Second World War.[7] 'People on the station went to try to get the radar equipment from it, but it was too late,' Sgt Vaysse remembers. 'I wanted to see the wreck but there was a guard round it and I wasn't allowed.'[8]

A total of twenty-two aircraft, several crewed by novices under training, were shot up or shot down by Luftwaffe intruders in the operation known as Gisella, stripping away any sense of security from the bucolic, rural setting of Britain's bomber airfields as the majority of those who lived there, the ground staff, now discovered they were in the combat zone. Even WAAFs had found themselves in the firing line.

LACW Jean Danford, a crew bus driver at Metheringham, south of Lincoln, had been waiting for 106 Sqn's Lancasters to land when the airfield lights went out. She decided to drive back to the crew room, where she normally picked up and deposited her cargoes, to ask what was happening. She remembers:

> I had just crossed one of the runways when I heard a plane which seemed too fast to be a bomber. Immediately there was the sound of rapid gunfire and as I looked back I saw the flash on the perimeter track just a few yards behind as the bullets hit the ground. I *flew* round the perimeter track to the crew room, parked the bus and dashed inside. There was a mass of people there, a WAAF officer told me that enemy aircraft had been waiting for our bombers to return, a warning had been Tannoyed all over the camp, but I hadn't heard it. After a cup of tea I watched, with the others, from the doorway. There was a right old battle going on as the gunners were firing at the fighters, which in turn were firing back.[9]

Twenty miles away at Spilsby, where 207 Sqn operated, WAAFs also found themselves under attack. Sgt Ken Freeman, a 19-year-old air gunner, had arrived on the squadron a few days before and was still waiting to take part in his first op. 'The Luftwaffe dropped a bomb right on the runway intersection and shot up the WAAF site,' he remembers. 'We aircrew jumped straight out of bed when we heard the machine-gun fire.'[10]

*

WAAFS now made up approximately 10 per cent of all the personnel on a bomber base. More than 180,000 had been called up into the RAF by 1945, fulfilling roles from telephonist to air traffic control assistant to mess waitress – often among the last female faces a young, doomed airman would ever see as the airwomen served his meal before take-off. WAAFs provided a shoulder to cry on sometimes for a young airman who believed his time was quickly running out. As crews ticked off the trips in their tour and approached the end WAAFs in the control tower too would keep a record, ready to congratulate a crew as they called up to join the circuit to land for the final time.

The RCAF, which operated its own bomber group in the area around Harrogate now known as 'Little Canada', also had its own female airwomen serving in Britain in the winter of 1945, volunteers for overseas service who had flown the Atlantic two years before and now staffed various posts at Allerton Park, the headquarters of 6 (RCAF) Group. The women, who wore a different blue uniform to their WAAF sisters, were known as WDs, which stood for Women's Division of the RCAF. Allerton Park, a sprawling collection of Nissen huts surrounding a Victorian Gothic mansion, had a poor record for amenities and was known as 'Castle Dismal' to the girls. That winter a reporter from the air force newspaper *Wings Abroad* was sent up to Castle Dismal to find out how the girls were faring. The subsequent article, printed in mid-March, put a cheerful spin on service life in which the new arrivals had had to cope with a bitter winter in snow-covered huts where a single stove took the place of the efficient central heating they had been used to in Canada.

'The girls work tremendously hard to make possible the night-by-night operations our airmen carry out over Germany,' a commissioned WD, Section Officer Elizabeth Engelson, reported on her charges. 'They have created their own homes away from home and have come to love them, under conditions that might make Canadian girls away from home sigh for home and mother.' 'Loving' their new living quarters might have stretched the degree of affection somewhat for what was still just a steel hut on a concrete base, but the airwomen had done their best with non-regulation knitted woollen bedspreads, iron bedside tables made from bomb fins, and pictures on the wall of the folks back in Canada and aircrew boyfriends now risking all.

'It's a wizard life,' says Cpl Lillian East, the article continued. 'There is something mighty exciting going on around here and we haven't time to think of our troubles.' The airwomen received many invitations to social events at the bomber bases around Harrogate. 'We can wear civilian clothes after duty on the station, to dances, bingo parties and movies – pardon me, cinemas,' says LAW Anne Starr. 'You should see the station in summer time,' says LAW Marion Simpson. 'It's loads of fun then. We bicycle a lot – into the little village over there for tea. The trees are beautiful and the grass here is a wonderful place for sun-bathing.'[11] But in winter it was hot-water bottles and a teapot on the stove that made life just about bearable.

To have her own previously prepared hot-water bottle waiting as the airwoman returned to her billet in the middle of the night was considered an essential by the WDs in early 1945. It was a story that could have been repeated at remote WAAF sites throughout eastern Britain. They were always built well away from the men's quarters at the bomber stations and that often meant a long bike ride to the duty section or even the mess. At Allerton Park there was a particularly lonely cycle ride in total blackness to and from the Victorian mansion where the girls tapped away at their teleprinters and typewriters in draughty great halls with wide oak staircases, surrounded by stained-glass windows from a more peaceful age. In the early hours of 5 March, as the intruders that had caused such mayhem east of the Pennines departed, the HQ teleprinters to the RCAF and RAF stations were hot with orders for the coming hours as Harris prepared to complete the instruction he had been given in February to destroy key industrial cities as part of Operation Thunderclap. Chemnitz, 45 miles to the south-west of Dresden, had been saved then from the true terrifying might of Bomber Command because of cloud cover. Now the forecast was promising. In fact the improvement in weather conditions that allowed the raid on Chemnitz after the bitter winter would contain one last quirk. It would strike at the Canadians in 6 Group and bring sudden destruction to the peaceful heart of Yorkshire's bomber country.

FOURTEEN

A COLD AND SILENT KILLER

IT was the sheer distance of flying to Chemnitz that daunted crews as the target was revealed in briefing rooms throughout eastern England on the chilly wet Monday that was 5 March. Some of them had been to the industrial city in east Germany before, on 14 February, the day after the long haul back from Dresden. Now two and a half weeks later there was the chance of a more successful attack. But as the young crews leaned forward earnestly on the hard benches to hear COs outlining the night's operation it was obvious again that the red ribbon across the map on the end wall was stretching an awful long way, about 600 miles in fact, nearly to what had been the border with the pre-war Czech Republic. It didn't help that the USAAF had attacked Chemnitz for the third time in three days that very day and now the Germans might be expecting Bomber Command at night to complete the punishment known in the press as round-the-clock bombing. The young crews couldn't help but reflect on their direct experience or what they had heard had happened the last time Harris's boys went to Chemnitz.

Flight engineer Alan Dearden, who was briefed for the St Valentine's Day raid on Chemnitz with 76 Sqn, remembers:

> It was all part of the Dresden job really. Most of the 88 anti-aircraft guns had been moved from the Dresden area to be used as anti-tank weapons against the Russians, but over Chemnitz we saw quite a bit of flak. Coming out of the target at about 18,000 feet I went to do a bomb bay check and discovered we had a hang-up of a 2,000-lb bomb. The mid-upper gunner, W/O Ken Hirst, had

called, 'Look, skipper, over to port a runway has just been lit up.' Then he saw a jet taking off from it and making a left circuit obviously being vectored onto us. He had never seen one before and he could see the flame coming out of the back. Ken could see the jet, which he identified as an Me 163, coming up from behind and below and ordered the skipper to corkscrew starboard as he opened fire on the fighter. He only fired about twenty-five rounds, but the enemy aircraft exploded. We had a crew of nine that night as we had a second pilot and a mid-under gunner and the action was witnessed by most of them. At debriefing we reported the action to the intelligence officer, but he showed little interest and we heard no more about it. Years later I read that the 163 couldn't land at night, but that the Luftwaffe lost twelve Me262s that night, so maybe it was one of those. Our hang-up was jettisoned over Dunkirk. The German Army was still holding out at the docks there and we had been told at briefing not just to jettison anywhere, but to drop any hang-ups over the Channel ports where the Germans were bottled up.[1]

Among the members of 101 Sqn at Ludford Magna who would be making a return trip to Chemnitz was Sgt Ken O'Brien, the rear gunner who had shot down a jet in January. He remembers:

The trip to Dresden on 13 February took nine hours and forty minutes in total and to Chemnitz and back the next night it was eight hours fifty-five. It was the cold in that winter that got to you rather than the quick turnaround, though. It took me about an hour to get dressed for an operation. First there were long johns, then my uniform and an electrically heated suit and the kapok suit on top. I looked like the Michelin Man in the old adverts when I had finished. Nearly all the Perspex had been removed from the Rose turret, with the twin .50 machine guns which we had. From the moment you reached operational height it was very cold indeed. If you didn't keep the turret moving constantly the hydraulic oil soon froze up. There was a little dribble tube at the back of the oxygen tube and as that froze you would break it off in lumps of ice and throw it out. You seemed to do that all the time. I don't know what would have happened if the electrically heated suit failed. One of my electric socks developed a short once and when I got back I found a little burn mark on my foot.[2]

Ludford's neighbouring airfield was Kelstern where Sgt Joe Williams was also just finding out he would be making another trip to Chemnitz. He remembered the surprise in February when his crew found themselves on the battle order for another Saxon city so soon after Dresden. 'We had only been in bed for a few hours before we were called again, for the operation on Chemnitz,' he remembers. 'We couldn't believe it after such a long trip.'[3] Now there were other things on his mind as he arrived for the new briefing for Chemnitz on 5 March. Earlier he had been turning over his jaunt to the pub with his crew the night before. He recalls:

Our Canadian pilot, Jim Alexander, had bought a Ford 8 car and most of the crew went with him to the Waterloo Arms at Laceby, near Grimsby, that night. The squadron commander turned up and the C Flight commander and the Station MO. The officers put in £1 towards the drinks and we non-coms got away with ten bob [50p]. We were drinking brown ale with whisky chasers and we were all inebriated, but in the course of the evening I heard somebody talk about a spare parachute. I had never heard of one, so I asked 'Where?' I was told 'Behind Jim's seat.' I have no recollection of coming back to Kelstern; apparently we were driven home by the Canadian navigator, Bill Petrachenko, who had never been known to drive a car.[4]

At wartime-constructed Tholthorpe, 12 miles north-west of York, the briefing room was large enough to accommodate the aircrew of two RCAF squadrons, 420 and 425. The 420 Sqn crew of P/O Earl Clark, now listening attentively to the met forecast, were all Canadian apart from the flight engineer, 20-year-old Sgt James Kirby, born in Windsor. Their Canadian comrades in P/O Roald Sollie's crew sitting nearby also had, as was usual, an RAF flight engineer, but 21-year-old Sgt Robert Dinnen came from Ballyjamesduff, Co. Cavan, and had left the neutrality of Eire to fight fascism. He was among the thousands of Irishmen now serving as aircrew in Britain. As many as 150,000 joined the British forces, despite the determined isolationism of President de Valera and the resentment of some of their countrymen towards such solidarity with the British Empire. Sgt Edwin Watson, the 630 Sqn flight engineer who had been officially told his operational tour would end this night, remembers that his squadron had three or more Southern Ireland bomber crew members and 'every time they went on leave they were provided with civilian clothes which had to be worn; all other servicemen had to wear uniform full-time. Most surprisingly all the Irish lads returned; if they hadn't the RAF couldn't have done much about it.'[5] Sitting among the more familiar members of the Sollie crew was a very experienced mid-upper gunner who would be flying with them for the first time. F/Sgt James Waugh was wearing the purple and white ribbon of the DFM on his battledress, awarded for shooting down an enemy night fighter over Oberhausen in November.

Four miles to the south at the pre-war station of Linton-on-Ouse the crews of 408 and 426 RCAF Sqns were also listening to the weather forecast for the evening, but in the greater comfort of a brick-built operations block. Facing the dais where the 426 Sqn CO stood was the crew of one of his flight commanders, Eric Garrett, a squadron leader at 24, sitting in front of the 426 Sqn crew of F/O Humphrey Watts. Behind them sat their comrades, the crew of F/Lt Ivor Emerson. Emerson was deputy flight commander of 426's B Flight, known as a cheerful type and considered one of the squadron's best captains with more than 2,400 flying hours. Among Emerson's crew was P/O John Low, his wireless operator, now busy taking in the route and leafing through his flimsies of signal codes for the operation. A few miles to the south–east Mrs Thompson and Mrs Helstrip went about their chores on traditional washday Monday at No. 28 Nunthorpe Grove in York, aware because of air tests earlier in the day that they would soon be hearing the thunder of Halifaxes climbing out for a heavy raid on Germany. Across the street as they hung out the washing they could see the gap where Nos. 19 to 25 had been until a German bomb had destroyed the four houses in the night blitz on York nearly three years before.

The scene of rows of air-force blue was repeated all through 6 Group in North Yorkshire, down through the neighbouring stations of 4 Group to the east and south of York, to those of 1 Group north of Lincoln, to 5 Group south of the city who would be going to a different target, to north Norfolk on the airfields of 100 Group where fifty-two crews were briefed for their radio countermeasures role, right down as far as 8 Group in Cambridgeshire and Huntingdonshire from where the Pathfinders would lead the Chemnitz attack. A total of 960 heavy bomber crews listened with rapt attention to the facts and figures that might save their lives or as easily snatch them away. While the details droned beneath smoke-filled rafters crews leaned almost imperceptibly towards both the telltale map as if to unlock secrets for a private talisman and also towards each other, drawing recognisable comfort from the unspoken comradeship of those they had joined with random uncertainty at Operational Training Unit and now knew so well. Joe Williams remembers that bond in his own crew of three RCAF officers and four RAF NCOs.

We were all friends and there was no division between us. The Canadians were commissioned, but we were all from the same strata of society. The wonderful thing about it, and it can't be emphasised enough, was the uniqueness of the crew in the RAF. In every other air force in the world aircrew were told, 'You will fly with so and so.' In the RAF you converged from your different training to OTU where you were going to form up into crews. You were put in a great big building, about 200 of you and then told, 'Get yourselves crewed up.' Now that was a unique experience and you chose each other. You became a crew and friends and each crew was an insular unit. It was a very important way of building morale. You trained together, you flew together and went out at night together. After an operation when you got back and had your breakfast and went to bed, you learned that so and so's crew didn't come back and you had to think. There was a distance

from them. There was one crew we knew very well, the Cunliffe*
crew we had known from OTU and they went missing on the first
raid to Chemnitz and their captain had bought an old second-hand
car. The next morning I saw the RAF police jemmying open the
doors and that was the only time I really felt something. They were
normally another crew I didn't know much about. There would be
an empty dispersal and the ground mechanics would be left with
nothing but the aircraft covers. What happened was the same day
a brand-new aircraft would be flown over and later on the nose and
the side would have painted on the same letters of the aircraft that
had gone missing and a lorry would arrive with another crew. It
was a case of 'D for Dog is gone, D for Dog is here'. You kept the
name of the aircraft, but personal feelings were diluted because of
the insularity of a crew. It was very clever, I think.[6]

This then was the scene for the nightly and daily drama that
was Bomber Command. Among the most vital nocturnal information was the forecast weather. What was waiting in the atmosphere could be as deadly as the enemy. The most cruel conditions
crews could encounter as the aircraft climbed out of base at the
heaviest weight in its long flight was atmospheric icing, water
droplets in the air freezing on contact, rapidly building up layer on
layer and changing the aerodynamics of the wings and tailplane,
causing the aircraft to stall. If a wing dropped during the stall, the
aircraft then went into a spin that could not be recovered from in
time at low height. Icing occurred because supercooled liquid
droplets existed in a cloud layer that wasn't cold enough for the
vapour to turn automatically to ice particles. Icing was rare at
minus 20°C for instance. The droplets were tiny, but together
could down a bomber in minutes. The forecast for all the squadrons in 6 Group that night was seven-tenths to ten-tenths strato-
cumulus in layers and altocumulus between 1,000 to 3,000 feet

---

* F/Lt Robert Cunliffe, lost on the Chemnitz raid of 14 Februay, is buried
in the Berlin War Cemetery with most of the crew of 625 Sqn's J2. Two are
commemorated on the Runnymede Memorial to the missing.

and 8,000 to 9,000 feet. The likelihood of icing was given as 'moderate' and there was nothing in the cloud, such as the presence of cumulonimbus which pilots feared because of the threat of severe, airframe-straining, up and down draughts, to spell out particular danger. At Tholthorpe one crew member specifically asked the base Met Officer F/O George Hancock if icing was likely. 'In response ... I said the icing would be moderate, not high,' F/O Hancock said later.[7]

From just after 4.30 p.m. the first aircraft had lined up before the stretching duty runway at their bases, their captains performing final nervous checks, then roared down the glistening concrete in the light rain and lifted laboriously towards the overcast 2,000 or 3,000 feet above. At Kelstern, north of Lincoln, F/O Jim Alexander's 625 Sqn Lancaster swept away at 4.39 p.m. and his rear gunner Sgt Joe Williams watched the runway dropping below and behind as Fox-2 climbed and the pilot retracted 15–20 degrees of flap at 500 feet. The waiting was over, another operation into the unknown was about to begin and each crew member went into his familiar routine. Sgt Williams later recorded what those first few moments of an operational flight felt like.

> As we climb out, turning to port the noise and reverberation pulsating through the airframe is acute, later our dulled senses will become accustomed to it. Looking down the tall spire of Louth Parish Church passes beneath us. I turn the turret to port and look up, the aircraft appears to be hanging in the sky. A thin film of petrol venting from the full tanks is spreading across the wings and flicks off the edge. I think of the eight tons of high explosive we are virtually sitting on, truly life was a little precarious. Turning, Jim brings us directly over base and reports to our navigator, 'On course. Now.'[8]

The Lancasters of 1 Group and 8 Group had no problems as they climbed through the overcast and reached for the late afternoon sun, but 6 Group, further north, did. At 4.28 F/O Earl Clark's W-William took off into rain at Tholthorpe and minutes later began to enter a band of icing, just as other 420 Sqn and 425

Sqn aircraft now would. From Linton-on-Ouse crews of 426 Sqn were also watching the rime of ice building on the wings of their climbing Halifaxes. F/O Clark's aircraft was now in deep trouble. His signaller, F/Sgt Robert Arnold, later reported:

> On the climb up we broke cloud and I saw the sun shining for a few seconds and then we were into cloud again which seemed to be similar to the cloud we had climbed through. Shortly after entering this cloud the captain said the aircraft was icing up and I looked out and saw ice on the propellor hubs and the air intakes, it was clear ice. A few seconds later the ice appeared to be building up rapidly and I heard loud banging noises which I took to be either large lumps of ice breaking off the propellors or the engines backfiring. The aircraft was shuddering and did not seem to be gathering any more height. The captain gave the order, 'Prepare to abandon aircraft', so I immediately left my set and put on my parachute. The aircraft was now shuddering violently and by this time the front escape hatch was open and the navigator [F/O Bert Freed] was himself baling out. I followed him out and my parachute opened satisfactorily and I made a good landing in a ploughed field.[9]

The mid-upper gunner in Clark's crew, W/O Harold O'Connor, was the last of the three survivors as the iced-up aircraft went into a spin, the G-force then pinning those remaining inside. He was thrown out as the aircraft broke up. He told RAF investigators later:

> The captain gave the order, 'Prepare to abandon aircraft.' I left the turret and put on my parachute and during this time the captain said 'Hurry' and asked if everyone was OK. I answered 'Mid-upper gunner OK, Skipper'. As I turned to approach the rear hatch I was thrown to the floor of the aircraft beside the mid-upper turret and had difficulty in moving. I tried to force myself along the floor towards the escape hatch but found it impossible due to the pressure forcing me down. During this time I heard a rasping, roaring sound followed by what sounded like an explosion. The next thing

I remember was dropping in mid-air. I pulled my parachute ripcord. Before my parachute opened I saw pieces of the aircraft falling above me. I made a good landing in a farmyard.[10]

S/Ldr Leonard Scott, the senior flying control officer at Dishforth, was looking westward from the control tower when he saw O'Connor come out of the 3,000-foot cloud base together with the two other survivors and pieces of the now-disintegrated aircraft. 'Three of these pieces turned out to be members of the crew whose parachutes opened at approximately 1,000ft while I was watching them,' he later reported. 'The other pieces fell to the ground and were scattered over a wide area.'[11]

It was ten minutes to five and the night's disasters were only just beginning. The area between York, Ripon, Harrogate and Tadcaster was crowded with eight airfields within a 10-mile radius of the base aerodrome of Linton-on-Ouse and eight minutes after F/O Clark's aircraft came down the Halifax of the young S/Ldr Eric Garrett collided with the 425 Sqn aircraft of P/O Mark Anderson from Tholthorpe and the wreckage of both fell to the south side of the Ouse near the Linton base. There were no survivors. Two minutes later the Halifax of F/O Humphrey Watts, who two hours before had been sitting behind Garrett at briefing, broke cloud in a spin over Westfield Lodge Farm, Hutton-le-Hole, near Pickering, after icing up. The farmer, William Strickland, who had been standing in his yard when his attention was caught by the sound of an aircraft overhead 'making a peculiar noise', described what happened next. 'The aircraft was in a flat spin to the right, spinning fairly slowly. As the aircraft lost height the speed of the spin increased and the nose dropped and it struck the ground at an angle of about 45 degrees. On impact the aircraft burst into flames. The bombs exploded about five minutes after the aircraft crashed, about 300 yards from where I was standing.'[12] No crew member could survive such an explosion.

But the price of the most costly icing calamity of the night had yet to be paid. It had unfolded over York just as Watts was coming down. F/Lt Ivor Emerson, flying 426 Sqn's Y-Yorker, had hit a band of icing cloud twenty minutes after take-off from Linton-on-Ouse. His wireless operator, P/O John Low, heard Emerson and his navigator F/O Alick Hutchison discussing the height of the aircraft as Y-Yorker climbed through the cloud, which was thicker than they expected. Low remembered:

> The captain said it was 9,400 feet. The navigator gave him a course to fly and the captain said it looked thick in that direction. The aircraft was still in cloud. I could see heavy icing on my window. The aircraft then started to yaw and I got the impression that alternate wings were dropping. I switched on my intercom and heard the Captain give the order to bale out. The movements of the aircraft were now more violent but I had no difficulty in putting on my parachute. At this time I saw the air bomber [F/O Thomas Campbell] go forward to get his parachute and the navigator opened the front escape hatch and was on the point of putting on his parachute when I baled out. I do not know the attitude of the aircraft when I left it or the height at which I baled out.[13]

Below him was the Nunthorpe housing estate in York, built just before the war. F/O William Mountjoy, a 6 Group flying control officer, was in the city when he heard the sound of 'roaring engines' at 5 p.m.

> A few seconds later I saw a Halifax come out of the clouds in a vertical spin. The cloud base was about 1500ft. The tail section of the aircraft seemed to be on the point of breaking up and shortly afterwards the tail unit broke away and one of the wings began to disintegrate. The aircraft disappeared behind houses and was still spinning when I last saw it. After impact I saw a large column of smoke and about three minutes later there was a small explosion which I took to be the fuel tank exploding.[14]

P/O Low remembered: 'I pulled the ripcord of my parachute, but it did not open and it was necessary to open the pack by hand. On the way down I saw the aircraft burning on the ground. I landed on my back on a wall about 40 yards from the crash in a built up area of York and was knocked unconscious.'[15] In fact his back had been broken.* The wireless operator was found by an RAF man on leave, Airman Oldridge, who had escaped into a garden through a window at the back of the house in Nunthorpe Grove when the bomber's arrival blew in the front. Oldridge was then astonished to see the parachute-equipped airman, who told him he was all right.[16]

The sound of the bomber in its death dive had also been heard by the Deputy Provost Marshall of York, W/Cdr Thomas Groves, in his office in Odeon Buildings in the city centre. 'I saw what appeared to be a large bomber at about 500ft, losing height rapidly,' he later reported. 'Almost immediately it began to disintegrate and two large pieces broke away on the starboard side. The aircraft appeared to roll to starboard then dived to the ground.'[17]

In those last minutes Emerson and most of his crew had been pinned inside the doomed aircraft by centrifugal force in the spin. The grating roar of the bomber's trajectory towards quiet Nunthorpe Grove rose to a crescendo which howled into the rooms of the houses below, sending some occupants diving for shelter and freezing others in terror. This wasn't like an air raid with a siren giving time to prepare. A cataclysm was about to arrive literally out of the blue and burst asunder the routine of the grove on a mundane washday afternoon.

The 30 tons of useless, distressed metal that had been the flying machine Y-Yorker arrived with explosive force. Most of the blow was directed against No. 28 where Mrs Thompson and Mrs Helstrip died immediately, as did Emerson and his crew apart from the badly injured Low. As the last of the brickwork and shattered beams crashed down and the dust began to settle W/Cdr Groves and his team of service police arrived on a scene of utter devastation. 'I found that the aircraft had crashed on two houses and several other houses were on fire,' he said. 'I saw two bombs lying in the road and two others I could see in the burning wreckage.

---

* Low's story had a happy ending. He is reported to have married his hospital nurse.

I telephoned for the fire brigade, civil police and bomb disposal squad. I ascertained that there were some injured in some of the adjoining houses and gave orders to my airmen and some soldiers who had arrived on the scene.'[18] But the tragedy, in which civilians were experiencing at first hand how fragile an airman's hold on life could be, wasn't over yet.

Groves, giving evidence to an enquiry later in the understated manner expected of a senior officer, reported: 'About 15 minutes later while this work was in progress one or more of the bombs exploded and killed three of the military standing near me. Civilians were removing furniture from the adjoining houses and were being assisted by the military. About half an hour later there was a much smaller explosion in the wreckage. I sustained a ruptured right ear drum and several splinter wounds in the back and legs.'

Another eight RAF police were injured in the blast, which – combined with the impact of the bomber crashing – damaged a total of 300 houses. Eight soldiers, two firemen and eight civilians were also hurt, as were two Italian POWs who were helping the removal of householders and furniture from the damaged buildings when the bombs went off. Two soldiers and an Italian POW were killed.

The carnage caused by the unexpected icing band was continuing across Yorkshire. S-Sugar of 425 Sqn, skippered by an American serving in the RCAF, F/O Arthur Lowe, came down twenty minutes into its flight from Tholthorpe. F/O Earl Brabbins, the navigator in Lowe's crew, told investigators later:

> We took off in a slight shower and climbed up to 7,000ft through cloud and at this height the ASI dropped back to 120mph and the pitot head heater was checked by the engineer [Sgt James Lynch] and found to be on. He said he had switched it on before take off. The captain said he was flying on gyro horizon. We continued climbing and struck a lane between two layers of cloud at 9,500ft where the pilot levelled off and the ASI built up to 180mph. On levelling off in this lane the aircraft began to shudder and I put on my parachute. I was in the nose of the aircraft working Gee.

The captain asked the rear gunner [P/O John Hyde], 'What is happening back there' and he replied, 'Everything seems OK'. At this time I was watching the captain who appeared to be fighting to control the aircraft and shortly afterwards he gave the order, 'Put on parachutes and abandon aircraft.' I opened the front escape hatch and jumped out. I was in cloud when I baled out and when my parachute opened I was below the cloud base. As I was gliding down I saw the aircraft pass underneath me and a parachute open near it. I landed about 50 yards from this parachute and found it was my captain whose parachute had opened too late to save him. The aircraft seemed to dive almost to the ground, zoom up again and then roll over to port and dive vertically to the ground. I made a good landing in an open field and was uninjured.[19]

Brabbins's succinct evidence to the later enquiry gives little indication of the terror that must have been felt in Lowe's or any of the crashing bombers in their final few airborne seconds. But the story of the crew's wireless operator, F/Sgt Kenneth McCuaig, does. RCAF interviewers found his mind had virtually blanked out the trauma of his escape. 'I remember taking off and that I was about to take a Group broadcast when I went off intercom,' he told them. 'The next thing I remember is when I put my parachute on and then I remembered looking out of the front escape hatch and preparing to go out the correct way, feet facing aft. I remember nothing more until I had landed by parachute.'[20] Only one other airman baled out to survive, the bomb aimer F/O J. Brownell.

There was an RAF witness to the crash, LAC John Fairbairn, a fire fighter. He reported:

I was standing by the fire tender on the airfield at Linton when I saw a Halifax aircraft just below cloud in a westerly direction flying in an erratic manner. The aircraft was carrying out a man-oeuvre similar to a falling leaf. After watching it for a few seconds the pilot appeared to dive the aircraft, pulled it out of the dive quite sharply and then the aircraft climbed almost vertically, rolled on to its back and spiralled to the ground. I saw no pieces break away from the aircraft and there was no fire in the air. On impact with the ground I saw a cloud of black smoke and flames and saw a terrific explosion ... I was standing just over one mile from the scene of the crash which was beside Little Ouseburn Church.[21]

S-Sugar in fact crashed 200 yards from Little Ouseburn, badly damaging the ancient Holy Trinity Church.*

The deadly droplets of supercooled air floating gently in cloud over North Yorkshire claimed their last victim eighteen minutes later. P/O Roald Sollie who had taken off from Tholthorpe in 420 Sqn's U-Uncle with the DFM winner F/Sgt James Waugh aboard for the first time, came down in Hayton Woods, three miles south-west of Tadcaster forty-nine minutes into his flight. F/Sgt Waugh, who had already cheated death once by winning the battle with the night fighter over Oberhausen, was the only one to escape. He said later:

After take off we climbed and entered cloud at about 2,500ft. We continued climbing and on the way I noticed ice forming on the aerials, some on the front of the mid-upper turret and a quantity around the air intakes. It appeared to be rime icing. We climbed to 10,000ft and at that height broke cloud and we were in clear air. On the climb up I heard the rear gunner [P/O Ralph Battles] ask the captain if everything was all right as he could see ice forming on the tailplane. The captain replied after looking at the wings, 'It's OK and nothing to worry about'. We flew in clear air at approximately 10,000ft for about five minutes and then flew through the top of a cloud which was a little above the general. Shortly after entering this cloud the port wing dropped suddenly and the captain tried to level out and the engineer [Sgt Robert Dinnen] said, 'Is everything OK, skipper' and the captain replied, 'Standby, I think it is the same trouble as I had before' ... The aircraft began to lose height quite gradually and at what I considered to be 7,000ft the captain said, 'OK fellows, abandon aircraft, jump'. I left my turret, put on my parachute, removed my

* The porch of the repaired church now contains a memorial window to the crew.

helmet and went back to the rear escape hatch. I opened the hatch and sat on the edge until the aircraft broke cloud at about 3,000ft. During this descent the aircraft seemed to be rocking fairly violently, but there did not appear to be any excessive 'G' and I had no difficulty moving my limbs. I saw the rear gunner turn his turret to beam and open his doors. The flight engineer was squatting just behind me. I do not know why other members of the crew did not bale out as there seemed to be plenty of time and the gyrations of the aircraft were not too violent.

I baled out and my parachute opened satisfactorily and I seemed to be floating down for two or three minutes. I made a good landing in a stubble field. I did not see the aircraft until it struck the ground and exploded. On breaking cloud at 10,000ft I took special notice to see if there was extensive icing on the wings of the aircraft and I did not see any although if it had been clear ice it might have been difficult to pick out as the sun was quite bright and dazzling. I don't know why I didn't bale out as soon as I got the order but I think it was because we were in cloud and I waited until the ground was visible.[22]

One other 420 Sqn crew had eventually to return to base after a frightening battle to control the aircraft because of icing. F/Lt Norman McHolm, who took off from Tholthorpe immediately after P/O Sollie, reported his windscreen iced up as soon as he entered cloud at 1,700 feet. He selected engine heat as he could hear ice being thrown off the propellers. He said:

I ran in hot air for about 30 seconds, changed to cold and the engines still ran normally. After climbing to 4,500ft the aircraft became very sluggish and the rate of climb dropped off. I could see heavy rime and clear icing on the wings, cowlings, windscreen and the air intakes which were completely iced over. On reaching approximately 6,000ft the aircraft stalled at 160mph with the engines all at full power. I checked the stall and continued to climb, but the aircraft was still very sluggish and stalled three more times, losing about 1,000ft on each occasion. The last stall was more vicious than the previous ones and the controls were snatched out of my hands and the control column was forced back into my stomach and the aircraft started to spin to the right. I put the nose of the aircraft well down before I was able to apply corrective measures. On recovering from this temporary loss of control I had gained sufficient air speed to assist me in climbing again and I reached 9,500ft where I broke cloud. I could then see that the aircraft was loaded with ice and it took full power to maintain this height. I continued to the French coast at approximately 9,500ft but considered I had used too much petrol so I returned to base, landing approximately five hours after take off and after landing the air intakes were still frozen.[23]

A total of seven Canadian Halifaxes had been downed by ice or collision within a few miles of their bases. Their comrades now would face the real enemy as they headed for Chemnitz

THE task that confronted the 750 or so crews continuing the long slog towards the far reaches of eastern Germany and the Russian Front was clouded by uncertainties about Luftwaffe resistance as well as weather. The usual complex spoofs, diversions and parallel raiding in force had been designed to confuse the enemy. In fact 248 Lancasters and 10 Mosquitos of 5 Group were part of the stream until a point north-west of Halle where they would make a 60-degree turn towards their target of the Böhlen oil refinery near Leipzig while the rest of the stream turned 50 degrees towards Chemnitz.

The Chemnitz-bound 1 Group crew of F/O Jim Alexander hit trouble as they were leaving the safety of England behind. The rear gunner Sgt Williams remembers:

The starboard outer began streaming smoke as we headed out over Beachy Head. The flight engineer thought it had blown a cylinder head gasket and it had to be closed down. We had a bit of a discussion about whether we should go on and the engineer said we could probably restart the engine when we reached bombing height. Not having that engine meant there was no power to the mid-upper turret, although the rear turret was powered by the port inner. We tried to restart the engine as we got further into France and then it showed all the symptoms of really being on fire and we had to operate the Graviner which filled the engine with foam, so from that point we were proceeding on three engines.[24]

The mighty stream of aircraft, occupying a block of sky 60 miles long and 5 miles wide, droned towards the area south of Bonn where the flak belts around Germany's industrial heartland thinned. It was known as the Cologne Gap and the Germans, aware for years that Bomber Command needed to choose it as a favoured route, had placed the night-fighter beacons of Ida and Elster above and below it with Beacon Otto further east. It had proved the killing ground on the Nuremberg raid of a year before when ninety-five bombers had been shot down. On this March night of 1945 the Luftwaffe controller, who had not been fooled by a Mosquito feint to Gelsenkirchen, correctly identified the main force and fighters of II/NJG2 were sent east of Koblenz to orbit the visual and radio beacon of Elster ahead of the Pathfinders 50 miles away. Another Mosquito spoof to Wiesbaden proved a distraction to the Luftwaffe, but some fighters made contact with the stream and destroyed three bombers east of the Rhine. The main force was heavily plotted from 8.20 onwards. The experts who compiled the RAF's raid analysis later reported that at 9.19 'night fighters were told Halle was the target, but soon after their attention was diverted to Dresden and to Chemnitz.'[25]

The engine problem with Sgt Williams's Lancaster Fox-2 meant it would now not reach its briefed bombing height and was falling behind its position in the stream for the attack on Chemnitz, timed to open with the first Pathfinders at 9.37 and to end thirty-four minutes later. It left the crew dangerously exposed. As the stream split near Halle four more bombers were shot down. There were then eight unsuccessful combats in the Böhlen area, but on the route in and out of Chemnitz there were nine attacks. One of them was directed against the Lancaster of F/Lt W. J. Buchan, a very experienced Canadian skipper on 12 Sqn with gunners who were proven marksmen. Buchan was awarded the DFC for what happened next. His citation read:

> Coolly and skilfully, F/Lt Buchan manoeuvred to a good position from which his gunners were able to bring their fire to bear on the attacker with great effect. The enemy aircraft was afterwards seen to be falling towards the ground with one engine on fire. On three other occasions, when over Pforzheim, Duisburg and Bottrop Wilhelm respectively, F/Lt Buchan's aircraft was attacked by fighters. In the ensuing fights, two of the attackers were undoubtedly destroyed and the third was driven off with both engines on fire.[26]

Buchan's Canadian mid-upper gunner, F/Sgt Cresswell Jones, was only 20 but had been engaged in six combats since his tour began, in one of which the Lancaster had been badly damaged and Jones had put out the ensuing fire. He was awarded the DFM.[27]

The spoofs, diversions and jamming of enemy night-fighter frequencies by 100 Group were divided many ways among its squadrons. The role of 192 Sqn was to investigate, record and later report on enemy radio navigational, control and plotting systems by use of equipment installed mid-fuselage in its Halifaxes and watched over by specialist radio operators. It meant flying a normal operation right to the target complete with a bomb load. F/Lt Jack Irvine had arrived over Chemnitz in his 192 Sqn Halifax twelve minutes into the raid when he also was attacked by a night fighter. He told RAF intelligence officers later:

> The target was well ablaze at this time and made a very bright patch on the undercast. Our bombs were dropped as ordered and at that moment the tail gunner spotted a Ju88 on the port quarter. There was no flak. A few seconds later the tail gunner gave me a corkscrew to port. This I did on instruments. At the bottom of the dive to port and just after the start of the climb to starboard I instinctively looked up to see the belly and tail of what I think was another Halifax directly above me and about 30ft away. There

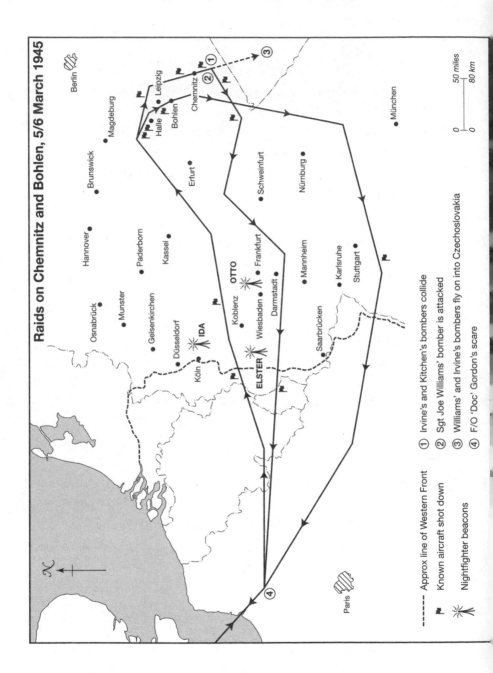

Raids on Chemnitz and Bohlen, 5/6 March 1945

① Irvine's and Kitchen's bombers collide
② Sgt Joe Williams' bomber is attacked
③ Williams' and Irvine's bombers fly on into Czechoslovakia
④ F/O 'Doc' Gordon's scare

----- Approx line of Western Front
Known aircraft shot down
Nightfighter beacons

was no time to avoid a collision and the nose of my aircraft struck the tail turret of the other aircraft. The impact took about five feet of the nose of my aircraft completely off. The other aircraft did not appear to be seriously damaged. The Ju88 had followed us into the corkscrew and at this point opened fire, scoring hits on the port wing.[28]

The aircraft was now vibrating badly, so Irvine, rapidly freezing in the gale whipping through the jagged nose, gave the order to put on parachutes. 'The Ju88 again attacked, but this time we lost it for good by a corkscrew to starboard given by the mid-upper gunner,' Irvine reported. The aircraft Irvine had collided with was not a Halifax, but a Lancaster from 434 Sqn, skippered by P/O J. Kitchen. P/O Kitchen had also just bombed the target from 16,500 feet when the Halifax rose up beneath his tail. The night-fighter crew then attacked Kitchen's bomber, damaging the hydraulic system and starboard wing, but Kitchen's gunners drove them off and he began the struggle to bring his damaged aircraft home. Irvine's ordeal would last much longer. 'We proceeded south of the target to our first turning point. It was there I decided to make for the Russian lines ... I had lost all of the instruments on my blind flying panel and I would never be able to stand the intense cold of the four or five hour trip to England. My feet and hands were already quite numb,' he revealed.[29] Irvine's report was made weeks later when he was returned to Britain. The story of two of his crew would not be told until the war had been over for two months and a former ally was showing signs of being the new enemy.

A total of four bombers were shot down just before or after the target in the Chemnitz area and because the city was so close to Czechoslovakia another two went down in that territory. The first was a Halifax of 102 Sqn. Three members of the crew baled out, but others had been injured and the pilot, 23-year-old F/O John Hurley, tried to land the aircraft near Strakonice to save them, but had crashed into trees and they had all been killed. The second aircraft to come down in Czechoslovakia was Fox-2. Joe Williams remembers:

By the time we got to Chemnitz every other crew had been and gone home. There didn't seem to be much flak actually as I think the Germans thought everybody had left by that time. We bombed and then on the way out scanning behind us I saw a fighter approaching in the light sky of the target. I told the pilot: 'There's a Junkers 188 starboard quarter down, converging on us.' He asked: 'What shall we do?' and I said, 'Do a gentle turn to port, to see if he's seen us.' He followed us round to port, so I ordered flat turns and opened fire.

The Junkers was rushing on to get underneath and was closing. He obviously had Schrage Musik, so I ordered a corkscrew to starboard. He went through the corkscrew with us. I was half standing in the turret, firing the guns fully depressed and the bomb aimer, Floyd Chapman, saw the fighter tucked in underneath us. The fighter opened fire. The mid-upper gunner later told me he could hear those cannon shells banging in all down the fuselage. Both wings were ablaze and the pilot ordered a bale-out. It was quite remarkable. Everything had stopped, there was no power or intercom and my turret was burning. I attempted to open the doors behind me. I managed to get the port door open, but I found the turret was slightly turned to the starboard beam and the flames were coming off the side of the fuselage in great sheets. I was later told by our engineer that the tail was falling off in lumps at that point.

I then had to rotate the turret with the hand gear to get it in line with the fuselage, but I couldn't get the starboard door behind me open. Later I found a 20-mm shell from the fighter had gone through my flying suit on the inside, entering by my right knee and exiting somewhere by my right shoulder, possibly damaging the door. I still couldn't get the door open and I really thought I was going to die. I sat back and I shouted: 'For God's sake get me out of here.' I turned round, tried again and this time it did open. I tried to enter the fuselage to get my chute, but my oxygen hose was still attached and pulled me back again. I ripped my mask off, which I shouldn't have done because I got my face burned. As I looked up the fuselage it was a long tunnel of flame, spiralling down in my direction and when I came abreast of my parachute in its stowage on the starboard side it was burning.[30]

In an instant Sgt Williams then remembered what he had been told in the pub only 24 hours – but what now seemed a lifetime – ago. There was a spare parachute behind the pilot's seat.

I lurched up the fuselage through the flames to get the spare parachute and I found out later the knees and seat of my Sidcot flying suit were burned out and all that was left of my flying suit sleeves was the electric-heating wires hanging down. I also found out later that the right-hand side of my parachute harness was nearly burned through. I managed to get over the main spar and reached the cockpit and everybody had gone out except the pilot, who was about to bale out by the front hatch. He told me many years after the war, what he did then was the bravest thing he ever did in his life. He could have gone out and nobody would have known, but the pilot (who was only just 20) got back in his seat and took control of the aircraft again, so that I could locate the spare parachute. I looked behind his seat, but couldn't find it. We both had thoughts of going down together on the same chute, but that never worked. I then found the spare chute under the navigator's table. I clipped it on both sides and I looked fleetingly out at the port wing. I shall never forget it. It looked like a lot of Bunsen burners shooting blue flame through the wing as petrol spurted out and burned. I dived head first through the front hatch and the pilot came behind me.

I pulled the ripcord and there was a tremendous tug on my shoulders and I knew I was alive. I felt as if God had wrapped up my life in a parcel and tucked it under my arm. I couldn't see much below. I felt my face and there were rolls of skin where I had been burned. The chute was oscillating and we had been told to pull on one riser or another to stop it, but it didn't seem to make much difference. I thought there was some way to go, but there was a bang on the back of my head and I found I was lying in snow. I was apparently 10 or 15 miles into Czechoslavakia. All of Main Force had turned, but we had gone straight on.

I walked until I came to this farmhouse. There was an outside lavatory with a light showing under the door, so I knocked on the door and opened it. It was shut again so I knocked on it again, saying 'Englander'. The man inside shot out, pulling up his trousers and took me into the house. His two buxom daughters were roused. They were Sudeten Germans apparently. They treated me very kindly, attending to my burned face. They weren't third-degree burns, not even second, but my nose and my eyes got the worst of it. The father kept on about Churchill being an 'Israelite'. One of the daughters* asked me if I loved Churchill. I said we did not love politicians, did they love Hitler, to which they replied, '*Ja, Ja*', so there was the difference. I was still feeling ecstatic about being alive.

The Volksturm were called for and I was taken to the local police house then the next morning taken to a large old building in the town of Kaadan and put in a cell. My eyes had by now all matted up and were stuck together and I had to crumble up the dried matter to see. But my burns later recovered although I had a brown face for about three years after the war.[31]

Late at night the door of the cell opened and in was pushed Sgt Williams's crew mate, Bob Pyett. He discovered that the mid-upper gunner had had his own remarkable escape from the burning aircraft. He had climbed down from his turret into the blazing fuselage, grabbed his parachute pack from its stowage and clipped it on as he made his way to the rear door, hearing the ammunition to the rear turret popping and banging in the burning feed tracks. He opened the exit door inwards and flung himself at the opening. The slipstream blew him back in again, but he had already pulled his ripcord and the chute spilled out at his feet. He gathered the

* Many years after the war Sgt Williams was reunited with the two girls he met that night when they traced him through an RAF magazine and accepted his invitation to visit him and his family in Devon.

silk in his arms, sat on the door sill and rolled out backwards. As he passed under the tailplane he let the silk go and the chute opened. He came down in a large tree and climbed down, quickly getting rid of a .38 pistol he was carrying in his flying boot, and was captured the next day. Amazingly all of F/O Alexander's crew had survived.

Eventually Sgt Williams was taken with other prisoners to the Dulag Luft interrogation centre near Frankfurt and on 4 April went behind the wire at Stalag Luft XIIID near Nuremberg. The next day he was evacuated with 300 other prisoners – all headed for Hitler's Bavarian redoubt, it was rumoured – and escaped with the navigator from his crew, F/O Petrachenko. Both of them would be on the run for ten days, dodging a fanatical enemy facing final defeat.

THE raid on Chemnitz had proved an accurate attack. The centre and south of the city were severely damaged by incendiary bombs and factories in the Panzer tank supply chain were burned out, adding to the destruction of previous raids. Two-thirds of the city – which had been known as the Saxon Manchester in the nineteenth century because of its engineering and industrial production – was now destroyed together with much of its transportation network, links that had been considered vital to the Germans in getting reinforcements to the Russian Front.

But it had been a night of heavy loss for Bomber Command: 31 (2.5 per cent) of the total of 1,223 aircraft of all types dispatched were missing. Of those 31 a total of 22 were downed in the Chemnitz operation and another 10, not counted in the Air Ministry raid loss figures for the press, crashed in England. The icing conditions had spread south during the night and the ice claimed a 419 RCAF Sqn crew near Aylesbury as they returned from Chemnitz, killing all on board in the subsequent crash. Another Canadian crew, from 429 Sqn, died in a crash in Kent. A third Canadian crew, from 432 Sqn, were all killed when they were shot down in their return flight by a British coastal battery in Essex. Problems had caused them to return later than the time the anti-aircraft unit had been warned Allied bombers would be passing through. Others ran low on fuel after such a long trip, one being abandoned over France, another crashing while trying to get into the airfield at Juvincourt near Reims.

F/O 'Doc' Gordon, the Canadian skipper of 158 Sqn's veteran Halifax named Friday the 13th, returned on three engines after the port outer throttle disconnected, as had the deicing pump, spraying fluid inside the cockpit. Icing had caused him to fly across France below the cloud base at 1,200 feet. He had been told the height of the local terrain was 350, which he assumed was in feet. After a while the gunners and flight engineer warned him he was so low they could see hedgerows. He later recorded:

> From my vantage point the ground was not visible, but directly ahead I could see two lights that resembled unshaded windows in a Frenchman's cottage. I remarked sarcastically, 'I'll show you how low we are', then I turned the aircraft towards the lights. As we approached the lights suddenly veered to my port side. They were, without doubt, the headlights of a vehicle whose passengers must have thought their time had arrived. This incident brought me to my senses with the realisation that I had accepted the reported elevation of the terrain as being measured in feet rather than in metres. Just how close we had come to parking on a point of high ground we will never know.[32]

The crew, now half an hour late on their ETA and flying through heavy rain, were diverted to RAF Blackbushe, near London. F/O Gordon wrote:

> As we approached Blackbushe visibility was extremely poor, so much so that I had trouble seeing the glide-path indicators. At this stage of the flight de-icer fluid was the last thing on anyone's mind. Only when we neared the perimeter on our final approach did we realise that the stuff had vaporised and condensed on every window and glass panel in the cockpit. It was then that my bomb aimer improved my view of the runway with one swipe of his hand.

Moments later we touched down. It was not one of my better landings.[33]

P/O Kitchen, who had collided over the target then been shot up, also made it back to Britain. He managed to bring his Lancaster into the emergency airfield at Carnaby, near Bridlington. It was written off on landing, without injury to the crew. Sgt Ken O'Brien made it back too, after nine hours and twenty minutes in the air. Sgt Edwin Watson also joyfully returned, his tour, which had begun the previous August, now ended. But the cost was being counted on the Canadian squadrons the next day. Twelve of the twenty-two aircraft that disappeared from the Chemnitz stream were Canadian, adding to the losses incurred just after take-off. In total that night 420 Sqn lost four aircraft, 425 Sqn three and 426 Sqn four. The often-restrained compiler of the operational record book for the squadron which had had to dispatch the night's spare aircraft and crew after losing three out of fourteen so quickly to icing, described it as 'a most disastrous' day and night.[34] Two days after the events that had brought home the air war so vividly to the people of North Yorkshire two courts of enquiry were opened at RAF Linton-on-Ouse, presided over by G/Cptn A. E. James. The first was into the plunging of F/Lt Emerson's Halifax into Nunthorpe Grove. Over the next few days statements were taken from witnesses, some of whom were in hospital. G/Cptn's James's conclusion on 14 March was, not surprisingly, that the pilot had lost control because of heavy icing. The summing-up continued: 'The reason for this severe icing appears to have been due to the aircraft flying through a cumulus or cumulo nimbus cloud embedded in the strato cumulus cloud. The crew were not warned of the likelihood of heavy icing but the court do not hold the No 6 Group meteorological forecasters to blame as it is the opinion of the court that these cloud conditions could not be foreseen.' But there was the added rider: 'The court cannot understand why more members of the crew did not bale out immediately the captain gave the order.'[35] As a result more ground parachute drills were ordered throughout 6 Group.

G/Cptn James also expressed the court's 'distress' at the end of his second, concurrent, hearing – into the crashes of P/O Sollie, F/O Clark, F/O Lowe and F/O Watts – 'that so few crew members survived these accidents and can only attribute it to the fact that the crews were not automatic in their emergency para-chute proceedure'.[36] No blame was attached to anyone for the crashes. There was no court of enquiry into the collision that claimed two aircraft near Linton-on-Ouse. Collision in the crowded skies of bomber country was too familiar an occurrence.

It would have been fortunate if crews could now consider that heavy loss over Germany's industrial areas of high population was in the past as the air war moved into its final weeks. But there were other raids on the Reich's well-defended cities in March – some at long range – and one in particular that a year before had signalled Bomber Command's biggest loss of the war. It would prove savagely costly once more.

FIFTEEN

OLD TARGETS, NEW LOSSES

THERE was much evidence in March that the Reich was collapsing and at the same time not enough as the Luftwaffe occasionally rallied to cause heavy losses to unfortunate squadrons. The month had begun promisingly with the final blow against the old target of Cologne, three days before its occupation by American troops. In the history of Bomber Command Cologne was prominent. The city and its heavy industry had been the subject of Operation Millennium, the first 1,000-bomber raid mounted by Harris in May 1942 as an attention-grabbing exercise to show what his Command, then under siege by the other services because of inefficient bombing in previous years, could achieve in containing the Nazi war machine if given the tools. Bomber Command had been back many times since, particularly in late October 1944 when it became both an industrial and transportation target as the Allied armies closed on Germany. Now, as General 'Lightning Joe' Collins and his VII US Corps stood poised to enter the city, Bomber Command would be called on again to link with USAAF raids and bury the last shreds of resistance from the German LXXI Corps and allow American troops to sweep through the rubble and beyond the cathedral to the Rhine, not crossed by an invader since Napoleon. March, among the most demanding four weeks for aircrew, would see 1945's highest monthly percentage of average FTRs per sortie at 2.1 and there was little time to relax. Harris was making up for lost time and rapidly increasing the pressure on Germany after the bad weather of January. But on the odd night or day they weren't called to risk all over the Reich crews and sometimes individual airmen headed off base for their favourite hostelry. For Laurie Godfrey, the wireless operator on 408 RCAF Sqn at Linton-on-Ouse, whose life had been saved by his gunners over Oberhausen in November, there was a fine choice and the nearest pub was within easy walking distance of his quarters. His accommodation was also among the best in the air force. He recalls:

On 408 Sqn the NCO aircrew were in Beningbrough Hall, a pretty posh billet. W/Cdr Leonard Cheshire had had it for his NCO aircrew when 76 Sqn was in Linton in 1943. Lady Chesterfield, the owner, complained to W/Cdr Cheshire at the time about the boys treading all over her plants and one chap rode a motorcycle down the main staircase. I was in the Blue Room on the corner of the first floor, with the two gunners from our crew and the flight engineer. You could see the River Ouse and the house was set in a marvellous park. It was a very peaceful and relaxing area and I think that helped a bit. The officers were living in their own mess. We were about three miles from our squadron base. A truck would collect us in the morning, or if we were late up we used to walk down. When we came back after an operation and had our eggs and bacon in the sergeants' mess a truck would take us up to our billet at the hall.

As a crew when not on ops we sort of went our own ways and thinking about it now I feel very lucky I was part of a very disciplined crew. There was one pub in Linton outside our base and two more in Newton-on-Ouse, which was just short of the entrance to the grounds of Beningbrough Hall. I used to go to the first pub in the village, the Dawnay Arms, some evenings and have a game of darts with the locals. It was very relaxing and the locals were very easy-going. I think they took care of aircrew. They knew you were on operations of course, but never asked about where you had been or anything. You knew, of course, that it wasn't a thing you should talk about during the war. It made a change to be with civilians and was very enjoyable to have a game of darts. The second pub in the village, the Black Boy, was quite small so was always full up. It was full of aircrew and ground staff. They had a

age from 12,000lb oy bombs on the mund–Ems Canal the raid of 23/24 ember1944. Point A s clear breaches of the ranch of the canal and 50-yard break in the branch. In both cases r has flooded out into ields alongside.

middle of the Hohenzollern Bridge at Cologne lies in the Rhine after it was finally ked by retreating German troops in March, 1945. It had been a difficult target for ber Command since the previous October, with crews being urged to spare the cathedral y, in the foreground of the picture.

The blasted and burnt-out centre of Bochum after the raid on the night of 4 November. It was after bombing the city that Australian pilot P/O Joe Herman plunged without a parachute when his Halifax exploded, yet he survived.

The searing scene from an RAF film unit Lancaster as a firestorm sweeps Pforzheim, ten days after the one which destroyed Dresden. South African Edwin Swales was awarded a posthumous VC for maintaining his bomb run to accurately drop his Pathfinder target indicators while his aircraft blazed from a battle with a night fighter.

ber Command maintained a constant pressure on Germany to force a surrender, despite illing weather conditions at RAF bases in the winter of 1944/45. Here aircrew of 630 join ground staff at East Kirkby in clearing the snow to mount another raid.

The glory of historic Dresden three years before Hitler came to power. The scene, looking along the Elbe, shows the Zwinger palace and Hofkirche in the foreground, then beyond the Augustus bridge the dome of the Frauenkirche.

Left One of Dresden's narrow streets, looking from the Brühl Terrace towards the Frauenkirche with the Landhaus museum tower in the distance.
Right The same scene weeks after the firestorm. Only the Landhaus on the right provides an indication of what once had been.

gaping ruins of the historic Aldstadt, heart of the firestorm. The camera is pointed towards the Hofkirche and the Marienbrücke beyond the barely visible arch of the ustbrücke.

Above The Ruhr Express, the first Canadian-built Lancaster, arrives in Britain for a photo call with the press. It was hoped to fly her back to Canada for a morale-boosting tour after she had completed 50 operations. But *below left* is the wreckage of the aircraft in the snow after she ran off the runway at Middleton St George and caught fire in January, 1945. It was her 49th op.

Below right P/O Wilson managed to bring this Halifax in to land after it lost its entire nose in a collision with a Free French aircraft after a raid on Saarbrücken in January. Wilson's bomb aimer and navigator fell out without parachutes.

most-destructive bomb of the war in Europe: Barnes-Wallis's 22,000lb Grand Slam,
ped by the Dambusters squadron in March, goes on display in blitzed Oxford St,
don, dwarfing the air cadet standing beneath it.

A fireman picks his way through the rubble of what had been a house in Nunthorpe Grove, York, hit hours before by an iced-up Canadian Halifax on its way to Chemnitz in March, 1945. Four other RCAF bombers were also lost to the conditions, all shortly after take off.

101 Sqn bombers hit a railway bridge at Bremen on 23 March. The flak coming up from the target struck the 101 Sqn aircraft of air gunner Ken O'Brien, damaging two engines and wounding the flight engineer.

piano going in there and we used to sing all the old wartime favourites. It was a very jolly atmosphere, with the boys drinking and having a good free and easy evening. The Canadians liked it, I think, because it was an English village pub and they liked the countryside and history.

The Alice Hawthorn pub was across the river from the airfield at Nun Monkton and it was seen as the main place to treat the crew who serviced your aircraft or to celebrate the end of your tour. There was an old boy who used to row aircrew across. He left the old boat tied up one night and some of the boys who had had a few beers came out of the pub, untied it and took it across themselves then just let it float away. We took the ground crew there one evening during our tour, to thank them for all their efforts.[1]

The favourite pub for 158 Sqn aircrew was the Brunswick in nearby Bridlington. The squadron had two veteran Halifaxes on its strength, the Wizard of Aus which had completed more than seventy operations and Friday the 13th, which had made its maiden operational flight on the crippling Nuremberg raid of 30/31 March and would complete 128 operations by the war's end. F/O 'Doc' Gordon was the Canadian skipper of Friday the 13th and remembers:

Although we were stationed at Lissett for only six months we met many Yorkshiremen and enjoyed the friendship of the people of Bridlington and the surrounding countryside ... That wonderful institution the English pub, in addition to being the local watering hole, was the social centre of the district. One was always sure of good company there. I believe every Canadian serviceman who served in England reserves a soft spot in his heart for his favourite pub and the friends he made there.[2]

For the Australians who made up most of 460 Sqn at Binbrook, north of Lincoln, the Marquis of Granby in the village was where ground crew were treated and end-of-tour parties took place. It was run by Rene Trevor, who found herself playing mother to hundreds of Australian airmen, sewing on buttons and serving the treat of a home-cooked meal to young men far from their loved ones. She would often sit at the pub piano singing favourites such as 'Goodnight Sweetheart'and 'Cowboy Joe' for the boys of the squadron, who suffered among the highest losses in Bomber Command. P/O Edney Eyres was an English bomb aimer who had just been commissioned in the winter of 1945 after months on 460 Sqn as a flight sergeant. He had returned from home leave in a stiff new officer's outfit. He remembers:

> One of the tailors in Folkestone did me proud. I had one uniform, one greatcoat, one peaked cap and one side cap. My crew said we would celebrate at the Marquis of Granby and insisted I bring my peaked cap. I wore my forage cap usually, but they were adamant I brought my peaked cap. They got me to put my cap on the table in the bar of the back room at the Marquis, then they each poured half a pint of beer in it. The damn thing never fitted me after that. They had set me up for it. When I went instructing after my tour I had to go on a lot of parades and I had a permanent red ring round my head because of that cap.[3]

On 2 March the newly commissioned P/O Eyres found himself on the battle order for a daylight raid on Cologne. A two-stage attack was planned, the first by 858 Lancasters and Halifaxes of several groups, the second by 155 Lancasters of 3 Group bombing on GH. As Cologne was now virtually a front-line city with its flak battalions intact to face the coming tanks it was that same flak that left an indelible impression on those who took part in the raid. P/O Eyres remembers:

> We were told our troops were only 4,000 yards away from the road bridge. We wanted to destroy that bridge right in front of the cathedral. I didn't see anything hit the cathedral, but there were two green markers burning on its roof, giving us a line to where the bridge was. The sky was so crowded with Lancs trying to line up for the target. Every time I tried to get a straight line at it another aircraft got in the way. The third time I had to bomb as we were

banking, but I reckon I got that bridge. My crew thought three times was a bit adventurous though. I was too busy to see if the flak was hitting aircraft, but there was plenty of it – lots of little black clouds appearing in the sky.[4]

F/O David Francis, the 460 Sqn navigator who had taken part in the Pforzheim attack, also remembers the fearsome artillery fire over Cologne.

The flak was very heavy, so thick we joked afterwards you could get out of the aircraft and walk on it to the next aircraft. Our aiming point was the centre of the railway yards to stop arms and men going to the front. The bombs had gone and the bomb doors were still open as we waited for the photoflash and there was a dirty big thump from a flak burst underneath and we shot about 50 feet in the air. We turned away and everything seemed to be all right then the mid-upper gunner called up and said, 'Cor, come and have a look at this.' I went up in the astrodome and I could see bits of the wings, tail and fuselage sticking up. But the aircraft was flying all right. There was a slight vibration from one of the engines, not enough to put it out. The day after we got back the ground crew told us they had stopped counting after finding 350 holes in the aircraft. Not one single fuel or oil line or control wire had been nicked and yet one little bit of flak could do all the damage. If your number's up, your number's up. We regarded it as pure blind luck. The vibration on one of the engines had been caused by damage to one of the propeller blades; about 2 inches had been taken off.[5]

F/Sgt James Wright, the 166 Sqn wireless operator who had taken part in the Dresden raid two weeks earlier, saw at first hand how effective the Cologne flak sites were that day. 'Standing in the astrodome of "C" for Charlie on the look out for German fighters I saw about half a mile away on the port side a Lancaster hit by an anti-aircraft shell under the wing root. Almost the complete wing fell off and the aircraft, for a fraction of a second, remained straight and level, then fell away on the one remaining wing like a falling leaf. Only two parachutes were seen.'[6] It was the sole daylight operation of Sgt Joe Williams, the 625 Sqn rear gunner who would be a POW four days later. He recorded:

> It was a splendid sight, up to 1,000 bombers in the air. Over the target, my first sight of the thousands of flak bursts, not as angry flashes of light as we knew them at night, but as black mushrooms of smoke which continued to hang in the sky. A huge black pall among the flak marked the place in the sky where a Lancaster, hit in the bomb bay, had disintegrated. The aiming point was the railway station on the north side of the cathedral. We turned and crossed the Rhine again; behind I counted four Lancasters all with engines on fire. One with three engines burning was going down and I lost sight of it.[7]

Sgt Williams learned later the aircraft was G2 from his own squadron, captained by F/O Thomas Downes. F/O Downes ordered his crew to come forward to bale out through the nose escape hatch. 'None of the crew were very anxious to go and were standing in the fuselage. P/O Bob Blackley the flight engineer saw that the fire in the starboard inner engine had turned to a brilliant blue flame and he knew what would happen when it reached the main fuel tank. He shouted "Go" and the bomb aimer and he jumped. As he passed under the Lancaster it exploded.'[*][8]

Among the 160 German soldiers killed by the carpet of high explosive were several SS men determined to fight to the last. As the Lancasters and Halifaxes flew home, less nine of their number, the Lancasters of 3 Group were on their way, but a failure by the GH signal meant that only fifteen bombed. GH stations were by now established in France, as were four Oboe stations, substantially increasing the range of a signal limited by the curvature of the earth. There were also two Gee chains to assist navigation. Setting up such mobile equipment to assist the bombing war was

---

* The bomb aimer, F/O A. J. Bloy, and P/O Blackley, one of the three RAF men in the mainly Australian crew, were the only survivors. The bodies of the others were recovered by American troops who entered Cologne a few days later.

not without its problems. One unit being established on the old First World War Marne battlefield lost a bulldozer which disappeared into an abandoned dugout.

Kenneth Turnham, the wireless operator who began his tour on the day Glenn Miller went missing, was now commissioned on 115 Sqn and was in the 3 Group attack. The flak was even more daunting for the smaller GH wave now that there were fewer bombers for the gunners. P/O Turnham remembers:

Going in to the target we could see a lot of flak coming up and the aircraft was vibrating. I was very apprehensive, worrying about fighters. I could hear the pings of the flak coming through the fuselage, which put the wind up you, and a piece came through where I was sitting at the radio and Fishpond set and one piece hit me in the arm and other pieces in the face. I could feel something trickling down and I didn't know how badly I was hurt. I reported I had been hit, as did the rear gunner, Jock Thompson, who had been wounded in the leg at the same time. He took his gloves off to investigate, getting frostbite in the fingers, but he didn't know then. We continued on the bombing run and the navigator went back to the rear gunner with a portable oxygen bottle to put a tourniquet on his leg and the flight engineer, Andy Glass, came to look at me. He told me it was just a flesh wound and I wasn't bleeding to death or anything.

When we landed at Witchford we discovered we had a burst tyre and later it was found there were forty-seven holes in the fuselage of the Lancaster. An ambulance was waiting for us and Jock Thompson and I were taken to sick bay. There was a piece of flak in my arm and in my nose and forehead. The doctor got me on the table and was waving a cut-throat razor and said, 'Close your eyes in case I slip.' I thought, My God, what's going to happen? but he shaved off my eyebrows and said there was a piece of flak in one eyebrow and a piece in the base of my nose too deep to extricate, so I told him to leave it. About twenty-five years later I started getting sinus problems and an X-ray showed I still had metal in my head. The rear gunner had two fingers amputated because of frostbite, but they weren't his trigger fingers so he continued flying with the crew and finished his tour. We always said we wanted to complete our tour as a crew, that was the camaraderie we had.[9]

On 5 March General Collins reached Cologne and the first elements of the US Ninth Army looked across a linkless river, the centre of the huge Hohenzollern rail and pedestrian bridge lying uselessly in the Rhine and further up river the wrecked road bridge, hit on the 30 October raid and now hit again. The cathedral behind the Hohenzollern bridge had survived, but the acres of rubble that had once been such an important centre of Nazi industry and commerce made a deep impression on the GIs and war correspondents now crunching over the debris and shuffling through the dust. It was visible evidence of what the combined RAF/USAAF bomber campaign was doing to the structure of the Reich. 'There was something awesome about the ruins of Cologne, something the mind was unwilling to grasp, and the cathedral spires still soaring miraculously to the sky only made the debacle below more difficult to accept,' wrote war correspondent Alan Moorehead in a contemporary account about the 'cemetery stillness' that was Cologne now the bombing and fighting were ended.[10] The fact that such an important symbol of Germany was now inside the front line wasn't lost on the Allied publicity machine. There were pictures in the British press of the wrecked bridges and *Wings Abroad* published a photo feature by RCAF photographers entitled 'Cologne Miracle', showing the intact cathedral with an American Sherman tank crew stationed outside. The story read that the cathedral 'is symbolic of a Germany long since dead, the Germany of Goethe and Luther, of Beethoven and Bach'. It also claimed that the 'miracle' of precision bombing had left the cathedral intact, a testimony to accuracy greater than could be achieved, as RCAF crews well knew.[11]

The fact that the third largest city in Germany was in Allied hands and its implication for the immediate future wasn't lost on Goebbels either. It shocked him out of the fantasy world into which he and other Nazis of the inner circle had retreated and – predictably, following the example of the Führer – turned his wrath on Germany's battered army which by now had lost more than 4 million men pursuing Hitler's twisted dream. 'I cannot understand that hardly any resistance was offered in Koln,' he wrote. 'It makes one blush to read reports that men found in Koln by the Americans were almost all fit for service . . . The situation in the West naturally gives rise to continuous and increasing anxiety, primarily because the Allies now have millions of German people under their thumb.' The next day he was writing: 'The greater part of Dessau is a sheet of flame and totally destroyed; yet another German city which has been largely flattened. In addition reports coming in from towns recently attacked, Chemnitz in particular, makes one's hair grow grey. Yet once more it is frightful that we have no defence worth mentioning with which to oppose the enemy air war.'[12]

Bomber Command's raid on the aircraft plant and rail links of the new target of Dessau on the night of 7–8 March had indeed been successful, but – despite Goebbels's disparagement – the Luftwaffe was rallying for a brief period and of 526 bombers that made the long journey to this virgin target in east Germany 18 were lost, a rate of 3.4 per cent. It was the final operation for P/O Eyres, back flying in his skipper's favourite aircraft R-Roger, which had been hit by incendiaries killing the mid-upper gunner while being flown by another crew on the Zeitz raid in January and had just been returned from the RAF repair unit. He remembers:

It was nine hours and five minutes to Dessau and back. We were there as back-up, but our spot-on navigator got us there in good time – not the thing to do to arrive either too late or too early. I was trying to map read in the nose over a snow-covered countryside trying to identify shapes with the target map when I identified what I thought was a dead right shape of the factory we wanted. We made our bombing run, released the bombs then I saw a lot of bombs going down a couple of miles away. I had picked the wrong target obviously and I was supposed to be one of the lead-the-way

301

boys. I think there is someone in the woods there still having a nervous breakdown, but on the outline map the shape looked just right. The trouble was you sometimes picked up a funny wind.[13]

The searchlights and flak over Dessau, not far from the Russian lines, proved fearsome. Sgt Reginald Bell, a gunner whose crew had joined 149 Sqn at Methwold only a few weeks before, recalls: 'We were caught by a master searchlight at the beginning of the bombing run and escaped at the end of the run. The skipper was injured during the steep dive, trying to avoid flak and searchlights and we were all relieved to have escaped. It meant I only did four ops out of my tour because of the pilot's injury.'[14]

Some crews reported seeing jets and rocket-powered fighters as they approached the target. The much sought-after Rose Bros rear turret with its twin .50 (12.7 mm) machine guns had by now reached 1 Group's 166 Sqn and New Zealand skipper F/O Ron Martin must have thanked his lucky stars to have had the extra range and punching power when he spotted a strange night fighter en route. His combat report, compiled in service style, the next day read:

> The pilot of Lancaster W sighted an enemy aircraft, suspected Me 163, on his starboard bow, slightly below, range 1,000 yards flying on a parallel course. He watched it for approximately two minutes, it then turned in towards our aircraft coming in from the starboard beam slightly down. The mid-upper ordered a corkscrew to starboard and both gunners opened fire simultaneously, range 300 yards, the rear gunner observing some strikes. As our aircraft passed over the enemy aircraft an explosion was seen and it fell towards the ground. The rear gunner and the engineer saw it hit.[15]

The considerable aircraft and crews now available to Harris meant he was able to mount two other large raids that night both to confuse the enemy and fulfil his obligations to Portal under the oil directive. The first, by 4 and 6 Groups on a refinery at Hemingstedt, missed the target by a couple of miles and four Halifaxes and one Lancaster went down. The second, by 5 Group alone on an oil refinery at Harburg near Hamburg, was accurate but cost 14 Lancasters of the 234 on the raid. It was a particularly disastrous night for the unlucky 189 Sqn which had lost one-fifth of the squadron on the Karlsruhe raid just over a month before. Now another four crews had gone in a twinkling.

Sgt Jack Shearing was a wireless operator on 49 Sqn, which shared the airfield of Fulbeck with 189 Sqn, and also lost a crew in the Harburg attack. In his diary he wrote the next day: 'When we started our bombing run all hell started up; we bombed and 20 seconds later we were hit by flak – the whole kite shuddered. The run out of the target was a nightmare, we saw five confirmed Lancs go down, one which a parachute came out of – saw several other kites that were probables. The flak was deadly, mostly light stuff sent up in a hosepipe form and fighters all around.'[16]

On landing at Fulbeck after a seven-hour flight Shearing and the rest of F/Lt Len Mellor's crew inspected the aircraft for flak damage and found that among the holes was one in the port wing that they could see was big enough for a man to climb through. Sgt Shearing continued:

> After a meal we went back to the hut. Castile [Sgt Ron Knight, w/op in F/O Elkington's crew] came in late ... I woke up ... he was in a terrible state (his battledress was saturated in Chestnutt's blood) ... he said they were hit by flak on the way to the target and Cyril Chestnutt was badly hit, dying just after (in Ron's arms) and Pat O'Keefe went out of the front hatch which was missing, but as his chute was gone and his helmet left we presumed he baled out ... although there was blood on his oxygen mask. Elkington was hit in the leg but got the kite back OK ... It made us all realise the horrors of war.*[17]

* F/Sgt Chestnutt, a 25-year-old pilot, though like many at this time serving as a flight engineer, is buried in Bournemouth, the second son his parents had lost in the war. The crew's bomb aimer, Sgt Daniel O'Keefe, is buried in Becklingen War Cemetery. He died aged 20 and had lately married.

A total of 41 aircraft were gone of the 1,276 sent over the Reich that night, an alarming 3.2 per cent. For Bomber Command the war was obviously far from over. P/O Eyres and his crew returned safely to Binbrook, his tour which had begun in September now completed. He remembers:

> I did thirty-seven ops because we wanted to finish as a crew. The rear gunner got mumps and missed a few; the navigator fell downstairs after one hilarious party and broke his arm, so he was off ops for a few days and eventually flew with his arm in plaster. It meant we had to do these extra trips to accommodate the rest. When we started on the squadron it was supposed to be a thirty-op tour, but then they upped it.[18]

In fact the new edict of a thirty-six-op tour introduced in February was changed back to thirty at this time as the numbers of new crews arriving on squadrons increased.

THE loss rate on several raids in March sliced through the ranks of particular squadrons. Occasionally only one bomber was shot down in an operation involving scores, but if the aircraft was from your squadron and you were friendly with the crew the loss could be felt as keenly as if scores had failed to return. F/Sgt Frank Horsley, the wireless operator whose aircraft had lost power in three engines evading a Ju88 on the night of the intruders, was now on 158 Sqn. He was part of a daylight force of 175 aircraft which bombed Gladbeck on the northern edge of the Ruhr on the 24th as Montgomery's set-piece crossing of the Rhine was taking place not far away in the Wesel sector. The target was devastated but only one aircraft was lost. It was the squadron's long-serving Wizard of Aus. F/Sgt Horsley remembers:

> It was about mid-day when I saw gliders landing and coloured parachutes. It is very vivid because I thought how lucky we were to be flying when the army had to fall out of the sky on such a dangerous mission. That was, of course, before we reached Gladbeck. W/O Ernest Yeoman (Yo-Yo) was flying some 50 yards or

so away at about the same height near the target when I saw a small puff of white smoke between his two starboard engines. Almost immediately the wing seemed as if it was burning like paper. I saw three of the crew get out before losing sight of the aircraft.*[19]

Then there were other operations that seemed as bad as anything that had taken place in five and a half years of war. On the night of 16–17 Bomber Command returned to Nuremberg, which had exacted the greatest price on the bomber boys a year earlier. Seven weeks before the blood-letting finally ended in Europe the long-distance target proved that yet again it was a deadly destination to be set against. This time all the losses were suffered by a single group, 1 Group based north of Lincoln.

F/O Kevin Muncer of 166 Sqn at Kirmington was briefed to fly in the leading edge of the three-wave attack just behind the Pathfinders. The crews of 1 Group were told there would be forty-six Lancasters and sixteen Mosquitos in the Pathfinder force and the first flares illuminating Nuremberg would go down at 9.26 p.m., quickly followed by red flares cascading green for bomb aimers to line up on. Another attack would be launched at approximately the same time, and only 55 miles away, on Würzburg, by the whole of 5 Group, who as usual would supply their own Pathfinders. Mosquito night fighters and intruders would be active within the stream. The Nuremberg force would fly across France then at Ulm, south of Stuttgart, turn north-east for Nuremberg. The 5 Group bombers would head across the Ardennes then over Germany turn south-east for the ancient cathedral city of Würzburg. A railway junction to the north of Würzburg, a virgin target, was given as the reason for the attack, but the greater truth was Bomber Command was running out of combustible targets and Würzburg was chosen as part of the general relentless pressure

* Scottish-born W/O Yeoman, his Scottish mid-upper gunner F/Sgt James Brown, his Welsh engineer Sgt John Williams and his Australian navigator P/O William Hulme all lie in European war graves.

to force a surrender. It would also provide a strong diversion for the Nuremberg force which would pass between the night fighter zones of Ulrich and Paula. Beacon Otto to the north of Stuttgart, which had proved so effective in gathering the night fighters to the killing zone a year before, would be available to receive the progress of the Würzburg bomber stream and at Nuremberg itself beacon Heinrich to the north of the city would provide an assembly point for the *Nachtjäger*.

It had been an unusual week for F/O Muncer. Four days before, the wife of the mid-upper gunner, eight months pregnant, had turned up in the village keen to be near her husband as the birth neared. F/O Muncer's Lancaster, appropriately coded M-Mother, lifted through the cloud at 5.14 p.m. Above was the worrying glare of moonlight, the very conditions that had caused such a savage loss on the Nuremberg raid of a year ago. The first indications that history was about to repeat itself came three hours later immediately after the stream flew out of the liberated territory of Strasbourg towards Stuttgart. Ahead the night sky suddenly showed the flaming trails of three aircraft on their last descent, teenage airmen desperately trying to escape as orange and blue flame gulped fuel from petrol tanks then burned the magnesium alloy of airframes themselves, the passions, hopes and dreams of twenty-one young men reduced to ashes within minutes.

Bomb aimer F/Sgt Frank Tolley of 625 Sqn remembers: 'It seemed that Jerry knew every turning point. The gunners kept calling in that they were seeing aircraft going down on fire and eventually Bruce Windrim said: "That's it, don't report any more." The navigator had enough to do without logging downed bombers.'[20]

Oberleutnant Eric Jung, who was directed towards the northerly stream while orbiting beacon Otto in his Ju88, went on to shoot down eight of the bombers in both forces with his crew. He later described to a post-war German veterans magazine the details of that night. As they flew south-east his contact-seeking radar operator looked sparingly into the cathode ray tube so as not to spoil his night vision. The night was so clear he was confident he would be able to pick up the outline of the bombers by looking outside.

> And so it was. After they had been airborne for about 20 minutes [7.34 p.m.] they saw the first *Kuriere* [Pathfinder] passing ahead of them from left to right. Visibility could not have been better. The Ju88 was in Planquadrat BS, between Strassburg [*sic*] and Stuttgart, right in the middle of the stream. There might have been between 290 and 300 of them, flying in loose formation. The Tommies must have taken the Ju88 for one of their own machines, because not a single one of them took evasive action.[21]

One by one Jung's aircraft picked off seven Lancasters within twenty minutes, mostly with Schrage Musik. Notwithstanding the developments there had been in the bomber war, with all the warning devices for crews and the strictures to gunners in 1 Group only the month before 'to guard against surprise attacks' there was no return fire, even when Jung attacked from the same level with his forward-firing guns. It was undoubtedly true that in the final stages of a pursuit the nimble night fighters held all the best cards.

But a worse mistake by a bomber crew in the Würzburg element was soon to be advertised. As Jung headed west-north-west looking for a place to land, his radar operator spotted a light in the sky above them, about 12 miles from Würzburg. The closing Ju88 pilot discovered it was a Lancaster with its navigation lights on. The error, possibly due to a greater fear of collision than of night fighters in a crowded sky or caused by the accidental brushing of a switch as instruments were checked, proved fatal. The account continues:

> Jung let [the Ju88] drop back a little so that he could begin his attack from astern, at the same time pulling the control column gently backwards. As he opened fire there was a burst of tracer from the rear turret – the first defensive fire he had met that night. [The Junkers crew] heard bullets striking home in the port wing. Ahead the bomber began to burn, with an ever-growing banner of flame behind it until it hit the ground.[22]

It was Jung's twenty-eighth and last victory of the war. There were now many ways the RAF could end an ace's career and his Ju88 crash-landed that night when a wheel went into a bomb crater on his chosen airfield.

F/O Muncer reached Nuremberg nearly four hours after take-off, the city's flak and searchlight sites putting up what seemed like a solid wall ahead. Then from port to starboard a night fighter raked the aircraft with cannon fire, its tracer flashing through the floor of the fuselage and into the cockpit. F/O Muncer felt a hard thump in his left arm as he instinctively rammed the control column forward and kicked left on the rudder, sending the bomber into a savage corkscrew to port. He heard the Canadian rear gunner, F/Sgt William Reynolds, call: 'We're on fire back here,' and out of the corner of his eye saw that both starboard engines were dead. F/O Muncer hauled back on the control column with his right arm and heard a loud crack as the Lancaster flicked over onto its back. The pilot was not strapped in and he was catapulted out of his seat and through the Perspex of the canopy escape hatch.

With difficulty he hooked his fingers into the D-ring of his ripcord and his seat-type parachute snapped open. As his left flying boot disappeared with the jerk he lost consciousness. He came to crashing through trees and hit the ground hard. He knew he was badly injured but not where and used the survival whistle all aircrew had hooked on their battledress collar. Minutes later F/O Muncer was sitting in a farmhouse kitchen looking at the bleeding stump of what had been his left arm. It had been shot off in the fighter attack. The German farmer's wife quickly applied a tourniquet of baling twine, thus saving his life.*[23]

---

* The only other survivor was F/O W. Gerard, the navigator, who had clipped his chute pack on immediately the fighter attacked. He also fell through the canopy hatch when the bomber flipped over. He was captured the next day and taken to a nearby village, passing the unmarked body of the mid-upper gunner who would never see his child. After the war F/O Muncer's inscribed watch was returned. It had been found on his severed arm by a French POW.

The Polish flight engineer and assiduous diarist F/Sgt Henryk Drozdz was on the raid with 300 Sqn, the second time he had been to Nuremberg in three months. He recorded in his journal:

It is possibly the worst target to bomb, because of the number of night fighters in that area . . . We arrive over the target a little early, so we fly around, which is very dangerous. When the target is on fire and thousands of flames and plumes of smoke fill the air between the ground and flight path, 17,000ft and higher, it is time for us. It feels like a jump into an abyss or hell. It is light as day, here and there a plane and underneath us a sea of fire and smoke. The city is clearly visible. We are over the centre of it. Artillery guns blast away, another moment the bomb aimer shouts and the plane is tossed up. Have we been hit? No it is the bombs going down. These are only short moments, but can there be anything more wonderful? No human eye could see nor memory retain these moments. Sometimes it is only hair-breadth and one plunges to earth – left, right and duck. I can find no words to describe the action. Action of moments and minutes involving thousands of human beings, where the strongest win. This time we belong to them and return safely to our base in Faldingworth.[24]

For F/Sgt Tolley the raid was among the most nerve-racking of his tour. He says:

We weren't attacked by a night fighter ourselves, but over the target I could hear flak pinging through the aircraft. We lost the use of our H2S radar and coming away from Nuremberg we got badly off track. I saw lights up ahead and realised it must be Switzerland. Their anti-aircraft defences fired at us, but it was just a token, and we were able to make a rough course back across to the Channel. We were not attacked by a fighter ourselves, though, on any raid. Our gunners never fired a shot in anger. They were told by group not to fire unless attacked, so as not to advertise their presence.[25]

However, not every crew on the Nuremberg raid followed the instruction. The New Zealand skipper F/O Ron Martin filed a combat report for the second time in eight days. It detailed that after bombing and while the pilot maintained his course and altitude amid the stomach-churning scene of aircraft falling to flak and fighters, the mid-upper gunner Sgt Matt Hudson

> sighted an Me110 directly above, range 75 yards, attacking another Lancaster on the starboard of our aircraft. The mid-upper opened fire with a short burst and then lost sight of the fighter for 2–3 seconds. The fighter then made its way to port level of another Lancaster coming towards our starboard beam. The mid-upper opened fire after giving the combat manoeuvre and the fighter passed across the front of our Lancaster and was lost from view.[26]

A total of 550 rounds of .303 had been fired, but no claim was made.

Hauptmann Wilhelm Johnen, a Luftwaffe night-fighter ace, had recently been recalled with his unit from Hungary as the Russians advanced and in March was based at Leipheim almost at the exact point where the inbound Nuremberg force would make its last turn towards the target. He found that the hunting nocturnal Mosquitos were now a constant threat to the *Nachtjäger*. On the night of the Nuremberg raid his unit had been at readiness since 6 p.m. after being told two large forces had been plotted leaving England. As they waited they were warned Mosquito intruders were in the area and runway lights would only be switched on when immediately necessary. After the war Johnen wrote:

> I taxied in the dark and took up my place on the runway. After a brief glance at the instruments and the engines I gave her full throttle. The flarepath lights went on and were switched off as soon as I was airborne. I had hardly levelled out the machine when Mahle [his radar operator] shouted, 'Look out, Mosquito!' I thought as much. The Tommies had waited until the fish was on the line. But I did not intend to make things easy for them. I hedge-hopped over the fields and shook off my pursuer. The British were very tough, but they did not propose to indulge in any near the ground aerobatics.[27]

Johnen's controller told him forces were heading for Würzburg and Nuremberg. Johnen elected to seek out the Würzburg-bound bombers and within minutes saw fire beginning to envelop the close-packed timber-framed buildings of the old city. 'A four-engined Lancaster crossed my path,' Johnen wrote. 'Without a thought I poured a long burst into its fuselage and wings. The crate exploded in the air and spun down with its crew. That was my only kill over Würzburg and incidentally my last kill of the war. It attracted the entire enemy night fighter pack on my heels. We could hardly watch the bomber crash on the ground before they set upon us.'[28] With his Naxos intruder alert system tick-ticking constantly in his headphones Hptmn Johnen escaped one attack to be suddenly hit by another. 'Even as I banked the burst hit my machine,' he wrote. 'There was a reek of smoke and fire. Terrifying seconds ahead, but I let my machine dive to be rid of my pursuer. The altimeter fell rapidly – 2,500 . . . 2,000 . . . 1,500, 1,000.' Johnen was free again, but as he came in to land at Leipheim Mosquitos were over the field once more. He positioned his Me110 onto the approach by one small light at the runway intersection with a red light positioned at the end of the landing strip. As he taxied to his dispersal pen a mechanic flashed a green-shaded torch which was seen by the orbiting intruders. They came into the attack cannons blazing and as Johnen and his crew leaped clear his Me110 became a blazing wreck.[29]

The Nuremberg raid F/Sgt Tolley and others found so alarming claimed two of his squadron's aircraft. The navigator in Tolley's crew, F/Sgt Bill Porter, remembers the struggle to make it home from southern Germany.

We had been hit by flak which caused skin damage to the aircraft wings and fuselage and damaged electrical cables, so I had no navigation equipment at all. The crew were on lookout for any navigation points and we got home by dead reckoning. I couldn't take star shots because the sky was too black then. We became very short of fuel and it was only by the skill of the pilot and flight engineer that we got back at all. We were an hour and a half late in returning to Kelstern, so late our names had been wiped off the board. When we taxied in to dispersal all the ground crew said was, 'Why have you damaged the aircraft?'[30]

At Wickenby five of the sixteen Lancasters 12 Sqn had sent on the raid were now missing – almost a third of the squadron gone in one night at this late stage of the war. The airfield was shared with 626 Sqn, who also lost an aircraft. Wickenby was a bare place indeed in the dawn of 17 March, six empty dispersals like lost teeth in the flight-line circle that was the bite of two squadrons. There were also three empty dispersals at Elsham Wolds where 103 Sqn operated from, three on 166 Sqn – including F/O Muncer's – three on 170 Sqn at Hemswell and three on 576 Sqn at Fiskerton. A total of 24 of the 231 Lancasters 1 Group had dispatched were missing, a horrifying 10.4 per cent. Ironically the nearest percentage Bomber Command debit to approach this in the past had been almost exactly a year before on raiding Nuremberg. But that had been when the Luftwaffe was at its peak, not in rapid decline. However, in the cold terms of profit and loss calculated by the Air Ministry the gain had perhaps been worth the price. Much of the city's Steinbühl district was ravaged by fire, the main railway station was out of action and the city's gasworks would never function again in wartime. The next occasion the Command would visit Nuremberg would be in daylight in mid-April and by this time Germany's defences would be in such disarray there would be no Allied aircraft shot down.

Another seven Lancasters had been lost from the Würzburg force. Würzburg itself was a smouldering ruin. The efficient 5 Group had dropped 1,217 bombs within seventeen minutes and 89 per cent of the built-up area was destroyed, killing up to 5,000 residents. Only ten of the seventy aircrew aboard the seven Lancasters lost survived. One of those who died was killed by local SS officials, determined, as some had also proved after the devastating Pforzheim raid, to avenge the loss of their townspeople, any moral questioning drowned out by Goebbels's hectoring. Sgt Peter

Roberts, the flight engineer in the crew of F/O John Gibson from 49 Sqn, remembers:

> We arrived in the target area a little too early for the Pathfinders. I was just pouring a cup of tea out of the flask when suddenly all hell let loose as cannon shells ripped into J-Jig. I had seen on previous raids that when fire started on a Lanc you had about 10 seconds to get out – our Canadian bomb aimer (Sgt Henderson) was having trouble getting the front hatch open, so I went to help him ... smoke and flames were everywhere.[31]

Sgt Roberts baled out and hid for three days 'frightened to death' before being found by Volkssturm and eventually being taken to a POW camp for GIs. A newspaper report in 1946 detailed what happened to the 20-year-old wireless operator in the crew.

> A third member of F/O Gibson's crew, F/Sgt Don Hughes, managed to escape from the burning aircraft successfully by parachute, landing by the banks of the River Main. In the morning he was found by two clergymen hiding in the church sacristy of Elbelstadt. He was handed over to a doctor who in turn took him to the Town Hall where he was interrogated. At 7.30 on Sunday 18th March, after two days in the police cells Don was removed from the cells by SS Kriminal-Sekretar Joseph Axt of the Würzburg Criminal Police and Obersekretar Johann Weber. He was then marched to the river, where Axt shot him in the back before throwing his body in the river; his body was recovered from the river next morning. Axt and Weber were charged before a military court at Iserlohn on June 11th, 1946, and both were convicted. Axt was sentenced to death by shooting and Weber to 20 years imprisonment.[32]

THERE were other heavy raids on German cities in March as Hitler's ambitions were finally ground into the dust. Often they were by record numbers of aircraft: Essen for instance was attacked on 11 March by 1,079 bombers and only 3 were lost; the next day it was Dortmund's turn. This time the stream consisted of 1,108 bombers, the largest force Harris would ever send to a single target. Sgt John Simpson, the Scottish flight engineer who had joined the RAF to 'have a go' at the Germans for bombing Glasgow and London and was shot down over Gelsenkirchen on 22 February, had been taken to Dortmund with other survivors of his crew. Luftwaffe officers were trying to arrange transport to the Frankfurt interrogation centre, amid the chaos. There was little accommodation in Dortmund to house anyone, even before the big raid, and the prisoners were put in the basement of bombed Luftwaffe barracks. Simpson remembers:

> The whole town was smashed, as far as you could see it was just rubble. It really was brought home to me. We'd read about these things, but until you saw it it was something else. Most of the bombed buildings seemed to have basements and people were living in them. You could see the smoke coming up from makeshift pipes where they had lit fires. In fact we had about thirty POWs living in them in the barracks.

As the sirens howled for the record raid in which nearly 5,000 tons of bombs would be dropped, Sgt Simpson and his comrades were taken to a makeshift shelter in underground cells.

> There was a Luftwaffe sergeant pilot guarding us who was flak happy. We could hear the bombs coming down and there was a continuous booming and shaking. It went on for what seemed a very long time. I thought the world had come to an end. I realised what I had seen when Glasgow and London were bombed was nothing compared to this. I had no real experience of raids and I remember thinking, This must be like a thousand-bomber raid, and in fact it was. But we were quite entertained by the antics of the German who was guarding us. We felt fairly secure because we were down fairly deep and thought unless it was a direct hit we would be OK.[33]

Only two aircraft were lost on the Dortmund raid out of more than 1,100 dispatched to the target. The resources available to Harris in these last weeks of the war were astounding. Lancasters and newly efficient marks of the Halifax were pouring out of Britain's factories and collectively few were being lost, so flight lines bulged with bombers and crews. The bombers didn't only come from Britain. Victory Aircraft of Canada was now producing all the Lancasters for the Canadian 6 Group. The first such Lancaster X had been flown over by S/Ldr Reg Lane in September 1943. It was christened the Ruhr Express, arrived with Bambi, a poodle pup, on board to give the press something cuddly to photograph and as 1945 began there were high hopes of the Lancaster being returned to Canada to go on permanent display once it had completed fifty operations. Unfortunately, as the Ruhr Express returned to Middleton St George from the Nuremberg raid of 2 January, its forty-ninth operation, it was found the flaps would not deploy properly and, after overshooting the runway, the aircraft ended up in a farmer's field where it collided with a trench digger. Amid exploding ammunition the crew escaped but fire destroyed the aircraft. Bambi fared better, *Wings Abroad* reporting at the end of January that the poodle, still under a foot high, was now the pet of the wife of veteran RCAF air gunner P/O Reginald Burgar, who was doing his tour with an RAF squadron.[34]

The contribution to victory made by Canadians in Bomber Command far exceeded the statistical proportion of volunteers one might have expected from a country with a pre-war population of 11 million. Not only had the Commonwealth Air Training Plan bases in Canada trained most of the pilots, navigators and bomb aimers in Bomber Command – even Australians and New Zealanders as well as British – and provided a whole bomber group, but Canadians also made up the largest Commonwealth group by far serving in RAF squadrons. The reciprocal sacrifices that statistically such a large contribution demanded was never more evident than in 1945. In fact 58 per cent of the Canadians who flew with Bomber Command were killed and losses on the Canadian squadrons of 6 Group continued right to the end. Sometimes it seemed they were downright unlucky, suffering casualties even from their own side. Canadian bomb aimer W/O

315

Teddie Hutton was coming back from a raid on the Ruhr metal-working town of Hagen on 15 March when the Canadian squadrons flew into a wall of Allied anti-aircraft fire. The night raid, the last operation of his tour with S/Ldr Wilbur Pierce which had begun the previous July, had already proved alarming enough. While on the bomb run as W/O Hutton leaned over his sight a Lancaster to the port side of their 433 Sqn Halifax was hit. He wrote later:

> Flames stream back along its fuselage until the large aircraft turns into a fireball and finally plunges to the ground. You see it and know what it is, but even at this stage of our tour it still seems unreal. I am all set to press the bomb release when I see the dark form of a Halifax emerging from the darkness directly below us, crabbing across the aiming point. It receives a direct hit, hurling chunks of flaming debris in all directions. The force of the explosion rocks our aircraft violently, but the skipper quickly recovers the bombing run. I press the release. 'Bomb gone' I shout, watching the blockbuster tumble towards the conflagration below.[35]

On the way home the crew began to relax their vigilance some time after crossing the Allied front line. 'Cruising over Belgium the tail gunner shouts, "Hey skipper, those dumb bastards are shooting at us",' W/O Hutton wrote. 'Of course we think he is kidding, but when some ack-ack shells begin bursting nearby, we can't believe it.' S/Ldr Pierce was asked if the Verey pistol in the fuselage roof should be fired, showing the colour of the day to prove it was friendly aircraft passing through. The skipper replied, 'No! Don't let them know where we are.' The rear gunner, F/Sgt G. McMurchy, then called out, 'Jeez, two more shot down' and a moment later reported that another aircraft had fired off the colour of the day.' 'Tell me what happens', orders the skipper,' W/O Hutton wrote. 'Within seconds the aircraft that had identified itself is hit by artillery shells, spirals down in flames and explodes. "Teddie direct me to open spaces", shouts the skipper. As he puts on more speed I switch on the H2S set, directing him around built-up areas, keeping to open spaces ... We don't feel secure until we are back over the Channel.'[36] Of the ten bombers lost on the Hagen raid, eight came from RCAF squadrons – four of those are believed to have been brought down by Allied anti-aircraft guns. The raid, which caused 1,500 large fires in Hagen, left 30,000 workers and their families homeless.

The night-fighter successes over Nuremberg, Würzburg and Hagen in mid-March signalled the swansong of the German night-fighter force, which in the two years of Harris's major bomber offensive had littered Europe with the pyres of shattered Wellingtons, Stirlings, Halifaxes and Lancasters and filled German cemeteries with their dead crews. There would be only one more occasion when the bombers downed in a single night would go into double figures. Half of them were lost on an attack on the oil refinery at Lutzkendorf as Harris fulfilled final obligations to the oil plan Portal had been urging him to make a priority since October.

SPRING

SIXTEEN

OIL, TOIL AND TROUBLE

THE failure of Harris to concentrate on the enemy's fuel supplies to the exclusion of virtually all other targets has been seen as his great mistake in the twenty-five months of his main bombing offensive. And there is no doubt that it *was* lack of oil that finally stopped the Nazi war machine. At Eisenhower's request he had carried out a night campaign against the enemy's Ruhr oil installations in the summer of 1944, then Portal had asked him to return to them in October. In November Portal had reminded him again and Harris had responded with further raids on oil installations. But it was not enough for the Chief of the Air Staff and after a flurry of letters to and fro in December in which Harris described the oil campaign as another 'panacea' like so many fruitless strategies in the past Portal had replied: 'Naturally, while you hold this view you will be unable to put your heart into it.' Harris suggested in January that, therefore, it might be best if Portal found another chief for Bomber Command.

Portal, who had great respect for Harris's abilities, not least his tenacity, immediately set out to defuse the situation. He had written on the 20th: 'I willingly accept your assurance that you will continue to do your utmost to ensure the successful execution of the policy laid down. I am very sorry that you do not believe in it, but it is no use my craving for what is evidently unattainable. We must wait until after the war before we can know for certain who was right.'[1] In fact Portal was right and in his immediate post-war book, *Bomber Offensive*, Harris admitted as much, but with the reservation: 'What the Allied strategists did was to bet on an outsider and it happened to win the race.'[2]

It was perhaps key to Harris's attitude at the time he was being badgered to concentrate more on oil and less on Germany's industrial cities that he did not have access to the most crucial intelligence of the war, the German Enigma coding machine decrypts known as the Ultra secret. Portal did and knew far better than Harris what Bomber Command's new precision in the final phase of the bombing war was doing to German means of propulsion.

As spring approached, however, it became obvious to Harris too that the German fuel supply was being effectively throttled. As the disciplined subordinate he was, once unequivocally ordered to carry out a specific campaign against oil, he had responded with a will while still attacking other targets to continue confusing the Germans to his daily and nightly intentions. In the poor weather conditions of January, his crews carried out six raids on oil installations. But in February it was sixteen, and in March, fifteen. The Germans had nonetheless always vigorously defended the lifeblood they needed to continue the war, and raids had often been at great cost, particularly if mounted at long distance against fuel plants in the eastern areas of Reich territory. On 8 February nearly 500 Lancasters had been sent to the important I. G. Farben hydrogenation plant at Politz, near Stettin on the Baltic. The route deliberately included Swedish airspace to avoid enemy flak and help to maintain the element of surprise. Sweden had often had its neutrality invaded by the RAF and by now irritation that diplomatic protests were being fobbed off was beginning to show. Since the previous autumn Bomber Command had been complaining that Swedish flak wasn't merely being used to warn off RAF bombers, but was actually shooting them down, though it was more likely that unexplained losses were due to previously damaged aircraft running out of fuel and coming down in the sea. In fact F/O Brian Curran of 619 Sqn had had to land his Lancaster in Sweden on the Politz raid of 13 January because he had insufficient fuel to return to England and he and his crew were interned until 10 March.[3] But on the final operation against the Politz plant on 8 February in which twelve Lancasters were lost, one of them went down to Swedish shellfire.

F/O Bruce Clifton, a 21-year-old former bank clerk, was en route to Politz when his 57 Sqn Lancaster was hit by flak over Helsinborg. 'Four of our bombs exploded and I was blown out of the aircraft and just managed to pull my ripcord,' the skipper reported when back home in mid-March. 'The remainder of the crew were killed in the aircraft. I came down about three miles from Helsinborg and went to a farmhouse from where I was collected by Swedish police. I spent the night at an army barracks.'[4]

By the time the war entered its penultimate month, however, Politz was a totally disabled ruin, thanks to the RAF, and Reich production of oil was now rapidly shrinking around Leipzig, where I.G. Farben had been producing synthetic petrol from brown coal since 1927. The USAAF considered the concentration of flak sites there was the highest in Europe and although the Leuna works for instance was attacked twenty times by the USAAF and twice by the RAF production was still maintained at 15 per cent of capacity from January until nearly the end of the war.[5] Seven miles from Leuna was another synthetic fuel plant, the Wintershall AG works at Lutzkendorf, set up in 1936. The RAF had first attacked it in mid-March, the whole of 5 Group being employed. Moderate damage was caused, but the flak gunners had swept through the squadrons of 5 Group, eighteen Lancasters being lost, a horrendous 7.4 per cent of those that had set out. The Spilsby-based 207 Sqn lost two of its crews. On the night of 4 April Bomber Command sent 1 Group to the refinery, losing 6 of 258. The aircraft of Sgt Ken O'Brien, the 101 Sqn air gunner who early in his tour had become certain he would not survive, was not one of them, to his surprise. He came home, his tour ended. He remembers:

We didn't know it was our last when we took off although it was our thirty-fourth trip. They had a glut of aircrew towards the end, but Bomber Command was going far into Germany and started to take losses again, so we did more trips than the thirty. We had to land away at North Creake because of bad weather. It was known as Shit Creek to aircrew and there was no accommodation for us. I had to sleep on a billiard table. We flew back to Ludford the next day and they told us then we were finished. I never thought I'd survive. It was stuck in my head that I wouldn't see the end of my tour. I was still 19 and with the rest of life ahead. There was one almighty party with our ground crew. We took them to the Black Horse pub in Ludford.

I think the only way the air force got us to go on ops was because we were so young. You didn't want to be put down as Lack of Moral Fibre and you knew that was at the back all the time, but I think the main reason you kept on was you didn't want to let the rest of your crew down. We were a family really, supporting one another. We used to go out to the pub together a lot. We would take the crew bus from Ludford to Grimsby, then into Cleethorpes to one particular pub. I didn't tell the rest of the crew that I was sure I wouldn't survive.[6]

It was also the last night operation for 625 Sqn's F/Sgt Bill Porter, who had lost all his navigation aids to flak over Nuremberg three weeks before. He recalls:

We were not aware of it but 4 April was also to be our last operation from Kelstern. We got airborne to Lutzkendorf at 11.20 p.m. and had an eight-hour trip before landing, debriefing and a meal. I don't recall what sleep we had that morning of 5 April, but I know that we packed and were airborne again at 4.15 that afternoon on our way to our new base at Scampton, a flight of fifteen minutes. Kelstern was closed as a base after we left. In March we did thirteen operations, which was pretty good going, and of course there were training trips in between. It was tiring, but it was a way of life you just got used to at that age. Our bomb aimer was the old man of the crew at 23. I was 21, the pilot was the same age, the flight engineer was 20 and the rest of the crew were 18 and 19. The first news on arrival at Scampton was not encouraging, since the then resident 153 Sqn had been involved in a mine-laying sortie while we were at Lutzkendorf and had lost crews. Mine-laying was extremely hazardous.*[7]

THE target-experienced 5 Group had not been asked to bomb the Wintershall AG works because that day they had been attacking the V-2 assembly plant at Nordhausen. But four nights later the group's squadrons found they were being asked to face the flak of Lutzkendorf once more.

Several of the crews who gathered for briefing were new to operations, the last batch of youngsters who had been persuaded by poster after poster of smiling airmen being used to sell everything from cocoa to war savings that the RAF might be the youngest of the three services but it was definitely the most glamorous to go for before the call-up papers dropped on the mat. However, once the initial square-bashing was over and an application for aircrew training had been filed, airmen quickly found any dreams they might have had of flying Spitfires were quickly dashed. There was a glut of pilots now and anyone who wanted to fly was rapidly diverted into the bomber programme and into the ranks of the air gunners.

Sgt Ken Freeman, the mid-upper gunner who had arrived on 207 Sqn at Spilsby in early March just in time for the night of the Luftwaffe intruders, had by April been in the air force for a year. He remembers:

I joined up at 18 and did all the aircrew tests, passing all the maths and physical exams to be graded PNB – Pilot, Navigator or Bomb Aimer. Then I went for final interview with a wing commander and all the brass. The first thing they asked me was: 'What can you tell us about the workings of the internal combustion engine?' My dad didn't have a car, so I replied, 'What's an internal combustion engine?' and they said, 'Right,

---

* Two 153 Sqn crews disappeared on the night of 4 April, believed to have been shot down in the Kattegat by a night fighter. They included the squadron commander, W/Cdr Francis Powley.

Wireless Operator/Air Gunner.' I was supposed to go to radio school, but was told I would have to wait six weeks. They said if I volunteered for straight AG I could go on an AG course right away, so I did.[8]

When Sgt Freeman was finally crewed up with Australian skipper F/O Warren Sharpe he found he wasn't the only one in an aircrew trade he hadn't initially expected. The flight engineer in his crew, like so many at this time, was also a qualified pilot.

It was not until 4 April 1945 that the seven men were sent on their first operation, the daylight raid to Nordhausen. Now, four days later, as Sgt Freeman listened to the briefing for his first night op, to Lutzkendorf, he could dwell on how uncertain life had become. The original rear gunner in his crew, 19-year-old Sgt Kenneth Clapperton, had already been killed, flying as a replacement with an experienced New Zealand pilot to an oil refinery at Hamburg on the night of 21 March. It was the second time in two nights running that 207 Sqn had lost a bomber on an oil target. Sgt Freeman remembers:

We were told about the op and went to look at the battle order but we found we weren't on because we were due to go on a week's leave the next day. Clapperton went to check himself and found he was down to fly with another crew. I thought then, foolishly, he would have one more trip than I had, so I went to see if I could join him. Then I realised it was the camp dance that night so I decided not to bother. It was a good dance, held every Wednesday. There were always a lot of WAAFs there and they used to bring in a lot of girls from Skegness.

A few hours later we were getting ready to go to the dance and Clapperton was standing on his bed pulling on his long underwear after getting a few hours' sleep. He gave me his little address book with all his girlfriends' names in and said, 'If anything happens to me just get rid of that, don't let it go home.' When we went to the mess the next morning we saw the WAAF serving breakfast – a girl who had been keen on him – was in tears and she said he was missing.*[9]

On the Australian 463 Sqn at Waddington a few miles to the north another 19-year-old air gunner, Sgt Dennis Broadhead, was listening to his recently appointed CO, W/Cdr K. M. Kemp. Sgt Broadhead, an ex-ATC cadet from Sheffield, was part of an international crew. His skipper F/O Thomas Baulderstone was Australian, as was the navigator F/Sgt James Hill. The bomb aimer F/O Robert Adrain and wireless operator W/O John Bomby were Canadian. Broadhead had been in the air force for just over a year. Among the aircrew listening to briefing at Skellingthorpe on the southern edge of Lincoln was F/Sgt James Chadwick, an air force regular. He had left his job as an assistant buyer in Manchester and joined up six months before the war. Now he was a bomb aimer on 61 Sqn in the crew of 20-year-old Canadian F/O John MacFarlane. Chadwick, at 34, was considerably older than most aircrew.

At Bardney rear gunner Sgt Elias Williams was thinking about his son Kenneth. The little boy had been five the day before. On the dispersal pans along the perimeter track of the bleak wartime airfield eighteen Lancasters were being bombed up from a snaking line of bomb trolleys with the Tallboys 9 Sqn's aircraft had been adapted to carry. The 12,000-lb bombs would be dropped from 18,000 feet, rapidly developing a vertical spin from their angled tail fins and penetrating the ground at 750 mph thirty-seven seconds later, to come to a halt approximately 25 feet below. Some had been fitted with a half-hour delay fuse to ensure the earthshaking effect that toppled buildings would go on long after the oil plant had been damaged by other bombs.

Crews at briefings across Lincolnshire were told theirs was the lesser attack of the night by Bomber Command. A total of 231

---

* Sgt Clapperton, of Carlisle, is buried in Becklingen War Cemetery with the rest of the crew of F/Lt Roland Werner, a married man. They were shot down by flak over Hamburg.

Lancasters of 5 Group would be going to Lutzkendorf led by 11 marker Mosquitos, but a mixed force of 440 Halifaxes and Lancasters of 4, 6 and 8 Groups would be following up an earlier USAAF raid on the shipyards of Hamburg. A small force from 5 Group would attack oil storage tanks in Hamburg the next day. As COs bade their final 'Good luck' there were the usual strictures to the rows of seated airmen about leaving all personal photographs, letters or even ephemera such as used bus or cinema tickets in their lockers. Lectures on wet and windy non-flying days had already alerted the aircrew as to how skilful the Luftwaffe interrogaters at Dulag Luft were at piecing together background material on a squadron and its personalities by what was found in the pockets of airmen, dead or alive. They were also urged never to fly without their identity discs around the neck. Bitter Nazis, surrounded by the wastes of what had been Hitler's much vaunted Reich, were now looking for any opportunity to shoot or lynch downed aircrew, particularly if they could claim they were spies because of the lack of a dog tag.

After a few hours' rest and a final pre-op meal of bacon and eggs the crews collected parachutes and Mae Wests and made their way to the locker rooms to struggle into flying boots, sheepskin Irvin jackets and for the gunners the bulky yellow Taylorsuit, amid the nervous banter of those about to meet the enemy, perhaps for the first time. The final act was to collect flasks of coffee and sandwiches, together with the special treat for aircrew, the confectionery ration to keep up their energy reserves. 'We used to get loads of sweets and chocolates in our flying rations,' Ken Freeman remembers. 'Barley sugars, Fry's chocolate creams, Crunchie bars and three or four bars of Cadbury's Dairy Milk. Some of it you ate, but there was a lot left.'[10] The Cadbury's ration chocolate in its wartime light blue on white oiled-paper wrapper, the Fry's Crunchie bars in their plain light orange covering and the brown-scripted Terry's 'Oliver Twist' bars with their logo of a smiling boy with a begging bowl rapidly filled battledress pockets. Then there was the nervous wait for the WAAF-driven bus to take encumbered crews out to their aircraft. The young and inexperienced Sgt Freeman, an amateur musician, had an extra piece of equipment to carry, his clarinet. 'I took it with me on ops because I thought if I was shot down it would be very useful in a POW camp,' he remembers ruefully now.[11]

Sgt Broadhead's was among the first of 5 Group's Lancasters to line up, engines booming, and bound away into the night sky just before 6 p.m. As an operationally inexperienced skipper, F/O Warren Sharpe, with Sgt Freeman aboard, was in one of the later waves. Ken Freeman recalls:

I had been excited to go on my first operation. The second one I had been a little more apprehensive about, particularly with it being a night op. You take off and see all these other aircraft milling around gaining height then they all start heading in the same direction. At that point the stream is probably 2 or 3 miles wide, but you know they are all coming together over the target. I was very worried about collision. It was part of my job to look for other friendly aircraft as well as night fighters and do a banking search every minute as the pilot weaved.

It took three and a half hours for the leading elements of the force to reach Lutzkendorf. By the time the final waves arrived the synthetic fuel was well ablaze. Ken Freeman remembers: 'You could see the target from a long way away, a bright orange, then it got bigger and bigger until the whole night was glowing orange. Then we could see the sparklers of flak.' High in the sky over Lutzkendorf itself the young musician achieved an ambition. 'As I scanned the sky from the mid-upper turret I picked up my clarinet and played a few notes off the intercom because I wanted to be able to say I had actually played over a target,' Ken Freeman recalls.[12]

The red burst of shellfire pumping up from the flak sites had already claimed F/O MacFarlane. 'Just over the target we were hit by flak and compelled to bale out,' F/Sgt Chadwick, one of only two crew members to escape the Lancaster in time, later reported. 'I landed on open ground about 200 yards east of Lutz-kendorf. I had noticed the position of three anti-aircraft posts and made my way between two of those towards the North and then turned West.'[13] The young Sgt Dennis Broadhead also soon found himself evading the enemy. 'We were hit by flak just before reaching the bombing run,' he recorded. 'We bombed the target and immediately afterwards found that the starboard wing was on fire. We carried on in a south westerly direction for about seven minutes when the order was given to bale out. It was then about 2315 hours. I landed in a tree, but managed to scramble down, leaving my parachute behind. I hid my Mae West and started to walk.' The rear gunner had been the only one of the crew to escape.[14]

Among the other aircraft brought down by the barrage of shell fire was the Tallboy-carrying Lancaster of 21-year-old Australian F/O Bernard Woolstencroft. The rear gunner F/Sgt Elias Williams was the sole survivor. He later related:

As the bomb aimer called, 'Bomb gone,' our aircraft lurched under a terrific flak barrage. There was an acrid smell of explosives in the fuselage and I heard the engineer call on the skipper to dive. Then the plane shuddered under a direct hit. The petrol tanks in the wings were on fire and they were streaming flame back towards my turret. I heard a shrieked 'Jump for it' then the intercom went dead. The Lancaster was now out of control and flames were all round me. It was such an intense fire I knew everyone else in the crew had had it. I tried to turn the turret to get out but the hydraulics weren't working. Frenziedly I turned it with the manual gear. By that time my clothing and parachute harness were burning, but I managed to turn the turret enough to leap into space.

I was falling from four miles up through the flak barrage and was hit behind the ear by a piece of shrapnel which stunned me and another piece hit my foot. By that time my clothes were no longer burning and I managed to pull the ripcord and the parachute opened, then I found myself swinging over what looked like a void. I thought it might be water, so I inflated my Mae West and waited to land on whatever it was. With a crash I hit a sloping roof which I rolled down while I frantically tried to grab something. I fell off and hit the ground in a shower of broken tiles. I lay there stunned. My face, hands and body were burned. There was blood coming from the wound in my head, I had a broken thumb and another shrapnel wound in my foot. I was terrified that I would be found by civilians. We had been warned they would tear us to bits.[15]

Night fighters also arrived in the target area. Sgt Ken Freeman remembers:

As we came away from the target after bombing I saw an Me110 above us on the port quarter. I knew it couldn't be a Pathfinder Mosquito because they would be well above or well below, it wouldn't be in the middle of us, so I shouted, 'Port, corkscrew, go,' which the pilot did immediately. As we went into the corkscrew I tried to test my guns and nothing happened. I found the electric switch in the middle was still off. Our training was to corkscrew without firing if you weren't attacked. As soon as we came back straight and level again I saw that we had lost him.[16]

A total of six aircraft were shot down from the Lutzkendorf force, including two from 463 Sqn and two from 49 Sqn, and another six were lost from the Hamburg raiders. But spring fog closed many airfields to the returning bombers and several crashed after being diverted. The aircraft of Sgt Freeman had to put into the training base of Gaydon in Warwickshire. 'They debriefed us, gave us a meal and then just turfed these airmen out of bed so we could get in,' Ken Freeman remembers. 'The beds were still warm because they had just got out. We slept for about four hours and then took off for base. I left two or three bars of chocolate under the pillow of the chap who had been turfed out.'[17]

In Germany the wounded and frightened Sgt Williams had already met the enemy. He related later:

As dawn came I was glad to be found by German soldiers. I was interrogated and learned I was in the town of Jena. They cut the signet ring off my finger. They asked me about my name Elias and asked if I was Jewish. I explained I was Welsh. I was then taken in a party of prisoners, including some in concentration camp clothing,* on a march which lasted eight days in all. My foot was very sore and I could only stagger. At one time a French doctor helped me by binding my wounds with paper bandages. One night we heard intense gunfire, then in the early hours of the next day we were found by forward tanks of Patton's Third Army. I had had my flying jacket taken from me and was wearing clothing given to me by the Germans, so I was then put under guard by the Americans and had some trouble convincing them I was a shot-down RAF man.[18]

The two Lutzkendorf evaders also eventually made it into the American lines. F/Sgt Chadwick, who had headed north then west, kept going across fields for two or three hours. He later told MI9 officers:

I came to a large quarry where I hid up all through the daylight period of April 9th. After dark I continued to walk in a westerly direction, skirting the town of Querfurt. I hid during April 10th in a large hayrick and continued walking west after dark, spending the daylight period of April 11th in a forest. I set out walking again at dusk and by dawn had reached a village about two miles east of Artern. Hearing gunfire in this town I decided to wait on the outskirts until American troops had broken through. At about 0930 hours on April 12th I met the leading tanks of the American 9th Armoured Division. I was repatriated on April 17th.[19]

The teenaged Sgt Broadhead who had started walking after ditching his Mae West kept it up for four hours then hid in a wood for the day. He told intelligence officers in Paris:

* These were probably prisoners from Buchenwald concentration camp only 30 miles from Jena. It was liberated on 11 April and the US journalist Ed Murrow made a broadcast from there the next day and a filmed record was made for America. Six days later a British film crew arrived in newly liberated Belsen, north of Hanover, and filmed piles of emaciated bodies being bulldozed into pits, the image of Nazi Germany that was then shown to cinema newsreel audiences in Britain. The Russians took their own film of Auschwitz's liberation, but didn't release it until January 1946, in time for the Nuremberg trials of the Nazi leaders.

When it was dark I started walking in a westerly direction and walked until dawn. I found some bushes where I was fairly well hidden and slept until about 10 the following morning. While I was hiding in the bushes a woman came up and looked at me, but did not speak. After she had gone away I thought it advisable to leave, so I began walking again until I came to a field where there were some people ploughing. I waited until evening when they had left the field then I started walking again. At about 2000 hours I met some American forces west of Erfurt.[20]

The same unit of those soldiers had come across the horrors of Buchenwald less than five hours before.

BOMBER Command raids on oil targets continued almost until the end of April in the final squeeze on Nazi supplies at the same time as communication centres were targeted as far away as Czechoslovakia to bottle up the halted military machine further. On the day after the second Lutzkendorf raid, as Air Ministry telegrams to the families of the missing were being presented in suburban avenues by boy Post Office messengers, the designated small force of Lancasters from 5 Group bombed Hamburg, in part to destroy oil storage tanks, the third Allied air attack on the city in 24 hours. The Luftwaffe arrived with Me262 jets to show it wasn't totally finished and two of the oil-target bombers were shot down, only two out of the fourteen men aboard surviving. It was the first operation in the second tour of F/O Graham Allen, a flight engineer who had won the DFM at the end of his first tour in the very different days of May 1943.* Now he was on the Australian 463 Sqn, which had lost two Lancasters over Lutzkendorf hours before. He remembers:

Only fifty-seven aircraft took part, seventeen Lancasters of 617 Sqn attacking submarine pens with Tallboys and Grand Slams. The remainder were after oil storage tanks near the main dock area. A squadron of Mustangs were to act as escort near the target. We

* See author's earlier book, *Bomber Boys*.

flew in a loose gaggle formation and all went well until about halfway from the Dutch coast to the target the starboard inner engine suddenly cut out. The prop was feathered and we later found out the drive shaft to the two magnetos had sheared. With only three engines we began to drop behind the main formation and by the time we reached the target we were on our own, the rest of the formation had bombed and were turning. My pilot, F/Lt McGregor, decided to press on and we dropped our bombs and turned for home, by now being about two miles behind. At the briefing we were told to fire flares if any enemy fighters were sighted and some now went up from the formation ahead. They were being attacked by several Me262 jet fighters. We saw one Lancaster go down slowly spinning, with the tail unit breaking off at the door.* Our gunners then saw a 262 behind us and we broke into a corkscrew as he came in firing his cannons. We were struck by several shells, one hitting the starboard outer engine which started losing coolant, leaving a stream of white vapour, another went straight through the main starboard petrol tank. The Perspex of the canopy above my head was hit and I have a large piece of it to this day. During the attack our wireless operator had fired several red flares and we were joined by two Mustangs from the escort. The Me262 broke off the attack and we then sorted ourselves out. The starboard outer was feathered and the fuel cock turned off, leaving us with two Merlins on the port side to get us home. I realised that the starboard tank was losing petrol and used the cross-feed to enable the port engines to feed off the damaged tank for as long as possible. By this time we had a Mustang on each wing tip and were escorted all the way to the English coast. We had radioed ahead and were given instructions to land at Woodbridge. The undercarriage and flaps were tested on the way because we did not want to have to make more than one attempt to land in our condition. F/Lt McGregor made a perfect landing, with a fire engine spraying foam

* This was S-Sugar of 50 Sqn, which crashed in the target area killing Australian F/O Vincent Berriman, a 25-year-old married man, and all his crew.

over the runway because of the still leaking tank. The ground crew who examined the tank told us that it must have been a 30-mm shell that hit us.[21]

This was not the last flourish of the Luftwaffe, but it was close to it. The once mighty force that had waged savage nightly destruction through Bomber Command in the winter of 1943–4 was now so short of fuel stocks and trained pilots that two days before the Hamburg attack it had been reduced to ramming its prey as a desperate predetermined tactic to try to stop the waves of daylight bombing raids on the Reich. Oberst Hajo Herrmann, who had formed the Wilde Sau fighters that had proved so successful in that winter of attrition for Bomber Command, organised a special unit of 120 volunteers who would pilot stripped-down Me109 fighters to fly into a USAAF air fleet, causing such destruction the Americans at least would be forced to stop bombing for a while, allowing the Luftwaffe to build up its Me262 force unhindered. A written request for volunteers on 8 March from Goering, the head of the Luftwaffe, promised 'immediate flight training' and demanded: 'I call you to an operation from which there is little possibility of returning.'[22] On 7 April a total of 1,257 USAAF B-17s and B-24s set out to attack various targets. The new Luftwaffe force of 120 raw young pilots took off in reply on their ramming mission. A total of thirteen bombers were lost, seven by ramming, but one-third of the new Luftwaffe recruits died in their crashing fighters. A total of 1,237 USAAF bombers continued on, to strike at their targets unhindered. Goering's dash for glory with Germany's remaining youth was over.

The oil refineries near Leipzig, at Leuna and Lutzkendorf, were overrun by American troops in the third week of April. The American broadcaster Ed Murrow was with them and his report of what the USAAF and the RAF had achieved was broadcast to British homes by the BBC on 22 April.

Acres and acres of twisted, rusted pipes – huge tanks ripped open – steel girders pointing to the sky. That is what had happened to the greatest petroleum-products plant in Germany, in spite of its being protected by more flak guns than there were defending Berlin. Leuna is an ugly monument to air power – it doesn't prove that bombers can win wars, but it does demonstrate that bombers can make it impossible for armies to move or for planes to fly.[23]

The RAF continued to attack the enemy's fuel supplies through April, usually by small forces and for little loss. Targets ranged from the benzol plant at Molbis, near Leipzig, to a fuel storage depot at Regensburg in Bavaria and even to Scandinavia, a raid by 107 Lancasters and 12 Mosquitos of 5 Group striking at the oil refinery in Tonsberg, on the night of 25 April, the final raid of the war by Bomber Command's heavies. The sole loss was a Lancaster of 463 Sqn, adding to the unit's considerable suffering in these last weeks. F/O A. Cox was at 19,000 feet in the target area when he was attacked by a Ju88 which blasted the front of the aircraft. Cox, his flight engineer Sgt G Simpson and bomb aimer F/O J. Wainwright were wounded, but despite frostbite setting in from the icy blast sweeping through the battered airframe Cox was able to make an emergency landing at an airfield in Sweden. He and the bomb aimer were later awarded the DSO, highly unusual for junior officers, and the flight engineer the CGM. F/Lt Gerry Mitchell, one of 5 Group's Pathfinders on 83 Sqn, remembers the raid because he got a ticking off. 'We had dropped route markers for Main Force and were at 18,000 feet not long after turning for home when I decided to try out my VHF radio to see how good it was,' he recalls, 'so I called up base, Coningsby. To my surprise they answered as clear as clear and asked what I wanted. The only thing I could think of was to say: "Tell my batman to light the fire in my hut." Did I get a rollicking for that.'[24]

There were other raids in April, almost as heavy as anything that had been seen before, as the enemy fought on to the last. A total of 969 Lancasters, Halifaxes and Mosquitos bombed the naval base, airfield and town of Heligoland on the 18th, which turned the target areas into something resembling a First World War battlefield landscape of overlapping craters. Three Halifaxes failed to return. F/Sgt Frank Tolley of 625 Sqn recalls the operation: 'We thought then the war was nearly over and we were put down for a daylight raid. The enemy ack-ack was very good and we were about the third wave. I saw aircraft being shot down ahead, but by the time we went in there was only one ack-ack gun firing. The others had been knocked out, so we didn't get much flak.'[25] Four days later Bomber Command was back to an old-style city attack with more than 750 Lancasters and Halifaxes en route to Bremen. Unlike the past, however, this operation was not designed to burn out factories and warehouses, but to prepare the way for the British XXX Corps, poised to engage from the southeast. In fact only 195 aircraft had bombed in thick cloud when the master bomber called off the raid because smoke and dust was now adding to the lack of visibility over the target and it was thought stray bombs might hit British troops. The whole of 1 and 4 Groups returned to base with full bomb loads. F/Sgt Tolley was on that raid too, the last of his twenty-two-op tour: He says:

> It was very scary because the master bomber kept calling us down. Going across to Germany we could see there were so many aircraft on the raid and then to be called down through cloud seemed very risky. We thought, Hell's bells, we might collide with another aircraft. We just prayed and hoped that we didn't. Then coming back with a full bomb load there was a worry about would the skipper get us down OK. The arming pins of the bombs were in and I did wonder if there would be a bumpy landing, but we did get down all right as all the others did. You didn't think about the fact you had gone all that way and brought the bombs back, you just thought, What the hell, orders are orders, another balls-up. I certainly didn't want to die. There was a saying, 'Often frightened, but never afraid.' You knew you had volunteered for operational flying and you were doing it, it was do or bust.[26]

There were 39 major operations carried out by Bomber Command in April, 16 by forces of more than 200 heavies and 5 by around 500 aircraft, sometimes many more. A total of 34,460 tons of bombs were dropped, but it was the combination of hectic day and night raids in March that would prove to have been the apogee of Bomber Command's long battle. A total of 67,637 tons of bombs were released then, a greater weight than in any other month and almost the same tonnage as the Command had dropped over the first three years of the war.

In these final few weeks there was a definite feeling that the anguish and anxiety for operational airmen and their families might soon be over if one could just hang on. But the savage irony of war had still to be played out in Bomber Command and this time upon those who were among the safer of its personnel: ground-based airmen. In the late afternoon of 17 April at East Kirkby, N-Nan of 57 Sqn was being prepared for a small operation on the railway yards at Cham in south-eastern Germany when a fire broke out under the Lancaster and eventually exploded its bomb load. Five other Lancasters were also destroyed in the blast and a hangar, in which incendiaries had been stored, was ablaze. Four airmen were killed and seven injured as explosion after explosion rolled across the station. Fire engines had to be called in from RAF Coningsby and from Spilsby, the nearest airfield to East Kirkby. Sgt Ken Freeman, who had returned to Spilsby from Pilsen earlier in the day, the last of his three operations, remembers: 'We were in the sergeants' mess having our evening meal and heard the crumps of explosions about four miles away. Apparently they had been loading with delayed-action bombs and one dropped off and became activated. The Lancaster went up, damaged the next one and airmen were scuttling around trying to unload planes.'[27]

It was the next day before East Kirkby was declared safe. Broken and burned-out bombers littered the sides of the perimeter track and debris was strewn across the hard standing outside No. 3 Hangar. Smudges of smoke stained the airfield from messes to admin buildings. Apart from the six bombers destroyed fourteen had been badly damaged. In the weeks following, several ground officers and airmen were subsequently awarded medals, including two George Medals, for their brave actions in trying to contain the waves of destruction. The incident was the last of a series of bomb explosions at air bases of Bomber Command in the furious pace of operations over more than two years. In March 1943, for instance, five Lancasters were wrecked in an explosion at Scampton when a flare went off in a 57 Sqn bombed-up Lancaster; the following month eighteen airmen were killed in a bomb dump explosion at RAF Snaith; in July 1943 a bomb load exploded at Binbrook sending a cloud of black smoke into the air clearly visible from neighbouring airfields and destroying two 460 Sqn Lancasters and damaging seven others being prepared for a Cologne raid; the next month as 103 Sqn crews boarded their Lancasters at Elsham Wolds for a Berlin operation a dropped incendiary caught fire and sparked off the aircraft's full bomb load, badly damaging Lancasters taxiing past the afflicted aircraft.

A bomb load falling through the open doors of an aircraft as a ground crew finished their raid preparation inside the fuselage was not as uncommon as it might have been. W/O Ted Hutton, the 433 RCAF Sqn bomb aimer who saw his comrades shot down by Allied anti-aircraft fire on 15 March, remembers how that operation to Hagen had begun, at Skipton-on-Swale. The crew had been driven to their Halifaxes dispersal to await the arrival of their flight commander skipper. The rule was aircrew could not enter the aircraft until the last of the ground crew were out. As an electrician left by the rear door he turned the Air-ground switch to the Flight position, which accidentally closed the jettison circuit and a Cookie and 1,500 incendiaries tumbled to the ground. 'Wib Pierce, our skipper, had driven up in his flight commander's van to find the aircraft and the area absolutely deserted,' W/O Hutton later wrote. 'All of them had taken off for the River Swale at speeds that would have left Olympic sprinters in the dust.' Luckily the 10-foot fall had not armed the bombs and a tractor train of bomb trollies was dispatched to the dump to get a new load.

> The skipper drove off to perform his duties as flight commander and returned to find an armament officer busy supervising the winching of the 4,000-pounder with a battered nose back into the bomb bay. 'What are you doing?' Wib asks. 'Putting this bomb back in the aircraft.' 'I don't want it on my aircraft.' 'Well,

we sure as hell don't want it on the station!' Time was moving
on so the skipper conceded the point; but there was not enough
time to load the incendiaries, so it was decided we take off
without them.[28]

The incendiaries were trollied away back to the bomb dump
without further incident. An accident that could have rivalled
many at the bomber airfields had been avoided by a twist of
fate. The East Kirkby blast the following month would hold the
record for accidental bomb destruction and so near to peace.
But five days later there was an even more unfortunate tragedy
at Fulbeck which took fifteen lives and injured a further nine
personnel. The resident 49 Sqn was being moved to Syerston
that day, a Sunday, and as aircraft lined up and took off
after breakfast 5015 Works Flight paraded outside the Motor
Transport Shed.

At 10 a.m. the sound of an aircraft at low level and high speed
drowned the noise of idling propellers as F/O George Elkington,
who had been wounded on the Harburg raid of 7 March by a
flak burst that killed his flight engineer, beat up the base before
departing for Syerston. The noise of Y-Yoke's four engines at full
bore rolled across the base as F/O Elkington arrived, diving, from
the south. His tail wheel struck the MT shed as he pulled up and
the Lancaster pitched forward, hitting the ground with the searing
sound of tearing metal. It ended in the familiar fireball, the blast
demolishing the clothing store and sending debris scything across
the parade ground. Elkington and five others of his crew died in
the aircraft, four more were killed on parade and five others died
from their dreadful injuries in the days that followed.

The end of the European war was a little more than two weeks
away and in fact the last of the fatally injured, 24-year-old LAC
Peter Moor, died on VE-Day itself. The torment and sacrifice that
so far had claimed the lives of more than 55,000 airmen was nearly
over for Bomber Command. Its survivors were not to know that
a new enemy was emerging from a former ally to begin a Cold

War that would threaten the world with annihilation for decades. Some RAF aircrew were already suffering in the grip of Stalin's Russian bear.

SEVENTEEN

ONE WAR ENDS, ANOTHER BEGINS

THE relationship between Britain and the Soviet Union had undergone a remarkable change since the German invasion of June 1941 and an equally vast, cleverly engineered, shift in the public perception of Stalin. For generations Russia had at best been viewed with suspicion by the majority in Britain, then with dread of Communist infection after the 1917 Revolution, Winston Churchill promoting the subsequent dispatch of a military force to Archangel two years later to aid the counter-revolutionaries. After the declaration of the Soviet-German non-aggression pact two weeks before the war, thus allowing the Nazis and Communists to divide up countries such as Poland between them, the 1939 newsreels were quick to play up the pluckiness of Finland in resisting the cruel Russian bear. But all that had changed overnight as Hitler's tanks rolled into Soviet territory. Red Menace newsreels in British cinemas were quickly replaced by ones showing determined Russian women building tanks; convoys to Murmansk fought desperate actions to deliver Lease-Lend material including as many as 5,000 Hurricane fighters; and in 1943 a specially cast Sword of Stalingrad was sent to Russia by King George VI in honour of the victorious defenders of that beleaguered city. The press and public relations industry had convinced the British public that any ideas they might have had of Josef Stalin as a mass murderer were totally unfounded and the dictator was a Good Joe after all, Uncle Joe in fact – a pilot on 44 Sqn so naming his Lancaster in tribute. There weren't any tributes on RAF bombers to Winston Churchill or President Roosevelt. In fact the title was considered so apposite 463 Sqn repeated it, with their own U-

Uncle becoming Uncle Joe Again. There was no end to Stalin's popularity.

It would be mere weeks after VE-Day that the public would be asked to perform a mental about-turn again, as Stalin so obviously flexed his muscles for European domination and the Cold War began. Those members of Bomber Command who had been unfortunate enough to fall into Russian hands already knew how the Soviet regime showed at best an indifference to its Allies and at worst sadistic cruelty. In February the Air Ministry was already displaying private suspicion about what shot-down aircrew might expect. At the briefing for the Chemnitz raid on the night of 14 February crews were warned that as they were flying so close to the Russian lines they should beware of Soviet soldiery. Just in case they bumped into them some safe-conduct passes in Russian were handed out.

Flight engineer Alan Dearden, who was briefed for the St Valentine's Day raid on Chemnitz, only 20 miles from the Czech border, remembers:

> We were told that if we finished up on the ground we had to make our way west. No way were we to go towards the Russians. Union Jacks were handed out to pin on our battledress, but there was only one for every two of us, so we were told to evade in pairs. Our 18-year-old rear gunner, Sgt Doug Begbie, asked me if I would pair up with him, so we went to look at the map to look where we would go. We decided we would head for Switzerland if shot down.[1]

But less than three weeks later as crews were briefed for Chemnitz again that fear seems to have been mollified as new suspicions were raised of what local Nazis were doing to downed Allied airmen. Crews were told to head for the Russian lines if they had to and the Union Flag safe-conduct passes were brought out again, this time with a more positive spin. W/O William Young, the special operator in the crew of F/Lt Jack Irvine whose Halifax collided with another bomber over Chemnitz on 5 March, remembers:

In the last-minute rush after briefing, I'd just grabbed one out of a box holding several hundreds and stuffed it into my trousers pocket ... The flag wasn't very impressive to look at; a small silk square liberally splashed on both sides with the Union Jack. A list of instructions warned me that the Russians might not accept the flag as positive proof of my bona fides. I was advised to learn the expression, 'Ya Anglichahnin'. This meant, 'I am English'.[2]

W/O Young would soon have to depend on the silk square to save his life. They were a recent innovation. On earlier raids in January and February on the Politz oil plant near the Eastern Front crews on some squadrons had been given a label to wear round their necks with the Union Jack on one side and the hammer and sickle on the other in case they came down in Russian-held territory.

W/O Young's skipper had turned east instead of west as the bomber stream had flown away from Chemnitz because he knew he could not make it back to base in the intense cold whipping through the shattered front of the Halifax. Back in Britain in April F/Lt Irvine gave intelligence officers an anguished account of his battle with the elements.

It was impossible to stand in the nose of the aircraft, so I ordered all of the crew except the two gunners to the rest position in order to keep as warm as possible. I flew east for an hour and a half until we figured we were well behind the lines of the Russian Front. At the same time I descended to try to lessen the cold. By this time both my legs were numb from the hips down. My left hand was also completely numb. My right hand I kept warm by sitting on it. At this point we ran into a snowstorm and had to turn back to the west. Soon afterwards I spotted the lights of a small town which I began to circle. It was then that both escape hatches were found to be jammed. Two of the crew used the aircraft's axes to chop open the fuselage door. This operation took about 20 minutes. When the door was finally opened I gave the order to bale out.[3]

W/O Young later related what a terrible ordeal the pilot had gone through as snow blowing in from the shattered nose had built up until it lay inches deep in the cockpit. 'Huddled over the controls, he was coated with a thin film of ice,' he said. 'It thawed and trickled down his face, only to freeze again when it reached his flying suit collar. Soon he had a thickening girdle of ice under his chin.'[4]

W/O Young was the first to bale out, coming down in a frozen landscape 40 miles west of Cracow, and at intervals as the Halifax continued to drone further west, back towards the German front line, the other six crew members followed beginning with the Canadian navigator F/Lt Jack Nixon. F/Lt Irvine knew he would not be able to bale out himself because of his frozen legs and hands. He said:

> I had to attempt a crash landing. It was still quite dark, but luckily I spotted a road with vehicles' headlamps moving along it. I descended over this to about 50ft with landing light on. By use of the light I found what seemed to be a decent field. I circled it twice, then dropped the flaps and came in for a belly landing. In doing so the aircraft took a chimney off a house and cut down two telephone poles which I did not see. The landing was OK, but I was knocked out by the impact. When I came to the aircraft was sitting in the field and had not caught fire. It took me some time to get my straps undone and as I couldn't stand up I fell from my seat and crawled to the front of the aircraft and out through the hole.[5]

F/Lt Irvine made contact with local people who had seen the aircraft come down and he and all but three of the crew were back in Britain by the third week in April. But the remainder were about to find out how unwelcome they were in territory now under Russian control. The Canadian mid-upper gunner F/Sgt W. J. McCullough was shot by a Russian sentry and spent weeks in a Polish hospital before being repatriated. The navigator F/Lt Nixon ran into a Red Army patrol and was incarcerated until after the war by his suspicious allies who said they wanted to check his story. But the 25-year-old special operator, W/O Young, entered a nightmare as soon as he hit the ground. He began trekking east through a desolate, snow-covered landscape in temperatures below zero, pursued by wolves. All he had was his escape compass and his safe-conduct pass. On the fourth day, as his strength was finally giving out, he came across a road and was seen by two soldiers in a Red Army lorry, who at first sped by then stopped. In an account for an RAF magazine nine years later, W/O Young related:

> I scrambled out of the ditch hands held high and fluttering my Union Jack. As I did so I heard the ominous click of safety catches. 'Ya Anglichahnin! Ya Anglichahnin!' My swollen tongue forced the words out. The taller of the two men spat on the ground. He seemed in favour of shooting me there and then, and kept jabbing his gun in my direction. His mate pointed down the road and said something I didn't understand. But, to my relief, the tall man nodded sullen agreement. They searched me, took my cigarette lighter, watch and Union Jack; then indicated they wanted me to get in the back of the truck.[6]

Young was taken to a war-battered country mansion where he was interrogated, all his requests for his details to be sent to the British military mission in Moscow being ignored. He was driven on to a small town where he was interrogated again and this time the female questioner issued her verdict: he was a German spy. He was taken to the town of Bielitz (now Bielsko-Biala) near Cracow and stood up before a Red Army tribunal who pronounced the death sentence. For days he worried in his rat-infested cell, awaiting the final summons for the firing squad.

> Then the questions started all over again. 'How could I be an Englishman; the British never flew over Germany! Only the Red Air Force was bombing the Germans into submission. Wasn't I a spy.' Over and over again the same questions were hurled at me. More truck journeys, more questions, more threats about a firing squad. I wondered how long it would go on. But one thing gave

me hope; the Russians had some doubts. If they hadn't I reasoned
I would be dead by now.[7]

Young was sent to a political prison at Pless (now Pszczyna) not
far from the Nazi extermination camp of Auschwitz discovered by
Soviet forces in January, but eventually after more questions and
denials he was transferred to a Soviet Army prison camp. There
he saw his comrade F/Lt Nixon: 'one of the happiest surprises of
my life', Young said.

> It was some days before we could talk together, but eventually we
> were able to compare notes. He told me that he too had jumped
> and like me had been picked up for questioning. But apparently his
> answers – or perhaps merely his accent – had convinced the Rus-
> sians that he wasn't a German. After that life became worth living
> again. We were allowed to remain together and we talked endlessly
> of escape. The Russians treated us a little better now, feeding us on
> weak raisin tea, even weaker stew and hunks of hard black bread.
> There came a final interrogation then Nixon and I were handed
> over to the Red Air Force.[8]

The two were driven to an airfield on the outskirts of Cracow
where they were imprisoned in a hut with sixty USAAF flyers
who had been 'shot down by mistake'. The climate changed considerably. Young was still interrogated, but now the special operator, whose last flight had consisted of searching the 300 to 4,200
megacycles waveband to locate enemy night-fighter transmissions,[9] was asked to join the Russian Air Force. He promptly
declined. Three weeks passed in which there was little to do
except read Russian newspapers, in which Allied gains were never
mentioned, and listen to Radio Moscow, which equally related
only Red Army successes. Meanwhile F/Lt Irvine had arrived
back in Britain and given his report of his last flight.

It was then that the RAF lost any faith in Young's survival, the
CO of 192 Sqn, W/Cdr D. W. Donaldson, writing letters of
sympathy to relatives of the two missing men on 21 April. His
letter to W/O Young's father in Glasgow read:

One member of your son's crew is now back in this country and has given us an account of what happened to the aircraft ... They were all seen to leave the aircraft, but unfortunately nothing was afterwards heard from your son. The remainder landed more or less safely. By the time they baled out the aircraft had been forced very low and it is possible that when your son jumped they were passing over some very high ground and his parachute would not have had time to open. It is, of course, impossible to say absolutely definitely that there is no hope, but I feel that if he was alive we should almost certainly have heard from him by now.[10]

In Poland the two airmen kept asking when they would be sent home and always the answer was 'Tomorrow'. The Americans organised a nocturnal escape attempt, hoping to steal a Lease-Lend Dakota they could see parked on the Cracow airfield. But before Nixon and Young could slide away from the hut, the Americans were discovered. All of them were thrown into prison, then transferred to Lvov (now Lviv) by another Lease-Lend Dakota. The Red Air Force insisted all such American aircraft were in fact Russian, given by the Communists to the Americans and English to help those countries' war effort. Eventually the war ended and they were sent on to Kiev in the Ukraine. Young and Nixon managed to sneak past a guard and find a representative of one of the British missions, now set up in several Polish towns with the major aim of getting the Russians to repatriate any British prisoners they found in German concentration camps. They were discovered and returned to custody, but their details were now known by the British. 'Then one morning came the great news that "Canada" Nixon and I were to leave for Odessa the next day,' Young reported.[11] The Black Sea port had a docking area for international ships. The journey took thirty-six hours by train in a reserved compartment in which they were escorted by a Russian officer. Young continued:

Slowly we chugged and puffed into Odessa where we were herded off to a reception centre. The place was full of French, Czech and Polish workers. A lot of them vanished overnight – possibly to die in front of an execution squad or linger in a salt mine. After a week, during which time the local British Mission worked wonders in getting us back into shape – Nixon and I embarked on a Norwegian ship. Four months of nightmare were over.[12]

VE-Day had come and gone eight weeks before.

THERE was some speculation after the war that other Britons had disappeared into Soviet camps never to return, but in the chaos of a changing political landscape in war-battered Europe it remained just a possibility and relations with the Soviets had reached such a low that no information would be coming from behind what was now being called the Iron Curtain. Many airmen who it was known baled out of their crashing bombers had disappeared, many of them to meet a lynching squad or Gestapo ready to administer a bullet in the back of the neck. In the months following the war various enquiries were begun with few conclusions. The major effort by the hard-pressed RAF investigating teams was devoted to bringing to justice killers of the fifty shot POWs from the Stalag Luft III escape in March 1944.

Three large POW camps in which RAF bomber crew were held in large numbers, Stalag Luft I at Barth, Stalag IIIA at Luckenwalde and Stalag IVB at Mühlberg, were liberated by Russian forces and the Red Army was certainly in no hurry to let the prisoners go back home. F/Sgt David Berrie, an RAF wireless operator, held at Stalag IIIA near Berlin, kept a diary from 22 April, the day he woke to hear cries of 'The Russians are coming', to 9 May when still under Russian guard while Britain's adult population nursed hangovers from VE-Day. He wrote: 'What I thought would be a little story of wonderful happiness has gradually deteriorated into a gloomy history of several thousand Allied ex-POWs.' The previous day after the Russians had ordered evacuation trucks sent to the camp to return empty he recorded: 'Boys leave camp in all directions. Some return later, others are interned etc.'[13] It wasn't until 20 May that F/Sgt Berrie and his comrades were finally taken in a Russian convoy to Wittenberg on the Elbe and handed over to the Americans.

W/O Dennis Slack, an RAF bomb aimer, had been a POW at Stalag IVB near Mühlberg north of Dresden since the autumn of 1943. At the war's end the 75-acre vastly overcrowded camp held 30,000 prisoners including thousands of Russians being slowly starved to death by their German captors. It was liberated by the Soviets on 23 April, but the 7,500 British prisoners were held in the camp for over a month. Individuals, including W/O Slack, escaped their liberator-captors and made their way on foot towards the American lines. How easily escaped prisoners were likely to be shot by Russians on sight was evidenced as he and his comrades sheltered overnight with an old German woman. 'In burst a Russian dressed in the local mayor's top hat and frock coat. The mayor had been shot. He stuck a gun in my ribs and asked, 'Who are you?' W/O Slack remembers. 'We told him who we were and he said, "If you are not looked after shoot her."'[14] At the Baltic Stalag Luft I the first Russians entered the camp on 2 May, but apart from eventually providing food ignored the prisoners, who did not reach home until 15 May.

Most RAF prisoners in Germany or its occupied territories were not freed by the Russians, however. To prevent that happening, as the Red Army advanced from the east the air force camps and others had been evacuated on Hitler's orders and the POWs sent on a march through the snow in the bitterest winter weather of the century. In April as the war entered its final stages they were at the end of their resources in an ordeal that had seen scores of their comrades die by the wayside.

EIGHTEEN

THE LONG DAY CLOSES

THE mixture of high excitement, fear, then memory-searing horror that had marked the final flight of the 9,922 RAF and Commonwealth aircrew of Bomber Command who became POWs in the Second World War gradually leached into a lethargic, depressive, overwhelming war of waiting as the weeks, months and eventually years ticked by. Some had been prisoners since 1940 and as the long day of the *Kriegesfangener* closed in the final weeks of April and the bitter weather of winter turned to a glorious spring there was at last genuine hope they would be home soon.

Most of them had shouldered their trials with patience and fortitude. Forced under guard to the Dulag Luft interrogation centre at the start of their incarceration, often threatened by vengeful civilians, practically all had refused to give any information to their captors except name, rank and number as required by the Geneva Convention. Despite the heat treatment and solitary confinement, the former in which the radiator controls in a 'sweatbox' cell would be turned up so high bunk rails were too hot to touch, the latter making a man feel desperate to talk to *anyone*, they had remained silent and spurned the fake Red Cross form prepared by the Luftwaffe which began with apparently harmless questions such as what squadron and group they flew with and even what pay were they getting. Shocked as they were by the loss of their comrades in the family bond of a crew and unable to come to grips with their own chance survival it was surprising how few of the airmen not long out of school had talked.

But a small number did crack. It was obvious to those who

came after them and were surprised by how much the Luftwaffe questioner knew about their own squadron and base that a few had spilled the beans in their terror. Now the RAF was looking for that tiny number who had helped the enemy. The monthly RAF magazine *Tee Emm*, avidly thumbed in RAF messes for its amusing cartoons and salutary tales about the latest happenings of the clueless P/O Prune, had printed a new warning to aircrew in December to divulge only name, rank and number if captured. Under the heading 'He Sold His Country For A Cigarette' it reported: 'Since the Invasion helped us to capture large numbers of German documents proof has been coming in that air crew members, when taken prisoner, are by no means the tight-mouthed oysters they should be. In fact some of them seem to fall over themselves to give vital information away.'[1]

Tee Emm even gave examples it had found from captured German documents.

> Here first is F/O — —, shot down in March 1944. He tells the Hun something he didn't then know, namely that German fighters were to be attacked with rocket ammunition. 'This advance information,' says the [German] report, 'was of great value to us; and then the prisoner, *without being in the least pressed*, went on to describe in detail experiments then actually being made in England with new methods of firing these rockets, which we found extremely useful'. Now comes F/Lt — —, pilot of a Halifax. 'Quite independently,' says his interrogator, 'he stated that Mosquitos had flown in the bomber stream, and when I argued it was impossible he described in complete detail his briefing on the subject'.

Tee Emm then left aircrew in no doubt about what would happen to the garrulous. 'You needn't imagine that, just because you're a prisoner and out of the war, no one over here is going to know what you say. They do already about many ... We're warning you ... KEEP YOUR DAMN MOUTH SHUT. Or else.'[2]

But it is a measure of how taciturn the average airman POW was that as the prisoners came home with the collapse of Germany there were just three court martials by the RAF of those it considered had assisted the enemy. Military Intelligence had been keeping tabs on the suspect prisoners for years, intercepting the mail they sent to relatives by the specially marked *Kriegefangerpost* envelopes, reading it, then posting it on. One RAF air gunner shot down in 1943 who spent two months at the Luftwaffe interrogation centre, being given much freedom, and made German propaganda broadcasts from Berlin until the end of March 1944, described to intelligence officers once back in Britain what he had discovered as he wandered around Dulag Luft. He had found a building containing registries 'giving particulars of groups, stations, squadrons and crews in this country, American and English, including the names of the commanders, flight commanders and the crews and the names of intelligence officers at the station'.[3]

He had his own theory, apart from the obvious, as to where the Germans' intelligence came from. 'When talking with one of the girl clerks one day I asked her how they got all this information,' he said. 'She told me that their spies in England took photographs of documents and sent them back by radio photographs.'[4] However incredible such a claim might have seemed it is a fact that interrogators at Dulag Luft had many sources of material with which to confront the new POW to convince him that they already knew a lot about his squadron and base. A Yellow File Room, for instance, collected biographical information from British and Commonwealth newspapers and magazines and the *London Gazette* award lists. There is also no doubt that while many Irish nationals fought bravely in the RAF some Irish labourers who helped to build the airfields of Britain, often staying on to complete them while operations were being flown, were unsympathetic to the British cause because of their recent history and went back and forth to neutral Ireland, where Germany had a legation. W/O Edwin Watson, the 630 Sqn flight engineer whose tour ended with the Böhlen raid of 5 March 1945, remembers: 'During intelligence briefings and lectures we were informed that an estimated two-plus spies could be on every operational station. Even in those days the IRA were active. In East Kirkby village there was one public telephone box. During ops an armed guard was stationed for up to 15 hours to prevent its use.'[5]

As the war with Japan came to an end in August the court martial of the 22-year-old air gunner who had helped the enemy also closed. He had pleaded not guilty to five charges, including being paid 350 marks a month by the German Foreign Office, but was found guilty on all counts and sentenced to five years in prison, though he was released from Dartmoor only three years later.

The Uxbridge court martial of another, older RAF air gunner shot down at approximately the same time in 1943 was told he had agreed to give his Dulag Luft interrogators details about his Halifax's speed, armaments and Gee box if allowed better quarters and parole. The evidence was that he was given a pass allowing him to wander round Frankfurt from dawn to dusk in civilian clothes and helped a 'Red Cross official' to get airmen to fill in the false Red Cross form, which the Air Ministry had known about since 1941. 'I realised what a fool I had been and demanded to be sent to a Stalag Camp,' the airman said. He got four years' penal servitude, later reduced by the Secretary of State for Air to two.[6]

The war of nerves conducted against shocked and disorientated aircrew in those first few days of captivity was always intimidating and could be extreme. Sgt John Simpson, shot down on 22 February, was interviewed by three separate interrogators at Dulag Luft over several days towards the end of March. The third was the nastiest. He remembers:

I was escorted to an office where the interrogator appeared in the uniform of a senior naval officer. He was a very tall and well-built man with a very autocratic demeanour. He became quite aggressive and got to the stage of accusing me of being a spy. By this time I was becoming apprehensive, but was able to reply I would have made a very poor spy as I only have a word or two of German and that he must have a record of my having baled out of a Lancaster which had been very badly damaged over Gelsenkirchen and later crashed. He then told me I was based at RAF Chedburgh near

Bury St Edmunds and flew with 218 Bomber Squadron. I was so amazed that he knew all this.[7]

Interrogations could become even more threatening at Dulag Luft, to the point of the uncooperative being promised a transfer to a concentration camp. It was not likely to happen once in the hands of the Luftwaffe despite the blustering by some of the Frankfurt interviewers, but if a shot-down airman was first captured by the Gestapo, usually after an evasion attempt in which he had been helped by the Resistance, it was a distinct possibility. F/Lt Alan Bryett, who had taken part in preparations for the Great Escape at Stalag Luft III in March 1944, remembers aircrew arriving at Sagan that October from such a camp.

> We didn't know about the concentration camps until the autumn of 1944. The way we found out was some aircrew had been shot down in France and been sheltered by the Resistance. They were all picked up together and sent off to a concentration camp. After a while the Allied authorities were able to protest they shouldn't be there and they were transferred to us. They arrived in trucks late at night and they were put two to a hut among us. We were asked by the Senior British Officer to give them a meal and look after them. They were in a terrified state and they told us there was a camp where Jews were being put in gas chambers.[8]

F/Sgt Albert Chinn, a mid-upper gunner on 207 Sqn, was among those who arrived at Stalag Luft III that night, transferred from Buchenwald, where he had been incarcerated with other RAF would-be evaders for two months. He had been shot down in July 1944 while attacking a flying bomb site south of Amiens. He had walked west for two days then a farmer had agreed to hide him. In the first week of August the local Resistance chief arrived. Back in Britain after the war F/Sgt Chinn told MI9:

> He told me that I would get back to the UK by the weekend if I was willing to go. I said 'yes'. My host took me to Beauvais by coach where I was handed over to two different Frenchmen and stayed three days with a postal worker. On August 11th I went by

coach to Paris where I met F/O Thomas Hodgson RCAF and F/Sgt L. Willand RAAF ... We were handed over to a Frenchman who kept us in his flat. Four other Allied airmen joined us. The next thing we knew was that the flat was surrounded and we were handed over to the Gestapo.

Chinn spent five days in the notorious Gestapo-run Fresnes prison in Paris, before being sent in a group to Buchenwald.[9]

Also in that group was S/Ldr Thomas Blackham, who had been hurled from his exploding Lancaster over the German Panzer base of Mailly-le-Camp in May 1944, and captured in Paris weeks later following various adventures with the Resistance. The first intimidation he suffered at Fresnes was to be stood up before a machine-gun firing squad for several hours, expecting a fusillade any second, while his guards fiddled with the loading mechanism at intervals. Eventually they simply took him back to a cell. In an article in an RAF magazine after the war he said that on 15 August the long train of Fresnes prisoners, including American flyers as well as British, left for Buchenwald to the sound of artillery fire as the Allies prepared to take Paris. Within hours of arriving at the concentration camp 'we were crushed into a large shower room and were relieved to see that water, not gas, came out.' Then he was singled out with other RAF officers for 'special' treatment. He wrote: 'We were called 'Terrorfliegers' because of the bombing the Germans had suffered, threatened with torture and beaten and kicked at every opportunity, often just to satisfy the whim of the SS guards.' But the most terrible daily ordeal, he said, 'was having to stand in line for so long while many of us had dysentery ... At 11 o'clock we received half a litre of soup, often just grass and water; and one eighth of a loaf with a small piece of margarine substitute. It was tragic to see men fighting like wild animals to scrape the bottoms of the food barrels. The strong beat the weak underfoot and the weak often died; nobody seemed to mind.' But there was occasional selfless goodness to be found among the orchestrated evil. 'The Russian prisoners were very kind to us,' S/Ldr Blackham wrote. 'At the risk of their own lives they brought us bread and clogs. They were treated on a different scale, but we British and Americans were given the same treatment as Jews.'[10]

There were individual horrors S/Ldr Blackham could not erase the memory of. 'A vehicle like a pantechnicon arrived one day and into it were crowded 250 little gypsy boys aged six to 16,' he wrote. 'The back of the van was closed and sealed. They were then gassed by connecting the exhaust pipe to the back.' In time a Dulag Luft interrogator arrived, who promised to transfer the British and American flyers to a POW camp if they could prove their identity.

> We signed certain forms giving our name, rank and number, and a few days later were given back our own clothes, less valuables, put in cattle trucks and transported to Stalag Luft III. We were all physically weak and our nerves were in bad shape. When the other POWs at Stalag Luft III saw us, they laughed their heads off. It seemed we looked so comical with our heads shaven. They were all very kind to us, but listened to our story with incredulity and a certain amount of disbelief. After a short period in this camp we were started on a series of forced marches across Germany.[11]

THE evacuation of the RAF POW camps from January 1945, as the Russians advanced, took place amid the harshest winter conditions in Europe of the century and would be ever remembered with distress by those subjected to it as the Long March. There were three main routes in which a total of 30,000 prisoners, air force and army, and eventually 50,000 Americans and other Allies, were being force-marched westward across Poland, Czechoslovakia and Germany in freezing weather. Rumours flew around the columns that the prisoners would be held hostage to help a peace deal with the Allies or that they were being moved to western German concentration camps such as Belsen for the SS to murder them in revenge for the bombing of Dresden and other German cities. The most likely rumour, however, was that Hitler wanted 35,000 prisoners held hostage in the Bavarian mountains for a last stand by the Nazis in the Bavarian redoubt centred on the Eagle's Nest at Berchtesgaden. Himmler had put SS General Gottlob Berger in charge of POW camps the previous autumn and in 1948 Berger told an American judge in Nuremberg that if a peace deal failed Hitler had given the order for them to be executed.[12]

The northernmost of the three RAF evacuation routes started at Stalag Luft IV at Gross Tychow, Pomerania, and went via Stettin to Stalag XIB and Stalag 357, both at Fallingbostel. Some prisoners were marched from here at the end of the war to Lübeck. The central route started from Stalag Luft VII at Bankau near Kreuzberg in what is now Poland, via Stalag 344 at Lamsdorf to Stalag VIIIA at Gorlitz and ending at Stalag IIIA, Luckenwalde. The southern route, in which some RAF POWs became intermingled mostly with British and American army prisoners, started at Stalag VIIIB not far from Auschwitz and led through Czechoslovakia to Stalag XIIID at Nuremberg and then on to the vastly overcrowded Stalag VIIA at Moosburg in Bavaria, which had contained a large number of RAF prisoners since 1943.

But as the long columns straggled across Germany in the driving snow of January and February and different parties tagged on to those from other camps in the chaos, the evacuation became one vast confused army moving south and north, but always generally westward away from the Russian advance. In most camps, the POWs were split up into groups of up to 300 men and because of the inadequate roads and in the ebb and flow of battle, not all the prisoners from the same camp followed the same route. The groups would march between 15 and 25 miles a day, resting at night where they could, in factories, farm buildings and even in the open. Stalag Luft III at Sagan, from where the Great Escape had taken place via the Harry Tunnel in the RAF and Commonwealth North Compound the previous March, was evacuated at short notice at 11 p.m. on 27 January. There were four compounds in all, two for USAAF personnel. All four compounds eventually staggered in to the town of Spremberg, once the geographical centre of the German Empire, but the Americans were then sent on to Moosburg in boxcars and the British from the North and East compounds were split, some being turned north towards Stalag IIIA at Luckenwalde, others being sent in cattle trucks to arrive finally at an old Merchant Navy camp at Westertimke, near Bremen. Another section of Sagan RAF prisoners were moved by rail to Nuremberg. Refugee civilians and different parties of POWs had been mixed up from the start. Prisoners who couldn't go on fell by the wayside, some to be dispatched by a guard's bullet, but most to succumb to chest infections in temperatures as low as minus 25° Centigrade, their numbers helping to make an eventual war total of 138 British and Commonwealth airmen who died in German captivity.

F/Lt Bryett remembers:

> On the Long March they didn't reckon on German civilians joining us, but from the first day they were tagging on the column looking for our protection against the Russians. It was dreadful, POWs were falling out with bronchitis and pneumonia. After a while the SBO [Senior British Officer] ruled that anyone who fell out had to have four or five able-bodied men fall out with him because they were less likely to shoot them all. I was in hospital in Brussels for six weeks with jaundice after being liberated.[13]

Even until the middle of March temperatures were often well below 0° Centigrade. Most of the POWs were ill-prepared for the evacuation, having suffered years of poor rations and wearing clothing ill-suited to the appalling winter conditions. Within a short time long columns of POWs were wandering over Germany with little or nothing in the way of food, clothing, shelter or medical care. At first they were glad to get out of the camps where most had lived a limbo-like existence for years. But as they trudged on there were lingering memories of the carefully built-up structure of the Stalags where, although the prisoners never knew what their ultimate fate would be, brother had met brother, or a friend from school days or the same civilian street had suddenly turned up to join them behind the wire.

As the POWs wandered on, belongings, which had often taken years to acquire, were tossed aside in the frozen mud as weariness took over from want. Bill Taylor, who had been a POW in Stalag Luft VII, remembered how before the Long March began a group of them in the camp had by great effort completed a blanket they had crocheted, with needles made from toothbrush handles, using cast-off woollies.

> One of our group embroidered the RAF wings as a centre piece. The blanket was duly raffled in front of the whole camp and we gained quite a lot of capital in the way of cigarette. On the second day after we were getting ready to move on after such a short rest I noticed the blanket lying in the snow along with other discarded articles. It had become too heavy to carry in our tired state. Hopefully some Russian soldier got some comfort from it.[14]

Prisoners from varied camps had different experiences. Sometimes the guards provided farm wagons for those unable to walk, but because there were no horses teams of POWs had to pull the wagons through the snow. In some cases the guards and prisoners became dependent on each other, other times the guards grew increasingly hostile. Passing through some villages, the residents would throw bricks and stones, and in others, individual Germans would share their meagre food.

F/Sgt Dick Raymond, a 20-year-old flight engineer, shot down the previous May in an 83 Sqn Lancaster, was in one of the columns from Stalag Luft VII at Bankau, which would end its march at Stalag IIIA, Luckenwalde, 20 miles south of Berlin. He remembers:

> We slept out in temperatures of minus 10 and minus 15. I think I only survived because I was young. Food was non-existent, we lived on raw sugar beet and raw spuds, whatever we could find. You could escape easily, but you would only freeze to death. I remember 1,500 of us queuing to get through a snowdrift, two at a time. The German guards were suffering as well. During one break I sat in the snow watching a guard eat a sausage. I must have

been staring at him because he shouted, 'Ach', picked it up and threw it at me.

Sometimes they put us in farm buildings at night with the guards on the outside. We used to get among the cows for warmth and look to see if they had left anything in their manger to eat. I saw a farmer's wife come out and throw some food refuse on the dung heap and the boys fighting to see if there was anything they could swallow. The last 80 miles we were crammed in cattle trucks. We were there three days and the Germans didn't open the doors. When we got out at Luckenwalde and staggered through the town the Germans were laughing at us because we were soiled. I suppose they had every justification, we had been dropping bombs on them for three or four years. I console myself that they knew all about the concentration camps.[15]

But there were other moments when the bomber boys could show their mettle. Bill Taylor remembers:

The 1500 Kriegies from Stalag Luft VII had been on the march for eight days. We were very cold, hungry, tired and a little despondent. The guards who were mostly older men and Volkssturm were also tired and getting increasingly irritable. As we entered a small town, the guards informed the local population who were lining the street, that we were 'RAF terror flyers'. This brought about a torrent of abuse from the local onlookers, and to heighten the tension, a column of Panzers had stopped close by. The crews sitting on top of their tanks decided to join in the crowd's derision, firing off a few rounds in our direction while giving the thumbs down sign.

Someone at the head of our column started to sing a Vera Lynn song *You Are My Sunshine*. The effect was dramatic and stimulating. The singing became louder and louder as it swept down the column. The Kriegies shook off their lethargy, formed themselves into lines of 'threes,' and with heads held high marched through that town singing loudly in defiance of our reception. It was a very proud moment.[16]

P/O Peter Thomson, the RAAF Camp Leader of Stalag Luft VII, made a report with the camp medical officer to the Swiss Protecting Power on 15 February detailing the hardship the prisoners had suffered on the Long March. 'On January 17th, 1945, at approximately 11 a.m. we received notice of one hour in which to pack our kit and be ready to leave the Camp by marching,' he reported. 'At the same time we were informed by Oberfeldwebel Frank that for every one man who fell out of the column on the march, five men would be shot. This order was never given in writing.'[17]

The start was postponed until 3.30 a.m. on 19 January and each man was issued with two and a half days' marching rations before leaving. The only medical equipment available was that carried by the medical officer and three orderlies in back packs. A diary was kept by P/O Thomson of the hardship of the march between 19 January and being entrained in cattle trucks for a camp at Goldberg – midway between Berlin and Lübeck – on 5 February. It begins:

> January 19th: Left Bankau and marched to Winterveldt, a distance of 28 Kms. This was done under extremely trying weather conditions and severe cold. The only accommodation at Winterveldt was small barns.
>
> January 20th: Marched from Winterveldt to Karlsruhe arriving at 10 am. We set off at 5 am and marched a distance of 12 kms. At Karlsruhe we were housed in an abandoned brick factory. Here for the first time we were provided with two field kitchens with which to cook for 1550 men. Each field kitchen was actually capable of cooking sufficient food for 200 men. The Medical Officer was also provided with a horse and cart for the transport of the sick. The cart was big enough to hold six sitting cases. Coffee was provided and after a rest period of 11 hours we were again ordered to move. The Camp Leader and the Medical Officer protested against further marching until the men were adequately fed and rested. We were told by the German Abwehr Officer that it was an order and must be complied with. The same night we left Karlsruhe and marched

to Schonfeld, arriving at 9 am on January 21st, covering a distance of 42 kms. The conditions during the night were extreme, the temperature being minus 13 degrees Centigrade. The Medical Officer's wagon was filled after the first five kilometres and from then onwards, men were being picked up at the roadsides in a collapsed and frozen state, and it was only by sheer will power that they were able to finish the march. After crossing the river Oder, a distance of 34 kms, we were told that we would be accommodated and that no move would be made for two days.

January 22nd: At 3 am orders were given by the Germans to prepare to march off at once. It was dark and there was some delay in getting the men out from their sleeping quarters because they could not find their baggage. The German guards thereupon marched into the quarters and discharged their firearms. The column was marching again by 5 am: Twenty-three men, it was ascertained at this stage, were lost and their whereabouts are unknown. They may have been left behind asleep, or they may have escaped. Also, thirty-one men were evacuated (we believe) to Lamsdorf, but nothing further has been heard of them; we marched to Jenkwitz, a distance of 34 kms and were housed at a farm in barns. Here we were issued with a total of 114 kgs of fat, 46 tins of meat, barley, peas, and three quarters of a pig. Soup was issued, the ration being about a quarter of a litre per man. No bread was issued.[18]

The diary continues in the same vein of hardship and misery telling of haphazard, inadequate rations, blizzards and exhaustion. Finally the column of 1,500 Kriegies arrived at a railhead. P/O Thomson's report continues:

We were put into cattle trucks, an average of 55 men to each truck. By this time there were numerous cases of dysentery and facilities for men to attend to personal hygiene were inadequate. The majority had no water on the train journey for two days. When the men were allowed out of the trucks to relieve themselves, numerous of the guards ordered them back inside again and we had to be continually getting permission for the men to be allowed out. We were on the train from the morning of February 5th until the morning of February 8th. Before commencing this journey, we were issued with sufficient rations for two days. The total distance marched was 240 kms.

Summary: As a result of this march and the deplorable conditions, the morale of the men is extremely low. They are suffering from an extreme degree of malnutrition, and at present, an outbreak of dysentery. There are numerous cases of frost bite and other minor ailments. They are quite unfit for any further movement. Food and better conditions are urgently required. We left Bankau with no Red Cross supplies and throughout the march all the rations were short issued, the most outstanding being bread, which amounts to 2,924 loaves.[19]

There were other hardships suffered by POWs in the Long March, perhaps the hardest to bear being shot up by their comrades in their own air force. Allied fighter aircraft now roamed at will ahead of the battle lines, harassing any Germans on the move. Sometimes the long columns of Kriegies were mistaken for the Wehrmacht. Near Westertimke in early April Typhoons shot up a column of POWs, killing a British officer and wounding many more. Several POWs were killed in a separate attack by a Mosquito on a barn they were sheltering in not far from Fallingbostel. In southern Germany Sgt John Simpson, who had experienced being on the receiving end of a 1,000 bomber RAF attack on Dortmund, also now found out what damage Allied fighters could cause. He had been moved from the interrogation centre at Dulag Luft to Stalag XIIID at Nuremberg. He remembers:

Soon we were on the move again and marched out of the camp about midday under a very dull and overcast sky. We weren't long out of Nuremberg when we were strafed by American Thunderbolts thinking, I believe, that we were retreating German troops. When it became obvious that we were about to be attacked the German guards scattered, closely followed by us. I later heard that some men had been killed. That experience was the most terrifying experience of my life and I have the greatest respect for our soldiers who had to suffer much danger as a matter of course.[20]

But it was outside a village called Gresse, near Lübeck, where the most tragic case of mistaken identity would occur. A long, straggling column of prisoners had halted for the welcome distribution of Red Cross parcels organised by the redoubtable Sgt James 'Dixie' Deans, a Whitley pilot shot down in 1940, who became a symbol of courage to RAF POWs as he took on responsibilities far beyond his rank to look after them. Most of the men had settled down to look for the welcome chocolate in the ration when a flight of six RAF Typhoons flew by, then turned back. They came in with cannons roaring and soon rockets too were slamming into the column, trees by the roadside exploding under the onslaught of fire. A total of thirty POWs were killed outright and several more died later.

F/Lt Al Wallace, an RCAF air gunner who was among those forced onto the choked byways by the evacuation of Stalag Luft III, remembers what it was like to be attacked by your own side.

We were straggling along the road, just having left a small town when I saw six RAF fighter aircraft fly across the front of the column at fairly low level then wing over. I saw the wings start to blink as their guns started firing and God, suddenly everybody was heading for the ditch. I lay there as flat as I could while these guys were strafing. They were mainly after the baggage wagons which were for guys who were too ill to carry their kit and some of them were riding on the wagons because they couldn't walk. Anything on wheels was a target for fighters. I could hear the cannons hitting the wagons and the planes screaming by and just hoped I would be OK.[21]

THE POW camps further west in Germany were not evacuated. Instead the numbers in them were vastly increased, adding to the hardship, as different columns from the Long March arrived to share the men's short rations. As airmen adapted to life behind the wire a disciplined society had been established where former aircrew conducted a different war against the enemy to the one they had been trained for. At Stalag I VB at Mühlberg the prisoners had remarkably even smuggled a woman into the camp in the final few weeks of the war to save her from the approaching rapacious Russians, intent on revenge. That she was the mother of one of the camp's RAF inmates was even more astounding. Sgt Winston Barrington, a 35 Sqn rear gunner, had been a prisoner for a little more than a year when his mother turned up.

W/O Dennis Slack had been on the camp escape committee for months and remembers:

> The English mother of Sgt Barrington went with him on holiday to Switzerland before the war where she fell in love with a Luftwaffe pilot. The following year she met the pilot in Switzerland again and they got married. She settled in Germany and her son returned to England. After the war started he volunteered for aircrew and was shot down in December 1943. He was in the same hut as me and told me about his mother. Sgt Barrington was able to make contact with her by letter and eventually she came to live in the village of Mühlberg so that she could be near to him. The Red Cross parcels used to arrive at the station and a party of army POWs was sent to collect them in a cart. The Germans wouldn't allow the RAF to go into the village because they knew we would escape, so Sgt Barrington used to change identity with a soldier and go in for the parcels where he would meet his mother.
>
> As the war went on and the Russians got nearer, Sgt Barrington got worried about what would happen to her, so in February 1945 it was decided to try to smuggle her into the camp. Sgt Barrington was able to warn her to prepare and the next time he went in for the parcels he took a spare army battledress uniform and he and the others were able to get his mother back into the camp. But the problem was where to hide her. We tried one or two places very unsuccessfully, then we had a brainwave. One of the huts had been converted into a theatre and it was decided to hide her under the stage. At evening time when prisoners were getting exercise an

escort would walk her round the compound in battledress and then she would go back under the stage again. Winston's mother was given the codename of 'Pete' in the camp to the handful of us who knew she was there. The Germans used to watch the shows put on by the POWs and never realised there was a woman hiding only six feet away from them.[22]

Both Sgt Barrington and his mother were flown safely back to Britain when the Russians finally agreed to release the Stalag IVB prisoners.

It was time to take risks as Germany collapsed and the cruelty of the Gestapo and SS became less efficient and more haphazard, now often being turned inward against Germans themselves who were not showing the right offensive spirit. For those RAF aircrew who had lately become guests of the Nazis, whether they lived or died by the actions of either side often became simply chance. Sgt Simpson, bombed by his own air force in Dortmund and shot up once by Allied fighters, had also been fired on by USAAF Thunderbolts on his way to Dulag Luft as they carried out their legitimate duty of destroying the last of Germany's means of moving men and supplies. He remembers:

We were put on a train in an open truck. Some newly captured American airmen told us that the Allies had crossed the Rhine and in fact Cologne had fallen. We were so busy celebrating this news that we had not noticed that the train had come to a halt in a cutting. The guards had disappeared and we realised the civilians in the carriages behind had disappeared and we suddenly realised why. Three American Thunderbolts came down to strafe the train and I saw the guns winking on the lead one. I realised he was aiming for the engine and we were just behind. We all scattered and fortunately no one was hurt, although the lead plane was badly damaged by flak by the flak car at the end of the train. The rest of the journey to Frankfurt was by foot, since the engine had been badly damaged, and took several days. We got nothing to eat, just drinks of water.[23]

When he was dispatched from Dulag Luft to its transit camp at Wetzlar he was bombed again. He remembers:

We were still in Frankfurt, by which time it was dark, when the air-raid sirens went on and we – there were about fifty of us – were escorted to a deep shelter where we became aware that we were surrounded by local civilians. Luckily, it was quite dark and we kept very, very quiet so we weren't sure whether they knew they were sheltering with some of the dreaded *Terrorfliegers* as we Allied bomber crews were called. After about two hours or so and after a lot of explosions and noise of ack-ack guns the all-clear was sounded and we continued on our way to Wetzlar.[24]

Sgt Simpson was then sent to Stalag XIIID at Nuremberg. He remembers:

Nuremberg was a very large camp built in what had been the stage for Hitler's rallies before the war. It housed many different nationalities including many Russians who were treated much worse than us, which was bad enough, and they were expected to be able to work despite their starvation diet. They were dying like flies. We were not kept long at this camp – about a fortnight or so.[25]

The march out of the camp, which led to the prisoners being shot up by Thunderbolts, continued throughout the night in heavy rain which lasted until the next day. Sgt Simpson recalls:

By early evening we were soaked through, having only our battle-dress tops to keep us dry ... My flying boots were badly worn by that stage, almost worn through, and the wool lining which had usually kept our feet warm soon became soaked and rucked. Eventually my feet were a mass of blisters so each step was an agony. We stopped early the next morning to rest in a forest. I think I was then at the lowest ebb of my time in Germany. My agony continued for another three days when I luckily met an American doctor who was able to supply me with Elastoplast strips which at least made life bearable. Some days later the weather improved as the further south we got into Bavaria the warmer it became and the less hostile attitude of the Bavarians, as against the locals from the heavily bombed areas of the north, became more pronounced.

In fact we had two memorable acts of kindness when tramping through Bavarian villages, the first when a German lady approached us with a large pail full of kippers and, in the other on a warm spring afternoon, an innkeeper came out of his inn with several pints of beer. In both cases the poor benefactors were almost crushed in the rush and really I was rather ashamed of our behaviour although we thanked them sincerely for their kindness. Eventually, after another few days, we reached our destination which was the German camp at Moosburg near Munich.

The conditions at Moosburg were really terrible and the thousands of POWs here were in a very sorry state and travel-weary; many of them had come from as far as Poland, experiencing the worst of severe winter weather, including men from Stalag Luft III. I had the good fortune to be billeted with these men, all officers, who were recognised by the black diamond they wore on the sleeve of their battledress in memory of their comrades who were executed.[26]

The US Fourteenth Armoured Division arrived at the gates of the teeming Moosburg camp on 29 April and liberated 110,000 prisoners of war of various nationalities.

As the Third Reich fell apart while its leaders desperately tried to prevent thousands of its prisoners joining up with their comrades once more, the opportunities for escape increased. Sgt Joe Williams, the 625 Sqn rear gunner who had to hunt frantically for a spare parachute in his blazing bomber on the Chemnitz raid of 5 March 1945, was one of those who saw his chance and took it. Like Sgt Simpson he also had been sent from Wetzlar to Stalag XIIID at Nuremberg, his train being shot up by a Mosquito intruder and then the truck he was transferred to being shot up by Thunderbolts. It meant he did not arrive at Stalag XIIID until 4 April and the very next day was marched out of the camp in a group of 300 which included the Canadian navigator from his crew, F/O Bill Petrachenko, bound, it was rumoured, for the Nazis' last stand at the Bavarian Redoubt.

Sgt Williams still had his silk map and small compass, issued in the escape kit collected by all aircrew before taking off on an operation, and within hours he and F/O Petrachenko escaped. Sgt Williams kept a fascinating daily diary of his adventures, written on a toilet roll. It begins:

> 5th April ... and away into the wood. We were about to enter a village (Ober-Baimbach) when we heard voices and heavy boots. We stumbled off the road, through a ditch and across a field behind the houses. A burst of Tommy-gun fire followed us. We kept going and hid in a wood. 6th April (Friday). Laid up in the wood all day, raining, wet through. Farmer ploughing with horses 100 yards away, but did not notice us. Moved off approximately 9pm, saw deer in the forest, sheltered from rain in deer hay-rack for a while, crossed main road and continued cross country NW. Crossed double railway track to Ammerndorf. Jerries in town, hid in timber yard by station and then in a garden while they passed. Still raining. Passed through the centre of Ammerndorf and hid in wood on high ground to north of town.[27]

The two continued to make progress, travelling by night and hiding up in woods during the day. On 8 April as they moved off again at 9 p.m. they fixed scarves round their heads to resemble the hats worn by soldiers of Hungary, Germany's ally. The diary continues:

> Came to Mkt Erlbach. It was the dead of night, 2–3am, and we decided to risk walking through. As we approached a large building on the right, two soldiers with Tommy guns slung over their shoulders walk out into the middle of the road. 'Halt,' they said. I threw up my arm and said, '*Heil*,' and kept walking to the left of the road. They took hold of Bill and swung him round. '*Magyar soldaten*,' (Hungarian soldier) he said. They let him go. Kept on NW, followed straight road through a forest for approx. 9–10 kilometres, then across a few fields to a belt of timber and laid up

in the bushy firs. Water bottle dropped from Bill's pocket while crawling into hide, found it in the morning.[28]

By 11 April they could hear small arms and shellfire nearby and as they laid up at night shell flashes were all around them. The diary goes on:

12th April (Thursday). Still in the hide, nothing doing in the morning. Found the rest of our meat was bad and threw it away. During the day, Bill went for a walk. After some time I went to the top of the wood to find him. He was sitting on the edge of a track, looking down to the valley where a tank was moving along. Wondered if it was American. I looked to our right. Less than 100 yards away a soldier with a rifle was approaching. We slid off the track and lay ready to put our hands up. He must have seen us, but passed feet away, looking straight ahead. Decided it was no good staying in the wood, but to head for the burning village, circle it and head NW. Set off at approx 9pm. Reached burning village. We heard a lot of voices and a bulldozer working. We got very close. Only German was being spoken so we turned away and headed NNE without circling the village.

Later on that night they came to a small orchard. 'I saw that there was a number of soldiers asleep and another with a rifle, standing against a tree. I swung Bill around and we walked silently away,' the diary reads. Later still, trying to reach high ground they had been aiming for, they entered a wood and sat down. 'Raining heavily,' the diary continues. 'Almost immediately a Tommy-gunner (German) started firing and further up the wood hedge a heavy machine gun was firing. The Tommy gunner was very close, approx. 50–60 yards. A few minutes earlier we just walked in front of both.'

The next day they came across some Sherman tank tracks and American K Ration wrappers. Further on there were signs of battle including a knocked-out German tank. Liberation was at hand and on 14 April the two came across abandoned German motorbikes. Sgt Williams wrote:

I selected mine, it was called a 'Wanderer', was quite new and full of petrol. I pedal started one for Bill and instructed him how to use it and off we both rode. This was approx. 10am. We drove 9–10 kilometres and entered a large town (Markbreit), meeting the Americans for the first time.

The soldiers were in a truck and looked at us with some curiosity when we stopped, put our bikes on the stand and walked up to them, scruffy, unshaven, our clothing covered in mud. 'I want to shake hands with you,' I said.[29]

The two were given food, reported to the Allied military government at the next town, Ochsenfurt, and were driven to Darmstadt, being flown from there to Paris, then taken onwards to catch a boat to Southampton. Sgt Williams was in Britain by 26 April.

THAT day the start of Operation Exodus began for Bomber Command to fly its Lancasters to Brussels to bring home the prisoners from liberated camps. But there were three holding thousands of RAF men where incarceration would continue as Stalin began his new game of bargaining his Allies' lives for those of Cossacks captured by the British and Americans while serving with the German Army. They were Stalag IIIA at Luckenwalde, near Berlin; the holding and transit camp at Goldberg, mid-way between Berlin and Lübeck; and Stalag IVB at Mühlberg, north of Dresden.

Stalag IVB was liberated on St George's Day, the day after Stalag IIIA, but it was over a month before the last of the Allied prisoners were evacuated by the Russians, who then used it as a prison camp for German POWs, 3,000 of whom died there over the coming months. Many of the RAF men in the camp slipped away when it became obvious the Red Army had no intention of letting them meet up with the nearby Americans anytime soon. W/O Slack and four others cut the wire on 2 May after hearing a rumour that a pontoon bridge had been built across the Elbe about 12 miles away. One of them had a pistol. W/O Slack remembers:

We managed to cross the Elbe by sheer luck over the pontoon bridge and continued walking west towards the Western Allies. We could hear gunfire still going on. By evening of the second day we arrived in a small village and knocked on the door of the first house. A terrified old lady came out. She thought the Russians had arrived. We explained who we were and she said we could stay the night.[30]

It was there that the Russian soldier burst in and suggested they shoot the old lady if she was any trouble. W/O Slack recalls:

The old lady was terrified and wanted us to stay for a few days, but we couldn't. She admitted her daughter was hiding in the loft. If the Russians found her she would be raped. A short time later we crossed into a place in the American Zone and found the local mayor there and told him we wanted accommodation. He took us to a house with no roof and straw on the floor and said, 'This is where you will sleep.' We pulled the gun out and told him, 'If anyone sleeps here it will be you.' He threatened to tell the authorities, but we told him he was in no such position and we were taken to the house of another old lady. She was marvellous to us. The war didn't exist as far as she was concerned. She looked on us as sons and treated us like royalty. Whether she had sons in the German forces I don't know, but she was a kind old lady. The next day we said goodbye and set off walking west along a main road. Eventually an American supply truck came along driven by a black soldier of the Red Ball Express.[31]

F/Sgt Lawrence Benson, a 635 Sqn flight engineer who had been shot down in June and had arrived in Goldberg after the march from Bankau, kept a diary of the final days of the war at the Goldberg camp. Russian trucks to take them to the American lines didn't arrive until 20 May, more than three weeks after the bomber boys in the camp first tasted freedom. He wrote:

One Friday morning we found Jerry had left us to look after ourselves. Two boys had been shot in earlier attempted escapes. With the news of Jerry's departure, there was great rejoicing. Flags of all nations appeared. Things quietened down very quickly, however, when we received an ultimatum from the SS unit in the neighbouring forest. A Russian unit was in the vicinity and there was great excitement when it arrived – guns, tanks, lorries, horse-drawn carts and women. This was a great moment for us, and especially for the Russian prisoners who had been so terribly treated.

On 29 April he recorded: 'Principal happening was the arrival of food,' and four days later:

> The past few days had been very strange. Obtained my Dulag Luft and Luft VII official record documents complete with photographs. Still no news of means of getting home. Some of our boys have been looting. Armchairs, clocks, wirelesses, cigars, swords, bikes – even horses have appeared in the barracks. An official German Document later reported the case of a Commando who had associated with a German prostitute. He was imprisoned because the price was irregular – one bar of chocolate. Another Commando was caught and admitted association with twelve women, all of whom denied the affair. He was accused of boasting and released.[32]

At Stalag IIIA at Luckenwalde RAF wireless operator F/Sgt David Berrie recorded on 30 April, eight days after the Russians first arrived: 'General Famen from Marshall Koniev's HQ says he hopes to move us to the Adolf Hitler Lager* as soon as possible it being a much superior camp and would be worth the difficulties if we stayed here for any length of time. This news seemed to indicate a long stay here which has us all fed up.' On 6 May the US Army sent a convoy of trucks to take away the British, American and other Allied prisoners, but the Russian commandant

---

* The Adolf Hitler Lager section of the camp was where the British Free Corps, an organisation of POWs – many of them ex-members of the pre-war British Union of Fascists – had been formed in the final months of the war to join the fight against the Russians. It never amounted to more than thirty-nine members.

refused to let them go and some truck drivers who had already loaded POWs had shots fired over their heads by the Red Army. Europe had been officially at peace for nearly two weeks before the men were eventually released.

As the prisoners languished behind the wire, their continued, unnecessary incarceration a particularly bitter blow in their long war of waiting, their comrades still flying had begun the final operational chapter of Bomber Command. They launched its last raid of the war on the heart of evil itself and began errands of mercy to a starving nation trapped by the German Army living off civilian food.

NINETEEN

DELIVERANCE BY BOMBER

THE final two weeks of the war as peace blossomed into a glorious spring were among the most satisfying for the men of Bomber Command Harris referred to as his 'Old Lags'. The bomb bays of their flak-scarred, oil-stained Lancasters and Halifaxes would now for the most part carry sacks of food for the starving instead of death by high explosive and fire. Equally rewardingly they would also bring back home RAF POWs who at times had never expected to see Old England again. But before these missions of mercy could begin there was a last day of destruction. One of the two major operations High Wycombe launched on that date was also deeply appeasing to the men who had suffered so much. It struck at the very centre of the evil ideology that had started it all and taken them away from their schools, offices and work benches so many years before.

The target route to the Eagle's Nest, Hitler's mountain retreat at Berchtesgaden where he had received Neville Chamberlain in 1938, was revealed to somewhat sleepy airmen in the early hours of 25 April. A total of 375 crews of 1, 5 and 8 Groups had been called, not long after they had stumbled into bed, to grope for battledress carelessly discarded the night before and weave towards ablutions blocks. There had been few aircraft on ops the previous day and at Wickenby the 626 Sqn mid-upper gunner F/Sgt Peter Bone had sunbathed in the afternoon sunshine. His excitement as he saw the target map for what would be his twenty-fifth operation was revealed in his diary. It read: 'Early call 1.30am Wed. Briefing 2.45am BERCHTESGADEN!!! Our AP SS barracks. Other AP Hitler's chalet Eagle's Nest.'[1] He recorded: 'The

Station Commander, G/Cptn Haines, announced with a faint smile before motioning to the airman to uncover the route map: "OK chaps, this will probably be your last kick at the cat".[2] A new CO had been appointed to 626 Sqn, W/Cdr D. F. Dixon, and F/Sgt Bone discovered he would be flying with him in T2. A few miles to the south at Woodhall Spa, Lancasters of 617 Sqn were being loaded with Tallboy bombs for the final time in the war. At nearby Scampton, where aircrew of 625 Sqn were still adjusting to the unaccustomed purpose-built comfort of a pre-war base after moving from the bleak and now closed Kelstern, eleven crews would be taking off for Berchtesgaden. P/O Knight would be making his first operational trip.

Dawn had just touched the horizon as the Lincolnshire Lancasters droned away and headed east into the rising sun of what would be a perfect spring day. F/Sgt Bone recorded cryptically in his diary:

> Flew down over Thames Estuary, across Dover-Channel-Pas de Calais. Crossed Rhine at 9,500! Clear weather all way. Picked up fighter escort Lake Constance. Wizard view of Swiss Alps, still snow covered. Got to target OK, no markers, can't hear M/B. Orbited like everyone else – slight heavy flak, no enemy fighters. Ours well in evidence and up to target, bombed smoke from 18,000! Flak from Salzburg.[3]

Communications over the target were generally poor. Mosquitos crews who had been tasked with bombing on Oboe found that the mountains of the Ober-Salzburg blanked out the transmission signal and the master bomber could not be heard at times. The operational record book of 460 Sqn details what happened.

> The master bomber had difficulty in locating the target and eventually turned to port where the target was located and marked with reds. This meant that nearly all the leading aircraft of the column had to orbit, some turning as far as Salzburg where they were engaged by heavy, moderate barrage flak. Bombing developed well. Initial stages were at starboard of the aiming point and the master

bomber called main force over to bomb to port and the whole target area was then well covered.[4]

The confusion affected the key group from 617 Sqn. Five of their Tallboys were seen to hit the corner of the SS barrack blocks, but the aircraft of F/Lt J. H. Leavitt was unable to line up properly. 'We did one run and were not satisfied,' he reported later. 'I called up the leader for permission to do a second run and could not contact him on Stud B. We found out afterwards he was on Stud A. By this time we were alone in the target area, the gaggle having departed. We then set course for home and dropped our bomb . . . at a viaduct over a road junction. The bomb undershot.'[5]

But for F/Sgt Bone, striking at the heart of National Socialism as the day of victory approached was the high point in his tour nothing could mar. He wrote in his memoir:

We have just bombed the SS barracks. By twisting myself round in my turret – no mean feat when one is encased in a bulbous, electrically heated suit – I can see mushrooms of dirty white smoke, flecked with orange, yellow and red, billowing up from the tiny buildings below. Concentric rings ripple outwards, as though we had just dropped pebbles into a pond. A few half-hearted flak puffs dot the picture-perfect blue sky. I notice a Lancaster way below us, descending slowly and streaming a long trail of white smoke behind it. I wonder, with the detachment that is second nature to us now, was this their first op or their last.* . . . My thoughts move on. It dawns on me as we draw away from the target that there is at last good reason to hope. I suddenly feel like singing: 'Roll out the barrel . . .'[6]

By the time the crews of T2 and the other 626 Sqn aircraft saw Lincoln Cathedral ahead in the sunshine and joined the circuit

---

* This was the aircraft of F/O H. G. Payne, RAAF, of 460 Sqn, which took off from Binbrook shortly after F/Sgt Bone's Lancaster climbed out over nearby Wickenby. Fortunately the whole crew survived and briefly became POWs.

378

for landing at Wickenby the radio in the sergeants' mess was announcing that the Red Army was only two miles from the Unter den Linden. All 617 Sqn's aircraft returned safely to Scampton as did ten of the aircraft of 625 Sqn. But P/O Knight, on his first operational flight, was missing. His aircraft finally appeared in the circuit a full two hours late because of engine trouble. 'He made base on two engines after putting up a grand show,' the adjutant recorded.[7]

Two aircraft failed to return: F/O Payne's and the Lancaster of Canadian F/O Wilfred Tarquinas De Marco of 619 Sqn. De Marco was killed with most of his mainly Canadian crew, their names being added to the roll of 9,980 Canadians who died flying with Bomber Command. They joined other Canadian comrades in the swollen legion of the dead who had been claimed in another operation that day, their deaths in accidents a particularly poignant postscript to the RCAF's war sacrifice.

The Canadians who died were among 482 crews of 4, 6 and 8 Groups ordered to bomb the coastal batteries at the pre-war resort of Wangerooge in the Frisian Islands, which controlled the approaches to Bremen and Wilhelmshaven. The day had begun well for at least one Canadian base. News was on the way from the Red Cross to 428 Sqn at Middleton St George that F/O D. M. Payne and nearly all his crew, missing since an operation to the U-boat yards of Kiel and long given up for dead, had drifted ashore in a dinghy after being tossed around on the North Sea for twelve days and were now POWs. Only the rear gunner, the newly promoted P/O Bert Vardy who had been interviewed by *Wings Abroad* after shooting down an Me262 over Hamburg, had been lost, going down with the sinking Lancaster. The aircraft had been hit by flak during the bombing run and the pilot wounded in the leg and left arm and hand. On the homeward route the Lancaster was hit by flak again, the engines having to be shut down one by one until Payne was left with a single power plant as he tried to make it across the North Sea and had to ditch. Only two of the crew were uninjured and the navigator F/O G. C. Riley was later awarded an MBE and F/O Payne a DFC for their actions in saving the crew in the dinghy. The squadron adjutant's assessment of Payne and his men on the day they went missing as a 'gen crew' was obviously accurate and long practices of dinghy drill had paid off.[8]

The attack on Wangerooge at first went according to plan, the area around the coastal batteries being saturated with bombs to prevent a repeat of what had happened in Antwerp the previous autumn when the port had been taken quickly in early September, but guns menacing the Schelde estuary leading to it had prevented its facilities being used for ten weeks. However, as more aircraft arrived of what was a huge force for such a small target disaster then struck among the squadrons trying to jockey into position for the bomb run. F/O A. L. Rose of 408 Sqn at Linton-on-Ouse saw M-Mother of his squadron collide over the target with W-William of 426 Sqn, which shared the base, and nobody from either aircraft was able to get out as the burning airframes plummeted. Both crews had been serving at Linton on the night seven weeks before when the base had lost one Halifax to collision and two more to icing shortly after take-off for the Chemnitz raid. As the Wangerooge bombers turned for home over the sea, A-Apple of 76 Sqn skippered by the 20-year-old Canadian W/O Joe Outerson flew into the Canadian-crewed T-Tommy of the same squadron. 'Crews report that "A" hit slipstream and collided with another aircraft and broke up in mid-air,' intelligence officers reported later. 'Three parachutes were seen, one of which was reported as damaged.'[9] In fact only the pilot of T-Tommy survived.

The Lancasters of two novice crews of 431 RCAF Sqn from Croft also then collided, eleven Canadians and three Englishmen, all with only one operation behind them, being killed. Two of the aircrew were only 19. The last of the seven aircraft to go down also carried airmen fighting a war from a foreign land. The entire crew of Halifax 'E' of 347 Free French Sqn were buried in the wreckage of their crashed aircraft on Wangerooge. There would perhaps have been some recompense for such tragic deaths within sight of peace if the attack had saved the lives of other servicemen in the army. However, the concrete of the Wangerooge batteries proved impregnable to high explosive and the guns were firing again within a few hours. It was a tragic epitaph to the sacrifice of Canadians in Bomber Command over six years of war.

THERE was little time for sadness, however, in messes at Croft, Middleton St George and elsewhere. Within 24 hours Bomber Command had turned away from war to begin two mighty missions of mercy. The relief effort known as Operation Manna was remarkable in that a local truce was arranged with the German army of occupation to allow it to happen. The failure of Arnhem and later the Allied drive to isolate the Ruhr pocket had left German troops in western Holland without the means of supply. They lived off the land in the last winter of the war while the indigenous Dutch population gradually starved. By spring, at which time the civilians had been reduced to eating tulip bulbs, 1,000 Dutch men, women and children a day were dying for lack of food. It took much negotiation with local German commanders by the Red Cross to broker a deal whereby the RAF had a one-hour window in the war to drop food to the Dutch people. It was planned to take place at Rotterdam racecourse on 28 April. The task fell to Bomber Command's 1 and 3 Groups and the Lincolnshire and Cambridgeshire bases had only one day to switch from loading ordnance to packing bomb bays with food. There was no time to organise parachutes. Hurriedly arranged practice drops, by the few aircrew let into the secret, quickly showed up the flaws of dropping without chutes. From 1,000 feet flour sacks burst like bombs and potatoes arrived ready mashed. It was just practical to go in at 500 feet, that was if the supplies had a wrapping of two sacks. The interior sack always burst, but not the exterior. That then created a shortage of sacks, and they were subsequently borrowed and stolen from miles around each RAF station. As it turned out, some German reluctance to agree to the truce saved the day. The operation was delayed until 29 April and there would now be three drop zones, not one – at The Hague and Leyden as well as Rotterdam, though it was still uncertain that the bombers would be safe from flak.

F/Sgt Bill Porter, the 625 Sqn navigator, who would be commissioned within weeks, learned his crew would be going to The Hague. He remembers:

April 29th was a great day. We were called to the briefing room around eight in the morning and listened, with some surprise, to the news that we were to drop food to the Dutch civilian population ... We were to transit at 1,500 feet, not the usual 15,000, and drop these supplies from 500 feet. The only time we flew this low was on the approach to a landing. After we arrived at our aircraft we were told to hold, clearance had not been received from the German High Command. About an hour later we were told to go; it was assumed that the clearance had arrived. It was more than forty years later that I learned that this was not the case. A/Cdr A. J. D. Geddes, who was the Air Commodore Ops and Planning at the Second Tactical Air Force headquarters in Europe, was part of the Allied group that met with the Germans and they didn't even meet to discuss the matter until 1300 hours on 30 April, by which time we were already briefed for our second trip. As we crossed the Dutch coast on 29 April we could see the German gunners standing by their guns, but the barrels were horizontal. We soon found our dropping zone at The Hague and offloaded the 800 lbs of supplies to an enthusiastic reception party. We were surprised at the number of flags being waved at us and being displayed on so many buildings.[10]

F/Sgt Frank Tolley, bomb aimer in the same crew, got a bird's-eye view of what low flying meant over what was still an enemy coastline. He remembers:

We were at extremely low level, in daylight, and as we went over the Dutch coast we were a bit apprehensive. We could see the German artillery positions and our rear gunner called up, 'I've got them in my sights if they open up.' The skipper told him: 'Don't you dare fire.' It was very difficult to map read across Holland because it was so flooded, but then we saw the civilians waving. They had been waiting for us. We had been briefed that they were starving in the western province and it was a great feeling that we were dropping food.[11]

The editor of the Netherland News Agency in Britain, H. G. Franks, flew in one of the Lancasters and later described the experience on the BBC for the benefit of Britons gathered round their wireless sets, avid for any news now that the end seemed so close.

Our squadron carried sufficient food – 42 tons of it – to feed one fifth of the population of The Hague for one day, but there were other squadrons as well. There was flour and yeast for bread-making; tins of meat and bacon, with pepper and salt and mustard to taste. The Dutch love for vegetables was met by tins of dehy-drated potato, as well as bags of peas and beans. Sugar, margarine, dried milk, cheese, dried egg and chocolate completed the order ... 'These were the best bombs we have dropped for years,' said Flight Officer [sic] Ellis, the bomb aimer of our aircraft.[12]

The Lancasters had flown in atrocious weather conditions of low cloud and rain, but F/Lt Robert Wannop, the skipper of another crew on The Hague drop, was able to describe what heart-rending joy was engendered by the mission both outside and inside the aircraft. 'Children ran out of school waving excitedly. One old man stopped at a cross roads and shook his umbrella. The roads were crowded with hundreds of people waving ... Nobody spoke in the aircraft. My vision was a little misty. Perhaps it was the rain on the Perspex.'[13]

The low cloud meant an even riskier return for the gaggle of bombers, aircrew anxiously looking out for any aircraft on a converging course. F/Sgt Porter recalls:

On the way home we were even lower, we had to climb to get over Cromer pier, while the fellows on our port side had to climb even quicker for they had the cliff to face. The tide was at an ebb as we approached the Lincolnshire coast and a fellow walking on the beach was soon face down eating sand as three low-flying Lan-casters came home. Once across the coast we had to climb and go back to base in an orderly fashion for the last fifteen minutes. We did three more of these drops, a second to The Hague on Monday 30th and then two at Rotterdam on 3 and 5 May.[14]

In a total of 3,300 sorties Bomber Command dropped 6,685 tons of supplies to the Dutch and the USAAF joined in with their own Operation Chowhound. Some RAF aircrew and ground crew slipped their names and addresses into the food parcels and letters of thanks were being received for weeks. Typical was the message from a young teenager, Annie Pebercoom, of Voorburg, Holland, to Johnny Reeves-Rowland, who took part in Operation Manna with 150 Sqn. It read:

> Innocent English friend. Perhaps, you will be very surprised to receive a letter from a Dutch girl as a consequence of your drop of a parcel of food. Your letter came in our neighbourhood. People were very glad with it and most of them would write you back. Perhaps you have received many letters from Holland. If you had seen the joy from us you would be deeply moved. We all had waved with pocket hankerchiefs and we had cried from joy to the flying machines ... We had endured and were so weak. Now it goes much better and we are more fit ... The war with Japan is very nearly over and we hope that the whole world will live in peace. The cinema play again and the tramway drive also. Everywhere there is peace and we can laugh again after five years. When the Moffen [a derogatory name for the Germans] were here it was a very unpleasant time and many of our men and boys were sent to Germany to work there, often suffering from hunger with their colleagues in the concentration camps. It was not to be forgiven, but also my respect for the English and Canadian soldiers. They have fought for us very heartily and also bought many sacrifices. Because of that we were very on tenterhooks and every time a town or city has fallen we say to each other, 'It goes very well'. That was a luminous point in the darkness. I hope you receive this letter and when you receive it will you give me best answer, so that I keep as a souvenir from the war ... I have forgotten so much from the English language.[15]

After so much anguish there were other heart-warming missions that the youngsters of Bomber Command would now be asked to fly. They struck a particular resonance with those who had seen so many comrades vanish in the earlier years of attrition. They gladly now took off to bring home some of those very same aircrew and other POWs from their liberated camps. For all the prisoners the final few days had been an anxious time of waiting. A total of 469 flights were made to Brussels in a two-week shuttle operation by Harris's bomber force to repatriate a total of 75,000 prisoners. The pathos of it all could sometimes be overwhelming both for the crews and the men seeing England's shoreline coming up again so many years and months after it had last faded behind them. F/Lt Douglas Jennings, the young 9 Sqn bomb aimer, who had been brought back to Britain himself in the autumn after a successful evasion, remembers those flights.

> It was very emotional. The former POWs were subdued getting into the aircraft. A lot of them were army, not necessarily aircrew, so hadn't flown before and were very apprehensive. They were just bedded down on the hard floor of the Lancaster, it was hardly posh. As a bomb aimer I had the maps down the front and could explain to them the different places we were going over and we usually flew over the south coast with the white cliffs. When they saw those it made them crease up. They were actually crying and it rubbed off on us.[16]

W/O Dennis Slack boarded a Lancaster at Brussels on the morning of 9 May.

> We were taken in batches of twenty to the airport. We were routed back to England right across the beaches where the invasion had taken place and taken on to RAF Cosford. I've never known organisation like we found there. We were checked in, showered and within 24 hours we had been innoculated, given medical examinations, had our teeth examined, had our hair cut, measured for a new uniform, issued with new shoes and given a railway warrant and back pay. At Birmingham there was a train waiting with a

special compartment just for ex-POWs. I got to Nottingham then onto Mansfield where my parents lived and I walked into their house eight days after leaving the camp. My old Irish setter Sandy knew I was coming. He had been pacing up and down all day and did he make a fuss of me when I arrived.[17]

Sgt Joe Williams, the 625 Sqn rear gunner who had escaped from the Germans marching him out of Stalag Luft XIIID on 5 April, had arrived home at his parents' mixed dairy and arable farm near Uckfield, Sussex, independently as Operation Exodus began. He remembers:

I got off the train at Isfield and the wife of the landlord of the Station Inn said I had to borrow their car to drive the two miles home. There had been a big question mark about whether I was dead. I arrived at the farmhouse and walked in. Just my mother was there. They had had the telegram saying I was missing, but fortunately someone in the RAF had contacted my mother only that day to say I had been seen in a camp and I was safe. I embraced my mother and then asked where my father and elder brother were. They were spreading manure in a field and I walked up to the gate and they stopped and stood up. I went across and shook hands. People weren't demonstrative in that time. There was simply relief that I was home and we just shook hands.[18]

Soon the whole country was to be overtaken by happy hysteria. VE-Day was about to arrive.

TWENTY

FINALE

THE news of victory came in typical understated British style, not with a bang but more of a whimper. Indeed the Germans were first to hear that they had lost rather than the British that they had won. The Russians were the ones holding up the announcement, the exercise of power a chill indicator of future relations with their former allies. Churchill, Stalin and the new US President, following Roosevelt's sudden death on 12 April, Harry Truman, had decided there would be a joint proclamation of peace in their capitals. On 4 May representatives of the German high command had agreed an armistice at Montgomery's HQ on Lüneburg Heath providing for all German forces in north-west Germany, Denmark and Holland to lay down their arms the next morning and on 7 May at Eisenhower's headquarters in Reims General Jodl signed the unconditional surrender of all German land, sea and air personnel. But Stalin, sticking to the point that there could be no proclamation until Marshall Zhukov in Berlin had accepted the German surrender on the Eastern Front, insisted no announcement be made before one minute past midnight on 9 May.

However the Reich Foreign Minister broadcast to all Germans on 7 May that the war was over, news avidly received by eavesdropping Allied military units. It wasn't until the evening that the BBC interrupted a programme to announce that the next day would be 'Victory in Europe Day and will be treated as a holiday'. In deference to the confusion caused by Stalin's intransigence the following day was declared a holiday too.

F/Sgt Henryk Drozdz, the Polish flight engineer who had longed for peace and a return to his occupied land, had been on leave and returned to Faldingworth while all this was going on. He was now waiting with the rear gunner in his crew, Wladek, to be posted to the Polish Air Force depot in Blackpool when he picked up his diary again for the first time since the end of March.

> Because our departure had been postponed Wladek and I are going to Sheffield, just equipped with toothbrushes. Even before the departure to Sheffield it feels that the war is finished. Everywhere on all the buildings flags are flying and banners with 'V'-day Victory etc. When we arrive in Sheffield there is a feeling of victory in the air. At 9 o'clock in the evening Mr Churchill announced that next day will be VE Day. It is difficult to describe – end of the war and so longed-for peace.[1]

The idea of peace was so strange after nearly six years of war that there had been no official planning of how it might be celebrated. It was left to the people of Britain to mark it how they may. As usual it was the housewives who made the practical arrangements between them. Street parties were organised so that the children might remember and rations were pooled to make a mountain of sandwiches and bowl after bowl of jelly. It came in one colour, orange, because children's ration orange juice was all that was available to add in thirds of a pint to the rest of the wartime recipe of two-thirds water, 1 oz of sugar and $\frac{1}{2}$ ounce of gelatine.

Long-hoarded bunting was strung out and there was a rush to find Union Flags to welcome home POWs. The night of VE-Day ended for most with impromptu bonfires in suburban gardens, usually for a whole street. The bonfire for my own small cul-de-sac in an industrial Yorkshire town was memorable because it was held in my family's garden. I was introduced to a new pyrotechnic that the firework manufacturers at least had had the foresight, and perhaps daring, to produce: a miniature RAF aeroplane, its fuselage a tiny rocket which when lit flew the small aircraft out of childish upheld fingers. It would be decades before Health and Safety legislation got a toehold on the landscape.

In London crowds gathered in Whitehall and Trafalgar Square from early morning, servicemen of all Allied nations taking advantage of girlish generous nature on such a momentous day and stealing kisses as they weaved among the throng. Wild flowers now grew among the blitzed ruins of office buildings around St Paul's and Fleet Street, their colours adding zest to streets full of drab blue and khaki. The temperature rose in conjunction with the excitement of the crowd and it was 75° Fahrenheit in central London by mid-afternoon. Canadian air gunner Sgt Patrick Bell, who had joined the RCAF straight out of high school and was still only 20, remembers: 'I was on leave in London and all the pubs were drunk dry that day. There were huge, huge crowds in Oxford Street and they were singing and dancing. It was a terrific atmosphere. Everybody treated us like heroes which I wasn't. I probably had my Pathfinder badge on, but don't even know if I had my Canadian operational wing on. Everybody was just as happy as can be and I was happy too. I knew I was going home.'[2]

On this day it seemed there were indeed Bluebirds Over the White Cliffs of Dover just as Vera Lynn had been promising for years. As the May blossom cast its petals over the fresh green lawns of Britain so many had died for, there was the prospect of golden days ahead in a land of peace and plenty. The harsh years of the austerity period in which rations would decrease rather than increase and a near bankrupt Britain would struggle to pay off its debt to America all lay ahead in the great unknown. For the moment it was time to enjoy the cheer and reflect on the prize. The greatest victor of them all was Churchill. At 3 p.m. he made a short triumphant broadcast from Downing Street then was driven the quarter of a mile to the House of Commons, his portly figure standing proudly on the front seat of an open car as he waved V-signs to the cheering crowd. It took half an hour for the car to travel the short distance. His personal, glorious journey, beginning with the pugnacious decision after the Fall of France that Britain would fight on alone when the sensible urged an accord with Hitler, would soon be halted with defeat in the coming general election.

His speech, ending with the words 'Advance Britannia', on which his voice faltered with emotion, was not specific in praise but paid tribute to the military might of Soviet Russia and the power and resources of America. Families listened through the crackle of static on living-room wireless sets and the speech was broadcast throughout the world. It was picked up by POWs at Stalag IIIA near Berlin, who had just discovered that American trucks had been sent to rescue them. 'Boys streaming to trucks but nothing official through yet,' the wireless operator F/Sgt David Berrie wrote in his diary, then later: 'Russians order trucks to return empty. Boys leave camp in all directions. Some return, others are interned etc. Barracks well below strength.' It was as a somewhat sad afterthought that he finished with: 'Heard Churchill and the King.'[3]

Flight engineer Lawrence Benson, guarded by Red Army troops at Goldberg, had managed to give them the slip the previous day, although the Russians would not release his comrades for almost another fortnight, and was in Brussels on VE-Day as was Dennis Slack. 'I was given some fresh clothing by the British authorities,' he recorded in his diary. 'As I was staying there overnight, I could not resist the claim of the dance floor, and set off that evening for the local Forces Dance.' He was flown home the next day.[4]

P/O Kenneth Turnham, the 115 Sqn wireless operator wounded by flak over Cologne only weeks before, was in hospital near his home in St Albans when peace arrived. 'I had a very sore throat, but my feelings were absolute elation,' he remembers. 'I had a brother in aircrew, who did forty-seven operations on Wellingtons and Halifaxes, and another brother in the navy and we had all survived. That was my mother's war effort, three sons in the services. We patients had a bit of a party with all the nurses on the ward. I think I could have done with staying in hospital a bit longer.'[5]

F/Sgt Peter Bone was on leave at his home in south London on VE-Day and celebrated with his family. He later wrote:

What better way than to light a bonfire in the back lane, just as bonfires had been lit on the hilltops across Britain in times gone by, to celebrate great victories. We invited some neighbours to our bonfire, but as far as I can remember, there was no dancing. No-one got drunk. I don't think we even spoke much. I think we were all suddenly tired. We seemed content to watch the flames gradually die down. Around midnight people started to drift away, with self conscious 'good nights'. By one o'clock Eden Way was fast asleep.[6]

On the stations of Bomber Command too there was a general feeling of anticlimax, a letting go after the tension of war. F/O John Greening, the pilot on 97 Sqn who had been a primary blind marker on Dresden, recalls: 'There wasn't one heck of a party at Coningsby. I think a lot of aircrew had seen so many of their comrades lost and there was no great euphoria. People felt a bit weary. The losses in Bomber Command had been tremendous.'[7] There was even time for sympathy to an enemy now. F/Sgt Frank Tolley says: 'I went on leave just before the end and saw a German for the first time. This Jerry POW was being brought out of Lincoln railway station by two soldiers and I thought, Poor bastard. It's over and done with and all for nothing for him.'[8]

In the villages of the bomber counties that had been shaken out of a rural routine by the war their most colourful canvas of the century was about to fade. Betty Manby was 15 when the war ended. Her mother had worked at the Marrowbone and Cleaver in Kirmington, the aircrew pub of 166 Sqn, and the previous summer Betty had often stood by the Kirmington perimeter track as the Lancasters queued for take-off, bidding farewell to the crews and receiving answering waves from gunners in their turrets. She recalls: 'The evening of VE-Day was fine and warm and I stood at our gate at dusk, watching the men and women going to the pub. One young Canadian stopped to talk to me. We chatted for a while then he gave me a kiss and a cuddle as he left.'[9]

But there were others that day for whom victory had a hollow ring. Kay Kirby, who the previous autumn had become a widow before she was 21 when her navigator husband went missing on the last trip of his tour, had by now been officially informed he was 'Presumed Killed' but could not believe it. She says:

For years I expected George to turn up. I couldn't reconcile myself to the fact that he wasn't coming back. I thought of all sorts of things. I thought, When he crashed he lost his memory, he doesn't know where he is, perhaps the underground movement have helped him. My parents' house near Stockwell was three storeys, but my bedroom was on the first floor and before George started his tour when he came back on leave unexpectedly he used to knock on my window with a clothes prop. After George went missing, many times I went to the door because I thought I heard him knocking at my window. Of course there was no one there.[10]

Others were still suffering physical injuries from the war. W/O Harry Stunell, the 21-year-old wireless operator who received extensive burns when his Lancaster crashed coming back from Munich in January, was in hospital at South Cerney where he had been taught to walk again after being given skin grafts at an American unit at Cirencester. He recalls:

On VE-Day I knew the Americans would be going home now, so I got in my uniform and went back to the hospital at Cirencester to say thank you for what they had done for me. While I was going along and, of course, it was obvious I had been wounded, I came across a man with his young son and he stopped and said to his boy, 'There you are, that's what the war was about, young men like these.' I was quite pleased by that.[11]

FIVE days after his victory speech the Prime Minister made another, fuller speech to the nation. Harris listened to it broadcast on the BBC with his old friend General Ira Eaker, by now Chief of the US Air Staff. They heard Churchill reflect on the Battle of Britain, the Blitz, the achievements of the Royal Navy and the entry into the war of Russia. They fully expected that at any moment would come the accolade for the bomber boys. They listened with growing incredulity as Churchill praised the invasion, the liberation of France and the further land battles in Germany. There were references to generals and admirals aplenty, but there was no mention of Bomber Command. The official cynicism and ingratitude that the bomber boys would suffer for decades had begun.

There were many statistics that Churchill could have mentioned if he had lingered at all on the bomber war. A final tally of 55,888 Bomber Command aircrew had died in six years of conflict and a further 8,403 had been wounded, their average age 22 before they reached journey's end. Bomber Command had made up only 7 per cent of Britain and its empire in uniform, yet had taken more than 20 per cent of the war's service casualties. Most had been Britons: 38,462 of the cream of the nation had gone, a similar denial of national potential as the attrition of officers in the First World War proved to be. But the Dominions too had made enormous sacrifices of the bright and brave they could not afford to lose. Notably Canada, which had trained so many from all over the world in its safe blue skies as well as its own, had lost 58 per cent of its youngsters who sailed the Atlantic to become part of Harris's bomber boys. A total of 9,980 of them would not be returning. Then there were the 4,050 Australians and the 1,703 New Zealanders who had come from the other side of the world to die in air-force blue. Once more the fatal percentages spelled out the scale of the sacrifice, the Australians in Bomber Command representing only 2 per cent of Aussies in wartime uniform, yet making up 23 per cent of the country's casualties. There were others too who might have been recognised, from occupied nations, not least the Poles, 977 of whom died fighting the war of the bombers for their freedom and ours. Not one got a mention in the public plaudits that rang out from Downing Street that day or in subsequent days.

F/Sgt Henryk Drozdz had guessed that as the conflict ended the reason for going to war at all would be forgotten, now that Stalin had a grip on Poland. He wrote as peace came:

Almost six long years of murderous struggles and now today arrived this moment of victory – Germany defeated. You could write for hours on this momentous fact. But the question remains –

how the end of the war affects us Poles. What have we gained and what is our future? It is difficult for me to write about it because it is so painful. When I watch the happy, dancing crowds of British people I feel a wave of sadness and pity or even maybe contempt at such shortsightedness. But then my thoughts are lost in this din, this roar of victory fanfares. For them the war is finished – for us calm and hope. This is therefore all I can say.[12]

A particular ingratitude would be heaped on the long-suffering Poles in a year's time. Two weeks after VE-Day the Labour Party left the wartime coalition government and won the subsequent general election on 26 July by a landslide. There were plans for a victory parade by the British Empire and its Allies to celebrate the hard work and sacrifice that had brought final defeat to Germany and eventually to Japan. But Stalin did not want the Poles included and said so. Clement Attlee, the new Prime Minister, bowed to Stalin's wishes, although Poland had been the fourth largest European ally of Britain in the Second World War. As a sop the Polish 303 fighter squadron, which had claimed the greatest number of kills in the Battle of Britain, was asked to send representatives. It declined because the invitation was not extended to any other Polish units. So there were no Poles for the grateful British people to cheer as the parade marched through London in the summer of 1946.

By then the austerity period had arrived, taxpayers of the United Kingdom paying for the war at the same time as the Government carried out brave social changes, such as the National Health Service and a guarantee of grammar school and university education by merit not family wealth. The nation of the mid-1940s was a foreign country compared to that of 1939. It was as if the patchwork blanket of class, deference and hierarchy that both supported and depressed society in pre-war Britain had been lifted and shaken. All the pieces fell back afterwards, but not in the same order. The class system had been split asunder. Many country houses had been requisitioned, and a great number of owners, beggared by death duties or lack of an heir, would never return.

Beningbrough Hall near Linton-on-Ouse, used to billet NCO aircrew during the war, would eventually be handed over to the National Trust. Young men who had left school at 14 would soon be demobbed from the services, particularly the air force, as senior officers. Meritocracy was in the ascendant in the new mood of egalitarianism under a Labour administration.

There would be a rally by the aristocracy in the late 1940s and early 50s to re-establish themselves, the glut of British war films of the period usually featuring officers with upper-class accents and other ranks as Cockneys, but the 1960s, as the war babies came of age, killed it off. The advent of the Beatles made a regional accent rather than a public school one the voice of choice. It was the RAF, the most junior of the three services, that had helped to effect that change.

The shifts in society were perhaps less obvious at first than the changes in the landscape. The bomber bases, both British and USAAF, that had littered eastern Britain were rapidly being closed, tin roofs of billets reacting surprisingly quickly to the elements and tufts of grass rapidly appearing between cracks in runways to spread and cover. S/Ldr Robert Vollum, the wireless operator who had completed his second tour with 158 Sqn at Lissett at the end of December, found himself posted back to the East Yorkshire base as Station Administrative Officer in July to close it down. He remembers:

All the men were taken up to Burton Agnes station and sent off to various destinations by rail and I returned to Lisset. It was quite eerie to see what had been a busy, noisy operational base where I had flown from so many times myself now silent. The aircraft had gone and the officers had left. It was a strange feeling as I looked across the airfield to where at one time the Halifaxes had lined up for take-off and I thought about all those nights I had set off from there. There would at one time have been about 1,200 personnel on the station and the buildings were now empty. Apart from myself there was just a flying officer who had been posted in to take over the care and maintenance with about twenty men.

There were so few of us now we all messed together in the officers' mess. I left Lissett in the hands of the flying officer and his party and then went off to Holme-on-Spalding-Moor where I did the same job of closing that down.[13]

The bombers, which contained such memories of youthful fear and courage, would themselves soon become scrap for the export drive without thought of preservation. G-George of the Dams Raid in which Guy Gibson had won his VC had surprisingly survived the war, but was scrapped like the rest in 1947. Most of the aircraft were broken up at RAF Silloth. LAC Ronald Ashbridge, an ex-erk at Waddington where the Australian 467 and 463 Sqns had operated their Lancasters, came from the Cumbrian town and cycled to the air base while he was on leave. 'I saw several of the 467/463 aircraft parked there with their proud PO and JO squadron letters,' he wrote. 'Through the mist of tears [I saw] men cutting these aircraft to bits ... Entire mainplanes hacked through and dropped, to be hacked up into smaller pieces then flattened by running steam rollers over them ... fuselages cut through and similarly flattened ... It was all just too much to take in.'[14]

While the physical evidence of the bomber boys' story was rapidly passing away, the final clues to what had happened to some of the men who had simply disappeared in the darkness was being put together. P/O Turnham joined the RAF Missing Research Enquiry Unit in Germany in 1946. He remembers:

I was stationed at Karlsruhe then moved to Regensburg and Heidelberg. I would get a file from the Air Ministry stating for instance the time an aircraft went missing on a particular raid to what target, based on the reports of returning crews at debriefing. We would then talk to the local village *burgomeisters* and they would tell us if any RAF aircraft crashed nearby and where the bodies were buried. It was a morbid type of job; sometimes there would be three or four legs and two arms and you had to try to identify who they were. We were meant to identify the body by the dog tags, laundry marks or the personal effects in the pockets. But the ultimate proof positive of identification, which happened in 90 per cent of cases, was by means of dental records. Fortunately all aircrew had to have their teeth in good order because of the pressure of flying at height, so a careful record was kept of the work done on an individual. We filled in the charts and the Air Ministry verified that person against their dental records as a positive member of that crew. The laundry marks weren't as good for identification because often aircrew borrowed a collar or whatever from a mate for a night out and the next night flew off wearing that collar.

It was very satisfying to identify missing airmen and that outweighed the morbid aspect. We passed the exhumed airmen over to the army who took them to the war cemeteries for re-burial and you knew relatives back home now knew where their loved ones were. There was myself and another officer with two drivers. We had Jeeps or Humber Snipes or 3-ton trucks to move around and we carried out the exhumations using local labour. I worked on as many as ten or twelve exhumations in a day. The army had searchlights on their vehicles which they would shine over the site to allow us to keep working. I worked on hundreds all told.

I was a bit queasy about going on my first exhumation, but the colleague I was with who was teaching me the job just threw some knives to me and said, 'Get on with it.' We didn't have any forensic or pathology training, it was a matter of carrying on. I had to cut away clothing to look for laundry marks, signet rings or any personal effects in pockets. Aircrew were always told to leave any personal effects behind before they went on an operation, but I found quite a lot of items – photographs and letters and so on. It seems many aircrew ignored that instruction and not all wore their dog tags as they were ordered to. I didn't for instance. I never found evidence of a war crime against an airman, but quite a few people on this job did go round the bend and start hitting the bottle.[15]

But for the majority of relatives of the missing such as George Kirby's widow there would be no comfort of a certain resting place for their loved ones. Only the second-dickey pilot and the rear gunner in her husband's crew have known graves, the rest are remembered on the Runnymede Memorial which commemorates the 20,000 missing RAF and Commonwealth airmen of the Second World War. The widow, who later remarried, says:

> Some time after the war someone sent a photograph to my mother-in-law showing the wooden crosses of four airmen in Germany. The middle one had Sgt Paul's and F/Lt Barlow's name written on it with the date 6 October and then either side also RAF 6 October, but no names. Later someone at the British Legion told me the aircraft had probably exploded and only two people could be identified. I always wanted to know more. Two years ago my younger son took me to Becklingen War Cemetery where Sgt Paul and F/Lt Barlow are now buried. There were several graves to unknown airmen, but I left the cemetery feeling George was not there. I feel there is still a gap in my life and I would like to know what happened, however horrible.[16]

As the last of the POWs came home in 1945 they brought with them the final certainty for relatives of the missing in Bomber Command and for their aircrew comrades that they were in fact dead. F/Lt Peter Johnson, whose wireless operator friend on 101 Sqn went missing on his twenty-ninth operation, not long after F/Lt Johnson finished his tour, says: 'Most aircrew in Bomber Command just went missing. I did hope for a little while that my friend Jock Mitchell would be found in a prison camp, that he would come back. Those you did know about you disregarded, but some you wondered where or what had happened. There weren't the connections then to find out.'[17]

It was hard to establish closure when so many had simply disappeared. The film selected for the first Royal Command Performance, in 1946, echoed the limbo-like chasm that opened for families when an airman was simply declared 'Missing', striking a chord with those who still sought an answer. *A Matter of Life and Death* told the story of a pilot in a burning Lancaster who bales out without a parachute and then has to be judged by a celestial court whether he has been counted dead by mistake and should really be in the land of the living. How many widows and mothers hoped beyond hope that there had been a dreadful Air Ministry error and Johnny would eventually come marching home.

As women grieved, the echoes of war would continue for years to remind them of their loss while Britain slowly rebuilt its blitzed cities and turned its out-dated, creaking industry from building tanks and aeroplanes to exportable goods. Sometimes those reminders of conflict were indeed explosive, a multiple blast at the vast bomb and shell dump of Clumber Park, Nottinghamshire, in 1947 destroying 1,000 acres of woodland; and mine clearance at Mundesley on the Norfolk coast claiming the lives of two Royal Engineer Sappers as late as 1953. As rationing continued for a decade and pictures appeared in British newspapers of the new, gleaming structures of Düsseldorf and other German industrial cities while the ruins of Sheffield or Manchester remained, the bomber boys waited in vain for some official recognition for their sacrifice. Harris had been lobbying Whitehall for the award of a separate Bomber Command campaign medal for two months before the day of victory. In June he wrote to Portal and the Air Secretary Sir Archibald Sinclair complaining of the slight to his men and it was clear he blamed Churchill for it. In fact he described Churchill's omission of any reference to the strategic offensive in his 13 May victory speech as 'an insult not to be forgotten, if it is forgiven'.[18] Harris's battle for his 'Old Lags' continued beyond Churchill's election defeat and he took up the cause again when Churchill returned to power in 1951. But when he was finally told in 1952 that the only recognition for his Command would be a baronetcy for himself Harris accepted he could make no further headway for his men. The lack of a medal is a stain on their comrades' memory that still rankles with the survivors of Bomber Command and the campaign continues.

So if the bomber boys were not to be honoured why not and what had they achieved? There is no doubt it was the bombing of Dresden and the subsequent foreign questioning, particularly from America – now taking Britain's pre-war place as the major power in the world – that denied Bomber Command its medal. It seems that Churchill, who had promoted the bomber offensive and had been among its most ardent supporters for much of the war, played a leading part in that denial. At the war's end Churchill the politician had taken over from Churchill the belligerent. Good relations with the new world order were paramount. The great war leader demonstrated the dexterity of decades in politics by apparently forgetting it was he who wanted Dresden bombed in February, not Harris. There would, therefore, be no reward for the courage of Bomber Command. How happy this would have made Goebbels, lately dead by his own hand after having his children poisoned, that the lies he had spread about Dresden had been so successful. They found rich soil among succeeding generations since the war and until quite recently brought a thoughtless condemnation of the bomber boys.

Yet it was the bomber offensive, by the USAAF and Harris's forces, that brought Germany to defeat in the field. It was the greatest single superiority of the Allies against the Axis, which had not invested in offensive, four-engined, long-range aircraft. All other successes on land had resulted from this advantage. At first the bomber had been the only way of taking the war to the enemy, then it had become the Second Front – supporting the Soviet Resistance which spent millions of Russian lives on the battlefield and off it. It had kept a cap on the expansion of German industry, paved the way for D-Day and allowed the campaign in Normandy to succeed by sealing off the German reinforcement and supply routes with the Transportation Plan. By the time D-Day arrived the German Air Force had been forced to turn to defence not offence, a strategy it had not initially planned for. In September 1944, 80 per cent of Luftwaffe fighters were based in Germany in a hopeless attempt to stop the bomber fleets instead of supporting the Wehrmacht. The Bomber Command and USAAF oil campaign put paid even to the Luftwaffe flying in that defensive role. In 1945 the resurrection of the Transportation Plan in Germany, together with the oil campaign, had remorselessly brought the Reich, its armies and any semblance of normal life by its productive people to a halt. RAF Bomber Command was essentially tasked with creating chaos and that is what it did.

The greatest mayhem had been caused in the final phase of the bomber offensive, beginning in September 1944 when the defence potential of the Luftwaffe was in rapid decline. In that period 45 per cent of the total bomb tonnage dropped by the Command in the whole war had fallen on Germany. In the last three months of 1944 a total of 163,000 tons had gone down. From January to April 1945 a total of 181,740 tons had blasted the Reich, 24,283 more than in the whole of 1943, when the offensive had truly begun. Most targets in 1945 had been oil and transportation centres, rather than cities per se, but often such targets were within urban areas. In those final four months of the bombing war the US Eighth Air Force, now with a bigger flight line, had exceeded Bomber Command's total, dropping 6,734 tons more.[19]

Creating that sea of rubble that the German cities had become in 1945 had demanded a terrible price, both in the toll among young aircrew and in civilian lives. In 1962 the Federal German Statistics Office put the total of civilian dead at 593,000.[20] This included the battalions of forced labourers from Occupied Europe, who did not have a priority for shelter space in Hitler's Reich, and the considerable number of civilians who died from Allied army shellfire, particularly in the taking of Berlin by the Red Army. It compares with the 63,635 British civilian dead in the blitzes by traditional Luftwaffe bombs and V-weapons. In the First World War 800,000 German civilians had died as a result of the Royal Navy blockade of the Fatherland.[21]

A total of 955,044 bombs were dropped by Bomber Command in the Second World War and three million homes as well as Germany's infrastructure and industry had been destroyed or damaged. Yet none of this misery would have been visited on Germany without the fanaticism of Hitler and his cohorts. A recent German study revealed that he was advised in 1942, before the true awesome might of Bomber Command and the USAAF was unleashed, that Germany could not win the war, but the dictator continued to exhort nothing less than total victory.[22] Vast numbers of Germans had been killed by the Germans themselves, the indescribable Holocaust apart; 71,000 physically and mentally challenged German children and adults had been liquidated in medical institutions under the Nazi euthanasia programme by the summer of 1941, a year and a half before what Harris called his main bomber offensive began.[23] Bombs on Germany eventually stopped such evil being perpetuated by cutting the head from the dragon. The German people were in fact liberated from tyranny by the effects of the bomber offensive, though undoubtedly not in a way they would have wished, and innocent as well as guilty paid a huge price for the support that had been given to Hitler. Who could not mourn particularly the lost children, trapped in the cities instead of being evacuated to the country? Unlike in Britain married women in the Third Reich were not conscripted for war work and mothers could have been forced to evacuate the cities with their children as they were not needed in the factories. The truth was it suited Nazi propaganda that women and children died in air raids and was thought to stiffen male resolve.

The last day of war finally ended the threat of a German atomic bomb being unleashed. Operation Alsos had already been launched to find the German Nobel prizewinner Werner Heisenberg and his fellow nuclear scientists. From the chaos of Germany they were taken to the former SOE training base of Farm Hall, near Cambridge, where their conversations were bugged for six months. It was only then that Britain and America discovered for certain that Allied development had superseded German nuclear plans by 1942. But until the war ended this was not known. For the Allies not to finish the conflict by all means in their power as quickly as possible and thereby possibly lose was unthinkable.

A price would also be paid by the man tasked with bringing such mayhem and misery to end the war. Harris was always honest about what the bomber offensive meant and he had written to the Air Council in December 1943 complaining that in the press they were presenting 'the aims of Bomber Command as the 'destruction of specific factory premises' rather than 'the destruction of German cities, the killing of German workers and the disruption of civilized community life throughout Germany'. Sir Arthur Street, the Permanent Under-Secretary of State for Air, whose bomber pilot son would be murdered by the Gestapo after the Great Escape, replied that it was necessary 'to present the bomber offensive in such a light as to provoke the minimum of public controversy'. If Harris didn't know before he certainly knew then that he was expected to wage a successful campaign and any post-war recriminations would be falling on his shoulders, not in Whitehall.[24]

Harris had certainly believed in 1943 that the war could be won by bombing alone and in 1944 had high hopes that enough aerial pressure would finally quash the Nazis. But so did his boss Portal and the Supreme Commander of the Allied Forces in Europe, Eisenhower. Both had urged Operation Hurricane, Harris merely followed orders. That he sometimes did so reluctantly by bombing industrial cities rather than oil targets in the autumn, for instance, caused a row in which he had to be brought to book. But the greatest damage to his reputation in the post-war years was the destruction of Dresden and that was a target he had not chosen. It had been urged on him by Portal and Churchill. It became a symbol in the post-war years for the bomber offensive and Harris shouldered the official distaste, as he always knew he would, in the peaceful post-war years of quiet academic debate.

There was little thanks for the man who had saved Bomber Command when he took over in 1942, a time when for lack of navigation aids and suitable aircraft the Command's bombing record was so poor it was in danger of being hived off to become an adjunct of the navy and the army. In common with all commanders Harris did have faults, not least in sometimes following a course beyond the point of usefulness. He was also wrong in not seeing in the final phase that the once costly oil targets provided the key to victory now Germany's defences were down and aircrew losses were falling. But it is difficult to think of any senior air force officer from 1942 onwards who would have had the single-minded ability to hold the Command together through its terrible years of attrition to become the efficient, war-settling weapon it proved in 1945. To paraphrase a famous Harris epigram, Churchill and Portal had sown the wind of the bomber offensive,

quite rightly, and Harris reaped the post-war whirlwind. Throughout all those years of attrition the aircrew of Bomber Command
had never doubted the strength that was emanating from the C-
in-C to them and in return Harris fought for his crews against
what at times seemed like a Whitehall carelessness with their lives
and how they should briefly live them. Even as the final phase of
the bomber offensive began Harris was sticking up for his crews
with the Air Ministry, who wanted to insist that all bomber personnel carry out a second tour, which Harris said would reduce
their chances of survival to about one in twenty.[25]

It was a mutual respect that continued in the post-war years.
Harris never forgot the young men who died and neither did the
survivors of their crews. An aircrew was a family to each other
and the links forged in the stress of wartime most of us cannot
know have not been forgotten. In October 2008 Sgt John Bremner,
a 21-year-old pilot on 102 Sqn missing since his Halifax was shot
down on a night raid to Berlin on 20 January 1944, was buried
with full military honours in the Heerstrasse War Cemetery simply
because his navigator, blasted out of the bomber when it exploded
in the air, would not rest until he found him. P/O Reg Wilson
returned to Germany with a metal detector in 2005 having established the crash site and in the wreckage were the remains of Sgt
Bremner.[26]

John Ladbrooke, a former navigator on 106 Sqn, thought
enough about his own crew that he travelled to Canada in 2009
at 86 to be reunited with the remaining known survivor, his RCAF
rear gunner, F/Sgt Donald Bowman. F/Sgt Ladbrooke's son had
tracked down the gunner the navigator had flown with over nine
months of war. Their tour had finished in November 1944, before
the Dresden raid. 'There has been a condemnation of Bomber
Command because of Dresden,' F/Sgt Ladbrooke says. 'Overall,
we were engaged in something that was bigger than us, so we had
to take part in it otherwise we would have lost. There would have
been no life for our people again so these things happen and it did
happen. That's war.'[27]

Many veterans of Bomber Command are left with terrible

memories of what they endured in that struggle for national survival, even sixty-five years later. The image – not uncommon – of a Lancaster burning from nose to tail and wingtip to wingtip as it slowly passed close beneath the stream, then exploding into a hundred pieces, was one that any crew member could not easily forget and could all too readily transfer to his own aircraft and crew. That such a crewman was prepared to go out again the next night and the next and face the same frightful scenes is extraordinary in these days of peace.

W/O Harry Stunell, who clawed his way out of an enclosure of flame when his Lancaster crashed, says:

> There aren't many days when I'm alone when I don't have flashbacks. I might be walking across a field with the dog when my mind is suddenly assailed by an image – in colour – of me trying to extricate myself from a blazing Lancaster in a burning forest. Just after the war I would get out of bed three or four times in the night to rake out the embers in the open fire grate, I was so afraid something would shoot out and set the house ablaze.[28]

The teenagers and other young men of Bomber Command were heroes to the British public when they carried the war to the enemy, in the beginning when no other nation could. The sound of hope in their passing was heard night after night over blacked-out Britain and Occupied Europe. A just reward for their sacrifice would be at least a campaign medal. The survivors of Bomber Command are still waiting.

Thousands of people have considered this lack of official recognition so shameful they have contributed by individual subscription in excess of £2 million for a central London memorial to be built, on which the names of the 55,888 Bomber Command aircrew who died will be inscribed. The people have spoken where politicians stayed silent.

THE AIRFIELDS the bomber boys flew from have mostly sunk back into the landscape now, the village pubs no longer ring to their youthful laughter and the wartime slang. Words and phrases such as wizard, popsie, wallop and a wad have made way for wicked, tottie and a bevvy and baguette. But standing in the leafy, summer silence at the side of cracked concrete that was once a runway it is easy to imagine an echo from the past as the prosaic airfield call signs come floating on the wind across the flat acres of bomber country: Silksheen, Peek-Frean, Coffee Stall, Dogbark. They are out there still. Now only the occasional roadside memorial marks the passing of so many who came from all corners of Britain and across the world to save civilisation. At Kirmington, where 166 Sqn operated, losing nearly 1,000 aircrew in the war, the memorial reads:

> *Ye that live mid England's Pastures Green*
> *Think on us and what might have been*

NOTES

OVERTURE

1. Interview with author
2. Juliet Gardiner, *Wartime: Britain 1939–45*, p. 559
3. National Archives: AIR 14–2697

1: A NEW AGE OF WARFARE

1. Juliet Gardiner, *Wartime*, p. 560
2. BBC News 24, 7 Sept. 2004
3. National Archives: W/O 208/3432
4. Daniel Flekser, 'Memoirs of the Great Escape,' Imperial War Museum 99/82/1
5. Ibid.
6. Interview with author
7. From Sgt Boness's unpublished account, 'A Short Trip,' via Jim Sheffield
8. Ibid.
9. Ibid.
10. Ibid.
11. Ibid.
12. Ibid.
13. Ibid.
14. National Archives: AIR 14–3412, Night Raid Report 722
15. National Archives: AIR 14–2799
16. Ibid.
17. Ibid.

18. Ibid.
19. W. R. Chorley, *Bomber Command Losses, 1945*, p. 57
20. National Archives: AIR 14–2799
21. Ibid.
22. Ibid.
23. Sir Arthur Harris, *Bomber Offensive*, p. 239
24. Interview with author
25. Bomber Offensive, p. 236

2: FROM ATTRITION TO PRECISION

1. Henry Probert, *Bomber Harris: His Life and Times*, p. 50
2. Kevin Wilson, *Men of Air: The Doomed Youth of Bomber Command*, p. 200
3. Interview with author
4. Ibid.
5. Ibid.
6. National Archives: AIR 14–3412, Night Raid Report 734
7. Ibid.
8. Ibid.
9. Interview with author
10. Ibid.
11. Martin Middlebrook and Chris Everitt, *The Bomber Command War Diaries*, p. 602
12. Kevin Wilson, *Bomber Boys: The Ruhr, the Dambusters and Bloody Berlin*, p. 28
13. Ibid., p. 225
14. Philip Gray, *Ghosts of Targets Past: The Lives and Losses of a Lancaster Crew in 1944–45*, p. 71
15. Ibid.
16. Sir Arthur Harris, *Bomber Offensive*, p. 227
17. Ibid.
18. National Archives: AIR 27–1352
19. National Archives: AIR 27–204
20. National Archives: AIR 25–79
21. National Archives: AIR 27–1352

22. National Archives: AIR 27–204
23. National Archives: AIR 25–79
24. Jorg Friedrich, *The Fire*, p. 225
25. *Bomber Offensive*, p. 241

3: RUINING THE RUHR AGAIN

1. Kevin Wilson, *Bomber Boys: The Ruhr, the Dambusters and Bloody Berlin*, p. 236
2. Hilary St G. Saunders, *Royal Air Force 1939–1945*, Vol. III, *The Fight Is Won*, p. 260
3. Sir Charles Webster and Noble Frankland, *The Strategic Air Offensive Against Germany 1939–45*, Vol. IV, pp. 172–3
4. DVD *Lancaster at War*, DD 20343, DD Video, 2004
5. Jorg Friedrich, *The Fire*, p. 343
6. Ibid., p. 263
7. Logbook quoted in letter to author
8. National Archives: AIR 27–1862
9. Ibid.
10. Ibid.
11. National Archives: AIR 14–3412
12. *Westfälische Landeszeitung*, 24 October 1944, quoted in Earl R. Beck, *Under The Bombs: The German Home Front 1942–1945*, p. 153
13. National Archives: AIR 14–2697
14. Chester Wilmot, *The Struggle for Europe*, p. 548, quoting Henry L. Stimson and McGeorge Bundy, *On Active Service in Peace and War*, 1948
15. Quoted in *The Struggle for Europe*, p. 550
16. Cordell Hull, *The Memoirs of Cordell Hull* (Hodder & Stoughton, 1948), p. 1606
17. National Archives: AIR 20–5513
18. Ibid.
19. Account to author
20. Interview with author
21. Wartime diary of Ernest P. Bone released to author

22. National Archives: AIR 27–653
23. W. R. Chorley and R. N. Benwell, *In Brave Company*, p. 98
24. Ibid.
25. National Archives: AIR 14–651
26. *In Brave Company*, p. 99
27. W. R. Chorley, *Bomber Command Losses, 1944*, p. 452
28. National Archives: AIR 14–3412, NRR 741
29. Ibid.
30. Ibid.
31. *The Fire*, p. 210
32. National Archives: AIR 14–3412, NRR 741
33. *Royal Air Force 1930–1945*, Vol. III, *The Fight Is Won*, p. 262
34. Ibid.
35. Ibid., p. 263
36. Interview with author
37. Account to author
38. *Bomber Command Losses, 1944*, p. 461
39. Interview with author
40. Ibid.
41. Ibid.
42. Ibid.
43. Chris Goss, *It's Suicide But It's Fun*, p. 131

4: BLOODY BOCHUM

1. National Archives: AIR 14–3412
2. National Archives: AIR 27–1742
3. Interview with author
4. Ibid.
5. Ibid.
6. *Flypast* magazine, November 2001
7. Ibid.
8. Ibid.
9. Ibid.
10. Ian Mackersey, *Into The Silk*, p. 131 and Internet sources
11. Jules Roy, *Return From Hell*

12. Account to author
13. Ibid.
14. www. Toronto Aircrew Association
15. Ibib.
16. National Archives: AIR 14–3412
17. Ibid.
18. National Archives: AIR 20–5513

5: A TORCH TO THE OIL

1. Hilary St G. Saunders, *Royal Air Force 1939–1945*, Vol. III, *The Fight Is Won*, p. 269
2. National Archives: AIR 20–5513
3. Ibid.
4. Roger A. Freeman, *The Mighty Eighth*, p. 180
5. Interview with author
6. Ibid.
7. National Archives: AIR 27–1862
8. Interview with author
9. Ibid.
10. Ibid.
11. Private operational diary of F/Sgt Henryk Drozdz
12. Interview with author
13. *Royal Air Force 1939–1945*, Vol. III, *The Fight Is Won*, p. 263
14. Ibid., p. 269

6: A BITTER SEASON TO BE MERRY

1. *The Times*, 5 Dec. 1944
2. Interview with author
3. Ibid.
4. Ibid.
5. Heilbronn Stadtarchiv
6. Wilhelm Steinhilber, *Heilbronn – Die Schwersten Stunden der Stadt*, Verlag Heilbronner Stimme, 1961
7. Stuttgart Staatsarchiv

8. *Lincolnshire Echo*, 5 Dec. 1944
9. Jorg Friedrich, *The Fire*, p. 123
10. Interview with author
11. Speer Papers, F/D 3063/49, Dept of Documents, Imperial War Museum
12. Interview with author
13. *Lincolnshire Echo*, 20 Dec. 1944
14. *Cambridge Daily News*, 16 Dec. 1944
15. *Yorkshire Evening Press*, 30 Dec. 1944
16. *The Times*, 4 Dec. 1944
17. Ibid., 5 Dec. 1944
18. Interview with author
19. Ibid.
20. John Castello, *Love, Sex and War*, p. 137
21. Interview with author
22. Ibid.
23. Ibid.
24. Ibid.
25. *The Swing Thing*, BBC 4 broadcast, 19 Dec. 2008
26. *Cambridge Daily News*, 15 Dec. 1944
27. *Yorkshire Evening Press*, 5 Dec. 1944
28. *Cambridge Daily News*, 16 Dec. 1944
29. *Lincolnshire Echo*, 4 Dec. 1944
30. *Love, Sex and War*, p. 137
31. Interview with author
32. *Yorkshire Evening Press*, 13 Dec. 1944
33. Ibid., 22 Dec. 1944
34. Christmas 1944 menu saved by RAF navigator Sgt Graham Scholes
35. Dennis E. Slack, *My Delayed Return*, Ch. II
36. *Lincolnshire Echo*, 23 Dec. 1944

7: FIRE AND ICE

1. E. P. Bone, *A Square Peg*, pp. 1 and 2
2. Ibid.

3. Interview with author
4. Ibid.
5. *Daily Herald*, 21 Feb. 1945
6. Ibid.
7. Private operational diary of F/Sgt Henryk Drozdz
8. Ibid.
9. Ibid.
10. Ibid.
11. Personal account by the late Don Thomsett in the possession of Eddie Hilton
12. Ibid.
13. Letter by Georg Greiner to Don Thomsett
14. Personal account by the late Don Thomsett
15. Interview with author
16. Account by F/O Weitendof via Eric Thomas
17. Ibid.
18. Ibid.
19. For a fuller account see W. R. Chorley and R. N. Benwell, *In Brave Company*, Back cover
20. Ibid., p. 107
21. Ibid.
22. Fey von Hassel, *A Mother's War*, p. 208
23. Interview with author
24. National Archives: AIR 27–494
25. Interview with author
26. National Archives: AIR 14–2799
27. Ibid.
28. Interview with author

8: TRACKING THE FUTURE

1. *Warplanes of the Third Reich*, p. 634
2. Roger A. Freeman, *The Mighty Eighth*, p. 184
3. *The Times*, 2 Oct. 1944
4. Hugh Trevor-Roper (ed.), *The Goebbels Diaries*, p. 152
5. National Archives: AIR 14–3412

6. Ibid.
7. Interview with author
8. National Archives: AIR 14–2799
9. Private operational diary of F/Sgt Henry Drozdz
10. Sgt Hymers's own account to the Nanton Lancaster Society
11. Ibid.
12. Private operational diary of F/Sgt Henryk Drozdz
13. Sir Arthur Harris, *Bomber Offensive*, p. 164
14. National Archives: AIR 40–2397, Night Fighters Interrogations Report 337/1945
15. Interview with author
16. Ibid.
17. National Archives: AIR 14–2766
18. Interview with author
19. Ibid.
20. *Wings Abroad*, Vol. IV, No. 157, 19 April 1945
21. Interview with author
22. Ibid.
23. Ibid.
24. Ibid.
25. *Wings Abroad*, 5 April 1945
26. Account to author
27. Kenneth K. Blyth, *Cradle Crew*, p. 141
28. National Archives: AIR 14–2766
29. Ibid.
30. National Archives: AIR 27–1834
31. National Archives: AIR 14–2766
32. Ibid.
33. Account to author

9: THE MAKING OF ASH WEDNESDAY

1. Norman Longmate, *Bombers*, p. 331
2. Charles Webster and Noble Frankland, *Strategic Air Offensive Against Germany, 1939–1945*, Vol. III, p. 55
3. National Archives: CAB 81/93

4. Dudley Saward, *'Bomber' Harris: The Authorised Biography*, p. 282
5. Ibid., p. 284
6. Ibid.
7. Ibid., p. 287
8. Ibid., p. 288
9. Gotz Bergander, *Dresden im Luftkrieg*, p. 99, and quoted in Frederick Taylor, *Dresden*, p. 158
10. Dresden, p. 169
11. Interview with author
12. Ibid.
13. Ibid.
14. National Archives: AIR 27–767
15. Alexander McKee, *Dresden 1945: The Devil's Tinderbox*, p. 137
16. *Dresden*, p. 158
17. National Archives: AIR 27–483A
18. Robert Lee with David Heaton, 'The Enemy My Friend', IWM 98/26A
19. Martin Chalmers, *To the Bitter End: The Diaries of Victor Klemperer 1942–45*, pp. 497–500 and quoted Barry Turner *Countdown to Victory*, p. 134
20. *Dresden im Luftkrieg*, p. 168
21. Otto Griebl, *Ich War Ein Mann Der Strasse* and quoted in *Dresden*, p. 299
22. 'The Enemy My Friend,' IWM 98/26A
23. Interview with author
24. Andrew Maitland, *Through the Bombsight*, p. 150
25. Ibid.
26. Ibid.
27. National Archives: NRR 837, AIR 14–3412
28. Interview with author
29. Ibid.
30. Ibid.
31. Account to author
32. www.spartacus.schoolnet.co.uk

33. (23 (=43) 5 (Klemperer.Victor) -2 99/2125, IWM Department of Documents
34. *Dresden*, p. 300
35. (23 (=43) 5 (Klemperer.Victor) -2 99/2125, IWM Department of Documents
36. Interview with author
37. National Archives: AIR 27–1923
38. Interview with author
39. Ibid.
40. Ibid.
41. National Archives: AIR 17–1858
42. CBC Digital Archives
43. *Dresden 1945: The Devil's Tinderbox*, pp. 170–74
44. *Dresden*, p. 329
45. 'The Enemy My Friend', IWM 98/26A
46. (23 (=43) 5 (Klemperer.Victor) -2 99/2125, IWM Department of Documents
47. Ibid.
48. 'The Enemy My Friend', IWM 98/26A
49. Internet: Wikipedia, Dresden casualties
50. *Dresden*, p. 413
51. Robin Neillands, *The Bombers' War*, p. 370
52. Ibid., p. 371
53. Saward, *'Bomber'Harris*, p. 290
54. Hansard, 2 July 1942
55. Saward, *'Bomber' Harris*, p. 292
56. Ibid., p. 294
57. *Daily Telegraph*, 3 Oct. 2008
58. Interview with author
59. Ibid.
60. Ibid.
61. Ibid.
62. Account to author
63. Quoted in Barry Turner, *Countdown to Victory*, p. 145
64. *Dresden*, p. 410

65. Sir Maurice Dean, *The RAF and Two World Wars*, quoted in *Dresden 1945: The Devil's Tinderbox*, p. 272
66. Geoffrey Brooks, *Hitler's Terror Weapons: From V-1 to Vimana*
67. Ibid.
68. Wolfgang Hirschfeld, *Hirschfeld: The Secret Diary of a U-boat*, p. 218
69. Compiled from W. R. Chorley, *Bomber Command Losses, 1945*

10: RECORD AND REVENGE

1. National Archives: AIR 27–1930
2. National Archives: AIR 14–3412, NRR 837
3. Talk by F/Lt Wood to the West Wales Branch of the Aircrew Association, 16 Jan. 1996
4. Interview with author
5. This example is quoted in M. R. D. Foot and J. M. Langley, *MI9: Escape and Evasion 1939–1945*, p. 226
6. Interview with author
7. Ibid.
8. Ibid.
9. National Archives: AIR 27–2143
10. Sound Archive account in Against the Odds Exhibition, Imperial War Museum North, 2006
11. Pforzheim Stadtarchiv
12. National Archives: AIR 27–2143
13. Interview with author
14. Ibid.
15. *Pforzheim, 23 Februar 1945: Der Untergang Einer Stadt*, Esther Schmalacker-Wyrich (1980), p. 154, and quoted by Jorg Friedrich, *The Fire*, p. 93
16. *London Gazette Supplement*, 24 April 1945
17. National Archives: AIR 17–1858
18. *Wings Abroad*, 8 March 1945
19. Marianna Pross, 'Die Einschlage Kommen Naher, Aus der Tagebuchern 1943–45 von FAK, 1945–7', Oberburgmeister

der Stadt Pforzheim, Kempowski Archive, Nartum, quoted in Barry Turner *Countdown to Victory*, p. 129

20. Website: RAF Bomber Command campaign diary
21. BBC News, 21 Dec. 2002
22. DD Videos, *Behind The Wire* video, 1997
23. From Oliver Clutton-Brook, *Footprints On the Sands of Time*
24. The Forgiveness Project, Internet
25. *Footprints On the Sands of Time*
26. The Forgiveness Project, Internet
27. Private operational diary of F/Sgt Henryk Drozdz
28. Peter Bone, *Night Flight to Germany: A Composite Picture, 1947*, recording
29. Interview with author
30. Ibid.
31. Ibid.
32. Account to author

11: STING OF THE MOSQUITO

1. Hugh Trevor-Roper (ed.), *The Goebbels Diaries*, p. xxviii
2. Ibid., p. 135
3. Ibid.
4. Albert Speer, *Inside the Third Reich*, p. 413
5. *Goebbels Diaries*, p. 11
6. Ibid., p. 19
7. Ibid., p. 206
8. Ibid., p. 213
9. Interview with author
10. *Flight*, 28, Dec. 1944
11. 01/1/1 8545, IWM Department of Records
12. Ibid.
13. For further details see James Goulding and Philip Moyes, *RAF Bomber Command and its Aircraft 1941–1945*, p. 98
14. US War Department, *Tactical and Technical Trends*, No. 30, 29 July 1943
15. Interview with author

16. *Goebbels Diaries*, p. 3
17. Ibid., p. 125
18. Interview with author
19. Account to author
20. Ibid.
21. Ibid.
22. Ibid.
23. Ibid.
24. Sir Arthur Harris, *Bomber Offensive*, p. 238

12: BREAKING THE CHAIN

1. National Archives: AIR 14–2799
2. Ibid.
3. Ibid.
4. Account to author
5. Ibid.
6. Ibid.
7. National Archives: AIR 27–1931
8. Interview with author
9. Ibid.
10. Account to author
11. Ibid.
12. John Ward, *Beware of the Dog at War*, p. 461
13. Ibid.
14. US Strategic Bombing Survey Summary Report (European War), 30 Sept. 1945: The Attack on the Railways and Waterways, Internet
15. Official report of the British Bombing Survey Unit
16. Interview with author
17. Report from Dr Helmut Schnatz, quoted in Martin Middlebrook and Chris Everitt, *The Bomber Command War Diaries*, p. 39
18. Operational diary of W/O Fred Haynes
19. National Archives: AIR 27–2128
20. *Wings Abroad*, Vol. III, No. 153, 22 March 1945

21. Interview with author
22. Ibid.
23. Ibid.
24. Ibid.
25. Ibid.
26. National Archives: AIR 27–1931
27. US Strategic Bombing Survey Summary Report (European War), 30 Sept. 1945, Internet

13: NIGHT OF THE INTRUDER

1. John Ward, *Beware of the Dog at War*, p. 449
2. Account to author
3. National Archives: AIR 27–1931
4. *Beware of the Dog at War*, p. 450
5. *Wings Abroad*, Vol. III, No. 153, 22 March 1945
6. Account to author
7. *Yorkshire Evening Press*, 5 March 1945
8. Interview with author
9. Richard Bailey, *In the Middle of Nowhere: The History of RAF Metheringham*, p. 87
10. Interview with author
11. *Wings Abroad*, Vol. III, No. 152, 15 March 1945

14: A COLD AND SILENT KILLER

1. Interview with author
2. Ibid.
3. Ibid.
4. Ibid.
5. Account to author
6. Interview with author
7. Proceedings of Court of Enquiry, RAF Linton-on-Ouse, held at Linton-on-Ouse Memorial Room
8. J. V. Williams's private account, 'No Turning Back'
9. Proceedings of Court of Enquiry

10. Ibid.
11. Ibid.
12. Ibid.
13. Ibid.
14. Ibid.
15. Ibid.
16. *Yorkshire Evening Post*, 6 March 1945
17. Proceedings of Court of Enquiry
18. Ibid.
19. Ibid.
20. Ibid.
21. Ibid.
22. Ibid.
23. Ibid.
24. Interview with author
25. National Archives: Night Raid Report 856, AIR 14–3412
26. *London Gazette*, 15 May 1945
27. *Wings Abroad*, Vol. III, No. 151, 8 March 1945
28. National Archives: AIR 14–1763
29. Ibid.
30. Interview with author
31. Ibid.
32. Aircrew Association, Vancouver Island Branch, *Aircrew Memories*, p. 141
33. Ibid.
34. National Archives: AIR 27–1843
35. Proceedings of Court of Enquiry
36. Ibid.

15: OLD TARGETS, NEW LOSSES

1. Interview with author
2. Aircrew Association, Vancouver Island Branch, *Aircrew Memories*, p. 143
3. Interview with author
4. Ibid.

5. Ibid.
6. Jim Wright *On Wings of War, A History of 166 Sqn*, p. 142
7. J. V. Williams's private account, 'No Turning Back'
8. Ibid.
9. Interview with author
10. Alan Moorehead, *Eclipse*, p. 200
11. *Wings Abroad*, Vol. III, No. 153, 22 March 1945
12. Hugh Trevor-Roper (ed.), *Goebbels Diaries*, 7 March, p. 68
13. Interview with author
14. Account to author
15. Copy of 8 March 1945 combat report supplied by crew member F/Sgt Jack Dunlop
16. John Ward, *Beware of the Dog at War*, p. 454
17. Ibid.
18. Interview with author
19. Account to author
20. Interview with author
21. *'Achtmal Pauke Pauke in einer Nacht'*, *Jägerblatt*, Aug./Sept. 1982
22. Ibid.
23. For a fuller account of F/O Muncer's remarkable escape see *On Wings of War*, p. 143
24. Personal diary of F/Sgt Henryk Drozdz
25. Interview with author
26. Copy of 18 March 1945 combat report supplied by crew member F/Sgt Jack Dunlop
27. Wilhelm Johnen, *Duel Under the Stars*, p. 193
28. Ibid.
29. Ibid., p. 198
30. Interview with author
31. Account by Peter Roberts in *Beware of the Dog at War*, p. 459
32. Newspaper cutting supplied to John Ward, author of *Beware of the Dog at War*
33. Interview with author
34. *Wings Abroad*, 25 Jan. 1945

35. *Aircrew Memories*, p. 157
36. Ibid., p. 158

16: OIL, TOIL AND TROUBLE

1. Portal Papers, Folder H83, Library of Christ Church, Oxford and quoted in Henry Probert, *Bomber Harris: His Life and Times*, p. 311
2. Sir Arthur Harris, *Bomber Offensive*, p. 225
3. National Archives: AIR 14–2073
4. Ibid.
5. United States Strategic Bombing Survey Summary Report (European War), 30 Sept. 1945
6. Interview with author
7. Ibid.
8. Ibid.
9. Ibid.
10. Ibid.
11. Ibid.
12. Ibid.
13. National Archives: AIR 14–2799
14. National Archives: AIR 14–2073
15. As told by F/Sgt Williams many years after the war to his son, Ted Williams
16. Interview with author
17. Ibid.
18. Related by F/Sgt Williams to his son
19. National Archives: AIR 14–2073
20. Ibid.
21. Account to author
22. Document shown and quoted in Adrian Weir, *The Last Flight of the Luftwaffe*, p. 46
23. Ed Murrow's CBS broadcast quoted in Desmond Hawkins, *War Report*, p. 306
24. Interview with author
25. Ibid.

26. Ibid.
27. Ibid.
28. Aircrew Association, Vancouver Island Branch, *Aircrew Memories*, p. 156

17: ONE WAR ENDS, ANOTHER BEGINS

1. Interview with author
2. Scotty Young, *Descent Into Danger*, p. 33
3. National Archives: AIR 14–1763
4. *Descent Into Danger*, p. 26
5. National Archives: AIR 14–1763
6. *RAF Flying Review*, Vol. 9, No. 9, June 1954
7. Ibid.
8. Ibid.
9. National Archives: AIR 27–1155
10. Letter reproduced in *RAF Flying Review*, Vol. 9, No. 9, June 1954
11. *RAF Flying Review*, Vol. 9, No. 9, June 1954
12. Ibid.
13. The Wartime Memories Project: Stalag IIIA, Internet
14. Interview with author

18: THE LONG DAY CLOSES

1. *Tee Emm*, Vol. 4, No. 9
2. Ibid.
3. National Archives: AIR 18–26
4. Ibid.
5. Letter to author
6. National Archives: AIR 18–27
7. Interview with author
8. Ibid.
9. National Archives: AIR 14–2073
10. *RAF Flying Review*, Vol. 9, No. 11, Aug. 1954
11. Ibid.

12. Wikipedia: Internet
13. Interview with author
14. Aircrew Association, Scottish Saltire Branch, Library No. 050
15. Interview with author
16. Aircrew Association, Scottish Saltire Branch, Library No. 039
17. Copy of report made available to Aircrew Association, Scottish Saltire Branch, Library No. 130, by George B. Thomson
18. Copy of P/O Thomson's march made available to Aircrew Association, Scottish Saltire Branch, Library No. 130, by George B. Thomson
19. Ibid.
20. Interview with author
21. Ibid.
22. Ibid.
23. Ibid.
24. Ibid.
25. Ibid.
26. Ibid.
27. 'Death of a Warbird', Sgt Williams's personal escape diary
28. Ibid.
29. Ibid.
30. Interview with author
31. Ibid.
32. Diary of former POW Lawrence Benson, contributed to Aircrew Association, Scottish Saltire Branch, Library No. 101 by fellow member Gilbert A. Gray
33.

19: DELIVERANCE BY BOMBER

1. F/Sgt Peter Bone's operational diary
2. F/Sgt Bone's memoir, 'The Last Kick at the Cat'
3. F/Sgt Bone's operational diary
4. National Archives: AIR 27–1910
5. National Archives: AIR 27–2128
6. 'The Last Kick at the Cat'

7. National Archives: AIR 27–2143
8. National Archives: AIR 27–1850
9. National Archives: AIR 27–1858
10. Interview with author
11. Ibid.
12. Desmond Hawkins, *War Report*, p. 338
13. Hilary St G. Saunders, *Royal Air Force* 1939–1945, Vol. III, p. 278
14. Interview with author
15. Operation Manna Display at RAF Helmswell
16. Interview with author
17. Ibid.
18. Ibid.

20: FINALE

1. Personal diary of F/Sgt Henryk Drozdz
2. Interview with author
3. The Wartime Memories Project, Internet
4. Diary of former POW Lawrence Benson, Scottish Saltire Branch, ACA, Library No. 101, contributed by Gilbert A. Gray
5. Interview with author
6. E. P. Bone, *A Square Peg*
7. Interview with author
8. Ibid.
9. Letter to author
10. Interview with author
11. Ibid.
12. Personal diary of F/Sgt Henryk Drozdz
13. Interview with author
14. Ronald Ashbride, *Yer Actual Erk*, p. 98
15. Interview with author
16. Ibid.
17. Ibid.
18. Henry Probert, *Bomber Harris: His Life and Times*, p. 347

19. Hilary St G. Saunders, *The Royal Air Force, 1939–1945*, Vol. III, p. 389

20. *Statistics Bundesamt Wirtschaft und Statistik*, Vol. III, pp. 139–42

21. Against the Odds Exhibition, Imperial War Museum North, 2006

22. *The German Reich and the Second World War*, quoted in the *Daily Telegraph*, 19 July 2008

23. Figures from BBC Timewatch programme, *Auschwitz*, by Laurence Rees

24. See author's previous work, *Men of Air*, p. 104

25. National Archives, AIR 20–2858

26. *Daily Telegraph*, 10 Oct. 2008

27. Account to author

28. Interview with author

ACKNOWLEDGEMENTS

I am particularly grateful to the following British, Commonwealth and Allied aircrew who participated in various ways in the preparation of this book. It is their unstinting help that made it all possible. Ranks and awards are those when they left the services and only air forces other than RAF are shown after names: 9 Sqn: F/Lt Douglas Jennings. 35 Sqn: F/Lt Sir William Hanham DFC. 49 Sqn: W/O Frank Campbell. 50 Sqn: W/O George Stewart (deceased). 51 Sqn: F/Lt Bill Morrish DFC. 75 Sqn: P/O Ron Brown; F/Lt Ron Mayhill DFC (RNZAF). 76 Sqn: S/Ldr Alan Dearden (deceased). 83 Sqn: W/O Dick Raymond. 97 Sqn: F/Lt John Greening; W/O Patrick Bell (RCAF); F/Sgt Bill Cotton. 100 Sqn: F/Lt Ron Clark DFC. 101 Sqn: F/O Dennis Goodliffe; W/O Jack Morley; Sgt Ken O'Brien DFM. 102 Sqn: W/O Alan Adams. 106 Sqn: W/O Harry Stunell; W/O John Harrison; F/O John Ladbrooke (deceased). 115 Sqn: F/Lt Ken Turnham. 138 Sqn: F/Sgt Ken Oakes (deceased). 139 Sqn: F/Lt Frederick Crawley DFC. 149 Sqn: W/O Derek Jackson (deceased); W/O Reginald Bell; F/Sgt Albert Miller. 158 Sqn: S/Ldr Robert Vollum DFC; W/O Dennis Slack; W/O Harry Irons DFC; F/Lt Alan Bryett; W/O Frank Horsley. 162 Sqn: F/Lt Ken Tempest DFC. 166 Sqn: F/Lt Jack Gagg DFC; S/Ldr James Wright; F/Lt Len Isaacson, Croix de Guerre (RCAF); F/O Jack Dunlop (RNZAF); F/Lt Sam Small DFC; F/Lt Eric Hadingham DFC and Bar (deceased). 1667 HCU: F/Lt Peter Johnson DFC. 189 Sqn: P/O Donald Clement. 207 Sqn: Sgt Ken Freeman. 218 Sqn: F/O Reg Johnson (RAAF); F/O Rowland Mason; Sgt John Simpson. 347 Sqn: Sgt Leonce Vaysse (FFAF). 408 (Goose) Sqn,

RCAF: F/O Kenneth Blyth (RCAF); F/Sgt Laurie Godfrey. 419 (RCAF) Sqn: F/Lt Al Wallace (RCAF). 420 (RCAF) Sqn: F/O Maurice Conway. 428 (RCAF) Sqn: F/O Lance Butler (RCAF). 433 (Porcupine) Sqn, RCAF: S/Ldr Wilbur Pierce DFC (RCAF). 429 (RCAF) Sqn: F/O Otto Sulek (RCAF). 460 (RAAF) Sqn: F/Lt David Francis DFC; P/O Edney Eyres; W/O Tom Howie. 463 (RAAF) Sqn: F/O Graham Allen DFM; Sgt Laurie Boness (deceased). 515 Sqn: W/O Alfred Rogers; F/Lt Alan Shufflebottom. 544 Sqn: W/O Francis Bayliss, CdG (Belge), AFM. 571 Sqn: W/Cdr Robert Bray DFC; F/Lt S. Perks DFC. 605 Sqn: S/Ldr Robert Muir DFC. 613 Sqn: F/Lt Tony Brandreth. 625 Sqn: S/Ldr Alex Flett DFC and bar; F/Lt William Porter; F/Sgt Frank Tolley; F/Lt Harold Sutton DFC; F/Sgt Bob Pyett (deceased); W/O Joe Williams. 626 Sqn: F/Lt Ron Wood (deceased); W/O Roy Ollerhead DFM; F/Lt Peter Bone. 635 Sqn: W/O John Silburn DFM (deceased). 692 Sqn: S/Ldr Tom Beal DFC. 630 Sqn: W/O Edwin Watson. 306th BG, USAAF: Lt Howard Roth.

I am also grateful to the following: Mrs Zofia Kwiatkowska and Mrs Halina Kwiatkowska for their great help with translations; Mrs Kay Polley, Mrs Mary Rogan; Mrs Betty Suiter; Herr Wolfgang Scholz; W/Cdr Alan Mawby, curator of the RAF Linton-on-Ouse Memorial Room; John Ward, author of *Beware of the Dog at War*; Jack Burgess, PRO of the Aircrew Association, Scottish Saltire Branch; Mr Ken Williams for the account from his father Elias Williams.

The following ex-Luftwaffe aircrew have also been generous with their assistance for which I am grateful: II/JG26: Uffz Ottomar Kruse, Iron Cross Second Class; VIII/NJG3: Major Paul Zorner, Knight's Cross; I/NJG2: Hptmn Heinz Rokker, Knight's Cross with Oak Leaves.

GLOSSARY

ABC	Airborne equipment for spot-jamming of night-fighter transmissions
AP	Aiming point
ASI	Air Speed Indicator
ASR	Air Sea Rescue
Corona	Ground-based listening and broadcasting system for sending false instructions to German night-fighter crews
Erk	Aircraftsman 2nd Class, the lowest RAF rank
ETA	Estimated time of arrival
DFC	Distinguished Flying Cross
DFM	Distinguished Flying Medal
DR	Dead reckoning (navigation)
DSO	Distinguished Service Order
Experten	A recognised Luftwaffe ace with five or more confirmed victories
Feldwebel	Sergeant in the Wehrmacht or Luftwaffe
FFI	French forces of the interior; the Resistance
FIDO	Runway fog dispersal system using burning petrol
Fishpond	Bomber radar set able to spot fighters up to 30 miles away
F/Lt	Flight Lieutenant
F/O	Flying Officer
FTR	Failed To Return, the final verdict on an operational bomber
F/Sgt	Flight Sergeant

FW190 — Focke Wulf single-engined fighter, a favourite of Wilde Sau pilots

Gee — Airborne device receiving signals from one master and two slave radio stations by which a navigator was able to plot his exact course on a grid

Graviner — Fire extinguisher device in an aircraft engine

Gremlin — Fictitious, RAF imp-like figure, expert at putting a spanner in the works

HCU — Heavy Conversion Unit

Himmelbett — Box fighter-control system introduced by General Kammhuber

H2S — Radar scanner carried underneath bombers supplying features of terrain below to operator inside

Jostle — Continuous wave-jamming of German R/T transmissions by equipment in 100 Group aircraft

Ju 88 — Twin-engined multi-purpose Junkers aircraft, often used in the Zahme-Sau night-fighter role

Korfu — Ground-based radar equipment that could lock onto bomber H2S transmissions

Kriegsgefang-ener — The German title for prisoner of war

LMF — Lack of moral fibre, the harsh judgement made by the RAF on those who felt unable to continue operational flying. Their files were stamped

Mandrel — Transmission equipment to jam enemy early warning radar

Me109 — Single-engined Messerschmitt day fighter adapted for Wilde Sau role

Me110 — Twin-engined Messerschmitt night fighter, lethal with Schrage Musik

Monica — Tail-mounted RAF device to warn of approaching night fighter

NAAFI — Navy, Army and Air Force Institutes – clubs cum cafés for other ranks. Airmen joked that the initials stood for No Ambition and F All Interest

Nachtjäger — Night-fighter aircraft or aircrew. The command structure was in Staffels of nine aircraft, three Staffels making a group, three groups making a Geschwader. In abbreviated form the Third Group of the First Night Fighter Geschwader would be III/NJG1

Naxos   Airborne radar equipment that could track bomber H2S transmissions

Newhaven   Pathfinder marking by visual identification of the target

Oboe   Highly accurate radar tracking and transmission system, signalling to a PFF aircraft the exact point at which to drop its TIs

Offset   Technique of dropping TIs outside an aiming point
marking   to avoid obscuring by smoke and setting bomb sights for an overshoot, so bombs actually hit the target

OKW   Wehrmacht high command

ORS   Operational Research Section at Bomber Command HQ

OTU   Operational Training Unit

Parramatta Pathfinder ground marking by the use of H2S

PFF   Pathfinder Flare Force

P/O   Pilot Officer

PR   Photographic reconnaissance

SA   Sturmabteilung (Storm troopers)

Schrage Musik Upward-firing guns in the fuselage of German night fighters

Screened   The process of releasing an airman from a squadron after a tour was completed

Serrate   Night-fighter airborne radar hunting *Nachtjäger* transmissions

S/Ldr   Squadron Leader

SN-2   Luftwaffe airborne radar operating on 90 megacycles that could not be jammed by Window

Sqn   Squadron

Stooging   RAF slang for idling, often over a target

T and D	A bombing technique developed by 5 Group where a force bombed blind after counting off the time from an identifiable, distant landmark
T I	Target indicator
U/S	Unserviceable
VC	Victoria Cross
WAAF	Women's Auxiliary Air Force. Members known by the same name
Wad	The air force name for a sandwich, invariably more bread than filling
Wallop	Airman's slang for a beer, though wartime restrictions meant it had less of an effect than the title suggests
Wanganui	Sky marking in very poor visibility. The prefix 'musical' meant the use of Oboe
W/Cdr	Wing Commander
Wilde Sau	Freelance night fighters, usually over targets and single-engined
Window	Metallised paper producing spurious responses on Luftwaffe radar
W/O	Warrant Officer
Zahme Sau	'Tame boar' fighters controlled by means of a running commentary

BIBLIOGRAPHY

AIRCREW ASSOCIATION, Vancouver Island Branch, *Aircrew Memories* (Victoria Publishing Company, 1999)

ANDREAS-FRIEDRICH, Ruth, *Berlin Underground* (Latimer House, 1948)

ASHBRIDGE, Ronald, *Yer Actual Erk* (Tucann Books, 1994)

BAILEY, Richard, *In the Middle of Nowhere: The History of RAF Metheringham* (Tucann Books, 1999)

BARDUA, Heinz, *Stuttgart in Luftkrieg 1939–45* (Klett Verlag Stuttgart, 1985)

BECK, Earl R., *Under the Bombs: The German Home Front, 1942–1945* (University Press of Kentucky, 1986)

BLYTH, Kenneth K., *Cradle Crew* (Sunflower University Press, 1997)

BONE, E. P., *A Square Peg* (Kwantlen University College, 2006)

BOWMAN, Martin W. and CUSHING, Tom, *Confounding the Reich* (Patrick Stephens, 1996)

BROOKS, Geoffrey, *Hitler's Terror Weapons: From V-1 to Vimana* (Leo Cooper, 2002)

BROWN, Ron, *Ron Brown's Per Ardua Ad Astra* (Publishers of Books for an Eclectic Readership, 2006)

CARRINGTON, Charles, *A Soldier at Bomber Command* (Leo Cooper, 1987)

CHALMERS, Martin (abr. and tr.), *To the Bitter End: The Diaries of Victor Klemperer 1942–45* (Phoenix, 2000)

CHORLEY, W. R., *Bomber Command Losses, 1944* (Midland Counties Publications, 1997)

CHORLEY, W. R., *Bomber Command Losses, 1945* (Midland Counties Publications, 1998)

CHORLEY, W. R., and BENWELL, R. N., *In Brave Company: The History of 158 Sqn, 1945* (Barnicotts, 1978)

COSTELLO John, *Love Sex and War: Changing Values 1939–45* (Collins, 1985)

DANCHEV, Alex and TODMAN, Daniel, *War Diaries 1939–1945, Field Marshal Lord Alanbrooke* (Weidenfeld & Nicolson, 2001)

DEAN, Sir Maurice, *The RAF and Two World Wars* (Cassell, 1979)

DOMINY, John, *The Sergeant Escapers* (Ian Allan, 1976)

ELLIS, L. F., *Victory in the West* (London, 1962)

FEST, Joachim, *Speer: The Final Verdict* (Alexander Fest Verlag, 1999)

FISCHER, Josef, *Köln 1939–45* (J. P. Bachem, 1970)

FOOT, M. R. D., and Langley, J. M., *MI9: Escape and Evasion 1939–1945* (Bodley Head, 1979)

FREEMAN, Roger A., *The Mighty Eighth* (Macdonald and Jane's, 1970)

FRIEDRICH, Jorg, *The Fire: The Bombing of Germany 1940–1945* (Columbia University Press, 2006)

GARDINER, Juliet, *Wartime: Britain 1939–45* (Headline, 2004)

GILBERT, Sir Martin, *The Day the War Ended: VE-Day 1945 in Europe and Around the World* (Harper Collins, 1995)

GOSS, Chris, *It's Suicide But It's Fun* (Crécy Books, 1995)

GOULDING, James and MOYES, Philip, *RAF Bomber Command and its Aircraft 1941–1945* (Ian Allan, 1978)

GRAY, Philip, *Ghosts of Targets Past: The Lives and Losses of a Lancaster Crew in 1944–45* (Grub Street, 2000)

GREEN, William, *Warplanes of the Third Reich* (Doubleday, 1970)

HARRIS, Sir Arthur, *Bomber Offensive* (Collins, 1947)

HASSLE, Fey von, *A Mother's War* (John Murray, 1990)

HAWKINS, Desmond (ed.), *War Report: From D-Day to VE-Day* (BBC Books, 1994)

HINCHLIFFE, Peter, *The Other Battle* (Airlife Publishing, 1996)

HIRSCHFELD, Wolfgang, *Hirschfeld: The Secret Diary of a U-boat* (Cassell, 1996)

HORSTMANN, Lali, *Nothing for Tears* (Weidenfeld & Nicolson, 1953)

HULL, Cordell, *Memoirs* (Hodder & Stoughton, 1948)

JACKSON, Robert, *Storm from the Skies* (Arthur Barker, 1974)

JENKINS, Roy, *Churchill* (Macmillan, 2001)

JENNINGS, Douglas, *Jump or Die* (Tucann Books, 2005)

JOHNEN, Wilhelm, *Duel Under the Stars* (William Kimber, 1957)

KARDORFF, Ursula von, *Diary of a Nightmare* (Rupert Hart-Davis, 1965)

LONGMATE, Norman, *The Bombers* (Arrow, 1990)

MACKERSEY, Ian, *Into the Silk* (Robert Hale, 1956)

MAITLAND, Andrew, *Through the Bombsight* (William Kimber, 1986)

MAYHILL, Ron, DFC, *Bombs on Target* (Patrick Stephens, 1991)

MCKEE, Alexander, *Dresden 1945: The Devil's Tinderbox* (Souvenir Press, 1982)

MCKEE, Ilse, *Tomorrow the World* (J. M. Dent, 1960)

MCKINSTRY, Leo, *Lancaster: The Second World War's Greatest Bomber* (John Murray, 2009)

MIDDLEBROOK, Martin and EVERITT, Chris, *The Bomber Command War Diaries* (Viking, 1985)

MOOREHEAD, Alan, *Eclipse* (Hamish Hamilton, 1945)

NEILLANDS, Robin, *The Bomber War* (John Murray, 2001)

OVERY, Richard, *The Air War 1939–45* (Europa Publications, 1980)

OVERY, Richard, *Why the Allies Won* (Jonathan Cape, 1995)

OVERY, Richard, *Bomber Command, 1939–45* (Harper Collins, 1997)

PARTRIDGE, Eric, *Dictionary of RAF Slang* (Michael Joseph, 1945)

POWERS, Thomas, *Heisenberg's War: The Secret History of the German Bomb* (Jonathan Cape, 1993)

PROBERT, Henry, *Bomber Harris: His Life and Times* (Greenhill Books, 2003)

RICHARDS, Denis, *Royal Air Force 1939–45*, Vol. I, *The Fight At Odds* (Her Majesty's Stationery Office, 1953)

RICHARDS, Denis, *The Hardest Victory* (Hodder & Stoughton, 1994)

RICHARDS, Denis and ST G. SAUNDERS, Hilary, *Royal Air Force 1939–45*, Vol. II, *The Fight Avails* (Her Majesty's Stationery Office, 1954)

ROY, Jules, *Return From Hell* (William Kimber, 1954)

RUMPF, Hans, *The Bombing of Germany* (Frederick Muller, 1961)

ST G. SAUNDERS, Hilary, *Royal Air Force 1939 45*, Vol. III, *The Fight Is Won* (Her Majesty's Stationery Office, 1954)

SAWARD, Dudley, *'Bomber' Harris: The Authorised Biography* (Cassell, 1984)

SLACK, Dennis E., *My Delayed Return* (Linney Print, Mansfield, 2006)

SPEER, Albert, *Inside the Third Reich* (Weidenfeld & Nicolson, 1970)

TAYLOR, Frederick, *Dresden: Tuesday, 13 February 1945* (Bloomsbury Publishing, 2004)

TERRAINE, John, *The Right of the Line* (Hodder and Stoughton, 1985)

TREVOR-ROPER, Hugh (ed.), *The Goebbels Diaries* (Secker & Warburg, 1978)

TURNER, Barry, *Countdown to Victory* (Harper, 2005)

WALLER, Maureen, *London, 1945: Life in the Debris of War* (John Murray, 2004)

WARD, John, *Beware of the Dog at War* (JoTe Publications, 1997)

WARD-JACKSON, C. H., and LUCAS, Leighton, *Airman's Song Book* (William Blackwood, 1967)

WEBSTER, Sir Charles, and FRANKLAND, Noble, *The Strategic Air Offensive against Germany 1939–45* (HMSO, 1961)

WEIR, Adrian, *Last Flight of the Luftwaffe* (Phoenix, 2000)

WHITING, Charles (ed.), *The Home Front: Germany* (Time-Life Books, 1982)

WHITING, Charles, *West Wall* (Pan Books, 2002)

WILMOT, Chester, *The Struggle for Europe* (Collins, 1952)

WILLS, Clair, *That Neutral Island* (Faber & Faber, 2007)

WILSON, Kevin, *Bomber Boys: The Ruhr, the Dambusters and Bloody Berlin* (Weidenfeld & Nicolson, 2006)

WILSON, Kevin, *Men of Air: The Doomed Youth of Bomber Command* (Weidenfeld & Nicolson, 2007)

WRIGHT, Jim, *On Wings of War* (166 Squadron Association, 1996)

YOUNG, Scotty, *Descent Into Danger* (Alan Wingate, 1954)

INDEX